Solaris® Troubleshooting Handbook

Troubleshooting and Performance Tuning Hints for Solaris® 10 and OpenSolaris®

Scott Cromar

Solaris® Troubleshooting Handbook
by Scott Cromar

Notice to the reader:
Author and publisher do not warrant or guarantee any of the products or processes described herein. The reader is expressly warned to consider and adopt appropriate safeguards and avoid any hazards associated with taking actions described in the book. By taking actions recommended in this book, the reader is willingly assuming the risks associated with those activities.

The author and publisher do not make representations or warranties of any kind. In particular, no warranty of fitness for a particular purchase or merchantability are implied in any material in this publication. The author and publisher shall not be liable for special, consequential, or exemplary damages resulting, in whole or in part, from the reader's reliance upon or use of the information in this book.

Trademarks:
Sun, Solaris, Java, Solstice DiskSuite, Solaris Volume Manager, Solaris JumpStart, NFS, and Java are trademarks or registered trademarks of Sun Microsystems, Inc and Oracle Corporation. All SPARC trademarks are registered trademarks of SPARC International, Inc. UNIX is a registered trademark exclusively licensed through X/Open Company, LTD. Symantec, Veritas, Veritas Volume Manager, VxVM, Veritas File System, VxFS, and Veritas Cluster Server are trademarks and registered trademarks of Symantec Corp. Other designations used by manufacturers and sellers to distinguish their products are also claimed as trademarks. Where we are aware of such a claim, the designation has been printed in caps or initial caps.

ISBN-13: 978-1463512415

ISBN-10: 1463512414

Published by Cromar & Cromar
St Augustine, FL 32092

2011 Printing by CreateSpace, North Charleston, SC

Comments, questions, and corrections welcome at
http://solaristroubleshooting.blogspot.com

This book extends and supplements information first published at
http://www.princeton.edu/~unix/Solaris/troubleshoot

Table of Contents

Table of Contents

1

Troubleshooting Methodology[1]

Most good system administrators have a secret passion: We like troubleshooting the hard problems. We like the adrenaline rush. We like the mental challenge. We like to be the hero.

But troubleshooting can be frightening too. It is no fun to have the boss asking the inevitable questions: "Is it fixed yet? What happened? Whose fault is it?"

And deep down, there's our unspoken fear: What if we're not good enough (or smart enough) to fix it?

This book will provide you a set of tools for troubleshooting problems on your Solaris systems. Some of the techniques we cover can be used for troubleshooting in any type of context. Some of them are usable on any Unix operating system. And some of them are specific to recent versions of Solaris (especially Solaris 10 or OpenSolaris).

At the end of the day, our biggest asset is something that can't be taught: a positive attitude. Every problem has a solution. (Not every solution is worth implementing, but that is a whole other story.) There are techniques that we can apply to our situation. But if we don't have a positive attitude, we are virtually guaranteed to fail.

People become better at troubleshooting with experience. We gain confidence in our abilities as we accumulate a history of successfully fixing problems. Techniques like the ones in this book are relatively easy to learn. Confidence and experience are much trickier.

Training in courses with a large lab component can be valuable in gaining both experience and confidence. For example, Sun offers two excellent lab-centered classes in *ST350—Sun Systems Fault Analysis* and *SA400—Solaris System Peformance Management*. Other vendors, such as Cisco and Red Hat, also offer classes with large troubleshooting and lab components.

Study and reading are also essential to becoming a good troubleshooter. We are not going to get anywhere without the tools to diagnose a problem. Subscribe to magazines or mailing lists which provide valuable tips, tricks, and case studies. Create and stick to a reading schedule to examine books on a variety of topics. Identify your knowledge gaps and seek out information to fill them.

And wherever possible, practice these techniques. Most shops have no shortage of problems that need to be solved.

---

1   Portions of this chapter were previously published in the August 2007 issue of SysAdmin Magazine as *Troubleshooting Methods*.

The Troubleshooting Process

"**Troubleshooting**" refers to the methods used to resolve problems. People who troubleshoot a lot come up with a set of habits, methods and tools to help with the process. These provide a standard approach for gathering the necessary information to zero in on the cause of a problem. This standard approach is known as a **methodology**.

Methodologies save time while troubleshooting. They allow us to organize our efforts in order to devote every available resource to resolving the problem.

On the other hand, a methodology only saves time when applied intelligently. It is possible to become so devoted to the process that we forget the purpose of the whole exercise—fixing the problem. It makes no sense to spend all our time writing logs and no time testing hypotheses.

Frequently, services must be restored before the real troubleshooting can begin. When this is the case, we must preserve things like core files, console output, and log files that we will need when we are allowed to begin to troubleshoot. We also must follow proper change control and documentation procedures for any changes we make while bringing services back online. It may make sense to turn on additional monitoring if the services are brought online before the root problem is identified and resolved. If we skimp on these steps, we may not be able to resolve the root problem, and we will be condemned to repeated outages as the problem surfaces again and again.

Good methodologies contain tools for coordinating efforts and organizing the troubleshooting process. The key is to focus our time and resources, minimize the cost of the problem, and find and fix the root cause. The effectiveness of these tools has been studied and verified (see, for example, Doggett in the "Resources" section).

Unfortunately, many otherwise good system administrators try to minimize the time spent resolving a problem by totally ignoring the importance of structuring and documenting the process. Structure keeps us from going in circles. Documentation provides useful information for avoiding wasted effort, fixing future problems, or evolving the design of our data environment.

Proper documentation also allows less experienced staff members to duplicate our methods and procedures. This is a key concern where these junior staff members are the primary support staff vacation coverage or disaster recovery operations. (Who wants to get called off a beach in Florida to resolve a problem in the home office? Some short-sighted administrators regard this scenario as job security. More mature admins regard it as a nuisance.)

Our techniques need to be seen as tools to be used to solve a problem. Not every home repair involves a wrecking bar and sledgehammer, and not every problem requires a full Ishikawa Diagram and formal set of probability calculations. With experience and maturity comes the judgment to decide which tools are appropriate for a particular problem. We have to practice the techniques so that we know how and where they will be most useful. Shortcutting the process unduly just causes us problems in the long run.

In broad outline, troubleshooting consists of three phases: Investigation, Analysis and Implementation. Presentations of troubleshooting methodologies sometimes present these steps with slightly different names, or emphasize slightly different aspects of the process, but the steps in Table 1-1 are one way to organize the process.

Table 1-1. The Troubleshooting Process

Step	Comments
Investigation Phase	
Problem Statement	A clear, concise statement of the problem.
Problem Description	List the symptoms of the problem, including what works and what doesn't. Identify the scope and importance of the problem.
Identify Differences and Changes	What has changed recently? How does this system differ from working systems?
Analysis Phase	
Brainstorm	Gather hypotheses. What might have caused the problem?
Rank the Likely Causes	How likely is each hypothesis?
Test the Hypotheses	Schedule testing for the most likely hypothesis. Perform non-disruptive testing immediately.
Implementation Phase	
Apply the Fix	Complete the repair.
Verify the Fix	Make sure that the problem is really resolved.
Document the Resolution	Save the troubleshooting information. Get a sign-off from the service owner.

Investigation Phase

The **Investigation Phase** consists of steps to identify the nature of the problem, gather information describing it, and find distinctions between working and non-working states of the system. The defining characteristic of the Investigation Phase is the collection of facts, not opinions.

For nontrivial problems, we save time over the long run by not jumping immediately to Analysis or Implementation. There is usually a lot of pressure to "just do something." Unfortunately, that is not the most effective use of time or resources. There is a universe of harmful or irrelevant actions that we can take, and only a very few actions that will improve or fix the situation.

Problem Statement

At the beginning of the process, we need to name the problem. A good **problem statement** defines the problem in a broad enough way that it accurately portrays the effects of the problem, but is narrow enough to focus our problem analysis.

Value judgments have no place in a problem statement. The goal of a problem statement is to produce a concise, correct, high-level description of the problem. To do this, focus on what *did* happen versus what *should* have happened.

Ideally, the problem statement will specify a defect in a particular object or service. The problem statement should

3

answer the questions "Where is the problem?" and "What is wrong?"

Problem Description

Once we have named the problem, we need to list as many symptoms as possible without becoming redundant. In particular, we should list dissimilar symptoms—their juxtaposition allows us to look at common threads between them.

It may even be helpful to list the things that are working fine, as contrasted with items that do not work. (For example, if we can `ping` the server from within the same subnet, but not from outside it, we immediately know that the network adapter is working and the IP address is set properly. We can focus on other aspects of the networking stack.)

When listing symptoms, we may need to speak to people from different areas of the user community for the failed service. We may need to get input from the service owner, an end user, a database administrator, or the help desk.

As obvious as it may sound, we have to look for and log any explicit error messages. (More times than I care to think about, I have wasted time chasing a problem whose solution is fully described in the text of an error message that I have overlooked.)

Core files and crash dumps may also be an important source of information. These should be gathered and provided to someone who knows how to analyze them (frequently the software vendor).

Solaris provides tools (eg `mdb`, `pstack` and `strings`) that can be used to perform simple or in-depth analyses of core files. We will look at some of these tools in Chapters 3 and 4. The core file or crash dump should be provided to the vendor's support engineer at the earliest opportunity; we can use the techniques from Chapters 3 and 4 to perform some elementary analysis ourselves, while we wait for the vendor response.

In some cases, hardware or software diagnostics may help to point the troubleshooter in the right direction. The relevant hardware and software vendors' documentation should be checked for any such tools. For example the Open Boot PROM on Sparc-based systems offers significant troubleshooting capabilities. (See the "OBP Command Line Diagnostics" section in Chapter 3.)

The start and end times of an outage should be nailed down as accurately as possible. This allows us to ask "What changed?" on a precise time window. We need this information for the next stage of the troubleshooting process.

We also need to get a handle on the scope and importance of the problem. While these might not be directly related to the root cause of the problem, they will determine the types of tests and resolutions that we might consider for the problem.

The importance of the problem will also determine how many resources we can spend in troubleshooting it. IT abounds with problems too expensive or too trivial to resolve. The role of IT is usually to advise the decision makers with appropriate estimates of costs and consequences of a problem or its resolution. Business requirements and resources will determine which of the universe of problems will get our full attention.

Identify Differences and Changes

We need to identify the differences between the broken system and a working system. The working system may be a prior state of the problem system. It may be another similar system. It may even be an architectural design of how we want the system to be.

With many emergency failures, we can find the problem by looking at recent system changes. When we do this step, we see how indispensable good change control practices are.

Nobody likes logging and documenting changes, but it is far worse to have to troubleshoot a system without any idea what changed recently. A working change control policy is a key to identifying recent changes on a system. At a minimum, all changes should have to follow testing, approval and documentation standards. (See "Change

4

Management" in Chapter 14.)

Analysis Phase

The **Analysis Phase** is focused on taking the facts from the Investigation Phase and explaining them. In this phase, we generate hypotheses from the information we have gathered, test the hypotheses, and report the results.

This stage of the troubleshooting process is all about the scientific method. Intuition and experience focus the investigation by identifying which possibilities are most likely to provide a solution.

Brainstorm: Gather Hypotheses

The **Brainstorming** step is where we try to identify all possible causes of the problem. We use the facts from the Investigation Phase to generate hypotheses about the cause of the problem.

The symptoms and problem statement can be turned around to provide hypotheses. We can ask ourselves questions like "How can this item have caused this problem?" The answers can be added to our list of hypotheses.

It is sometimes useful to have a system diagram or other mental model of the system before thinking about possible causes. Each component of the system should be considered as a possible cause.

(A common example of such a mental model is the OSI network stack in Table 1-2. Some network troubleshooting methodologies focus on eliminating portions of the stack as the cause of the problem.)

Table 1-2. OSI Network Reference Model—Example of a System Model

Level Name	Description
Application Layer	Application programs using the network.
Presentation Layer	Data presentation to the applications.
Session Layer	Manages sessions between cooperating applications.
Transport Layer	End-to-end error detection and correction.
Network Layer	Manages connections and addressing on the network.
Data Link Layer	Reliable data delivery across physical network components.
Physical Layer	Network media characteristics.

In this context, "components" need to be considered at an appropriate level of abstraction. Depending on the nature of the problem, a diode, a computer, a network service, or the Internet may be considered to be components. For our purposes, we define a "**component**" as an entity that can testably be eliminated as the source of the problem.

If we can eliminate a component, it makes no sense to spend time eliminating subcomponents. The level of abstraction can make a huge difference in the amount of time spent in a troubleshooting exercise. (In an idealized situation where we can eliminate half of the system at each step, for example, we can narrow a problem down to one component out of a million in only 20 steps.) Figure 1-1 illustrates several different levels of abstraction that might be used to examine a problem.

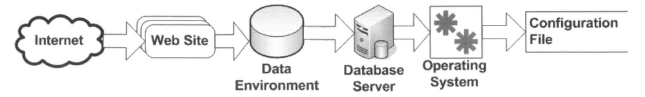

Figure 1-1. Levels of Abstraction

There are several tools to help organize brainstorming sessions. One such tool is the **Ishikawa Cause-and-Effect Diagram** (see the "Ishikawa Cause-and-Effect Diagrams" sidebar). A key to a successful brainstorming session (especially one involving a team of people) is that everyone focuses on identifying possible causes rather than starting to drill down on a particular hypotheses. Ishikawa Diagrams help make sure that each system component is examined as a possible cause of the problem.

Ishikawa Cause-and-Effect Diagrams

Ishikawa Cause-and-Effect (or "Fishbone") Diagrams are a tool that allows us to focus a brainstorming session. We generate an Ishikawa Diagram by drawing a "backbone" arrow pointing to the right at a rectangle containing our problem statement. Then attach 4-6 "ribs," each of which represents a major broad category of items which may contribute to the problem. Each of our components should fit on one or another of these ribs.

The next step can be done by the troubleshooting team leader or by the whole team. Specific causes are attached to the appropriate rib, and more detailed potential causes are listed as branches of their related causes.

Figure 1-2 shows an example of an Ishikawa Diagram. The four categories chosen for this diagram were "Computer System," "Computing Environment," "People and Procedures" and "Application." Several secondary potential causes have been attached to each of the main categories.

Appropriate primary categories for the diagram may be different from situation to situation. Common paradigms presented in the literature include "materials, methods, machines and manpower" or "people, procedures, plant and parts." Whatever we choose, our major categories should represent the universe of issues that may have caused our problem.

The main advantage of an Ishikawa Diagram for our purposes is that it can organize the brainstorming process so that significant hypotheses are not ignored. A well-organized diagram can focus the troubleshooting team's attention on each potential issue to help avoid the problem of overlooked hypotheses.

Remember that your goal is not the production of a pretty diagram. The Ishikawa Diagram is a tool to facilitate brainstorming. The goal is to make sure to cover all the possible causes of our stated problem.

Not every problem requires anything as formal or organized as an Ishikawa Diagram. There is no point in trying to swat a fly with a sledgehammer. But when a problem is big enough to involve multiple people and several different areas of inquiry, something like an Ishikawa diagram provides needed structure to a brainstorming session.

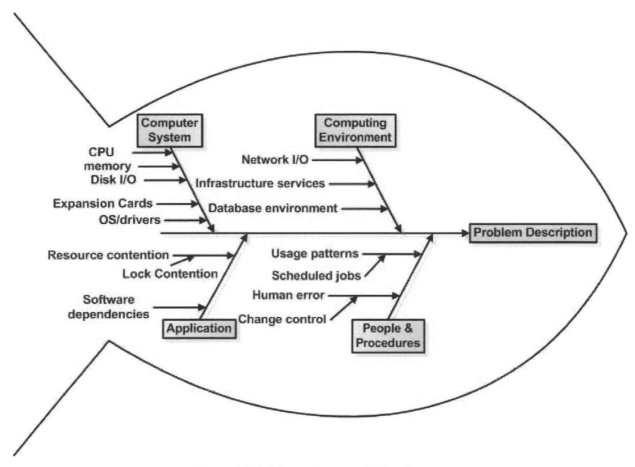

Figure 1-2. Ishikawa Cause-and-Effect Diagram

Rank the Likely Causes

Once we have a list of possible explanations for the problem, we need to decide which of them are most likely to be correct. We also need to look into any assumptions that are implicit in the hypothesis statements.

Only eliminate hypotheses when they are absolutely disproved. This step is about ranking the probabilities of the different hypotheses being the correct explanation. Unlikely hypotheses should not be discarded, though they may be characterized as "very unlikely" or "corner cases."

In some cases, the best way to test the hypotheses is by looking at information gathered during the Investigation Phase. For example, a bug report may closely match the symptomology of your problem. If this is the case, we should look closely at that bug report.

For more complex problems with more moving parts, it may be useful to use formal tools to help identify which potential causes are more important than others. **Interrelationship Diagrams** (see the "Interrelationship Diagrams" sidebar) are tools developed to help organize and think about the relationships between these potential causes. They are useful in looking for ultimate vs proximate causes.

(**Ultimate causes** are the "root" causes of the problem. While they may not be directly indicated by the symptoms, we will continue to have these problems until we address the ultimate causes. **Proximate causes** are the causes of the problem that are immediately, directly responsible for the symptoms.)

7

As with the Ishikawa diagrams, not every problem will require the use of this sort of formal technique. On the other hand, complex problems with lots of moving parts may benefit from their use.

Interrelationship Diagrams

Interrelationship Diagrams (IDs) are a tool to look at a collection of possible explanations and identify which of them might be a root cause. IDs are particularly useful when hypotheses are interrelated in nontrivial ways. Their purpose is to identify which of several interrelated items are causes and which are effects.

IDs use boxes containing phrases describing the potential causes. Arrows between the potential causes represent influence relationships between the issues. Each relationship can only have an arrow in one direction. (Where the relationship's influence runs in both directions, the troubleshooters must decide which one is most relevant.) Items with more "out" arrows than "in" arrows are causes. Items with more "in" arrows are effects.

Figure 1-3 shows a simple example of an Interrelationship Diagram. The real benefit of an ID comes when we are looking at the relationships between the possible causes. In particular, they are helpful in distinguishing between the apparent (proximate) causes and the root (ultimate) causes.

Researchers provide several suggestions for using IDs effectively (see Mizuno, 1988):

1)Collect information from multiple distinct sources.

2)Phrases with a noun and a verb are recommended in each box.

3)Diagrams must reflect a group consensus.

4)Redo diagrams several times if necessary.

5)Don't get distracted by intermediate factors.

A common way to use IDs is to write each box's description on a Post-It note, arrange them on a white board, and draw in the arrows. This can be a useful way to deal with a large number of interrelated hypotheses.

In more complicated implementations, arrows may be weighted in order to try and rank the causes in order of importance. As a practical matter, that is probably overkill for most troubleshooting exercises of the sort that system administrators face.

Usually, the diagram's main benefit is in helping the troubleshooting team to focus on the issues and their relationships. In particular, it helps distinguish between the causes and symptoms of a problem. The relative importances of the competing hypotheses and the relationships between them are often a side-benefit of this discussion.

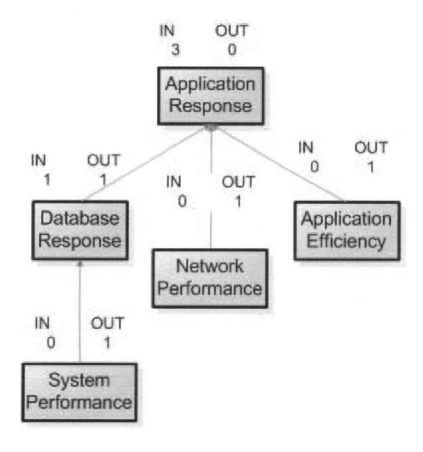

Figure 1-3. Interrelationship Diagram

Fault Profiles

Hardware and software faults tend to have distinct profiles. There is enough difference between the profiles that they can be useful in distinguishing whether a particular problem is likely to be a hardware or a software fault. Fault profiles are not a smoking gun, but they are a useful tool. Table 1-3 contains lists of characteristic symptoms of hardware and software faults.

Table 1-3. Problem Profiles

Hardware Fault Profile
Hardware faults tend to arise suddenly, with no prior change in the environment.
Hardware faults tend to occur at random intervals.
Hardware faults tend to be more frequent and severe as time goes on.
Watchdog resets are usually caused by a hardware problem. (See "Watchdog Resets" in Chapter 3 for a discussion of exceptions.)
Error messages on the console or in the system logs may indicate a hardware fault.
• Asynchronous memory errors usually indicate a DRAM module problem.

Hardware Fault Profile
Hardware faults tend to arise suddenly, with no prior change in the environment.
• Asynchronous memory faults usually indicate a problem on the bus between the memory and the CPU.
• Ecache parity errors indicate a problem synchronizing memory between the CPU cache and the physical memory.
• If there are disk error messages and a stack trace lists UFS routines, there is probably a disk hardware problem.
Hardware faults may follow traumatic events such as power surges, environmental problems, or rough physical treatment of the hardware.

Software Fault Profile
Software faults frequently emerge during a change in the environment.
Software faults are often predictable and repeatable.
Panics are usually the result of a software fault (though hardware faults can also cause panics).

Test the HypothesesOnce we have identified which hypotheses are most likely to be correct, we need to schedule them for testing immediately. This does not necessarily mean that they can actually be tested immediately. Some hypotheses require disruptive testing, which may need to be scheduled during a maintenance window. Nevertheless, testing should be *scheduled* immediately for any hypotheses that are considered to be fairly likely to be the cause of the problem.

Other hypotheses do not require disruptive testing. Those tests should be carried out immediately, from most likely to least likely.

As with doctors, the rule for troubleshooters is "First, do no harm." Our testing should be the least disruptive possible under the circumstances. We need to minimize costs associated with downtime, service instability, time, money, and technical resources. We should never do anything without knowing how to reverse the change.

If a failover solution exists, we should fail over. At a minimum, service outages should be confined to scheduled maintenance windows where possible. Data needs to be backed up to prevent data loss. In particular, configurations should be preserved before they are changed. No test should be carried out that cannot be reversed.

In some cases, it may be possible to test the hypothesis directly in some sort of test environment. This may be as simple as running an alternative copy of a program without overwriting the original. Or it may be as complex as setting up a near copy of the faulted system in a test lab. If a realistic test can be carried out without too great a cost in terms of money or time, it can assure us that we have identified the root cause of the problem.

Depending on the situation, it may even be appropriate to test out the hypotheses by directly applying the fix associated with that problem. If this approach is used, it is important to only perform one test at a time, and back out the results of each failed hypotheses before trying the next one. Otherwise, you will not have a good handle on the root cause of the problem, and you may never be confident that it will not re-emerge at the worst possible moment.

As we design tests, we should try to have a "smoking gun" level of certainty about whether we have nailed the cause (or at least narrowed it down).

It is frequently best to start with the most likely cause for the failure, based on the troubleshooting team's understanding of the system. The history of similar faults may also indicate the most likely problem. The "most likely first" approach is especially valuable if one of the possible causes is considered to be much more likely than the others.

On the other hand, if investigating the most likely cause requires disruptive or expensive testing, it makes sense to eliminate some of the possibilities that are easier to test. This is particularly the case if there are several easily testable hypotheses.

The best approach is to schedule testing of the most likely hypotheses immediately. Then start to perform any non-disruptive or minimally disruptive testing of hypotheses. If several of the most likely hypotheses can be tested non-disruptively, so much the better. Start with them.

The key is to start eliminating possibilities as soon as possible. It makes no sense to waste time arguing about the most likely cause. Prove it. At this stage, the troubleshooting team has spent a lot of time thinking about the problem. Don't start with the corner cases, but start narrowing the list down.

Intermittent problems are especially difficult to troubleshoot. See the "Dealing with Intermittent Problems" sidebar for suggestions on handling this type of problem.

Dealing with Intermittent Problems

Intermittent problems are very difficult to troubleshoot. Reproducible problems can be troubleshot; each false possibility can be disproved. Problems that aren't reproducible can't be approached in the same way.

We have no way to know that a problem is not reproducible until after we have tested the available hypotheses. Even so, our testing regime should be able to eliminated some areas of concern:

Problems present as intermittent because:

1) We have not identified the real cause of the problem.

2) The problem is being caused by flaky hardware.

The first possibility should be addressed by going back to the brainstorming step. It may be helpful to bring a fresh perspective into the brainstorming session, either by bringing in different people, or by sleeping on the problem.

The second problem is tougher. There are hardware diagnostics tests that can be run to try to identify the failing piece of hardware. The first thing to do is to perform general maintenance on the system. Re-seat memory chips, processors, expansion boards and hard drives. Use an approved vacuum cleaner to clean the dust out of the case. Look for cracked traces or stress fractures on the system boards.

If OS patches are out of date, it also makes sense to apply a current patch set to resolve driver issues that may have since been fixed. Keep track of which patches are applied when so that we can back them out if new problems emerge.

Once general maintenance has been performed, test suites like SunVTS can perform stress-testing on a system to try to trigger the failure and identify the failing part. Ideally, we want to pull the failing system out of production long enough to be able to run the tests and perform the repair. Perhaps this can be done during a maintenance period or the system can be replaced temporarily with a piece of failover hardware.

It may be the case, however, that the costs associated with this level of troubleshooting are prohibitive. In this case, we may want to attempt to shotgun the problem.

Shotgunning is the practice of replacing potentially failing parts without having identified them as actually being flaky. Usual practice is to replace parts by price point, with the cheapest parts being replaced first. (Litt, 2005) Though we are likely to inadvertently replace working parts, the cost of the replacement may be cheaper than the costs of the alternatives (like the downtime cost associated with stress testing).

When parts are removed during shotgunning, discard them rather than keep them as spares. Any part we remove as part of a troubleshooting exercise is questionable. (After all, what if a power surge caused multiple parts to fail? Or what if there was a cascading failure?) It does not make sense to have questionable parts in inventory; such parts would be useless for troubleshooting or replacement.

Shotgunning may violate your service contract if performed without the knowledge and consent of our service provider. (To get consent, we may need to apply leverage to the service provider. We can speak candidly with a manager about the impact of the problem and whether the provider's usual strategies are working. It may even be necessary to purchase the parts ourselves in order to perform shotgunning.)

No matter how we deal with an intermittent problem, we have to keep good records. Relationships between our problem and other events may show up when we look at the history of our environment. Unless we can demonstrate that we've gone well beyond the usual re-occurrence frequency without the problem re-emerging, we can't really be sure that the problem is fixed.

Implementation Phase

The **Implementation Phase** is where we finally resolve the problem and recover the system to a working state. We also make sure that we have really fixed the problem and where we document our results.

Apply the Fix

Once our testing has identified the source of the problem, we need to fix it. This includes fixing any required documentation, Jumpstart setup, or configurations on other systems.

A key concern in applying the fix is that we do so in the least-disruptive, lowest-cost manner possible. (Lowest-cost means that we have to consider all the costs. This includes the cost of downtime on the affected service, the cost of instability on the system prior to the fix, as well as direct costs associated with the repair.)

Ideally, we want to carry out the fix in a way that we can verify that the problem is actually resolved. Especially where reboots are required, it is sometimes hard to tell whether the problem has actually been fixed, or whether the reboot just cleared up the symptoms.

Verify the Fix

We need to make sure that we have actually resolved the problem. We also need to verify that we have not introduced any new problems.

In a well-organized environment, each service should have a test procedure or test suite associated with it to identify when the service is working properly. (Test suites will never be 100% complete, but they can evolve into extremely useful tools.) As new failure modes emerge, tests for them must be integrated into the suite.

Part of this step may be a root cause analysis to make sure that we have nailed the cause of the problem, as opposed to applying a Band-Aid to a symptom. Root cause analyses are discussed in more detail in Chapter 2.

Document the Resolution

Information on troubleshooting incidents needs to be stored in a central repository. This doesn't necessarily mean an expensive web-enabled trouble ticket database solution. In many environments, it is enough to have a wiki or a shared directory with an appropriate subdirectory structure and file naming scheme.

(Where a shared directory is used as the repository, I strongly recommend that each problem have its own subdirectory with a name that indicates at least the date of the problem occurrence as well as a name indicating the general nature of the problem.)

A key document that needs to be included in this repository is a sign-off from the service owner agreeing that the problem has been resolved. This may seem like administrivia, but the discipline of getting a sign-off ensures that we have understood and addressed the end user complaint. It also ensures that the end user spends the time to check it out (or at least takes some ownership for future occurrences of the problem). We don't have to write up a contract that requires approval from Legal. In many environments, a copy of a thank-you email from the service owner is good enough.

At a bare minimum, the problem resolution documentation needs to include the following:
- Problem statement.
- Problem description documents, including dates and times of occurrences.
- Any vendor service order or correspondence associated with the problem.
- Information about the hypotheses generated during brainstorming, including any diagrams or documents used to organize them. (If a white-board discussion has been a central part of the process, take a digital photo of it and save it as part of the problem history.)
- Descriptions and results of testing. (This may be as simple as a checklist or a collection of saved emails.)
- A confirmation and acceptance document from the service owner.

For many environments, it is enough to save copies of the emails between members of the troubleshooting team. The key thing is that they be organized in a way that they can be found if we need to reference them in the future.

Over time, the collection of data on resolved problems can become a valuable resource. It can be referenced to deal with similar problems. It can be used to track recurring problems over time. Or it can be used to continue the troubleshooting process if it turns out that the problem was not really resolved after all.

Case Study

Here is how we might apply these techniques to a system crash.

soltest, a Sun X4200 server, crashed on Thursday morning at 1:32 am. Fortunately, this system is part of a high-availability cluster of web servers, so services were not interrupted. We have the freedom to work on soltest immediately, rather than having to try to bring the system online by any means necessary in order to limp through to a maintenance window.

Problem Statement

Our problem statement in this case is very straightforward: "soltest panicked on Thursday morning at 1:32am." Note that this problem statement does not include any value judgments about difficulties caused by the system panic, it does not include any hypotheses as to the cause, and it does not include a list of immediately observable symptoms.

Problem Description

Our next task is to fully describe the problem by collecting as many symptoms as possible. We end up with the following:

1) A core file was generated by the system panic. A quick examination (see Chapter 3 and 4) shows that httpd was active at the time of the panic.
2) POST reports "Hypertransport Sync Flood occurred on last boot." SunSolve identifies this as a memory error.
3) BIOS and service processor System Event Log information report errors on the DIMM at CPU0, slot 1.
4) The fault LEDs are lit for CPU0, slots 0 and 1.

Identify Differences and Changes

Our records for the system show that memory was upgraded 6 months ago.

Brainstorm

The obvious conclusion is that the cause of the problem is a bad DIMM. Rather than jumping immediately to replacing the DIMM, we take the time to think through the Ishikawa Diagram in Figure 1-4.

(Note that some of the items on the diagram are extremely low probability events. The purpose of a brainstorming exercise is to generate possible explanations, not to filter them. We want to encourage hare-brained speculation in this step. Sometimes those oddball hypotheses end up being the real cause or at least triggering a thought that leads to the root cause.)

Since we are disciplined enough to think through each aspect of the system, we make several interesting observations:

1) Sometimes an error reported on one DIMM is actually a result of a bad memory chip elsewhere in the same bank.
2) The DIMM may be poorly seated, not failed. This can be due to a faulty slot on the system board, or it may be due to a poorly installed DIMM.
3) CPU or cache errors sometimes manifest as "memory errors."
4) An OS or driver bug might have falsely reported a memory error.
5) Bad power supplies sometimes cause failures of other components.
6) Could high network traffic have caused the problem?
7) Sometimes we purchase "gray market" DIMMs (ie, DIMMs from other than a certified VAR, as opposed to "black market" DIMMs which might be stolen.) Should we be more careful about which suppliers we use?
8) Can the Fault Management Facility handle errors more gracefully?
9) Might the httpd process be at fault? It was active at the time of the crash.

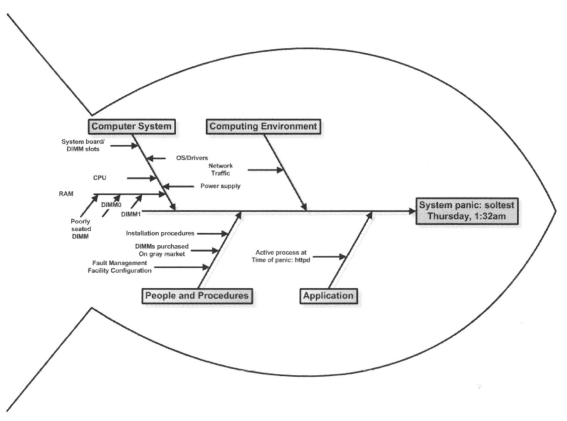

Figure 1-4. Ishikawa Diagram

Rank the Likely Causes

We have generated quite a few hypotheses. It makes sense to look for possible relationships in order to make sure that we examine any possible root causes.

In the real world, Interrelationship Diagrams are frequently generated by writing the various proposed causes on Post-It notes on a white board, then rearranging them and drawing relationship arrows between them. Working through this process in this case yields a few observations, which are illustrated in Figure 1-5:

1) One relationship that jumps out is the possibility that our purchasing policy (gray market DIMMs) may have led to the installation of a bad part. In this case, we have a possible ultimate cause (purchasing policy) and a possible proximate cause (bad DIMM) that both need to be examined.

2) Another possible relationship is that our installation procedure may have damaged a DIMM. In this scenario, our ultimate cause would be poor installation procedures, and our proximate cause would be the resulting bad DIMM. (Since the upgrade was six months ago, this is a low probability hypothesis.)

3) A bad power supply may have led to a DIMM being zapped.

15

4) High network traffic or some activity of httpd may have resulted in exercising the back area of memory, but they can't reasonably be considered to be the "cause" of the problem in any reasonable sense.

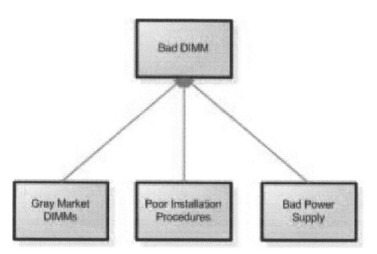

Figure 1-5. Memory Error Interrelationship Diagram

Based on this, the ranking of the most likely hypotheses are:

1) The DIMM in slot 1, CPU 0 is faulty. (The most obvious candidate is usually the right one.)

2) The DIMM in slot 0, CPU 0 is faulty.

3) The DIMMs in the bank are improperly seated or have a bad DIMM slot.

4) CPU 0 has a problem.

5) An OS or driver problem is improperly reporting a memory error.

In addition, we need to examine the possible ultimate causes of the gray market parts or the poor installation procedures. Both of these are possible problems with broad ramifications, and they should be examined.

Test the Hypotheses

Sun outlines a procedure for investigating memory errors in the diagnostics manual for these servers. When investigating a hardware error, we should always check vendor documentation for their recommendations about how to proceed with testing. Sometimes there are built-in testing facilities that we are unfamiliar with, and sometimes there are hardware-specific issues that we don't know about.

In this case, Sun recommends the following procedure for identifying whether it s a bad DIMM, a mis-seated DIMM, a system board problem or a CPU problem:

• Switch to standby power mode and pop off the cover.

• Make sure that the DIMMs are in a legal configuration, using certified parts. (Since we have been running fine for six months, this is almost certainly the case. Our gray market parts may even have Sun part number stickers on them.)

• Check the fault LEDs on the DIMM slots and the CPUs. (We did this earlier as part of the Problem Description step, and noted that the fault LEDs are lit for slots 0 and 1 on the CPU0 side.)

• Disconnect the power cords and hook up an anti-static wrist strap. (This goes back to our installation procedures. Any time we are fiddling with the innards of the system, we need to be careful about static electricity.)

• Remove the DIMMs from the problem bank and visually inspect them for damage (scratches, cracked leads or plastic, dirt, etc).

• Inspect the slots to look for damage.

• Use compressed air or a specially designed vacuum to clean out the slots. (Don't blow into the slots with your mouth; your saliva is not an approved system cleaning agent. And don't use the floor vacuum. If you aren't sure if your vacuum is designed for systems work, it is not.)

• If there is no visible damage to the chips or the slots, exchange the positions of the two DIMMs, reconnect the power and reboot. Re-run system diagnostics (including a memory stress test from SunVTS if the boot proceeds okay). If the memory stress test comes up okay, the problem was probably due to a mis-seated DIMM.

• If an error is generated during boot or the stress test, see if it moved to the other DIMM slot in the bank. If so, the DIMM is bad and should be replaced. If the error is still on slot 1, the CPU or the DIMM slot is bad.

• Shut down the system and re-connect the anti-static strap. Move the DIMMs to the slots on CPU1's side. Reboot and repeat the diagnostic tests. If the error moves to the CPU1 side of the system, the DIMMs are bad and need to be replaced. If the error stays on the CPU0 side of the system, the CPU is bad. If the error does not re-occur (but can be prompted by running diagnostics with the DIMMs in the original slots), the problem is with the DIMM slots on the system board.

In addition to the fun with hardware, we need to take the time to examine the other two potential root causes. (We can do this while the memory stress test is running.)

We can examine the quality issues with our gray market vendor by looking at the repair history of parts purchased through them. We may also want to consider whether we may have voided service contracts or system warranties by purchasing non-approved parts, and whether the extra costs and risks associated with our decision are justified by our cost savings.

And our installation procedures should be reviewed in any case. Everyone should be reminded to take proper anti-static and hygenic precautions (wash hands, clean work area, etc) and to install parts in a manufacturer-approved manner.

The power supply should also be investigated, since power supply problems can be very difficult to track down. General practice is to start looking at the power supply as a possible culprit when there have been multiple part failures over a relatively short period of time. Unless there is actually a fault light on the power supply, it is difficult to pin down power supply problems, especially intermittent ones.

The steps outlined by Sun are involved. In some cases, (with the concurrence of our service vendor, if any), it might make sense to shotgun the problem by replacing suspected parts one at a time. After each replacement, diagnostics (including a stress test) should be run. Parts removed during a shotgunning session should always be discarded, even if we don't think they are bad (see "Dealing with Intermittent Problems" above). The usual practice when shotgunning is to replace parts in order of cost (cheapest first), rather than likelihood. Individual cases may be handled differently.

Apply the Fix

In this case, our failed part has been replaced as part of our testing regime. The ultimate cause, however, may still be out there. Any changes to our purchasing and installation procedures also need to be implemented.

Verify the Fix

Our diagnostic tests, especially the SunVTS stress test, are a good way to validate our fix. Procedural changes also need to be verified and approved by the relevant managers.

Document the Resolution

In most enviroments, it is enough to bundle together the logs and documents generated during the troubleshooting session and put them in a directory share with a defined structure. In this case, for example, perhaps we could create a directory for the soltest server, with a subdirectory named according to the date and a brief problem description (yyyymmdd-ProblemDescription). Our diagrams, notes and emails can be saved to this directory. We should also include a document containing any service order numbers created with our service provider.

In larger environments, it may be worthwhile to set up a problem resolution database to allow searches of problem resolution information.

We also need to include a sign-off document from the system owner verifying that the problem is resolved. (This may seem like overkill, but I don't care to think of the number of times that I had thought a problem was resolved, only to discover that I forgot to re-start some obscure service or other.)

Resources

- Cromar, Scott. (2007). *Solaris Troubleshooting at Princeton University.* Princeton, NJ: Princeton University. (http://www.princeton.edu/~unix/Solaris/troubleshoot/index.html)
- Cromar, Scott. (August 2007). Troubleshooting Methods. SysAdmin Magazine.
- Doggett, Dr Anthony Mark. (February-April 2004). A Statistical Analysis of Three *Root Cause Analysis Tools.* Journal of Industrial Technology. (http://www.nait.org/jit/Articles/doggett010504.pdf)
- Hunt, Craig. (April 2002). *TCP/IP Network Administration, 3rd Edition.* Sebastopol, CA: O'Reilly.
- Ishikawa, K. (1982). *Guide to Quality Control, 2nd Edition.* Tokyo: Asian Productivity Press.
- Litt, Steve. (October, 2005). *Shotgunning.* Troubleshooting Professional Magazine, Fall 2005. (http://www.troubleshooters.com/tpromag/200510/200510.htm)
- Mizuno, S., ed. (1988). M*anagement for Quality Improvement: The Seven New QC Tools.* Cambridge: Productivity Press.
- Sun Microsystems. (June, 2006). *SunVTS 6.2 Test Reference Manual for SPARC Platforms.* Santa Clara, CA: Sun Microsystems, Inc. (http://docs.sun.com/app/docs/doc/819-6455)
- Sun Microsystems. (June, 2006). *SunVTS 6.2 Test Reference Manual for x86 Platforms.* Santa Clara, CA: Sun Microsystems, Inc. (http://docs.sun.com/app/docs/doc/819-6456)
- Sun Microsystems. (June, 2006). *SunVTS 6.2 User's Guide.* Santa Clara, CA: Sun Microsystems, Inc. (http://docs.sun.com/app/docs/doc/819-6454)
- Sun Microsystems Training. S*T-350: Sun Systems Fault Analysis.* (http://www.sun.com/training/catalog/courses/ST-350.xml)
- Sun Microsystems Training. S*A-400: Solaris System Performance Management.* (http://www.sun.com/training/catalog/courses/SA-400.xml)

2

Root Cause Analysis

Too often we see people who think that they have "fixed" the problem because the immediate emergency is over. People who don't resolve the root problem are condemned to a continual break/fix treadmill. The discipline of root cause analysis was invented to help us break the firefighting cycle and actually get the problem fixed for once and for all.

Systems administration is not the only discipline to have problems that need us to dig down to the ultimate causes. Fortunately, root cause analysis is general enough to be applied to a broad range of problems.

5 Whys

The simplest version of root cause analysis is sometimes called the "**5 Whys**" method developed by Toyota Motor Corporation. This method proposes that for most problems, by asking "why" a problem occurs, and asking "why" each successive explanation occurs, we can arrive at the root cause within 5 iterations. There is nothing magical about the number 5; the exercise should be repeated until we get to something that is recognizable as a root cause. Example 2-1 illustrates:

Example 2-1. 5 Whys

```
Problem Statement:  The system crashed.  (Why?)
A memory chip failed.  (Why?)
The machine room temperature exceeds recommendations.  (Why?)
The HVAC unit is undersized given our heat load.  (Why?)
Our projections for heat load were lower than what has been observed.  (Why?)
We did the heat load projections ourselves rather than bringing in a qualified expert.
```

There are some serious weaknesses to the 5 Whys method:
- The results are not repeatable. We may well end up with different results depending on who runs the exercise. For example, what if we had answered the second "why" with some other plausible explanation? (Eg, "The chip was installed improperly." Or perhaps "The manufacturer's quality control is inadequate.")
- We are limited to the participants' knowledge of the system. In particular, we aren't going to find any answers that the participants don't already suspect.
- We may not ask "why?" about the right symptoms of the problem.

- We may stop short and not proceed to the actual root cause of the problem. For example, people may stop at the point about the HVAC unit being undersized, run the estimates themselves, and promptly purchase a larger (but still undersized) unit.

These problems can be addressed, usually by reaching a group consensus about the appropriate answer for each "why" and by performing rigorous testing wherever possible.

Current Reality Tree

Eliyahu Goldratt presented a "**Theory of Constraints**" (TOC) to resolve issues with organizational problem-solving. One of the cornerstones of the Theory of Constraints is a type of diagram known as a **Current Reality Tree** (CRT).

The Current Reality Tree has a number of similarities with the Interrelationship Diagram we discussed in Chapter 1. As with the ID, the CRT's primary components are boxes describing symptoms and arrows representing relationships between them. There are several key distinctions between an ID and a CRT:
- Arrows may flow in both directions if necessary. In particular, this allows us to identify a negative feedback loop.
- Symptoms are divided into **Undesirable Effects** (UDE) and **Neutral Effects** (NE). This allows us to recognize the effects of things in our environment that are not viewed as undesirable, but which may contribute to a UDE.
- Two or more symptoms may have their arrows combined with an ellipse. In a CRT, this means that the combination of those symptoms is sufficient to provoke the following UDE, but that all of them are required to ensure that the following UDE occurs. (In other words, the combination of UDEs and NEs is both necessary and sufficient to provoke the following UDE.)
- Because of the emphasis on identifying combinations of effects that are both necessary and sufficient, CRTs can sometimes flush out symptoms that are not obvious at first glance. As a result, CRTs can be better at getting to a real root cause than either Ishikawa diagrams or Interrelationship Diagrams. (See the "Summary of Other Findings" in Doggett 2004, for example.)

Building a CRT

Building a CRT has a lot in common with the Ishikawa and Interrelationship Diagrams we explored in Chapter 1. First, we ask a **Key Question** with our Problem Statement. The question will usually be of the form "Why is this happening?" or "Why did this happen?"

Next, we need to create a list of several Undesirable Effects which are related to the Key Question. Each of these UDEs gets a box (or perhaps a Post-It note on a white board). These are arranged from top to bottom, where the top symptoms are the result of the symptoms from lower rows.

Wherever we can say something like "If A, then B," we would draw an arrow from A to B. Where we can say something like "If A is combined with B, then we get C," we would draw arrows from A and B to C, then group the arrows with an ellipse.

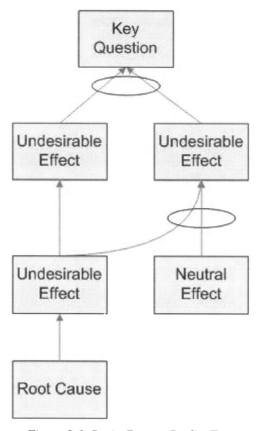

Figure 2-1. Basic Current Reality Tree

We may also identify a feedback loop, where an effect has a direct impact on one of its own causes. Figure 2-2 illustrates such a loop.

In Figure 2-2, we consider the case of a CPU-bound service on a system with inadequate memory. The system starts to swap, which slows down the process because data is stored in swap space rather than memory, and CPU resources are required to run the page scanner and perform swapping.

During this exercise, we may find it necessary to add more symptoms, either Undesirable Effects or Neutral Effects. We should not add UDEs or NEs that are not part of a key causality chain, or that are simply "Facts of Life." We want to try to keep the diagram clean enough that it can be used to spur thinking about how to resolve the root causes; it doesn't make sense to put in items which are tangential or environmental.

We will likely have two or more branches of the tree. Wherever possible, we should try to identify connections between the branches, such as symptoms that would cause the lowest-level effects of both branches.

At the lowest level of the CRT, we should ask "Why?" and continue to build the tree down until we are at the **Root Causes**, also known as "**Problems**." If the lowest level boxes are still just symptoms of an underlying problem, build down as far as possible by asking "Why?" at each stage.

It is possible to have more than one root cause for a problem. In this case, we would want to identify which of the causes is predominant. If one of the root causes is responsible for more than 70% of the UDEs, it is designated the **Core Problem**; it should receive our attention first. (Pareto Diagrams, discussed later in this chapter, may help us to identify the Core Problem.)

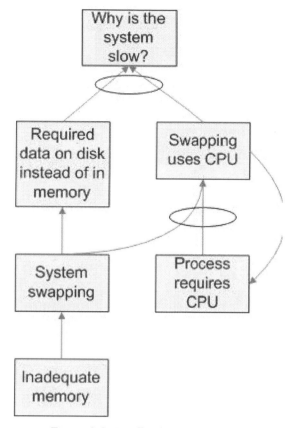

Figure 2-2 Feedback Loop in a CRT

In Figure 2-2, for example, the core problem is that we have inadequate memory. We could argue that an alternative root cause is that we don't have enough CPU resources to swap efficiently, but a reasonable system administrator would have to admit that more than 70% of the problem is due to the memory shortage.

It is also possible that at the lowest level, we will end up with a **Core Conflict** between two or more otherwise Neutral Effects. The combination of these two NEs, or the conflicts between them may end up causing the UDEs further up the diagram. Figure 2-3 illustrates a core conflict.

Evaporating Cloud

The **Evaporating Cloud** refers to Goldratt's method for dealing with conflicts. In particular, Goldratt discusses the **Core Conflict Cloud** representing the Core Conflict in our CRT.

The cloud metaphor describes the sense of unease we feel when faced with a seeming choice between two necessary conditions. Most of the time, we feel that we are caught in a situation where the best we can do is get away with some sort of unsatisfactory compromise.

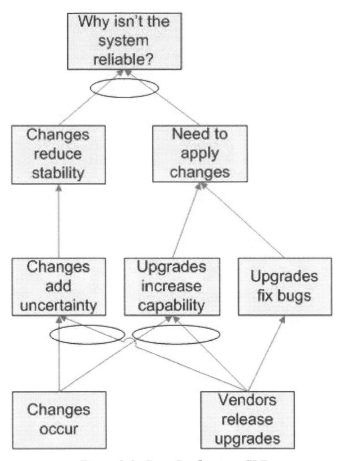

Figure 2-3. Core Conflict in a CRT

In an Evaporating Cloud Diagram, the end goal (aka the Systemic Objective) is placed in a box on the left. The two conflicting Prerequisite Conditions are placed in boxes at the right hand side of the drawing, with a lightning bolt arrow between them. The Necessary Conditions for the Systemic Objective are placed in boxes next to their respective conflicting prerequisite conditions. See Figure 2-4, for example.

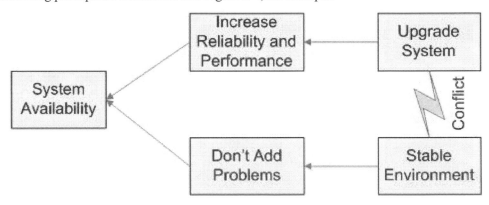

Figure 2-4. Evaporating Cloud

Many conflicts can be resolved by defining the Necessary Conditions as narrowly as possible to reach the Systemic Objective, then seeing if this allows a redefinition of the Prerequisite Conditions that eliminates the conflict. The

24

goal of a Theory of Constraints thinking exercise is to reach a win/win solution to a problem that leverages constraints rather than viewing them as obstacles.

Figure 2-4 illustrates the age-old conflict between upgrades and system stability. On the one hand, upgrades will usually increase the system reliability and performance. Neglecting upgrades for too long will eventually result in system problems or delays when placing service calls. On the other hand, changes always carry some risk, so there is a strong desire to avoid the pain of changes, including upgrades.

In this case, we need to recognize the end goal of providing a reliable service. Upgrades need to be performed, but should be performed in a way that allows for adequate planning and testing in order to avoid introducing problems to a working system.

This sort of solution "**evaporates**" the cloud. In the Theory of Constraints, we can now build a **Future Reality Tree**, which is like a Current Reality Tree, except that it will represent the system with the changes we recommended to evaporate the cloud. These additional changes are called **injections**. Figure 2-5 includes an example of a Future Reality Tree with our injections.

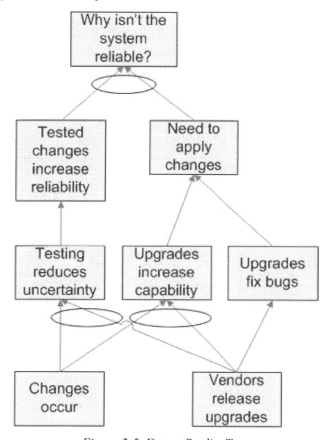

Figure 2-5. Future Reality Tree

Pareto Diagram

Pareto Diagrams are designed to help us identify which of several items is responsible for most of the problems we face. The Pareto Principle is an observation that states that in many real world cases, 80% of the problems come from 20% of the components.

25

We would create a Pareto Diagram by identifying "buckets" of factors into which we will sort incidents. Each incident is assigned to only one bucket. Based on which buckets are responsible for the most incidents, we know where we should focus our efforts. In the case of buckets assigned to different root causes in a CRT, the Pareto Diagram tells us which cause is the Core Problem.

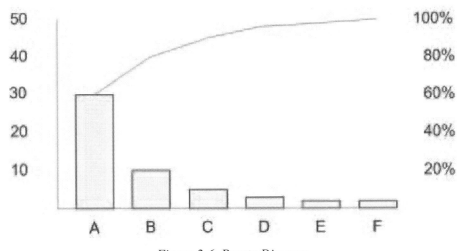

Figure 2-6. Pareto Diagram

In Figure 2-6, the numbers on the left side of the graph indicate the raw number of incidents associated with each bucket in the bar graph. The numbers on the right side indicate the cumulative percentage of incidents reflected by the buckets to the left of each point on the upper line graph.

One way to interpret Figure 2-6 is that cleaning up cause A will eliminate 60% of the problem occurrences. Eliminating A and B will eliminate 80% of the incidents.

> Analyses like a Pareto analysis are only possible if information on past incidents have been collected. This is an example of why it is so important to document incidents as discussed in Chapter 1.

Resources

- Doggett, Anthony Mark. (February-April 2004). A Statistical Analysis of Three *Root Cause Analysis Tools*. Journal of Industrial Technology. (http://www.nait.org/jit/Articles/doggett010504.pdf)
- Goldratt, Eliyahu M. (1997). Critical Chain. Great Barrington, MA: North River Press.
- Goldratt, Eliyahu M. (1994). The Goal. Great Barrington, MA: North River Press.
- Goldratt, Eliyahu M. (1994). It's Not Luck. Great Barrington, MA: North River Press.
- Goldratt, Eliyahu M. (1990). Theory of Constraints. Great Barrington, MA: North River Press.
- Mosley, Henry. (January 2006) *Current Reality Trees: An Action Learning Tool for Root Cause Analysis*. Baltimore, MD: Strategic Leadership Seminar for Population and Reproductive Health. (www.jhuccp.org/training/scope/starguide/toc/rootcauseanalysis.ppt)
- Ohno, Taiichi. (1988) *Toyota production system: beyond large-scale production*. Portland, OR: Productivity Press.
- Patrick, Francis S. (May 2001) *Taking Advantage of Resistance to Change (and the TOC Thinking Processes) to Improve Improvements*. Hillsborough, NJ: Focused Performance. (http://www.focusedperformance.com/articles/resistanceslides.pdf)
- Schwalbe, Kathy. (2006) *Information Technology Project Management*. Boston, MA: Thompson.

- Shelford, Thomas J. and Remillard, Gregory A. (October 2002) *Real Web Project Management.* Boston, MA: Addison-Wesley.
- US Department of Energy. (February 1992) DOE Guideline: *Root Cause Analysis Guidance Document.* Washington, DC: US Department of Energy, Office of Nuclear Energy. DOE-NE-STD-1004-92.
- Youngman, Kelvyn. (2007) *A Guide to Implementing the Theory of Constraints (TOC).* (http://www.dbrmfg.co.nz)

3

Errors, Logs and Diagnostics

Sometimes the best clues are the most obvious. Every troubleshooter can tell you a story about the error message that meant exactly what it said. It is easy to spend hours looking for obscure causes when the "file not found" error means that the stinking file wasn't found.

This chapter describes the different types of error messages and the different facilities that collect them. It also includes descriptions of several of the different facilities that Solaris provides to assist in troubleshooting problems.

We will spend several pages at the beginning of this chapter defining different types of error messages and when they occur. There is a lot of technical detail here summarized in lists and tables so that they are easy to reference when looking at a particular error message.

We will also spend time discussing how to set up a serial connection to SPARC-based systems, and how to use the OBP diagnostics and console messages to find the cause of a problem. At the end of the chapter, we discuss the boot process and how to use boot messages to diagnose problems.

Appendix A contains a listing of the most common error messages, along with an English-language interpretation of each message and some suggestions about what caused the error in the first place.

Logs can be found in any number of places, but the most important ones are found in */var/adm*, */var/log*, and */var/svc/log*. In particular, the */var/adm/messages* file is the default location for the most critical error messages.

Signals

Signals are an operating system mechanism to notify processes or threads of events. Signal handlers can be defined at a thread level to perform non-default actions when a signal is received, but our focus in this section is to look at what types of errors correspond to different signals.

Signals may be synchronous or asynchronous to the execution of the process. As we discuss in the "Traps" section below, **synchronous signals** occur as a result of an action of the process itself. They come from the kernel trap handler.

Asynchronous signals are sent to the process based on external events. A common example is when one process sends another process a signal via a `kill()` or a `sigsend()` system call. This type of signal is also called an **interrupt**. They can come from a user command, another process or from the kernel.

The `signal.h(3HEAD)` man page includes a full listing of signals. Table 3-1 below the lists the most relevant signals for troubleshooting purposes.

Table 3-1. Common Signals

Signal Name	ID #	Default Action	Description
SIGHUP	1	Exit	Hang up. (See the `termio(7I)` man page.)
SIGINT	2	Exit	Interrupt. (See the `termio(7I)` man page.)
SIGQUIT	3	Core	Quit. (See the `termio(7I)` man page.)
SIGILL	4	Core	Illegal instruction.
SIGABRT	6	Core	Abort.
SIGEMT	7	Core	Emulation Trap.
SIGFPE	8	Core	Floating Point Arithmetic Exception.
SIGKILL	9	Exit	Killed.
SIGBUS	10	Core	Bus Error.
SIGSEGV	11	Core	Segmentation Fault.
SIGSYS	12	Core	Bad System Call.
SIGPIPE	13	Exit	Broken Pipe.
SIGCHLD SIGCLD	18	Ignore	Child Status Change.
SIGPWR	19	Ignore	Power Fail or Restart.
SIGSTOP	23	Stop	Stopped (by a signal).
SIGTSTP	24	Stop	Terminal stop. (See the `termio(7I)` man page.)
SIGCONT	25	Ignore	Urgent Socket Condition.
SIGTTIN	26	Stop	Stopped, tty input. (See the `termio(7I)` man page.)
SIGTTOU	27	Stop	Stopped, tty output. (See the `termio(7I)` man page.)
SIGXCPU	30	Core	Exceeded CPU time limit. (See the `getrlimit(2)` man page.)
SIGXFSZ	31	Core	Exceeded the file size limit. (See the `getrlimit(2)` man page.)
SIGLOST	37	Exit	Resource lost. (A lock, for example.)
SIGXRES	38	Ignore	Resource control exceeded (see the `setrctl(2)` man page.)

Signal handling for a process can be displayed using the **psig** command. Example 3-1 shows edited output of a **psig** command for `picld`:

Example 3-1. psig Output

```
# psig 94
94:     /usr/lib/picl/picld
HUP     caught  0x12298         SIGINFO
INT     default
QUIT    default
...
ALRM    blocked,default
TERM    default
...
CLD     default                 NOCLDSTOP
...
```

The DTrace demo program **/usr/demo/dtrace/sig.d** provides a count of which processes receive how many of each signal. See Example 3-2:

Example 3-2. Signals by Process

```
#  dtrace -s /usr/demo/dtrace/sig.d
^C
            SENDER          RECIPIENT       SIG COUNT
            sshd            dtrace          2 1
            sched           xntpd           14 15
```

Types of Error Messages

Before we get into the specifics of how to deal with particular types of errors, we need to understand where they come from. Any application or service may issue its own error messages; those messages can be tracked down by examining the product documentation. In this section, we look for the types of messages that the OS provides for issues with basic system operation.

The main types of system error messages are traps, bus errors, interrupts, and watchdog resets. Each of these facilities reports on a specific sort of problem, with particular characteristics.

Table 3-2: Types of Error Messages

Error Message Type	Characteristics
Traps	• Synchronous signals. • Documented in *trap.h* and *machtrap.h*.
Bus Errors	• Processor references a location that cannot be accessed. • Synchronous signals. (A type of trap.)
Interrupts	• Asynchronous signals. • Handled by dedicated interrupt-handling kernel threads.

Error Message Type	Characteristics
Watchdog Resets	• Fault condition deemed as potentially dangerous. • Immediately drops to the PROM monitor. • Usually no core dump.

Traps

Traps are synchronous messages generated by the process or its underlying kernel thread. Examples include SIGSEGV, SIGPIPE and SIGSYS. They are delivered to the process that caused the signal. (See Table 3-1 in the "Signals" section above for definitions of the most common types of signals.)ECC (Error Checking and Correcting) interrupts are reported as traps when a bit error is corrected. While they do not crash the system, they are frequently a signal that the memory chip in question needs to be replaced. They can also be caused by environmental factors such as cosmic rays. Common practice is to wait for two or more occurrences of ECC errors before replacing the memory chip.

Critical errors include things like fan/temperature warnings or power loss that require immediate attention and shutdown.

Fatal errors are hardware errors where proper system function cannot be guaranteed. Fatal errors result in a panic or watchdog reset.

Trap messages can be discovered in a number of places, including error logs, mdb output, and console messages. The following files define the most important types of traps:
• */usr/include/sys/trap.h* (software traps)
• */usr/include/v7/sys/machtrap.h* (hardware traps, 32 bit)
• */usr/include/v9/sys/machtrap.h* (hardware traps, 64 bit)

The **trapstat** command provides a way to monitor the level of activity for different run-level traps. **trapstat -l** provides a full list of traps available on the system; Table 3-3 contains a list of summary of several important UltraSPARC traps and the signals that correspond to them.

Table 3-3. Traps and Corresponding Signals

Trap	Corresponding Signals	Meaning
async_data_error	SIGBUS	Unrecoverable error in attempting the access.
data_access_error	SIGBUS	Unrecoverable error in attempting the access.
data_access_exception	SIGSEGV, SIGBUS	No valid user mapping to specified address.
data_access_MMU_miss	SIGSEGV	Access to mapping denied.
data_access_protection	SIGSEGV	Type of access denied.
division_by_zero	SIGFPE	Division by zero attempted.
fp_disabled	SIGILL	Floating Point Registers State FEF bit is 0
fp_exception_ieee_754	SIGFPE	Arithmetic exception.

Trap	Corresponding Signals	Meaning
`fp_exception_other`	`SIGFPE`	Arithmetic exception.
`illegal_instruction`	`SIGILL`	Undefined opcode attempted.
`instruction_access_error`	`SIGBUS`	Unrecoverable error during instruction.
`instruction_access_exception`	`SIGSEGV, SIGBUS`	No valid user access to instruction.
`instruction_access_MMU_miss`	`SIGSEGV`	Unrecoverable error during instruction.
`mem_address_not_aligned`	`SIGBUS`	Illegal memory address specified.
`privileged_action`	`SIGILL`	Privileged action attempted.
`privileged_opcode`	`SIGILL`	Privileged opcode attempted.
`tag_overflow`	`SIGEMT`	Arithmetic overflow.

Bus ErrorsBus errors are traps in the sense that they are associated with synchronous signals. They merit their own section because the profile of bus errors is distinct.

A **bus error** is issued to the processor when it references a location that cannot be accessed. Bus errors are frequently accompanied by core files or crash dumps, which can be examined with **mdb** or provided to the software vendor (or both). Hardware causes for these errors include a memory mismatch, or the error may indicate failing, misconfigured, or corrupted storage in memory, disk devices, boot blocks, or cache. Software causes include invalid file descriptors, bad memory allocation, data structure misalignment, or illegal I/O requests. (These software problems may be due to the code itself or to a compiler bug.)

- **Illegal Address:** Usually a software or firmware failure.
- **Instruction Fetch/Data Load:** Device driver bug.
- **Virtual Memory Addressing:** data_access_exception, for example.
- **Synchronous Data Store:** data_access_error (valid mapping and permissions, but unrecoverable error during access.)
- **Asynchronous Data Store:** async_data_error (valid mapping and permissions, but unrecoverable error during access.)
- **MMU:** Memory Management Unit: Can be hardware or software errors, but are frequently system board problems.

Interrupts

Interrupts notify the CPU of external device conditions. These conditions are asynchronous to normal operation, since the devices typically operate in a request-and-response manner. Interrupts are delivered to the responsible process or kernel thread.

In Solaris, interrupts are handled by dedicated interrupt-handling kernel threads, which use mutex locks and semaphores to handle potential conflicts and collisions. The kernel will block interrupts in a few exceptional circumstances (for example, during the acquisition of a mutex lock protecting a sleep queue). Fault-related interrupts include:
- Device Done or Ready.
- Error Detected.
- Power On/Power Off.

Watchdog Resets

A **watchdog reset** occurs upon a fault condition that the system deems as potentially dangerous. On OBP-based systems, when such a fault occurs, the system immediately drops to the PROM monitor without taking a core dump. If the `watchdog-reboot?` OBP parameter is set to **true**, the system will reboot. No further diagnostics will be possible, unless an error message appears either in the system logs (from immediately before the watchdog reset was executed) or on the console (during hardware diagnostics during the reboot).

If the `watchdog-reboot?` parameter is set to **false**, some limited diagnostics are available that may point to a culprit.

Further complicating the issue, watchdog resets may be caused by either hardware or software problems. A software-triggered watchdog reset occurs when two trap errors take place so close together that the first one does not have time to complete before the second one is received by the system. This type of watchdog reset is sometimes called a "CPU" watchdog reset, since it occurs when the CPU receives a trap while the register bit to receive traps is not set. Since hardware faults may cause traps, a CPU watchdog reset may be caused by either hardware or software failures.

A second type of watchdog reset is a "system" watchdog reset. These are almost always caused by a hardware fault that the OS cannot handle in a safe way.

If the system is still at the PROM monitor prompt following the watchdog reset, it is possible to execute the following commands to attempt to gather some information about the system state prior to the reset. If at all possible, the system should be observed through a console or `tip` session that can be used to preserve the output of the PROM monitor session.

Post-Reset Diagnostics

Immediately after a watchdog reset, there are some diagnostics that may help to identify the cause of the problem. The following commands may be particularly useful:

- `.registers`: Displays kernel internal registers.
- `.locals`: Displays the registers in the current register window.
- `.psr`: Displays the Processor Status Register.
- `f8002010 wector p`: (Note that the word is *not* "vector.") This command displays messages similar to those in dmesg. They represent any final messages that may have occurred before the reset.
- `ctrace`: Displays the trace of the current thread.

Additional debugging information can be made available to the **ctrace** command via a module called obpsym. This can be loaded in one of two ways:

1. `modload /platform/`uname -i`/kernel/misc/obpsym`
   from the root command line. This method loads the module for the current boot session only.
2. `forceload: misc/obpsym` in the */etc/system* file. This method loads the module during future reboots.

Sun recommends using both methods so that the obpsym module is reloaded on each reboot until the problem is diagnosed and resolved.

Once the PROM monitor diagnostics have been run, use **sync** at the ok> prompt to generate a crash dump. This can be analyzed as suggested in Chapter 4. If a dump file is not saved, follow the troubleshooting suggestions in that section.

Watchdog resets are often caused by a hardware failure requiring a system board or CPU replacement. Less frequently, memory replacements may clear up the problem. These are just rules of thumb; any hardware that can send a trap is potentially responsible for a watchdog reset. I have even seen cases where shortening a SCSI path eliminates watchdog resets. Pay attention to all the error messages, even the ones that seem irrelevant at first.

Hardware faults may leave traces in log or console error messages. In particular, check for the following:

- **Asynchronous Memory Error**: Indicates a memory problem.
- **Asynchronous Memory Fault:** May be a bus problem between the memory and CPU. Try replacing the system board first, then the CPU, then the memory.
- **Ecache Parity Error:** Indicates a problem with the CPU's onboard cache. Replace the CPU.

syslog

The `syslog` facility is a critical piece of the logging infrastructure. It is relatively easy to set up a central `syslog` server to aggregate logs from several different machines. From there, the central logs can be processed, monitored, or archived.

The /etc/*syslog.conf* file controls the level of logging for each of the different facilities, as well as the action or file to which log entries are sent. (To send logs to a remote log server, the action is set to `@logserver`)

The format of /etc/*syslog.conf* is of lines defining how different log messages should be handled. Each line consists of a comma-separated list of `facility.level` pairs separated by whitespace from an action.

The actions in an /etc/*syslog.conf* file are log file names or the names of remote log servers. The facility defined in the `facility.level` pairs contains a `syslog` **facility**, which is usually defined as one of the following:

- **auth**: For authentication events.
- **daemon**: Daemon service events.
- **kern**: Kernel events.
- **local[0-7]**: Designed for local use.
- **lpr**: Print events.
- **mail**: Mail-related events.
- **user**: User processes.

The levels define the lowest level event that are logged by that rule. Any event of that level or higher for the specified facility is logged. **Levels** may be defined as `emerg`, `alert`, `crit`, `err`, `warning`, `notice`, `info`, `debug` or `none`. Either facility or level (or both) may contain an asterisk to match any facility or level.

The `syslog` output can be overwhelming in size. Fortunately, there are several reporting scripts available to help process `syslog` output. Two good freely-available solutions are `logcheck` and `logwatch`. (URLs to both are provided in the "Resources" section at the end of the chapter.)

The `syslog-ng` package allows auditability and flexibility that is not included in the standard `syslog` package. If `syslog` does not provide enough flexibility, `syslog-ng` is worth a look.

Log Rotation

Log rotation is controlled by the **logadm** command in the root crontab. (In previous versions of Solaris, the **newsyslog** command was used to do the file rotation.) The configuration file for **logadm** is /etc/logadm.conf. The entries in logadm.conf can specify that an individual file be rotated based on `-s` *size* or `-p` *period*. Unless otherwise specified, **logadm** creates a new file with the same ownership and permissions as the old file and rotates the old file. Files are permitted to expire based on the specified `-A` *age*, `-C` *count*, or `-S` *size* options. Compression may be specified for older log files by specifying the number of old log files to remain uncompressed with `-z` *count*. In addition, each logadm.conf entry may contain a `-a` *post-command* option to specify a command to be run after the rotation has occurred (such as a daemon restart). The `-w` option is used to write or edit a **logadm** configuration to the logadm.conf file so that it is called when **logadm** runs from the root crontab. The exact syntax can be found in the `logadm(1M)` man page.

Example 3-3 below demonstrates how the **logadm** options work. The period is set to zero to allow us to rotate even though no real amount of time has passed. Figure 3-1 demonstrates graphically what this sequence of options does.

Example 3-3. Log Rotation

```
soltest# ls -l
total 8
-rw-r-----   1 root       sysadmin        713 May 18 19:33 logfile
-rw-r-----   1 root       sysadmin       1293 May 18 19:32 logfile.0
-rw-r-----   1 root       sysadmin         32 May 18 19:26 logfile.1.gz

soltest# logadm -p 0w -c -C 2 -z 1 logfile
soltest# ls -l
total 4
-rw-r-----   1 root       sysadmin          0 May 18 19:34 logfile
-rw-r-----   1 root       sysadmin        713 May 18 19:33 logfile.0
-rw-r-----   1 root       sysadmin        604 May 18 19:32 logfile.1.gz
```

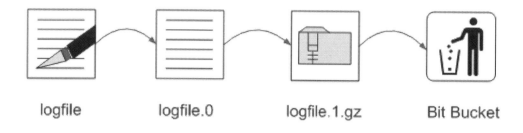

logfile   logfile.0   logfile.1.gz   Bit Bucket

/path/logfile -c -C 3 -z 1

Figure 3-1. Log Rotation

Console Messages

Console messages are displayed to the location selected by the **consadm** command. The current settings can be displayed by running the command without options. The **consadm -a /dev/devicename** adds console devices and the **consadm -d /dev/devicename** option removes them. Persistent console connections can be enabled or disabled by adding the **-p** option to the addition or deletion command.

The console may be applied to the frame buffer, a serial port, or the System Controller card. (See the "LOM" section below for a discussion of the SC card.)

Console logging output consists of two parts:
1. Kernel and syslog messages written to */dev/sysmsg*, as specified in the *syslog.conf*.
2. rc script output is written to */dev/msglog* .

Serial Port Management

Relatively inexpensive serial console servers are available to permit remote console access. The instructions to connect and configure these console servers are usually provided by the vendor.

Cabling Serial Connections

The most difficult part of managing the installation is finding the pinouts for the ports on the console server and the different pieces of server hardware being connected. Make sure to check the documentation for both sides of the serial connection to line up the pins to allow for proper communication. See the "DTE vs DCE" sidebar for a discussion of serial communications.

Table 3-4 summarizes the serial pin assignments that are used to connect a terminal to a computer or a computer to a computer. The "Null Modem Connection" specifies the pin on the remote side that each pin needs to connect to. (Note that most real-world implementations do not wire up the FG or SG ground connections.)

The DB-25 connector is the "standard" serial port seen on most older servers. On most newer servers, it has been replaced by an RJ-45 connector. There is no standard pinout for RJ-45 connectors, so the hardware documentation will need to be consulted for a particular piece of hardware.   (DB-25 and DB-9 connectors are rhomboid, with 25 or 9 pins, respectively. DIN-8 connectors are circular with 8 pins. RJ-45 connectors are the clip-type connectors familiar to most ethernet users.)

Table 3-4. Important Serial Pin Assignments

Pin Description (local)	DB-25 Pin #	DB-9 Pin #	DIN-8 Pin #	Netra RJ-45	Null Modem Connection (remote)
Frame Ground (FG)	1				FG
Transmitted Data (TD)	2	3	3	3	RD
Received Data (RD)	3	2	5	6	TD
Request To Send (RTS)	4	7	6	1	CTS
Clear To Send (CTS)	5	8	2	8	RTS
Data Set Ready (DSR)	6	6		7	DTR
Signal Ground (SG)	7	5	4,8	4,5	SG
Data Carrier Detect (DCD)	8	1	7		DTR
Data Terminal Ready (DTR)	20	4	1	2	DCD and/or DSR

I've included the pinout for a Netra RJ-45 port as an example, but there is no guarantee that this will be consistent, even between different Netra models. There is no RJ-45 pinout standard, so don't make the mistake of assuming that one exists. Always check the system documentation for each type of server you work with.

Figure 3-2 gives a graphic representation of a serial connection pinout from a DB-25 to a Netra's RJ-45 serial port.

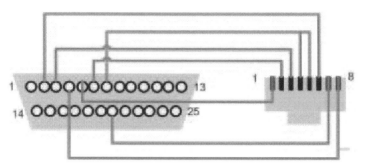

Figure 3-2. DB-25 to Netra RJ-45 Serial Pinout

DTE vs DCE

Most of the confusion in wiring up serial connections comes from the fact that the specification (RS-232) specifies two types of serial devices. **DTE** (Data Terminal Equipment) devices are the ones that we most frequently deal with; they include computers, terminals, and printers. **DCE** (Data Communications Equipment) devices include modems. If you are not sure which class a particular piece of hardware belongs to, check the documentation.

In the standard, it is assumed (for historical reasons) that data will be transmitted from a DTE device to a DCE device. This means, for example, that pin 2 ("Transmitted Data" or "TD") means data that is transmitted from a DTE device and to a DCE device, even though both specify pin 2 for this connection.

Cables for use between a DTE and a DCE device are called "modem" or "straight" cables.

When we are talking about a connection between two DTE devices (as when we connect a server to a serial terminal), we need to cross-connect three different items, creating a "null-modem" or "crossover" cable:

1. Each side's TD (Transmitted Data) must be connected to the other side's RD (Received Data).
2. Each side's RTS (Request To Send) must be connected to the other side's CTS (Clear To Send).
3. Each side's DTR (Data Terminal Ready) must be connected to both the DCD (Data Carrier Detect) and DSR (Data Set Ready) pins on the other side, if both exist. If both do not exist, use the one that does exist. (See Table 3-2.)

When the serial connection is run over a twisted pair cable, the key rule to remember is to not include both the TD and RD wires in the same twisted pair. This can lead to cross-talk and reduce the range and reliability of the connection.

Most shops establish and stick to a wiring standard in order to be able to switch around cables and reduce the amount of time charting pinouts when a new connection is needed. (Nemeth, et al in the "Resources" section of this chapter has an excellent section on serial cabling over RJ-45.)

Managing Serial Connections with tip

The `tip` command can be used to allow one Unix workstation to act as a serial terminal for another Unix system.

The following must be in place to allow this to work between two Sun systems:

- The system to be observed should be halted. If a keyboard needs to be removed from the system, the system should be powered off. (Some older models will even blow a keyboard fuse if the keyboard is removed while the system is powered up.)
- The */etc/remote* file on the observing machine needs to have the **hardwire** line pointing to the correct serial port.
- By default, the file points at port b. In this case, the line should look like:
  `:dv=/dev/term/b:br#9600:el=^C^S^Q^U^D:ie=%$:oe=^D:`
- If serial port a is to be used, change the line to look like:
  `:dv=/dev/term/a:br#9600:el=^C^S^Q^U^D:ie=%$:oe=^D:`
- A null modem cable should be run between serial port a on the system under observation and the serial port configured in the */etc/remote* file's **hardwire** line on the observing system. (A null modem cable interchanges wires 2 and 3 on one end. The pinouts of the systems on each end of the connection may need to be looked up in their hardware documentation.)

On the observer system type `tip hardwire` in a window. (It is best to use a windowed environment so that control of the system can be regained in case of a session hang.) A "*connected*" message should be echoed to the window. If not, use `admintool` or another utility to see if the serial port is already in use.

A `tip` session should not be closed by killing the process, the shell, or rebooting the observer machine. In these cases, a /var/spool/locks/*LCK* file may not be cleaned up properly, which may prevent further `tip` sessions. If the `tip` session will not start; check to make sure that no old lock files are clogging up the works.

Some common `tip` commands are:
- ~. (End session.)
- ~# (Break—same as STOP-A.)
- ~? (List all `tip` commands.)

Other commands may be found on the `tip` man page.)

The system to be observed/controlled can be powered up. If the `diag-switch?` PROM environment variable is set to `true`, hardware diagnostic data will be displayed to the `tip` window.

LOM

The **Advanced Lights Out Manager** (ALOM) or **Integrated Lights Out Manager** (ILOM) that comes with current server hardware allows us to manage the console over the network as well as through the serial port. ALOM can be configured to send email alerts of hardware failures, hardware warnings and other events related to the health of the server.

The **System Controller** (SC) runs independently of the rest of the server, on standby power. It continues to work even when the server itself is powered off.

The ALOM can monitor a number of system components, including fans, CPUs, power supplies, temperature, electrical environment and server front panel.

The default for the network port on the SC is for DHCP with SSH enabled. The SSH session requires the administrative password or a default, system-specific password (like the last 8 characters of the serial number) for connection. Obviously, the default password needs to be changed immediately.

The specifics of the SC vary across server platforms. The individual server's documentation should be consulted for details.

PROM Monitor Diagnostics

OpenBoot PROM (OBP) based Sun hardware comes with some pretty significant hardware diagnostic capabilities built in. Using it will require a console connection, but the hardware diagnostics can save time and money by quickly pinpointing the failed part.

Sometimes the part does not show up as failed during a diagnostic run. In that case, a stress test may help to push the piece of hardware to fail. Sun provides the SunVTS suite for stress testing.

Sun's OBP has several features that can be useful in troubleshooting:
- It can read device drivers and diagnostics for probed devices.
- A FORTH interpreter is included.
- It is organized with a data structure hierarchy for easy navigation.
- A number of environment variables can be set.

The POST-based hardware diagnostics only check out the devices and buses required to access I/O devices; they do not check the devices themselves. Even so, the onboard hardware diagnostics can often pinpoint the source of a hardware failure.

To run the Sun hardware diagnostics, perform the following at the **ok>** prompt:

```
ok>    setenv auto-boot? false
ok>    setenv diag-switch? true
ok>    setenv diag-level max
ok>    setenv diag-device disk net
ok>    reset
```

Now, watch the results of the diagnostic tests. There is a ton of output to the console, but it can be very specific in pinning down a bad piece of hardware.

The diagnostics increase the amount of time for each boot, so most environments like to keep them turned off when they are not actually in use:

```
ok>    setenv diag-switch? false
ok>    setenv auto-boot? true
```

Hardware and Drivers

We can get some of this same information by running

```
/usr/platform/`arch -k`/sbin/prtdiag -v
```

on a running system. Results on **prtdiag** should be compared to log entries in */var/adm/messages* or console error messages.

`/usr/sbin/prtconf -v` and **sysdef** may be used to identify which devices are attached to the system. They may display a "`driver not attached`" message if the driver is unavailable, no device exists at that node, or that device is not in use. The **fuser** command can be used to identify processes that are accessing a device.

OBP Command Line Diagnostics

Some additional PROM diagnostics are available at the `ok>` prompt. To discover what additional diagnostics are available for your hardware, type **help diag** at the `ok>` prompt. The output will include the appropriate syntax for all available PROM diagnostic functions.

Note that **reset** should be run as above before running tests. Also keep in mind that **test-all** may hang the system, requiring a power cycle.

PROM environment variables can be set at either the root user prompt or the `ok>` prompt. Most (but not all) PROM environment variables can be set with the **/usr/sbin/eeprom** command. When invoked by itself, it prints out the current environment variables. To use **eeprom** to set a variable, use the syntax:

/usr/sbin/eeprom *variable-name=value*

Remember that variable names that include a "?" will need to escape the question mark: "\?"

All PROM environment variables can be set at the `ok>` prompt. The **printenv** command prints out the current settings. The syntax for setting a variable is:

```
ok>   setenv variable-name value
```

x86 systems do not have an OBP. Instead, they simulate the EEPROM variables via the */boot/solaris/bootenv.rc* file. Solaris x86 systems allow for the inclusion of the `acpi-user-option` and `console` variables to specify power management settings and console location (respectively).

The OpenBoot firmware provides for two command line interfaces:

- Restricted Monitor: This interface is signalled by the > prompt. It provides for the execution of the **b** (boot), **c** (continue), and **n** (new command mode) commands. The Restricted Monitor is used to implement PROM security via the `security-mode` PROM environment variable
- PROM Monitor: (Also known as the "Forth Monitor" or the "New Monitor.") This interface provides additional control, including a FORTH command interpreter. The PROM Monitor is signalled by the `ok>` prompt.

Once in the `ok>` PROM monitor mode, it is possible to examine the tree of hardware devices known by the system. The following are the crucial commands to remember:

- **cd** changes location in the device tree.
- **ls** lists the contents of the present node.
- **pwd** gives the current location in the device tree.
- **dev** *device-pathname* selects a particular node of the tree for examination.
- **.properties** shows the properties for a particular node.
- **device-end** unselects a node.

The device names are cryptic, but they are closely related to the names of devices in the Operating System's */devices* directory. The */etc/driver_aliases* file may also be useful when trying to identify a device.

A full device path node name has the following form:

name@address*:arguments*

One example of such a name of a boot device is:

/pci@1f,0,pci@1,1/ide@3/disk@0,0:a

To identify the devices on a system, we need to turn off autobooting and reset the PROM so that system registers are cleared. Remember to re-enable autobooting at the end of the process by setting the parameter back to "true."

```
ok>   setenv auto-boot? false
ok>   reset-all
```

To list available probing commands available on this system, run a **sifting probe** command:

```
ok>   sifting probe
```

Some typical probing commands are:

- **probe-ide**
- **probe-scsi-all**

- `probe-pci`
- `show-disks`
- `show-tapes`
- `show-nets`
- `show-devs`

The ability to navigate the device tree on such a primitive level is useful for troubleshooting. If the device in question is not present, we have a physical connectivity issue. At that point, we might try a `reset` or power cycle, then check cables and terminators, then examine the device itself.

If the device shows up on the PROM hardware tree (but not in the Operating System) we could try a `boot -r`, examine the /dev and /devices directories, and look at the relevant device drivers. The `drvconfig` command allows us to rebuild `/devices` entries online; the `disks` and `tapes` commands create `/dev` links for new devices.

In addition, the following commands can be used to examine the CPUs or switch to another CPU:

```
ok>    module-info
ok>    processor-number switch-cpu
```

Sometimes additional information can be obtained by navigating the PROM device tree. We can also hit the Sun documentation web site for additional information on PROM monitor diagnostics.

Some special key sequences can be used to run OBP commands after the system is powered on and before the keyboard flashes the second time. These sequences can come in handy if the NVRAM becomes corrupted.

(Note that the "L1" key is labelled as "Stop" on most modern Sun keyboards.)

- **L1-f** invokes FORTH command mode on the serial port before the hardware is probed. F`exit` continues the initialization.
- **L1-n** resets NVRAM contents to the default.
- **L1-d** sets the `diag-switch?` to true for this boot only.
- **L1** runs POST in INIT mode, regardless of security settings.

SunVTS Stress Testing

SunVTS is Sun's validation test suite. It may have been included in the OS installation; if not, the installation is very straightforward, and only involves a few `pkgadd` commands. The `sunvts` command starts up an interface (either graphical or text-based) allowing different test suites to be run.

The main drawback to SunVTS stress testing is that it takes a long time to run a thorough test. The cost of having the machine unavailable for that long may be higher than is appropriate for a particular environment. On the other hand, I have found SunVTS stress testing to be helpful in flushing out intermittent hardware bugs in the past.

Some of the tests that can be run through SunVTS are:
- **cmttest**: Chip multi-threading test.
- **disktest**: SCSI disk test.
- **fputest**: Floating point test.
- **iptest**: *Fibre channel test.*
- **mptest**: Multiprocessor test.
- **pmemtest**: Physical memory test.
- **ramtest**: Test for each DIMM.
- **sptest**: Serial port test.

- **nettest**: Network test.
- **vmemtest**: Virtual memory test.

Fault Management Facility

The Solaris **Fault Management Facility** is designed to be integrated into the Service Management Facility (SMF, see Chapter 13) to provide self-healing capability on Solaris 10 systems.

The fmd daemon is responsible for monitoring several aspects of system health. It receives telemetry information regarding problems detected by the OS, performs analysis of this information, and may initiate self-healing actions in conjunction with the SMF. The **fmadm config** command shows the current configuration for fmd.

Fault Manager logs can be viewed with **fmdump -v** and **fmdump -e -v**. **fmstat** shows statistics gathered by fmd. Example 3-3 shows the output from some of these commands.

Example 3-3. Fault Management Facility Output

```
#  fmadm config
MODULE                  VERSION STATUS   DESCRIPTION
cpumem-diagnosis        1.5     active   UltraSPARC-III/IV CPU/Memory Diagnosis
cpumem-retire           1.1     active   CPU/Memory Retire Agent
eft                     1.16    active   eft diagnosis engine
fmd-self-diagnosis      1.0     active   Fault Manager Self-Diagnosis
io-retire               1.0     active   I/O Retire Agent
snmp-trapgen            1.0     active   SNMP Trap Generation Agent
sysevent-transport      1.0     active   SysEvent Transport Agent
syslog-msgs             1.0     active   Syslog Messaging Agent
zfs-diagnosis           1.0     active   ZFS Diagnosis Engine
#  fmstat
module             ev_recv ev_acpt wait    svc_t  %w  %b  open solve  memsz  bufsz
cpumem-diagnosis         0       0 0.0      2.5     0   0     0     0   3.0K      0
cpumem-retire            0       0 0.0      1.4     0   0     0     0   1.4      0
eft                      0       0 0.0      1.4     0   0     0     0   713K      0
fmd-self-diagnosis       0       0 0.0      0.7     0   0     0     0      0      0
io-retire                0       0 0.0      0.6     0   0     0     0      0      0
snmp-trapgen             0       0 0.0      0.8     0   0     0     0    32b      0
sysevent-transport       0       0 0.0     44.5     0   0     0     0      0      0
syslog-msgs              0       0 0.0      1.9     0   0     0     0      0      0
zfs-diagnosis            0       0 0.0      0.9     0   0     0     0      0      0
```

The messages provided from the **fmdump** command can be entered into a web query engine at http://www.sun.com/msg in order to find out what the message means. This may not be necessary, since the Fault Management messages are intended to be English language and specific enough to direct us to perform the right action.

(Example 4-8 in Chapter 4 includes output from a situation where **fmdump** is used to diagnose a problem.)

When appropriate, the FMF provides error messages to the syslog facility. As more things become instrumented for the Fault Management Facility, we can expect that error lists (like the one in Appendix A) will become obsolete. Instead, we will use the **Universal Unique Identifier** (UUID) assigned to each distinguishable problem description, enter it into the web site, and get a plain-language description of what the problem is and how to address it.

At the time of this writing, Fault Management facilities for x64 were being implemented. In the future, they will give us a way to monitor and react to correctable errors. (In the past, we were wholly dependent on the BIOS for monitoring, and the OS remained unaware of any correctable errors.)

Core File Management

Core files are memory images of applications which terminate abnormally. We can customize when and where core dump files are created, as well as what they will be named. This configuration is controlled by the **coreadm** command.

Run without any options, **coreadm** shows the current core dump configuration. The **-e** option enables a specified type of core dump (global or process), and **-d** disables it. Example 3-4 demonstrates how to use **coreadm**:

Example 3-4. coreadm

```
# coreadm
     global core file pattern:
     global core file content: default
       init core file pattern: core
       init core file content: default
           global core dumps: disabled
       per-process core dumps: enabled
        global setid core dumps: disabled
 per-process setid core dumps: disabled
     global core dump logging: enabled
# coreadm -d process
# coreadm
  ...
       per-process core dumps: disabled
  ...
# coreadm -e process
# coreadm
  ...
       per-process core dumps: enabled
  ...
```

The **-g** option allows us to set a target directory for global core dumps, and the -p option allows us to set per-process targets. coreadm allows us to customize the core dump target by user, process, machine name, etc, as defined in the coreadm(1M) man page.

Core File Analysis

We have several tools available for looking at process core dumps.

At a minimum level, the file command tells us the name of the process that generated the core file (in this case "*test.pl*"):

```
# file core
core:           ELF 32-bit MSB core file SPARC Version 1, from 'test.pl'
```

The most intuitively useful commands for examining core dumps are the "p-commands" from */usr/proc/bin*. Each of these displays the name of the calling process and its PID, as well as the following:

*   **pstack** displays the process stack.
*   **pmap** displays the address space map.
*   **pldd** lists the linked libraries associated with the process.
*   **pflags** displays the */proc*-related flags for each lwp in the process.
*   **pcred** shows the effective and real UIDs and GIDs associated with the process.

Some sample output from running the p-commands against our core file is shown in Example 3-5:

Example 3-5. p-command Output

```
# pstack core
core 'core' of 19613:   /usr/local/bin/perl -d ./test.pl
 ff0d47b0 realfree (64ec74, 3030299, 93b28, ff16cbc0, 0, ff16fad4) + 68
 ff0d46d8 realloc  (64ec04, 60, 64ec0c, 0, 3, 64ec64) + 374
 0006f8fc Perl_safesysrealloc (64ec0c, 60, 64ec0c, 154d40, 11b400, ff1709b0) + 38
 00071f50 Perl_my_setenv (12ca38, 124ce8, 62dbf8, 11b400, 154d40, 1) + 170
 00075c00 Perl_magic_setenv (124ce8, 607400, 75b60, 65, ffb12878, 4) + a0
 000744f8 Perl_mg_set (62dc28, 404c007, 2, 2edd4dcb, 120b50, 120b50) + 78
 00080794 Perl_pp_sassign (62dc28, 0, 0, 380d54, 80, 0) + b8
 000802a0 Perl_runops_standard (118800, 12ad08, 5f9cc0, 800000, 11b4e0, ff16b3d4) + 30
 00028528 S_run_body (1, 11b400, 11b400, f1e30, ff362000, 2) + 14c
 00028158 perl_run (0, fffffffc, 3, ffbffd44, 0, 8) + 8c
 00024db8 main     (3, ffbffd44, ffbffd54, 11b4e0, ff360100, ff360140) + a4
 00024bdc _start   (0, 0, 0, 0, 0, 0) + 5c
# pmap core
core 'core' of 19613:   /usr/local/bin/perl -d ./test.pl
00010000    960K r-x--  /usr/local/bin/perl
0010E000     48K rwx--  /usr/local/bin/perl
0011A000   5720K rwx--    [ heap ]
FE690000     32K r-x--  /usr/local/lib/libgcc_s.so.1
FE6A6000     16K rwx--  /usr/local/lib/libgcc_s.so.1
FE6B0000    168K r-x--  /lib/libcurses.so.1
FE6EA000     32K rwx--  /lib/libcurses.so.1
FE6F2000      8K rwx--  /lib/libcurses.so.1
...
FF350000      8K rwx--
FF360000     24K rwx--
FF370000     48K r-x--  /lib/libsocket.so.1
FF38C000      8K rwx--  /lib/libsocket.so.1
FF3A0000      8K r-x--  /lib/libdl.so.1
FF3B0000    184K r-x--  /lib/ld.so.1
FF3EE000      8K rwx--  /lib/ld.so.1
FF3F0000      8K rwx--  /lib/ld.so.1
FFBF8000     32K rw---    [ stack ]
 total    17328K
# pldd core
core 'core' of 19613:     /usr/local/bin/perl -d ./test.pl
/lib/libsocket.so.1
/lib/libnsl.so.1
/lib/libdl.so.1
/lib/libm.so.2
/lib/libc.so.1
/platform/sun4u-us3/lib/libc_psr.so.1
...
/usr/local/lib/perl5/site_perl/5.8.7/sun4-solaris/auto/Term/ReadLine/Gnu/Gnu.so
/usr/local/lib/libreadline.so.5
/lib/libcurses.so.1
/usr/local/lib/libgcc_s.so.1
# pflags core
core 'core' of 19613:   /usr/local/bin/perl -d ./test.pl
        data model = _ILP32   flags = MSACCT|MSFORK
 /1:    flags = 0
        sigmask = 0xfffffeff,0x0000ffff   cursig = SIGSEGV
# pcred core
core of 19613:  e/r/suid=1029  e/r/sgid=14
```

The **mdb** debugger allows us to drill down into the guts of a core dump. We'll take a more detailed look at **mdb** in Chapter 4. For our current purposes, it will be enough to use the `::status` dcmd to examine the core in **mdb** in order to identify the arguments to `test.pl` and the type of error (Segmentation Fault) in Example 3-6:

Example 3-6. Checking core File with mdb

```
# mdb core
Loading modules: [ libc.so.1 ld.so.1 ]
> ::status
debugging core file of test. (32-bit) from soltest
file: /usr/local/bin/perl
initial argv: /usr/local/bin/perl -d /export/home/scromar/test.pl
threading model: multi-threaded
status: process terminated by SIGSEGV (Segmentation Fault)
status: SIGSEGV (Segmentation Fault)
> $q
```

Crash Dump Management

When a system panics, it attempts to write an image of its memory to a special file. This file is called a crash dump, and it is stored in the "dump device." Upon reboot, the crash dump is copied by the **savecore** program to a particular target directory, known as the "savecore directory." The configuration for this process is managed via the **dumpadm** utility; by default the "savecore directory" is */var/crash/hostname* and the "dump device" is swap. **dumpadm** stores its configuration in */etc/dumpadm.conf*.

The crash dump is written as a pair of files, named `unix.N` and `vmcore.N`, where N is a sequence number. The `unix.N` file is the memory image, and the `vmcore.N` file is the symbol table.

If the system crashes to the `ok>` prompt, a crash dump can be attempted by running the **sync** command. Immediate core dumps can be generated from a running system by running **savecore -L** or **reboot -d**.

Crash Dump Analysis

In-depth crash dump analysis requires more patience and time than most administrators have. Unless we have a guru on staff, it is unlikely that we will be able to analyze a system crash dump thoroughly. On the other hand, most of the time, we don't need to do anything anywhere nearly so complicated. Usually it is enough to extract error conditions and look at the last active process before things blew up.

The best way to handle a system crash dump is to open a case with Sun and get the core file to them as soon as possible. Once that is done, it may be worth our while to pick off some low-hanging fruit.

Solaris' Modular Debugger (**mdb**) is a wonderful facility for drilling down to almost any level of detail of our formerly running system. We'll take a deeper look at **mdb** in Chapter 4, but it is worth looking at some of its base functionality for looking at a crash dump.

At a minimum, we will want to do is look at the message buffer and find out what command was active at the time of the panic. Most of the items in the message buffer will have made it to the system logs, but some things may not have made it across the road before the crash. To examine a core file, run the following for a particular pair of core file and symbol table:

```
mdb -k unix.# vmcore.#
```

Within **mdb**, we can examine the messages with the command:

```
::msgbuf
```

The messages in the buffer may be interesting on their own. Any messages can be compared against the common error messages listed in Appendix A (or checked out on http://www.sun.com/msg if the message reports a UUID). For SPARC systems, the message buffer may also contain the following items of interest: **g7** (current thread address), **rp** (register pointer), **sp** (stack pointer), and **pc** (program counter).

We can also find these locations of interest by dumping the registers with the $r macro, if they are not in the message buffer. The instructions in the program counter can be displayed with *pc_address*/40ai once we find the program counter's address.

To find the last command that started running before the panic, we should use g7. First, we find its t_procp by running *g7_address*$<thread against g7's address. Then we look at psargs in *procp_address*$<proc2u. Table 3-5 lists several **mdb** commands that are useful for crash dump analyses.

Table 3-5: Basic Crash Dump Analysis

mdb Command	Description
$c	Dump the stack trace.
rp_address$<regs	Dump the registers at *rp_address*
pc_address/40ai	Display the instructions in the pointer counter at *pc_address*
g7_address$<thread	Find thread information for the current thread located at *g7_address*
procp_address$<proc2u	Display process information for processor at *procp_address*
::msgbuf	Display message buffer.
::panicinfo	Displays information on register and message buffer entries useful for examining a crash dump.
::regs or $r	Dump the contents of the registers.
::stackregs	Displays stack register entries.
::status	Display status, including error information.
!	Command escape; especially useful for **grep**ping out strings of interest.

An example crash dump analysis is performed in Chapter 4's Example 4-7, using additional tools presented there.

Boot Sequence

"The system won't boot" is a common symptom for certain types of problems. We can use our knowledge of the boot process to pin down exactly where the problem lies.

There are a lot of similarities between the boot processes of Sparc and x86 versions of Solaris. But there are also some significant differences. In order to make the discussion clearer, each type of boot process has been given its own section.

OBP/Sparc Boot Sequence

The following represents a summary of the boot process for a Solaris 10 system on Sparc hardware.

- **Power On:** Depending on the system involved, you may see some output on a serial terminal immediately after power on. This may take the form of any of the following:

```
Hardware Power ON
'
,
```

These indications will not be present on a monitor connected directly to the server.

- **POST**: If the PROM's `diag-switch?` Parameter is set to `true`, output from the POST (Power On Self Test) will be viewable on a serial terminal. The PROM `diag-level` parameter determines the extent of the POST tests. (See the **"OBP Command Line Diagnostics" section above for details.) If a serial terminal is not connected, a `prtdiag -v`** will show the results of the POST once the system has booted. If a keyboard is connected, it will beep and the keyboard lights will flash during POST. If the POST fails, an error indication may be displayed after the failure.

- **Init System**: This consists of the following activities:

  OBP: If `diag-switch?` Is set, an "Entering OBP" message will be seen on a serial terminal. The MMU (memory management unit) is enabled.

  NVRAM: If `use-nvramrc?` Is set to `true`, read the NVRAMRC. This may contain information about boot devices, especially where the boot disk has been encapsulated with a volume manager such as Veritas Volume Manager (VxVM).

  Probe All: This checks for disk drives and other devices.

  Install Console: At this point, a directly connected monitor and keyboard will become active, or the serial port will become the system console access. If a keyboard is connected to the system, the lights will flash again during this step.

  Banner: The PROM banner will be displayed. This banner includes a logo, system type, PROM revision level, the ethernet address and the hostid.

  Create Device Tree: The hardware device tree will be built. This device tree can be explored using PROM Monitor commands (as discussed in "OBP Command Line Diagnostics" above.)

  Extended Diagnostics: If `diag-switch?` and `diag-level` are set, additional diagnostics will appear on the system console.

  If the `auto-boot?` PROM parameter is set, the boot process will begin. Otherwise, the system will drop to the **ok>** PROM monitor prompt, or (if `sunmon-compat?` and `security-mode` are set) the > security prompt.

  The boot process will use the `boot-device` and `boot-file` PROM parameters unless `diag-switch?` is set. In this case, the boot process will use the `diag-device` and `diag-file`.

- **bootblk**: The **OBP (Open Boot PROM) program loads the** `bootblk` primary boot program from the `boot-device` (or `diag-device`, if `diag-switch?` is set). If the *bootblk* is not present or needs to be regenerated, it can be installed by running the `installboot` command after booting from a CDROM or the network. A copy of the `bootblk` is available at `/usr/platform/`arch -k`/lib/fs/ufs/bootblk`.

- **ufsboot**: The secondary boot program, `/platform/`arch -k`/ufsboot` is run. This program loads the kernel core image files. If this file is corrupted or missing, a message like the following will be returned:

```
bootblk:  can't find the boot program
```

- **kernel**: The kernel is loaded and run. For 32-bit Solaris, the relevant files are:
  `/platform/`arch -k`/kernel/unix`
  `/kernel/genunix`

  For 64-bit Solaris systems, the files are:
  `/platform/`arch -k`/kernel/sparcV9/unix`
  `/kernel/genunix`

  As part of the kernel loading process, the kernel banner is displayed to the screen. This includes the kernel version number (including patch level, if appropriate) and the copyright notice.

  The kernel initializes itself and begins loading modules, reading the files with the `ufsboot` program until it has loaded enough modules to mount the root filesystem itself. At that point, `ufsboot` is unmapped and the kernel uses its own drivers. If the system complains about not being able to write to the root filesystem, it is stuck in this part of the boot process.

  The `boot -a` command takes single steps through this portion of the boot process. This can be a useful diagnostic procedure if the kernel is not loading properly.

- **/etc/system file**: The */etc/system* file is read by the kernel, and the system parameters are set. The following types of customization are available in the */etc/system* file:
  `moddir`: Changes the path of kernel modules.
  `forceload`: Forces the loading of a kernel module.
  `exclude`: Excludes a particular kernel module.
  `rootfs`: Specify the system type for the root file system. (UFS is the default. At the time of this writing, ZFS is not supported, but it will be supported in a future release.)
  `rootdev`: Specify the physical device path for root.
  `set`: Set the value of a tunable system parameter.

  If the */etc/system* file is edited, it is strongly recommended that a copy of the working file be made to a well-known location. In the event that the new */etc/system* file renders the system unbootable, it might be possible to bring up the system with a `boot -a` command that specifies the old file. If this has not been done, the system may need to be booted from CD or network so that the file can be mounted and edited.

- **kernel initialized**: The kernel creates PID 0 (`sched`). The `sched` process is sometimes called the "swapper."

- **init**: The kernel starts **PID 1** (`init`). The `init` process reads the */etc/inittab* and */etc/default/init* and follows the instructions in those files. This file is now maintained out of the **Service Management Facility** (SMF) rather than by directly editing it. Some of the entries in the */etc/inittab* are:
  `fs`: sysinit (usually `/etc/rcS`)
  `is`: default init level (usually 3, sometimes 2)
  `s#`: script associated with a run level (usually `/sbin/rc#`)

- **Service Management Facility** (SMF): The Service Management Facility starts up the bulk of the services on the system. `init` runs `/lib/svc/bin/svc.startd` to start processes to mount the filesystems, configure the network and other devices, perform system tasks and start services.

- **rc scripts**: The rc scripts execute the files in the */etc/rc#.d* directories. They are run by the `/sbin/rc#` scripts, each of which corresponds to a run level.

  (We can add debugging to the rc scripts by adding *echo* lines to a script to print either a "I got this far" message or to print out the value of a problematic variable or setting.)

x86/x64 Boot Sequence

Most of the Solaris-specific steps in the x86/x64 boot sequence are the same as for Sparc-based systems. Some of the hardware-specific portions of the boot sequence, especially surrounding the BIOS and GRUB, are distinct.

The x86 and x64 boot sequence runs as follows:

- **BIOS:** The BIOS runs self-tests to verify the system hardware. Any additional hardware BIOS's on the system are run at this time. Your system hardware manuals may contain comments about the specific tests carried out during this step.

- **mboot**: The BIOS reads the first disk sector from the boot device. The first sector on this device contains the mboot master boot record. mboot contains the disk information needed to find the active partition and the location of the pboot Solaris boot program.

- **pboot**: The Primary Boot Subsystem displays a choice of available OS installations on the system (if multiple installations are configured into GRUB).

- **bootblk**: pboot loads bootblk, the primary boot program.

- **fdisk**: If there are multiple valid bootable partitions, bootblk checks the fdisk table to find the default boot partition. bootblk then builds a menu of valid partitions. An alternative partition may be selected within 30 seconds, or bootblk proceeds to the default boot partition.

- **Secondary Boot Subsystem**: The Secondary Boot Subsystem menu appears when the Solaris release is chosen (or selected by default). The autoboot process can be interrupted to run the Solaris Device Configuration Assistant, which allows us to boot from a different device, configure or reconfigure hardware, or perform some other device or boot tasks. (To enter the Device Configuration Assistant, we must hit the ESC key.) If started, the Device Configuration Assistant displays a list of potential boot devices, with the default marked by an asterisk.

- **Secondary Boot Program**: The secondary boot program, boot.bin or ufsboot, runs a command interpreter to execute /etc/bootrc. bootrc allows 5 seconds to set a non-default boot option. (The Current Boot Parameters Menu appears and allows an opportunity to select boot options.)

- **Mount root partition**: The kernel initializes by using boot.bin or ufsboot to read module files. Once it has loaded enough of these modules to mount the root partition, the secondary boot program is unmapped and the kernel proceeds with the boot process.

  The boot -a command takes single steps through this portion of the boot process. This can be a useful diagnostic procedure if the kernel is not loading properly.

- **/etc/system file**: The /etc/system file is read by the kernel, and the system parameters are set. The following types of customization are available in the /etc/system file:
  moddir: Changes the path of kernel modules.
  forceload: Forces the loading of a kernel module.
  exclude: Excludes a particular kernel module.
  rootfs: Specify the system type for the root file system. (UFS is the default. At the time of this writing, ZFS is not supported, but it will be supported in a future release.)
  rootdev: Specify the physical device path for root.
  set: Set the value of a tunable system parameter.

  If the /etc/system file is edited, it is strongly recommended that a copy of the working file be made to a well-known location. In the event that the new /etc/system file renders the system unbootable, it might be possible to bring up the system with a boot -a command that specifies the old file. If this has not been done, the system may need to be booted from CD or network so that the file can be mounted and edited.

- **kernel initialized**: The kernel creates PID 0 (`sched`). The `sched` process is sometimes called the "swapper."

- **init**: The kernel starts PID 1 (`init`). The `init` process reads the *etc/inittab* and *etc/default/init* and follows the instructions in those files. This file is now maintained out of the **Service Management Facility (**SMF) rather than by directly editing it. Some of the entries in the *etc/inittab* are:
  `fs`: sysinit (usually `/etc/rcS`)
  `is`: default init level (usually 3, sometimes 2)
  `s#`: script associated with a run level (usually `/sbin/rc#`)

- **Service Management Facility (**SMF): The Service Management Facility starts up the bulk of the services on the system. `init` runs `/lib/svc/bin/svc.startd` to start processes to mount the file systems, configure the network and other devices, perform system tasks and start services.

  If SMF does not start up on its own, it may be because of a failure of `svc:/system/boot-archive:default`

  To resolve this problem, select the Solaris failsafe archive option in the GRUB boot menu during the next reboot. The failsafe boot option provides instructions for rebuilding the boot archive. Once that is complete, the boot can be continued by clearing the SMF boot archive with the **`svcadm clear boot-archive`** command.

- **rc scripts**: The rc scripts execute the files in the *etc/rc#.d* directories. They are run by the `/sbin/rc#` scripts, each of which corresponds to a run level.

  (We can add debugging to the rc scripts by adding **echo** lines to a script to print either a "I got this far" message or to print out the value of a problematic variable or setting.)

Service Initialization During the Boot

Boot messages are much less verbose than with the old `init` scripts. To get verbose output, boot with the **`boot -v`** or **`boot -m verbose`** commands. **`svcadm`** can be used to change the run levels. The service identifiers (known as **FMRIs**) associated with the different run levels are:

- **S**: `milestone/single-user:default`
- **2**: `milestone/multi-user:default`
- **3**: `milestone/multi-user-server:default`

The current run level can be displayed with **`who -r`** To step through the run levels, use the following series of commands:

```
boot -m none
svcadm milestone svc:/milestone/single-user:default
svcadm milestone svc:/milestone/multi-user:default
svcadm milestone svc:/milestone/multi-user-server:default
```

Startup for a Particular Service

Several things should be examined if a service fails to start:
- Is the service in maintenance mode? (**`svcs -l FMRI`**)
- If so, why? Check the log file specified in the **`svcs -l FMRI | grep logfile`** output, and run **`svcs -xv FMRI`**
- If the problem has been resolved, clear the fault with **`svcadm clear FMRI`**
- Check for service dependencies with **`svcs -d FMRI`** The output from **`svcs -l`** distinguishes between optional and mandatory dependencies.
- Check the startup properties with **`svcprop -p start FMRI`**

50

- The startup for the process can be **truss**ed to get some visibility into where it is failing by inserting a **truss** into the start or exec statement for the service. To do this, just add

```
truss -f -a -o /path/service-truss.out
```

to the beginning of the start or exec statement with an **svccfg -s** statement.

Resources

- Bauer, Kirk. *logwatch*. Logfile viewer. (http://freshmeat.net/projects/logwatch/)

- Crawford, Craig. *logcheck*. Logfile viewer. (http://logcheck.org/)

- Cromar, Scott. (2007) Solaris Troubleshooting and Performance Tuning at Princeton University. Princeton, NJ. (http://www.princeton.edu/~unix/Solaris/troubleshoot/index.html)

- Drake, Chris and Brown, Kimberley. (May 1995) *Panic! UNIX System Crash Dump Analysis*. Prentice Hall.

- McDougall, Richard and Mauro, Jim. (July 2006) *Solaris Internals*. Upper Saddle River, NJ: Prentice Hall & Sun Microsystems Press.

- McDougall, Richard, Mauro, Jim and Gregg, Brendan. (October 2006) *Solaris Performance and Tools*. Upper Saddle River, NJ: Prentice Hall & Sun Microsystems Press.

- Nemeth, Evi; Snyder, Garth; Seebass, Scott; Hien, Trent R. (2001) Unix System Administration Handbook, 3rd Edition. Upper Saddle River, NJ: Prentice Hall PTR.

- Sun Microsystems. (November 2006) *Advanced Lights Out Management (ALOM) CMT v1.3 Guide*. Palo Alto, CA: Sun Microsystems, Inc. (http://docs.sun.com/app/docs/doc/819-7981-10)

- Sun Microsystems. (June 2006) *man pages section 1: User Commands*. Palo Alto, CA: Sun Microsystems, Inc. (http://docs.sun.com/app/docs/doc/816-5165)

- Sun Microsystems. (June 2006) *man pages section 1M: System Administration Commands*. Palo Alto, CA: Sun Microsystems, Inc. (http://docs.sun.com/app/docs/doc/816-5166)

- Sun Microsystems. (June 2006) *man pages section 2: System Calls*. Palo Alto, CA: Sun Microsystems, Inc. (http://docs.sun.com/app/docs/doc/816-5167)

- Sun Microsystems. (February 2002) *OpenBoot 4.x Command Reference Manual*. Palo Alto, CA: Sun Microsystems, Inc. (http://docs.sun.com/app/docs/doc/816-1177-10)

- Sun Microsystems. (August 2004) *OpenBoot PROM Enhancements for Diagnostic Operation*. Palo Alto, CA: Sun Microsystems, Inc. (http://docs.sun.com/app/docs/doc/817-6957-10)

- Sun Microsystems. (February 2000) *Solaris Common Messages and Troubleshooting Guide*. Palo Alto, CA: Sun Microsystems, Inc. (http://docs.sun.com/app/docs/doc/806-1075)

- Sun Microsystems. (January 2005) *Solaris Modular Debugger Guide*. Palo Alto, CA: Sun Microsystems, Inc. (http://docs.sun.com/app/docs/doc/816-5041)

- Sun Microsystems. (June, 2006). *SunVTS 6.2 Test Reference Manual for SPARC Platforms*. Santa Clara, CA: Sun Microsystems, Inc. (http://docs.sun.com/app/docs/doc/819-6455)

- Sun Microsystems. (June, 2006). *SunVTS 6.2 Test Reference Manual for x86 Platforms*. Santa Clara, CA: Sun Microsystems, Inc. (http://docs.sun.com/app/docs/doc/819-6456)

- Sun Microsystems. (June, 2006). *SunVTS 6.2 User's Guide*. Santa Clara, CA: Sun Microsystems, Inc. (http://docs.sun.com/app/docs/doc/819-6454)

- Sun Microsystems. (May 2006) *System Administration Guide: Advanced Administration*. Palo Alto, CA: Sun Microsystems, Inc. (http://docs.sun.com/app/docs/doc/817-0403)

4

Probing Processes

The process is one of the fundamental abstractions of Unix. Every object in Unix is represented as either a file or a process. (With the introduction of the */proc* virtual file system, there has been an effort to represent even processes as files.)

In this chapter, we look at some of the tools that Solaris provides for examining processes. Hardware-related problems are actually the easiest ones to fix. There are a limited number of components, and the diagnostics on modern computing equipment are quite good (and getting better all the time). Software-related problems, on the other hand, are much more difficult. Probing processes means getting our hands dirty and looking at what is happening in the guts of the software.

Solaris is an incredibly useful environment that allows us the flexibility to do almost anything we can imagine. The downside of this flexibility is that it provides us with an almost unlimited number of ways to mess things up. Sometimes we can find our problem by doing things like source code inspection. More frequently, we have to examine a failing process in detail to see where we went wrong.

Introduction to Processes

A **process** owns pages of physical memory containing all of the instructions, data and memory structures required for program execution. The **process state** is the set of information which is used by the kernel to manage the process.

One way to define a process is as a container for **threads**, which are the pieces of a process that can execute independently of each other. **Kernel threads** are the tasks that are actually performed by the kernel; they are the objects that are scheduled and executed within Solaris. **User threads** are created within the process and associated with a **lightweight process** (LWP). Each LWP is, in turn, associated with a kernel thread. The LWPs are kernel objects which allow the user threads to be executed independently of each other.

Each process is uniquely identified by a positive integer known as a **Process ID** (PID). The sched (memory scheduler) process has a PID of 0; the init process has a PID of 1. Other processes are assigned available numbers from the process table as they are created.

Solaris, like other Unix systems, provides two modes of operation: user mode, and kernel (or system) mode. Kernel mode is a more privileged mode of operation. Processes can be executed in either mode, but user processes usually operate in user mode.

The /proc Virtual File System

/proc (or `procfs`) is a virtual file system that allows us to examine processes like files. This means that */proc* allows us to use file-like operations and intuitions when looking at processes. */proc* does not occupy disk space; it is located in working memory. This structure was originally designed as a programming interface for writing debuggers, but it has grown considerably since then.

To avoid confusion, we will refer to the virtual file system as */proc* or `procfs`. The man page for `procfs` is `proc(4)`. `proc` will be used to refer to the process data structure discussed in "Process Structure" below.

Under */proc* is a list of numbers, each of which is a Process ID (PID) for a process on our system. Under these directories are subdirectories referring to the different components of interest of each process. This directory structure can be examined directly, but we usually prefer to use commands written to extract information from this structure. These are known as the "**p-commands.**" The most important of these are listed in Table 4-1.

Table 4-1. The p-Commands

Command	Description
`pcred`	Display process credentials (eg EUID/EGID, RUID/RGID, saved UIDs/GIDs)
`pfiles`	Reports `fstat()` and `fcntl()` information for all open files. This includes information on the inode number, file system, ownership and size.
`pflags`	Prints the tracing flags, pending and held signals and other */proc* status information for each LWP.
`pgrep`	Finds processes matching certain criteria.
`pkill`	Kills specified processes.
`pldd`	Lists dynamic libraries linked to the process.
`pmap`	Prints process address space map.
`prun`	Starts stopped processes.
`prstat`	Display process performance-related statistics.
`ps`	List process information. (In particular, **/usr/ucb/ps -auxww** can be useful to see the full command string.)
`psig`	Lists signal actions.
`pstack`	Prints a stack trace for each LWP in the process.
`pstop`	Stops the process.
`ptime`	Times the command; does not time children.

Command	Description
ptree	Prints process genealogy.
pwait	Wait for specified processes to complete.
pwdx	Prints process working directory.

Example 4-1 demonstrates the use of several of these p-commands to examine a process. (In this case, the process is an **ls** of the */usr* directory piped through **more** and waiting for the user to hit a key to continue.)

Example 4-1. Using p-Commands

```
# ps -ef | grep more | grep -v grep
    root 18494  8025    0 08:53:09 pts/3        0:00 more
# pgrep more
18494
# pmap -x 18494
18494:  more
 Address    Kbytes    RSS    Anon  Locked Mode   Mapped File
00010000       32     32       -       - r-x--   more
00028000        8      8       8       - rwx--   more
0002A000       16     16      16       - rwx--     [ heap ]
FF200000      864    824       -       - r-x--   libc.so.1
FF2E8000       32     32      32       - rwx--   libc.so.1
FF2F0000        8      8       8       - rwx--   libc.so.1
FF300000       16     16       -       - r-x--   en_US.ISO8859-1.so.3
FF312000       16     16      16       - rwx--   en_US.ISO8859-1.so.3
FF330000        8      8       -       - r-x--   libc_psr.so.1
FF340000        8      8       8       - rwx--     [ anon ]
FF350000      168    104       -       - r-x--   libcurses.so.1
FF38A000       32     32      24       - rwx--   libcurses.so.1
FF392000        8      8       8       - rwx--   libcurses.so.1
FF3A0000       24     16      16       - rwx--     [ anon ]
FF3B0000      184    184       -       - r-x--   ld.so.1
FF3EE000        8      8       8       - rwx--   ld.so.1
FF3F0000        8      8       8       - rwx--   ld.so.1
FFBFC000       16     16      16       - rw---     [ stack ]
-------- ------- ------- ------- -------
total Kb     1456   1344     168       -
# pstack 18494
18494:  more
 ff2c0c7c read     (2, ffbff697, 1)
 00015684 ???????? (0, 1, 43858, ff369ad4, 0, 28b20)
 000149a4 ???????? (ffbff82f, 28400, 15000000, 28af6, 0, 28498)
 00013ad8 ???????? (0, 28b10, 28c00, 400b0, ff2a4a74, 0)
 00012780 ???????? (2a078, ff393050, 0, 28b00, 2a077, 6b)
 00011c68 main     (28b10, ffffffff, 28c00, 0, 0, 1) + 684
 000115cc _start   (0, 0, 0, 0, 0, 0) + 108
# pfiles 18494
18494:  more
  Current rlimit: 256 file descriptors
   0: S_IFIFO mode:0000 dev:292,0 ino:2083873 uid:0 gid:0 size:0
      O_RDWR
   1: S_IFCHR mode:0620 dev:284,0 ino:12582922 uid:1000 gid:7 rdev:24,3
      O_RDWR|O_NOCTTY|O_LARGEFILE
      /devices/pseudo/pts@0:3
```

```
   2: S_IFCHR mode:0620 dev:284,0 ino:12582922 uid:1000 gid:7 rdev:24,3
      O_RDWR|O_NOCTTY|O_LARGEFILE
      /devices/pseudo/pts@0:3
# pcred 18494
18494:  e/r/suid=0  e/r/sgid=0
        groups: 0 1 2 3 4 5 6 7 8 9 12
```

In example 4-1, we run **pmap** and **pstack** commands that allow us to examine the process's memory space and stack, respectively. The **pfiles** and **ps** commands inform us that the process is running on terminal pts/3. **ps** and **pcred** tell us that it is running as user root; the ownership of the terminal session in the **pfiles** output tells us that the terminal session owner has UID 1000.

The **pfiles** output is somewhat awkward to use because it reports an inode rather than a human-readable file name. We can work around this when we want to look at a particular file, since we can find out its inode with **ls -i** */path/filename* and compare it to the **pfiles** output for processes of interest. (The DTrace Toolkit's **iosnoop** (Example 5-7) or **opensnoop** (Example 5-8) may provide a more flexible way to look at open file information.)

We look further into the **prstat** command in Chapter 6. It is a tremendously useful command that allows us to identify a CPU or memory hog.

The implementation details of the procfs system are beyond the scope of this chapter. Basic information is available in the proc(4) man page.

> While it can be fun to explore */proc* with tools that read file system objects, attempting to write to */proc* may lead to catastrophic results.

Examining the Guts of a Process

In the most intuitive sense, **processes** are the result of us running a program. For several very good reasons, not every program is allowed to perform every function on the computer. In particular, processes are not allowed to interact directly with the computer hardware. The kernel controls all hardware access. Each process requests services from the kernel (and ultimately from the hardware) via system calls. **System calls** allow user processes to request that the kernel perform privileged operations on their behalf.

Tracing the progress of system calls and their results gives us a very useful view of what is happening inside of a process. As we will see later in the chapter, it is not a complete view of what the process is doing, but most of the time it is good enough.

Sun provides some useful resources for looking into the guts of an executing program. The **truss** utility allows us to look at the system calls and their results as the program runs. The **mdb** facility allows us to look at all of the structures that make up a running process, including the contents of all of the memory structures used by that process. **DTrace** provides flexible monitoring at any level of detail required.

Tracing System and Library Calls with truss and apptrace

truss traces library and system calls and signal activity for a given process. This can be very useful in seeing exactly where a program is choking. With the "**-o** *filename*" option, the output is saved to a log file for later analysis. Other useful options are "**-p** *PID*" to specify a process ID, "**-f**" to include child processes in the output, "**-c**" to look at the time spent on each call, and "**-d**" to include timestamps. Several options are listed in Table 4-2 for easy reference:

Table 4-2. Useful truss Options

Option	Purpose
-c	Seconds spent on each call and number of times each call is made.
-d	Include timestamps.
-D/-E	Show time delta between system calls.
-e	Shows environment strings passed in to new processes.
-f	Include information from child processes.
-l	Includes thread number for each call.
-o *filename*	Log session to a file.
-p *PID*	Specify a process.
-x *syscall*	Display arguments to specified call(s).

In order to understand **truss** output, it is important to understand the common system calls. The section 2 man pages contain detailed information on these calls, including definitions of arguments and return values. Table 4-3 describes the system calls most commonly seen while troubleshooting with **truss**.

Table 4-3. Common System Calls

System Call	Description
brk()	Requests memory during execution.
exec() execve()	Opens a program.
exit()	Terminate a process.
fcntl()	Performs control functions on open files.
fork() fork1() vfork()	Spawn a new process.
fstat()	Obtains information about open files by file descriptor.
getdents64()	Reads directory information.
ioctl()	Performs terminal I/O.
kill()	Sends a signal to a group of processes.
lseek()	Moves read/write file pointer.
lstat()	Obtains file attributes.

System Call	Description
mmap()	Maps a process's address space to a file or shared memory object..
open() openat()	Opens a file. Returns a file descriptor number which is referenced when the process references the file.
poll()	Multiplexes reads and writes across multiple file descriptors.
pread()	Reads from an open file without changing the file pointer.
pwrite()	Writes to an open file/device without changing the file pointer.
read() readv() readlink()	Reads from an open file or symbolic link.

Table 4-3 only represents a subset of the system calls seen in **truss** output, but these are usually enough to give us a good idea what is going on. The section 2 man pages contain information on other system calls that may come up during troubleshooting sessions.

In most cases, we will be looking for error messages in the **truss** output. These entries will contain the string "Err" in the last column of the output. (Appendix A includes a list of the most common error message codes, along with a brief description. A full list with comments is found in the */usr/include/sys/errno.h* file.) Most errors can easily be characterized as either system call errors or missing file errors.

It is also useful to look at signals reported by the **truss** output. Processes or threads can be notified of events through **signals**. Signal handlers can be defined to perform non-default actions when a signal is received. (A common example is when SIGHUP causes a process to re-read its configuration file.) Signal masks can be defined on a per-thread basis.

Signals may be synchronous or asynchronous to the execution of the process. **Synchronous signals** (also called traps) occur as a result of an action of the process itself. Examples are illegal instructions or address references that require the termination of the thread performing the action.

Asynchronous signals are sent to the process based on actions outside of its execution flow. A common example is when one process sends another process a signal via a kill() or a sigsend(). This type of signal is also called an **interrupt**.

Sometimes we need to understand a signal that is sent. The *signal.h(3HEAD)* man page includes a full listing of signals. Table 3-3 in the "Signals" section of Chapter 3 lists the most relevant signals for troubleshooting purposes.

A process's signal actions can be viewed by using the **psig** command.

Many missing file errors are the result of a library not being in a directory in the LD_LIBRARY_PATH or something of the sort. If the **truss** output shows a successful manipulation of the file with open(), that file is not your culprit.

truss output can be a bit difficult to interpret. Since it tracks every single system call, the sheer volume of data can be overwhelming. The best way to handle things is to dump the output to a log file and review it afterwards.

There are several strategies for reviewing **truss** output. One of the best is to look for the final error message and work up from there to see what the program was trying to do. A lot of the time, it is something as basic as a missing file (which may just mean a missing entry on a PATH or LD_LIBRARY_PATH environment variable). Example 4-2 shows the output of an attempt to ls a nonexistent file:

Example 4-2. truss Output

```
soltest > truss ls /bogusfile
execve("/usr/bin/ls", 0xFFBFFA2C, 0xFFBFFA38)  argc = 2
resolvepath("/usr/lib/ld.so.1", "/lib/ld.so.1", 1023) = 12
resolvepath("/usr/bin/ls", "/usr/bin/ls", 1023) = 11
stat("/usr/bin/ls", 0xFFBFF808)              = 0
open("/var/ld/ld.config", O_RDONLY)          Err#2 ENOENT
stat("/usr/lib/libc.so.1", 0xFFBFF328)       = 0
resolvepath("/usr/lib/libc.so.1", "/lib/libc.so.1", 1023) = 14
open("/usr/lib/libc.so.1", O_RDONLY)         = 3
mmap(0x00010000, 8192, PROT_READ|PROT_EXEC, MAP_PRIVATE|MAP_ALIGN, 3, 0) = 0xFF3A0000
mmap(0x00010000, 991232, PROT_NONE, MAP_PRIVATE|MAP_NORESERVE|MAP_ANON|MAP_ALIGN, -1, 0) =
0xFF280000
mmap(0xFF280000, 881573, PROT_READ|PROT_EXEC, MAP_PRIVATE|MAP_FIXED|MAP_TEXT, 3, 0) =
0xFF280000
mmap(0xFF368000, 29469, PROT_READ|PROT_WRITE|PROT_EXEC, MAP_PRIVATE|MAP_FIXED|MAP_INITDATA,
3, 884736) = 0xFF368000
mmap(0xFF370000, 2592, PROT_READ|PROT_WRITE|PROT_EXEC, MAP_PRIVATE|MAP_FIXED|MAP_ANON, -1,
0) = 0xFF370000
munmap(0xFF358000, 65536)                    = 0
memcntl(0xFF280000, 139692, MC_ADVISE, MADV_WILLNEED, 0, 0) = 0
close(3)                                     = 0
munmap(0xFF3A0000, 8192)                     = 0
mmap(0x00010000, 24576, PROT_READ|PROT_WRITE|PROT_EXEC, MAP_PRIVATE|MAP_ANON|MAP_ALIGN, -1,
0) = 0xFF3A0000
getcontext(0xFFBFF500)
getrlimit(RLIMIT_STACK, 0xFFBFF4E0)          = 0
getpid()                                     = 16464 [16463]
setustack(0xFF3A2088)
brk(0x000270F0)                              = 0
brk(0x000290F0)                              = 0
stat("/platform/SUNW,Sun-Fire-V240/lib/libc_psr.so.1", 0xFFBFEF90) = 0
resolvepath("/platform/SUNW,Sun-Fire-V240/lib/libc_psr.so.1", "/platform/sun4u-
us3/lib/libc_psr.so.1", 1023) = 37
open("/platform/SUNW,Sun-Fire-V240/lib/libc_psr.so.1", O_RDONLY) = 3
mmap(0x00010000, 8192, PROT_READ|PROT_EXEC, MAP_PRIVATE|MAP_ALIGN, 3, 0) = 0xFF390000
close(3)                                     = 0
mmap(0x00000000, 8192, PROT_READ|PROT_WRITE|PROT_EXEC, MAP_PRIVATE|MAP_ANON, -1, 0) =
0xFF380000
stat("/usr/lib/locale/en_US.ISO8859-1/en_US.ISO8859-1.so.3", 0xFFBFEC70) = 0
resolvepath("/usr/lib/locale/en_US.ISO8859-1/en_US.ISO8859-1.so.3",
"/usr/lib/locale/en_US.ISO8859-1/en_US.ISO8859-1.so.3", 1023) = 52
open("/usr/lib/locale/en_US.ISO8859-1/en_US.ISO8859-1.so.3", O_RDONLY) = 3
mmap(0x00010000, 8192, PROT_READ|PROT_EXEC, MAP_PRIVATE|MAP_ALIGN, 3, 0) = 0xFF270000
mmap(0x00010000, 90112, PROT_NONE, MAP_PRIVATE|MAP_NORESERVE|MAP_ANON|MAP_ALIGN, -1, 0) =
0xFF250000
mmap(0xFF250000, 14902, PROT_READ|PROT_EXEC, MAP_PRIVATE|MAP_FIXED|MAP_TEXT, 3, 0) =
0xFF250000
mmap(0xFF262000, 8914, PROT_READ|PROT_WRITE|PROT_EXEC, MAP_PRIVATE|MAP_FIXED|MAP_INITDATA,
3, 8192) = 0xFF262000
munmap(0xFF254000, 57344)                    = 0
memcntl(0xFF250000, 6912, MC_ADVISE, MADV_WILLNEED, 0, 0) = 0
close(3)                                     = 0
munmap(0xFF270000, 8192)                     = 0
time()                                       = 1168368283
ioctl(1, TCGETA, 0xFFBFF954)                 = 0
brk(0x000290F0)                              = 0
```

```
brk(0x000330F0)                                        = 0
lstat64("/bogusfile", 0xFFBFF8D0)                    Err#2 ENOENT
/bogusfilewrite(2, " / b o g u s f i l e", 10)          = 10
: write(2, " : ", 2)                                   = 2
write(2, " N o   s u c h   f i l e".., 25)    = 25
write(2, "\n", 1)                                      = 1
_exit(2)
soltest > grep "ENOENT" /usr/include/sys/errno.h
#define ENOENT   2          /* No such file or directory          */
```

(Notice that we were able to find the English translation of the obscure error code in */usr/include/sys/errno.h*.) In Example 4-2, the first ENOENT (No such file or directory) message is a result of a missing *ld.config* file:

```
open("/var/ld/ld.config", O_RDONLY)            Err#2 ENOENT
```

This sort of thing is common during the initial stage of a process's output, when the process is looking for the different dynamic libraries and such that are required. (In this case, it just means that we are using the defaults for the dynamic linker configuration.)

The second ENOENT message, however, is more interesting:

```
lstat64("/bogusfile", 0xFFBFF8D0)              Err#2 ENOENT
```

Here we see that an `lstat()` (which checks that the file attributes are appropriate) reports that it can't find the file. Immediately after that, we see that the error message "No such file or directory" is written to the screen, and we `exit()` with error code 2. (Non-zero `exit()` codes are usually an indication that things did not work out for the process.) Not surprisingly, the problem is that */bogusfile* does not exist.

truss -c -p *PID* provides a summary of a process's system call activity. It can also track functions that the dynamic linker is able to see (which may exclude binaries that have been optimized). This is done with the **truss -u a.out -p** *PID* command.

Example 4-3 demonstrates the output of **truss -c** and **truss -D**. The amount of time spent on different system calls may point to a culprit in a performance problem. It may also be useful to find out which system calls are responsible for errors during a program's execution.

Example 4-3. truss -c and truss -D Output

```
soltest > truss -c grep teststring /etc/passwd

syscall            seconds   calls   errors
_exit               .000        1
read                .000        2
open                .000        5       1
close               .000        5
brk                 .000        6
stat                .000        5
getpid              .000        1
execve              .000        1
getcontext          .000        1
setustack           .000        1
mmap                .000       18
munmap              .000        6
getrlimit           .000        1
memcntl             .000        3
resolvepath         .000        6
open64              .000        1
                  --------   ------   ----
sys totals:         .003       63       1
```

59

```
usr time:              .003
elapsed:               .050

soltest > truss -D ls
 0.0000 execve("/usr/bin/ls", 0xFFBFF9DC, 0xFFBFF9E4)  argc = 1
 0.0102 resolvepath("/usr/lib/ld.so.1", "/lib/ld.so.1", 1023) = 12
 0.0009 resolvepath("/usr/bin/ls", "/usr/bin/ls", 1023) = 11
 0.0004 stat("/usr/bin/ls", 0xFFBFF7B8)           = 0
 0.0003 open("/var/ld/ld.config", O_RDONLY)           Err#2 ENOENT
 0.0005 stat("/usr/lib/libsec.so.1", 0xFFBFF270)   = 0
 0.0003 resolvepath("/usr/lib/libsec.so.1", "/lib/libsec.so.1", 1023) = 16
 0.0004 open("/usr/lib/libsec.so.1", O_RDONLY)     = 3
 0.0003 mmap(0x00010000, 8192, PROT_READ|PROT_EXEC, MAP_PRIVATE|MAP_ALIGN, 3, 0) =
0xFF3A0000
...
 0.0004 openat(-3041965, ".", O_RDONLY|O_NDELAY|O_LARGEFILE) = 3
 0.0004 fcntl(3, F_SETFD, 0x00000001)              = 0
 0.0002 fstat64(3, 0xFFBFF760)                     = 0
 0.0003 getdents64(3, 0xFF3A4000, 8192)            = 48
 0.0002 getdents64(3, 0xFF3A4000, 8192)            = 0
 0.0002 close(3)                                   = 0
 0.0003 _exit(0)
```

truss does have a performance impact on the process being examined. It is implemented by repeatedly stopping and starting the process in order to monitor it. The DTrace Toolkit program **dtruss** allows much of the same functionality, without the performance hit.

Shared library calls can be traced via **apptrace** in a similar way. Functions of interest can have full details exposed by using the -v option:

```
apptrace -v function-name command
```

Process Structure

In order to get real value out of **mdb** and **dtrace**, we need to have some understanding of the internal structure of a process and some of the names of objects inside a process structure. The following discussion is limited to the minimum necessary for a general Solaris admin to troubleshoot a local problem. Readers who would like a more in-depth discussion should look at *Solaris Internals* by McDougall and Mauro or *Unix Internals: The New Frontiers* by Vahalia. (See "References" at the end of this chapter.) Readers who feel comfortable with Solaris internal structure may wish to skip ahead to "Examining Processes with mdb" later in the chapter.

Process structure is defined in the *usr/src/uts/common/sys/proc.h* file. Some key elements are listed below. Several elements of the proc structure are related to chains of objects. Chains are a common organizing mechanism in Unix. In a **chain**, or **linked list**, each element points to the previous element in the chain and the next element in the chain. This allows the number of these elements to grow without the overhead of resizing a table.

Different types of structures, such as memory structures, locks and threads, are discussed in following sections.

Binary Executables and the Linker

Ultimately, a process is created when fork() (or one if its relatives) creates a process structure and exec() populates the structure with the new process's image. When this happens, the runtime linker ld.so.1 resolves references to shared library functions.

Binary executable files are in Executable and Linking Format (ELF). We can examine the headers of an ELF file with the `elfdump` utility. `elfdump -c` reveals the ELF header, including the location of the Section Header Table (SHT, located at `e_shoff`) and Program Header Table (PHT, located at `e_phoff`). The SHT provides information on the linkable sections of the executable, and the PHT tells us about the program segments of the executable.

We can debug linker operations by setting the `LD_DEBUG` and `LD_DEBUG_OUTPUT` environment variables before calling the executable. Setting `LD_DEBUG` to "`help`" provides a list of available options, including "`all`." `LD_DEBUG_OUTPUT` specifies a logging file.

Process Virtual Memory

Each process has its own virtual memory space. References to real memory are provided through a process-specific set of address translation maps. The computer's Memory Management Unit (MMU) contains a set of registers that point to the current process's address translation maps. When the current process changes, the MMU must load the translation maps for the new process. This is called a **context switch**.

The MMU is only addressable in kernel mode, for obvious security reasons. The kernel text and data structures are mapped in a portion of each process's virtual memory space. This area is called the kernel space (or system space).

In addition, each process contains these two important kernel-owned areas in virtual memory: u area and kernel stack. The **u area** contains information about the process such as information about open files, identification information and process registers. The **kernel stack** is provided on a per-process basis to allow the kernel to be **re-entrant** (ie, several processes can be involved in the kernel, and may even be executing the same routine concurrently). Each process's kernel stack keeps track of its function call sequence when executing in the kernel. The kernel can access the memory maps for non-current processes by using temporary maps.

The kernel can operate in either process context or system (or interrupt) context. In process context, the kernel has access to the process's memory space (including u area and kernel stack). It can also block the current process while waiting for a resource. In kernel context, the kernel cannot access the address space, u area or kernel stack. Kernel context is used for handling certain system-wide issues such as device interrupt handling or process priority computation.

Each process's virtual memory space is divided into the following sections:

- **Kernel**: While this is part of the process's memory space, it is not directly addressable by the process. It must be accessed via system calls.
- **Stack**: Used by the program for variables and storage. It grows and shrinks in size depending on what routines are called and what their stack space requirements are. (Each thread in a process has its own stack.) The stack grows downward into the hole.
- **Shared Libraries**: Shared libraries are position independent so that they can be shared by all programs that want to use them. One common example is `libc.so`
- **Hole**: This is the address space that is unallocated and unused. It does not tie up physical memory. For most processes, this is the bulk of the virtual memory for the process.
- **Heap**: Used for some types of working storage. It is allocated by the `malloc()` function. The heap grows upward into the hole.
- **BSS**: Uninitialized variables. These are not part of the executable file and their initial value is set to zeros.
- **Data**: Initialized data such as global variables, constants and static variables from the program.
- **Text**: Instruction stream from the executable file.

Each process maps either 2^{32}, 2^{44} or 2^{64} bytes of memory (depending on whether the OS is running in 32 or 64-bit mode and the hardware environment). (The UltraSPARC I and II processors are limited to 2^{44} in 64-bit mode.) 2^{32} is about 4GB, 2^{44} is about 16TB and 2^{64} is about 16EB. Not all of this memory is allocated (used); the virtual memory is used as address space that can be mapped to actual memory resources.

The entire process virtual memory space is not mapped. The process is only permitted to access memory locations with valid mappings. If attempts are made to access a memory location that is not mapped, a page fault results.

Physical memory is not actually assigned to virtual address space until the first time that it is referenced. At that time, physical memory is allocated, one page at a time. Calls to free() do not actually release the physical memory that has been mapped. Instead, they mark the area as available for use. Such memory pages may be taken by the page scanner if there is a system memory shortfall, but will be left alone otherwise. As a result, process memory will tend to grow over time unless there is a system memory shortfall.

The virtual memory map for a process can be displayed using the **pmap -x** *PID* command. This command shows several aspects of the process's virtual memory, including the address and the amount actually resident in physical memory (RSS). Heap and stack segments are flagged as anonymous (Anon).

Process Context

A **process's context** consists of information that identifies the process and its state. This includes several key elements, such as the user address space, control information, credentials, environment variables, accounting information and the hardware context. The **hardware context** consists of the process's state information, including the program counter, stack pointer and registers. The hardware context is copied from the CPU to the u area of the process structure during a process **context switch**.

Processes are usually created with fork() or alternatives such as fork1(), vfork() or forkall(). forkall() duplicates the entire process context, while fork() and fork1() only duplicate the context of the calling thread. (vfork() does even less than this; it effectively borrows the calling process context. The use of vfork() is deprecated in most cases due to the danger of a race condition between the processes sharing the context.)

> In previous versions of Solaris, fork() implemented the same strategy as forkall(). In Solaris 10, fork() implements the same strategy as fork1(). As of this writing, the man page has not quite caught up to the new reality.

Previous versions of Solaris were vulnerable to a problem known as a "fork bomb" where a loop in code resulted in a process forking out of control. (Any number of geeky inside jokes have described the results of this problem, none of which are appropriate for a G-rated book.) Now, Solaris attempts to resolve this problem by applying a throttle to the forking process. If the kernel discovers that there is no available process table entry, the process issuing the fork() is forced to sleep for an extra clock tick. This has the effect of limiting the number of forking failures to one per CPU per clock tick. As the number of failures increase, so does the imposed delay. An "out of processes" message will appear on the console, and **sar -v** will have non-zero values in its ov column.

Context Switching

A **context switch** occurs when the Memory Management Unit (MMU) loads a new thread's translation maps. This is a relatively expensive procedure. Too many context switches can dramatically hurt performance.

Context switching is monitored directly by **vmstat** or **mpstat**. Of particular interest is the icsw value for **mpstat**, which reports on the number of involuntary context switches. (**Involuntary context switches** occur when a thread is forced from the CPU in favor of another thread.) A large number of involuntary context switches may indicate CPU saturation.

DTrace can also provide a way to look at which processes are contributing to the involuntary context switches. We will discuss this in Example 5-2 (Chapter 5) and in "System Calls and Context Switches" (Chapter 7).

proc Block

In the "Process Context" section, we discussed some of the contents of a `proc` structure (or "`proc` block") in a general way. In order to be able to understand what we are seeing inside the process, we need to know what some of these objects are called.

Table 4-4 lists several of the most important objects from the `proc` block in the order that they appear in the output of a `::print proc_t` command in **mdb**. This list is far from complete; check the *proc.h* and *user.h* files for a complete list. (The "Resources" section at the end of this chapter includes links to the OpenSolaris site's listing of *proc.h* and *user.h*.)

(For our purposes, the u area is included in Table 4-4, since it is displayed that way by **mdb**. Traditional Unix architecture considers it to be a separate structure, but Solaris brings it into the `proc` structure via an include clause in the *proc.h*.)

Table 4-4. proc Block Elements

Element	Description
p_exec	Vnode pointer to the executable file.
p_as	Pointer to process address space.
p_cred	Location of process credentials structure.
p_swapcnt	Number of swapped-out processes.
p_stat	Process status. (Distinct from thread state, though a "representative" thread's state is reported by ps.) The status may be one of the following: 1. SSLEEP: Waiting for an event. 2. SRUN: Running. 3. SZOMB: Zombie; terminated but not waited for. 4. SSTOP: Stopped by debugger. 5. SIDL: Intermediate state in process creation. 6. SONPROC: On a processor.
p_ppid	Parent Process ID (PID)
p_parent	Pointer to parent process.
p_child	Pointer to first child process.
p_sibling	Pointer to next sibling process on the chain.
p_psibling	Pointer to the previous sibling process on the chain.
p_lwpexit	Waiting for an LWP to exit.
p_proc_flag	*/proc* related flags.
p_utime	This process's user time.

Element	Description
p_stime	This process's system time.
p_cutime	Sum of user time for child processes (reported upon child exit).
p_cstime	Sum of system time for child processes (reported upon child exit).
p_bssbase	Base address of last BSS below heap.
p_brkbase	Heap base address.
p_brksize	Heap size in bytes.
p_sig	Pending signals for this process.
p_stksize	Process stack size, in bytes.
p_user	User structure; considered part of *proc.h* in Solaris.
u_start	Microstate time at process start.
u_comm	Executable file name from exec().
u_psargs	Arguments from exec().
u_cdir	Current directory vnode pointer.
u_rdir	Root directory vnode pointer.
u_mem	Accumulated memory usage.
u_mem_max	Maximum RSS over the life of the process, in KB.
p_task	Pointer to containing task.
p_pagep	Pointer to sc_page_ctl structure of process's shared pages.
p_rctls	Pointer to resource controls.
p_stk_ctl	Currently enforced stack size.
p_fsz_ctl	Currently enforced file size.
p_vmem_ctl	Currently enforced address space size.
p_fno_ctl	Currently enforced file descriptor limit.
p_pool	Pointer to containing pool.
p_zone	Pointer to containing zone.

Each process's open files may be identified by moving through structures associated with the process. The open file structure u_finfo points at contains a pointer to f_list, which is itself a pointer to an array of uf_entry_t structures, indexed by file descriptor. For each descriptor, the `uf_file` points to a file structure. This includes a link to the vnode (`f_vnode`). The vnode is specific to a particular type of file system and uniquely identifies the file. (In UFS, the inode is the vnode identifier.)

The number of files a process can have is not limited by the number of `uf_entry` structures associated with it. When the process runs out of these structures, an additional set is allocated to bring the total number to ((`fi_nfiles` x 2) +1), with a hard limit set by the max-file-descriptor resource control. (See the "Resource Controls" section in Chapter 6.) When this happens, the old list becomes part of the new list of structures, and the new list is moved to the structure indicated by `fi_rlist` (the "retired" file list).

The full `psinfo_t` structure is defined in the `proc(4)` man page. Some of the more interesting elements of the `psinfo_t` structure are listed in Table 4-5.

Table 4-5. Elements of psinfo_t Structure

Element	Description
pr_nlwp	Number of active Lightweight Processes in the process.
pr_pid	Process ID.
pr_ppid	Parent process ID.
pr_uid/pr_gid	Real user ID/group ID.
pr_euid/pr_egid	Effective user ID/group ID.
pr_addr	Process address.
pr_ttydev	tty to which the process is bound.
pr_start	Process start time.
pr_fname	Executed file name.
pr_psargs	Initial characters of argument list.
pr_argc	Initial argument count.
pr_envp	Address of initial argument vector.
pr_taskid	Task ID.
pr_projid	Project ID.
pr_poolid	Pool ID.
pr_zoneid	Zone ID.

Kernel Services

The Solaris kernel may be seen as a bundle of kernel threads. It uses synchronization primitives to prevent priority inversion, such as mutexes, semaphores, condition variables and read/write locks.

The kernel provides service to processes in the following four ways:

- **System Calls**: The kernel executes requests submitted by processes via system calls. The system call interface invokes a special trap instruction.
- **Hardware Exceptions**: The kernel notifies a process when it attempts illegal activities such as division by zero or user stack overflows.
- **Hardware Interrupts**: Devices use interrupts to notify the kernel of status changes (such as I/O completions.)
- **Resource Management**: The kernel manages resources via special processes such as the page daemon.

In addition, some system services (such as the NFS service) are contained within the kernel in order to reduce overhead from context switching.

Threads

An application's **parallelism** is the degree of parallel execution achieved. In the real world, this is limited by the number of processors available in the hardware configuration. **Concurrency** is the maximum achievable parallelism in a theoretical machine with an unlimited number of processors. Threads are frequently used to increase an application's concurrency.

A **thread** is a control point within a process, and represents a relatively independent set of instructions within a program. It shares global resources within the context of the process (address space, open files, user credentials, quotas, etc). Threads also have private resources (program counter, stack, register context, etc).

The main benefit of threads (as compared to multiple processes) is that the context switches are much cheaper than those required to change current processes. Even within a single-processor environment, multiple threads are advantageous because one thread may be able to progress even though another thread is blocked and waiting for a resource.

Interprocess communication also takes considerably less time for threads than for processes, since global data can be shared instantly.

Kernel Threads

A **kernel thread** is the entity that is scheduled by the kernel. If no lightweight process is attached, it is also known as a **system thread**. It uses kernel text and global data, but has its own kernel stack, as well as a data structure to hold scheduling and synchronization information.

Kernel threads can be independently scheduled on CPUs. Context switching between kernel threads is very fast because memory mappings do not have to be flushed. See Chapter 7 for information on scheduling.

> Old-timers will remember that we used to look carefully at the context switching rate as an indication of an overloaded system. With current hardware, context switching is much faster, and is not usually a problem on its own. Context switching rates should be used to help generate a holistic picture of how the system is behaving; they should not be used as a standalone indication of a problem.

Lightweight Processes

A **lightweight process** can be considered as the swappable portion of a kernel thread.

Another way to look at **lightweight processes** is to think of them as "virtual CPUs" which perform the processing for applications. Application threads are attached to available lightweight processes, which are attached to a kernel thread, which is scheduled on the system's CPU dispatch queue.

LWPs can make system calls and can block while waiting for resources. All LWPs in a process share a common address space. Interprocess Communication (IPC) facilities exist for coordinating access to shared resources.

By default, one LWP is assigned to each process; additional LWPs are created if all the process's LWPs are sleeping and there are additional user threads that `libthread` can schedule. The programmer can specify that threads are bound to LWPs.

Lightweight process information for a process can be examined with **ps -cL -p *PID***, as in Example 4-4.

Example 4-4. Lightweight Process Information from ps

```
soltest/ > ps -cL -p 501
   PID   LWP  CLS PRI TTY          LTIME CMD
   501     1   TS  59 ?            0:00 sshd
```

(Since there is a 1-1 correspondence between LWPs and kernel threads in Solaris 10, the kernel threads are assigned the same ID as the LWP.)

> Older versions of Solaris did not necessarily have a 1-1 correspondence between LWPs and kernel threads. The newer threads model was introduced as a patch in older Solaris versions.

Both Solaris/Unix International and POSIX APIs are supported in Solaris 10 for developing threaded applications, but the implementation code is the same for both. The current recommendation is to default to the POSIX standard as being more portable, but the same kernel code will be referenced either way.

Each lightweight process is represented by a `ulwp_t` data structure. The linked list of these structures are referenced by the process's `uberdata`. Within **mdb**, these can be examined by using the address specified for `all_lwps` from the `::uberdata` dcmd and following the chain. Example 4-5 demonstrates this process in the "Examining Processes with mdb" section.

The full `lwpsinfo_t` structure is defined in the `proc(4)` man page. Some of the more relevant objects in an `lwpsinfo_t` structure are listed in Table 4-6.

Table 4-6. Elements of lwpsinfo_t Structure

Element	Description
pr_lwpid	Lightweight process ID.
pr_addr	Internal thread address.
pr_wchan	Wait address for sleeping thread.
pr_stype	Synchronization event type.
pr_state	Numeric thread state. (S=sleep, R=runnable but not running, Z=zombie, T=stopped, I= intermediate state or O=on CPU.)
pr_nice	Nice value for CPU usage.
pr_syscall	System call number.
pr_pri	Priority value.
pr_clname	Scheduling class name.
pr_onpro	Processor which last ran this thread.
pr_bindpro	Last thread processor binding.

Element	Description
`pr_bindpset`	Processor set binding for thread.

User Threads

User **threads** are scheduled on their LWPs via a scheduler in `libthread`. This scheduler does implement priorities, but does not implement time slicing. If time slicing is desired, it must be programmed in. Locking issues must also be carefully considered by the programmer in order to prevent several threads from blocking on a single resource.

User threads are also responsible for handling of `SIGSEGV` segmentation violation) signals, since the kernel does not keep track of user thread stacks.

Each thread has the following characteristics:

- Has its own stack
- Shares the process address space.
- Executes independently (and perhaps concurrently with other threads).
- Completely invisible from outside the process.
- Cannot be controlled from the command line.
- No system protection between threads in a process; the programmer is responsible for interactions.
- Can share information between threads without IPC overhead.

Zombie Processes

When a process dies, it becomes a **zombie process**. Normally, the parent performs a wait() and cleans up the PID. Sometimes, the parent receives too many SIGCHLD signals at once, but can only handle one at a time. It is possible to resend the signal on behalf of the child via **kill -18 *PPID*** Killing the parent or rebooting will also clean up zombies. The correct answer is to fix the buggy parent code that failed to perform the `wait()` properly.

Aside from their inherent sloppiness, the only problem with zombies is that they take up a place in the process table. The **preap** command performs cleanup on zombie processes.

Examining Processes with mdb

A detailed description of a program as complex as **mdb** is beyond the scope of this book. Sun provides a complete manual on its web site, and the OpenSolaris Community links to a number of real-world debugging sessions using **mdb**. (See the "Resources" section below.)

mdb has the following basic **command syntax**:

[*address*] [, *count*] command [*arguments*]

Commands in **mdb** are called **dcmds**. A few of the more common dcmds are listed in Table 4-7. A full list can be obtained by running the `::dcmds` command in an **mdb** session.

Table 4-7: mdb Verbs

Verb	Description
?	Examine code or variables in executable object file.

Verb	Description
!	Shell escape.
/	Examine value.
=	Translate value to a different format.
$<	Invoke commands, including macros.
<	Read value from a variable or register.
@ or \	Format data from physical address space.
$C or $c	Stack backtrace.
$Q	Quit mdb session.
$v	Print non-zero variables.
::dcmds	Provides a listing of dcmds.
::help [cmdname]	Provides usage notes on a specific dcmd.
::kmastat	Print kernel memory allocations.
::mappings or $m	Print address space mappings.
::memstat	Report memory statistics.
::msgbuf	Display message buffer.
::nm	Print symbol table.
::objects	Print load objects.
::panicinfo	Presents useful register and message buffer contents for examining a crash dump.
::pmap	Print memory mapping of specified process.
::print [type]	Display object of specified type.
::ps	List processes, including address of proc_t.
::rctl	Prints a resource control table (rctl_t) if the specified address points at an rctl_t structure.
::rctl_dict	Print system default resource controls.
::rctl_list	Print resource controls for a specified process.
::regs or $r	Print general registers.

Verb	Description
`::seg`	Print address space segment.
`::stack`	Print the stack backtrace.
`::stackregs`	Print the stack backtrace, including registers.
`::status`	Display status, including error information.
`::system`	Display system variable customizations
`::thread`	Display a summary of `kthread_t`.
`::threadlist`	Display a list of threads and their C stack traces.
`::typeset or >`	Assign value to a variable or register.
`::uberdata`	LWP information for a process.
`::walk`	Walk the specified data structure.

In this example, we look for the memory location of `ulwp_one` as the appropriate place to begin a walk through the LWPs. Each LWP is then asked to report on its own address. Given the address of an LWP, we can identify its lwpid by finding its `ul_lwpid`.

Example 4-5. mdb Examination of LWPs

```
soltest/ > mdb -p 104
Loading modules: [ ld.so.1 libc.so.1 libnvpair.so.1 libavl.so.1 ]
> ::uberdata
libc.so.1`_uberdata:
            &link_lock          &fork_lock          fork_owner
+0x0        0xff2ecbc0          0xff2ecc00          <NULL>
...
            ulwp_one            all_lwps            all_zombies
+0x1098     0xff3a2000          0xff3a2000          <NULL>
...
> 0xff3a2000::walk ulwps | ::print ulwp_t ul_self
ul_self = 0xff3a2000
ul_self = 0xff3a2400
ul_self = 0xfed50000
ul_self = 0xfed50400
ul_self = 0xfed50c00
ul_self = 0xfed51000
> 0xff3a2400::print ulwp_t ul_lwpid
ul_lwpid = 0x2
> 0xff3a2400::print ulwp_t ! grep "lwpid"
    ul_lwpid = 0x2
> $Q
```

Example 4-6 demonstrates the use of some other commands by specifying the running kernel with **mdb -k**. The **ps** command allows us to find the address of a particular `proc_t` structure, which can then be examined. Of particular interest is the fact that `u_psargs` contains the original command used to create the process, and **::pfiles** allows us to look at process open files:

70

Example 4-6. mdb Process Examination

```
soltest/ > mdb -k
Loading modules: [ unix krtld genunix specfs dtrace ufs sd ip sctp usba fcp fctl nca lofs
zfs random logindmux ptm md cpc fcip sppp crypto nfs ]
> ::ps ! grep more
R   5534   5393   5534   5388      0 0x4a004000 0000060001338c00 more
> 0000060001338c00::pmap
                SEG            BASE       SIZE     RES PATH
0000030005941a70 0000000000010000    32k          /usr/bin/more
00000300059419e0 0000000000028000     8k      8k /usr/bin/more
0000030005b47d40 000000000002a000    16k     16k [ anon ]
000003000586fc68 00000000ff200000   864k          /lib/libc.so.1
0000060001e770e0 00000000ff2e8000    32k     32k /lib/libc.so.1
000003000586fcb0 00000000ff2f0000     8k      8k [ anon ]
0000030005c786c0 00000000ff300000    16k          /usr/lib/locale/en_US.ISO885
0000030005c78288 00000000ff312000    16k     16k /usr/lib/locale/en_US.ISO885
0000030005c78a68 00000000ff330000     8k          /platform/sun4u-us3/lib/libc
0000030005c78870 00000000ff340000     8k      8k [ anon ]
0000030005b47cb0 00000000ff350000   168k          /lib/libcurses.so.1
0000030005c11008 00000000ff38a000    32k     24k /lib/libcurses.so.1
0000030005c785a0 00000000ff392000     8k      8k [ anon ]
0000030005915878 00000000ff3a0000    24k     16k [ anon ]
00000300059417e8 00000000ff3b0000   184k          /lib/ld.so.1
000003000586e990 00000000ff3ee000     8k      8k /lib/ld.so.1
0000030005c10000 00000000ff3f0000     8k      8k [ anon ]
00000300059158c0 00000000ffbfc000    16k     16k [ anon ]
> 0000060001338c00::print proc_t
{
    p_exec = 0x6000442b5c0
    p_as = 0x600009b31c0
    p_lockp = 0x600006b0300
    p_crlock = {
        _opaque = [ 0 ]
    }
    p_cred = 0x60000800300
    p_swapcnt = 0
    p_stat = '\002'
    p_wcode = '\0'
    p_pidflag = 0
    p_wdata = 0
    p_ppid = 0x1511
    p_link = 0
    p_parent = 0x60001e80c08
...
> 0000060001338c00::print proc_t ! grep psargs
        u_psargs = [ "more /etc/name_to_major /etc/name_to_sysnum" ]
> 0000060001338c00::pfiles
FD   TYPE          VNODE INFO
   0 CHR 00000600010bfec0 /devices/pseudo/pts@0:2
   1 CHR 00000600010bfec0 /devices/pseudo/pts@0:2
   2 CHR 00000600010bfec0 /devices/pseudo/pts@0:2
   3 REG 0000060008a6eac0 /etc/name_to_major
> $Q
```

The expression used to generate the address may be formatted any of several different ways. Table 4-8 contains several of the more interesting for our current purposes. Appendix D discusses some other forms of **mdb** expressions.

Table 4-8: mdb Expressions

Expression	Description
0t*integer*	The integer may be expressed as binary (0i), hexadecimal (0x) or decimal (0t).
<*identifier*	Value of the indicated variable.
identifier	The value of the indicated symbol.
.	The value of the current location.
&	The value of the location most recently used to execute a dcmd.
+	Incremented value of the current location.
^	Decremented value of the current location.

Variables

Variables are assigned using the > or ::**typeset** dcmds. Variables may use non-reserved names consisting of sequences of letters, digits,underscores or periods. The value of a variable is a 64-bit unsigned integer.

The following variables are persistent:

- **0**: Most recent value printed by / \ ? or =
- **9**: Most recent count from $<
- **b**: Virtual address of the base of the data section.
- **d**: Size of the data section (bytes).
- **e**: Virtual address of entry point.
- **hits**: Number of times the event specifier has been matched.
- **m**: Magic number of target's primary object file.
- **t**: Size of text section (bytes).
- **thread**: Current representative thread's identifier.

Sparc Registers

Several Sparc registers may be of interest when looking at system state, especially when looking at a crash dump:

- %g0-%g7: General Registers.
  g0=Zero.
  g7=Address of current thread.
- %i0-%i7: Input registers.
  i6=Frame pointer (for tracing previous function through stack.)
- %o0-%o7: Output registers.
  o6=Stack pointer (sp).
  o7=Program counter (pc).
- %l0-%l7: Local registers.

In Example 4-7, we examine a crash dump to look for the command that provoked a panic.

Actually, we are looking for the command that was active at the time of the panic. It just sounds

72

better the other way. In this case, they are the same thing, but a hardware-involved panic is not necessarily the fault of the active process.

The g7 is an address of a current thread, so we look for its pointer back to the proc block of the calling process. Once we have that, we can look for the u_psargs to find the name of the command that was active at the time of the panic. (In this case, the crash dump was provoked by a **reboot -d** command.)

Example 4-7 mdb Finds Active Process at the Time of a Crash Dump

```
soltest/var/crash/soltest > mdb -k unix.0 vmcore.0
Loading modules: [ unix krtld genunix specfs dtrace ufs sd ip sctp usba fctl nca lofs random
cpc fcip nfs ]
> ::regs ! grep g7
%g7 = 0x0000030000fa52c0                 %17 = 0x0000000000000002
> 0x0000030000fa52c0$<thread ! grep procp
    t_procp = 0x6000137e020
> 0x6000137e020::print proc_t ! grep psargs
        u_psargs = [ "reboot -d" ]
$Q
```

In Example 4-7, note the use of the exclamation point to call **grep** in order to find what we want quickly. The volume of output can quickly become overwhelming unless we do something to focus it.

Crash Dump Examination

mdb offers some additional functionality that may be useful when drilling deeper into a crash dump. For example, **::regs** provides a full register listing, the **::panicinfo** macro provides summary information about the circumstances of the dump's creation, and the **$c** macro provides a stack trace of the running process.

Example 4-8 examines a crash dump resulting from a memory error.

Example 4-8 mdb Examination of a Crash Dump

```
soltest/var/crash/soltest > mdb -k unix.0 vmcore.0
Loading modules: [ unix krtld genunix specfs dtrace ufs sd md ip sctp usba random fcp fctl
nca logindmux ptm cpc fcip sppp crypto nfs ]
> ::regs
%g0 = 0x0000000000000000                 %10 = 0x0000000003ffffff
%g1 = 0x00000000011eda64 clear_errors+0x78 %11 = 0x00000000ff0f3c00
%g2 = 0x00000000011fa000 ecache_flush_line+0x3b8 %12 = 0x0000000003fffc00
%g3 = 0x03efffff8000000                  %13 = 0x0000000000000000
%g4 = 0x00000000fbffffffe                 %14 = 0x000000023fdafdc0
%g5 = 0x0000000000000001                 %15 = 0x0000000000000000
%g6 = 0x0000000000000000                 %16 = 0x0000000000000000
%g7 = 0x0000030004560980                 %17 = 0x0000000000000000

%o0 = 0x00000000011fa220                 %i0 = 0x00000000011fa220
%o1 = 0x000002a100b0e438                 %i1 = 0x000002a100b0e460
%o2 = 0x0000000000000000                 %i2 = 0x0000000000000000
%o3 = 0x0000000000000000                 %i3 = 0x0000000000000000
%o4 = 0xfc30ffffffffffff                 %i4 = 0x03efffff8000000
%o5 = 0x03cf000000000000                 %i5 = 0x0000000001855000
fhead_vn_spec+0x230
%o6 = 0x000002a100b0db01                 %i6 = 0x000002a100b0dbb1
%o7 = 0x00000000010e988c    fm_panic+0x30 %i7 = 0x00000000011eb9a8
cpu_deferred_error+0x568
```

73

```
  %ccr = 0x00 xcc=nzvc icc=nzvc
 %fprs = 0x00 fef=0 du=0 dl=0
  %asi = 0x80
    %y = 0x0000000000000000
   %pc = 0x0000000001041f4c vpanic
  %npc = 0x0000000001041f50 vpanic+4
   %sp = 0x000002a100b0db01 unbiased=0x000002a100b0e300
   %fp = 0x000002a100b0dbb1

 %tick = 0x0000000000000000
  %tba = 0x0000000000000000
   %tt = 0x0
   %tl = 0x0
  %pil = 0xf
%pstate = 0x016 cle=0 tle=0 mm=TSO red=0 pef=1 am=0 priv=1 ie=1 ag=0

      %cwp = 0x00  %cansave = 0x00
%canrestore = 0x00 %otherwin = 0x00
   %wstate = 0x00 %cleanwin = 0x00
> ::panicinfo
             cpu                 0
          thread       30004560980
         message UE Error(s)
          tstate          80001600
              g1            11eda64
              g2            11fa000
              g3   3effffff8000000
              g4           fbfffffe
              g5                 1
              g6                 0
              g7       30004560980
              o0           11fa220
              o1         2a100b0e438
              o2                 0
              o3                 0
              o4 fc30ffffffffffff
              o5   3cf000000000000
              o6        2a100b0db01
              o7           10e988c
              pc           1041f4c
             npc           1041f50
               y                 0
> 0x0000030004560980$<thread ! grep procp
    t_procp = 0x6000224cc20
> 0x6000224cc20::print proc_t ! grep psargs
       u_psargs = [ "/usr/local/tw/tripwire -initialize -c /usr/local/tw/tw.config.SunOS5
-v" ]
> $C
000002a100b0db01 vpanic(11fa220, 2a100b0e460, 0, 0, 3effffff8000000, 1855000)
000002a100b0dbb1 cpu_deferred_error+0x568(ecc1ecc100000000, 3, 1000040000019d,
400000000, 0, 30000ef8560)
000002a100b0e651 ktl0+0x48(30000096859, 0, 60006436540, 2a100b0f678, 2a100b0f680
, 60000839a40)
000002a100b0e7a1 kmem_depot_alloc+8(3000008bdc0, 30000096870, 90e, 3000008be00,
30000096858, 0)
000002a100b0e851 kmem_cache_alloc+0xfc(300000966c8, 0, 0, 6, 1f8, 180c000)
```

```
000002a100b0e901 ufs_alloc_inode+0x18(300000b0040, 2d13d2, ff, 0, 18bc800, 40)
000002a100b0e9b1 ufs_iget_internal+0x200(600010f3440, 2d13d2, 13d2, 0,
60001327b80, 300000b0040)
000002a100b0ea71 ufs_dirlook+0x2ac(2, 2a100b0f680, 2a100b0f458, 2d13d2,
60009996470, 60006436540)
000002a100b0eba1 ufs_lookup+0x2ac(60006436540, 2a100b0f680, 2a100b0f678, 0, 0,
60000800d18)
000002a100b0ec81 fop_lookup+0x28(60006436540, 2a100b0f680, 2a100b0f678, 121e0d8
, 0, 60000813380)
000002a100b0ed51 lookuppnvp+0x344(2a100b0f940, 0, 60006436540, 2a100b0f678,
2a100b0f680, 60000839a40)
000002a100b0ef91 lookuppnat+0x120(60000839a40, 0, 0, 0, 2a100b0fad8, 0)
000002a100b0f051 lookupnameat+0x5c(0, 0, 0, 0, 2a100b0fad8, 0)
000002a100b0f161 cstatat_getvp+0x198(ffd19400, ffbf88c8, 1, 0, 2a100b0fad8, 0)
000002a100b0f221 cstatat32+0x40( fffffffffd19553, ffbf88c8, 1000, ffbf82d0, 1000
, 0)
000002a100b0f2e1 syscall_trap32+0xcc(ffbf88c8, ffbf82d0, 5, ff265072, ffbf88eb,
7fffffdc)
> ::stackregs
000002a100b0db01 vpanic(11fa220, 2a100b0e460, 0, 0, 3effffff8000000, 1855000)
    %l0-%l3:        3ffffff       ff0f3c00        3fffc00               0
    %l4-%l7:       23fdafdc0              0              0               0
  cpu_deferred_error+0x568:call       -0x10214c      <fm_panic>

000002a100b0dbb1 cpu_deferred_error+0x568(ecc1ecc100000000, 3, 1000040000019d, 400000000, 0,
30000ef8560)
    %l0-%l3:       23fdafdc0              1         184c4d0         184c400
    %l4-%l7:      80d00000000         203400         ecc1ecc1        ecc1ec00
  ktl0+0x48:            jmpl        %l3, %o7

000002a100b0e651 ktl0+0x48(30000096859, 0, 60006436540, 2a100b0f678, 2a100b0f680,
60000839a40)
    %l0-%l3:              5           1400            1604         11eb440
    %l4-%l7:      60000800d18      60000839a40              0      2a100b0ef00
  kmem_depot_alloc+8:     call       -0xbb384       <mutex_tryenter>

000002a100b0e7a1 kmem_depot_alloc+8(3000008bdc0, 30000096870, 90e, 3000008bc00, 30000096858,
0)
    %l0-%l3:             36             2f      60000839a40              35
    %l4-%l7:             22             75      60000800d18      2a100b0f940
  kmem_cache_alloc+0xfc:  call       -0x2cc        <kmem_depot_alloc>

000002a100b0e851 kmem_cache_alloc+0xfc(300000966c8, 0, 0, 6, 1f8, 180c000)
    %l0-%l3:              1      30000096898              0      30000096870
    %l4-%l7:      300000968c0              3              0             1f8
  ufs_alloc_inode+0x18:   call       -0x117000      <kmem_cache_alloc>

000002a100b0e901 ufs_alloc_inode+0x18(300000b0040, 2d13d2, ff, 0, 18bc800, 40)
    %l0-%l3:              1      30000071f18              0      30000071ef0
    %l4-%l7:      30000071f40         18a8400              0             1f8
  ufs_iget_internal+0x200: call       -0x38c        <ufs_alloc_inode>

000002a100b0e9b1 ufs_iget_internal+0x200(600010f3440, 2d13d2, 13d2, 0, 60001327b80,
300000b0040)
    %l0-%l3:      600002e3d20      60001340000      600007b9e90      5500000010
    %l4-%l7:           1000      600002e3d20              1               1
  ufs_dirlook+0x2ac:      call       +0x53d0       <ufs_iget_alloced>
```

```
000002a100b0ea71 ufs_dirlook+0x2ac(2, 2a100b0f680, 2a100b0f458, 2d13d2, 60009996470,
60006436540)
    %l0-%l3:      60009996470       60009996470       60009996470       300000b00f0
    %l4-%l7:                1           2d0f0e        5d88002d13d2       300000b0040
    ufs_lookup+0x2ac:        call      -0x106b8      <ufs_dirlook>

000002a100b0eba1 ufs_lookup+0x2ac(60006436540, 2a100b0f680, 2a100b0f678, 0, 0, 60000800d18)
    %l0-%l3:      60009996470               f                 6                45
    %l4-%l7:      30000071f40               0       60000800d18                 2
    fop_lookup+0x28:         jmpl      %i3, %o7

000002a100b0ec81 fop_lookup+0x28(60006436540, 2a100b0f680, 2a100b0f678, 121e0d8, 0,
60000813380)
    %l0-%l3:      60006436540               0       600010f3440              2420
    %l4-%l7:             2000               2       3000581fee0                 1
    lookuppnvp+0x344:        call      +0xc078c      <fop_lookup>

000002a100b0ed51 lookuppnvp+0x344(2a100b0f940, 0, 60006436540, 2a100b0f678, 2a100b0f680,
60000839a40)
    %l0-%l3:          18a87f0       60006436540               0                 0
    %l4-%l7:      60000800d18       60000839a40               0                10
    lookuppnat+0x120:        call      +0x14         <lookuppnvp>

000002a100b0ef91 lookuppnat+0x120(60000839a40, 0, 0, 0, 2a100b0fad8, 0)
    %l0-%l3:               36              2f       60000839a40                35
    %l4-%l7:               22              75       60000800d18       2a100b0f940
    lookupnameat+0x5c:       call      +0x84         <lookuppnat>

000002a100b0f051 lookupnameat+0x5c(0, 0, 0, 0, 2a100b0fad8, 0)
    %l0-%l3:          e913718          ff36fa40               0                 0
    %l4-%l7:          ffbf88c8       2a100b0f940               0          18a8400
    cstatat_getvp+0x198:     call      -0x565ac      <lookupnameat>

000002a100b0f161 cstatat_getvp+0x198(ffd19400, ffbf88c8, 1, 0, 2a100b0fad8, 0)
    %l0-%l3: fffffffffd19553               0               0                 0
    %l4-%l7:                0          18a8400               0       60000800d18
    cstatat32+0x40:          call      -0x95c        <cstatat_getvp>

000002a100b0f221 cstatat32+0x40(fffffffffd19553, ffbf88c8, 1000, ffbf82d0, 1000, 0)
    %l0-%l3:                0       2a100b0fad0               1                 0
    %l4-%l7:                0       2a100b0fad8               0                 0
    syscall_trap32+0xcc:     jmpl      %g3, %o7

000002a100b0f2e1 syscall_trap32+0xcc(ffbf88c8, ffbf82d0, 5, ff265072, ffbf88eb, 7fffffdc)
    %l0-%l3:          100742c       2a100b0fb90       300074fb8b8           104220c
    %l4-%l7:          185b448          7fffffff       30004560980       2a100b0fb90
mdb: failed to read instruction at 13008: no mapping for address

>::msgbuf
...
NOTICE: SUNW-MSG-ID: SUNOS-8000-0G, TYPE: Error, VER: 1, SEVERITY: Major


panic[cpu0]/thread=30001884000:
UE Error(s)
```

```
000002a1009f0700 SUNW,UltraSPARC-IIIi:cpu_deferred_error+568 (ecc1ecc100000000,
3, 1000040000019d, 400000000, 0, 30000ef8560)
   %l0-3: 000000022f171780 0000000000000001 000000000184c4d0 000000000184c400
   %l4-7: 0000080d00000000 0000000000203400 00000000ecc1ecc1 00000000ecc1ec00
000002a1009f11a0 unix:ktl0+48 (6000026dd00, 0, 18ab800, bb9e, 3e8a, fa28)
   %l0-3: 0000000000000007 0000000000001400 0000009000001606 00000000011eb440
   %l4-7: 0000000000000000 000002a1009f1ad8 0000000000000000 000002a1009f1250
000002a1009f12f0 genunix:dnlc_lookup+80 (60004ca1900, 2a1009f1680, 8, 6000026dd0
0, 2a1009f1688, 6000026dcf0)
   %l0-3: 000006000b571780 0000000000007fff 0007c76c02f73e8a 0000000001863c00
   %l4-7: 0000000000000001 0000000000000008 000000004e593e8a 0000000000000002
000002a1009f13a0 ufs:ufs_lookup+1b0 (60004ca1900, 2a1009f1680, 2a1009f1678, 0, 0
, 60001bbb0b0)
   %l0-3: 00000600068f0e88 000000000000000f 0000000000000007 000000000000004e
   %l4-7: 0000030000071f40 0000000000000000 0000060001bbb0b0 0000000000000002
000002a1009f1480 genunix:fop_lookup+28 (60004ca1900, 2a1009f1680, 2a1009f1678, 1
21e0d8, 0, 60000813380)
   %l0-3: 0000060004ca1900 0000000000000000 00000600010ff500 0000000000002420
   %l4-7: 0000000000002000 0000000000000002 000006000c432b28 0000000000000001
000002a1009f1550 genunix:lookuppnvp+344 (2a1009f1940, 0, 60004ca1900, 2a1009f167
8, 2a1009f1680, 60000839a40)
   %l0-3: 00000000018a87f0 0000060004ca1900 0000000000000000 0000000000000000
   %l4-7: 0000060001bbb0b0 0000060000839a40 0000000000000000 0000000000000010
000002a1009f1790 genunix:lookuppnat+120 (60000839a40, 0, 0, 0, 2a1009f1ad8, 0)
   %l0-3: 000000000000003a 000000000000002f 0000060000839a40 0000000000000039
   %l4-7: 0000000000000023 0000000000000075 0000060001bbb0b0 000002a1009f1940
000002a1009f1850 genunix:lookupnameat+5c (0, 0, 0, 0, 2a1009f1ad8, 0)
   %l0-3: 000000000e2c0f80 00000000ff36fa40 0000000000000000 0000000000000000
   %l4-7: 00000000ffbf88c8 000002a1009f1940 0000000000000000 00000000018a8400
000002a1009f1960 genunix:cstatat_getvp+198 (ffd19400, ffbf88c8, 1, 0, 2a1009f1ad
8, 0)
   %l0-3: fffffffffffd19553 0000000000000000 0000000000000000 0000000000000000
   %l4-7: 0000000000000000 00000000018a8400 0000000000000000 0000060001bbb0b0
000002a1009f1a20 genunix:cstatat32+40 (fffffffffffd19553, ffbf88c8, 1000, ffbf82d
0, 1000, 0)
   %l0-3: 0000000000000000 000002a1009f1ad0 0000000000000001 0000000000000000
   %l4-7: 0000000000000000 000002a1009f1ad8 0000000000000000 0000000000000000

syncing file systems...
 3
 done
dumping to /dev/dsk/c1t0d0s1, offset 65536, content: kernel

> syscall_trap::dis ! grep i0
syscall_trap+0x18:              mov       %i0, %o0
> $Q
```

The stack trace (reported in the $C and ::stackregs output) is in reverse chronological order (most recent event at the top). Note that the last command in the top of the stack trace before things go bad is an attempted kernel memory allocation.

::panicinfo reports that the specific type of problem is a UE Error. ::msgbuf reports a specific message ID associated with the crash: SUNOS-8000-0G. This message ID can be entered at the Sun web site to obtain more details about how to respond to the crash.

The web page associated with this message basically tells us to examine console output and message logs. The meat of this message is:

```
The Message ID:  SUNOS-8000-0G indicates errors detected by the Solaris kernel required
immediate reboot to preserve system integrity.

The system will attempt to save the error information and then perform diagnosis as the
system reboots. The system administrator should look for further diagnosis information that
pertains to the actual system fault in the system messages after reboot. Any further action
would be dictated by those messages.

In the event that the system is unable to save or process the information and system
diagnosis fails, the information from the system console may be useful in trying to manually
diagnose a system failure. Please have this information available when placing a service
call for additional help.
```

The following error messages were placed in the /var/adm/messages file during the boot:

```
Apr 10 00:11:13 cnylim01 fmd: [ID 441519 daemon.error] SUNW-MSG-ID: SUN4U-8000-3
5, TYPE: Fault, VER: 1, SEVERITY: Minor
Apr 10 00:11:13 cnylim01 EVENT-TIME: Tue Apr 10 00:11:12 EDT 2007
Apr 10 00:11:13 cnylim01 PLATFORM: SUNW,Sun-Fire-V240, CSN: -, HOSTNAME: cnylim0
1
Apr 10 00:11:13 cnylim01 SOURCE: cpumem-diagnosis, REV: 1.5
Apr 10 00:11:13 cnylim01 EVENT-ID: 7858b050-cf36-4e88-ad0d-f994c748a1ee
Apr 10 00:11:13 cnylim01 DESC: The number of errors associated with this memory
module has exceeded acceptable levels. Refer to http://sun.com/msg/SUN4U-8000-3
5 for more information.
Apr 10 00:11:13 cnylim01 AUTO-RESPONSE: Pages of memory associated with this mem
ory module are being removed from service as errors are reported.
Apr 10 00:11:13 cnylim01 IMPACT: Total system memory capacity will be reduced as
 pages are retired.
Apr 10 00:11:13 cnylim01 REC-ACTION: Schedule a repair procedure to replace the
affected memory module. Use fmdump -v -u <EVENT_ID> to identify the module.
```

The output of the suggested **fmdump** command identifies the problematic module. (See "Fault Management Facility in Chapter 3 :

```
soltest> fmdump -v -u 7858b050-cf36-4e88-ad0d-f994c748a1ee
TIME                        UUID                                    SUNW-MSG-ID

Apr 10 00:11:12.8968 7858b050-cf36-4e88-ad0d-f994c748a1ee SUN4U-8000-35
   95%  fault.memory.bank

          Problem in: mem:///unum=MB/P0/B1:B1/D0,B1/D1
             Affects: mem:///unum=MB/P0/B1:B1/D0,B1/D1
                 FRU: mem:///unum=MB/P0/B1:B1/D0,B1/D1
```

The web page output on http://www.sun.com/msg/SUN4U-8000-35 includes a description of the error message and detailed instructions on how to handle it:

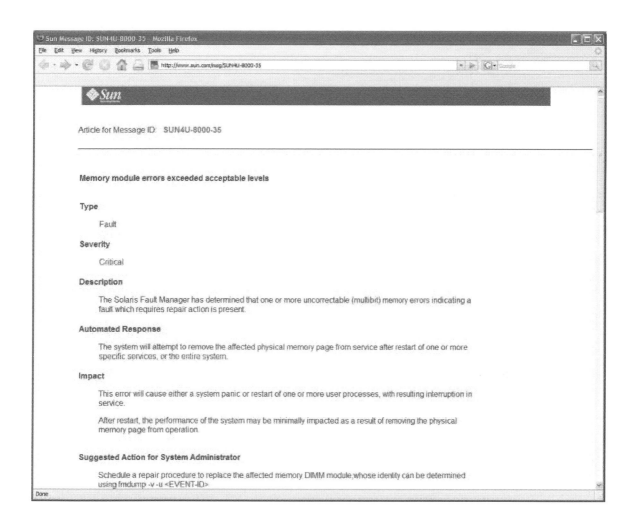

Figure 4-1. Sun Web Page for Error SUN4U-8000-35

Input and Output Commands

Table 4-9 lists several of the most important **mdb** input and output commands.

Table 4-9. mdb Input and Output Commands

Command	Description
$< $<<	Replace input with a macro or source a macro.
$>*filename*	Log session to a file.

Command	Description
address/format-spec	Read the value from address formatted as format-spec. If no address is specified, use the current address (dot or .)
address/W value	Write the value in the four bytes starting with the address. If no address is specified, use dot. V, w or Z may be used instead of W to write 1, 2 or 8 bytes, respectively.
address=format-spec	Format the immediate value of the address.
?	Read/write primary object file.
@format-spec	Read/write physical address as format-spec.
\format-spec	Read/write physical address as format-spec.

The difference between / and = is subtle. For example, to find the address holding the value of the maxphys symbol in decimal, we would run:

maxphys=D

To find the value inside the above address, we would use / like:

maxphys/D

mdb can be used to display or change system variable settings on the fly. Any changes to variable settings are only valid until the next reboot, so these changes should also be made in the relevant configuration file (usually */etc/system*).

Example 4-9 demonstrates how to view and change these variables. To view them in decimal, we will want to use the "D" format string. (Other formats can be viewed with the **::formats** dcmd.) Printing the var structure resulted in the parameters being displayed in hexadecimal, which is the default within **mdb**. The = operator makes it easy to translate between hexadecimal and decimal. A decimal number can be specified by starting it with the string "0t".

Example 4-9. Viewing and Changing System Variables with mdb

```
soltest/ > mdb -kw
Loading modules: [ unix krtld genunix specfs dtrace ufs sd ip sctp usba fcp fctl nca lofs
zfs random logindmux ptm md cpc fcip sppp crypto nfs ]
> maxusers/D
maxusers:
maxusers:       2022
> maxuprc/D
maxuprc:
maxuprc:        29995
> max_nprocs/D
max_nprocs:
max_nprocs:     30000
> v::print "struct var"
{
    v_buf = 0x64
    v_call = 0
    v_proc = 0x7530
    v_maxupttl = 0x752b
    v_nglobpris = 0xaa
    v_maxsyspri = 0x63
    v_clist = 0
    v_maxup = 0x752b
```

```
      v_hbuf = 0x800
      v_hmask = 0x7ff
      v_pbuf = 0
      v_sptmap = 0
      v_maxpmem = 0
      v_autoup = 0x1e
      v_bufhwm = 0xa1c8
}
> 800=D                                      .
                2048
> maxusers/W 800
maxusers:          0x1000          =          0x800
> maxusers/D
maxusers:
maxusers:          2048
> maxusers/W 0t2022
maxusers:          0x800           =          0x7e6
> maxusers/D
maxusers:
maxusers:          2022
> ::formats
...
B - hexadecimal int (1 byte)
C - character using C character notation (1 byte)
D - decimal signed int (4 bytes)
E - decimal unsigned long long (8 bytes)
...
```

In example 4-6, the **mdb** session was started with the "**w**" flag to make it writable: **mdb -kw**

Locking

Four types of locking are available on Solaris:

- Mutex locks.
- Semaphores (counters). (Not the same as IPC semaphores.)
- Condition variables (generalized semaphores).
- Multiple-reader, single-writer locks.

The following types of locking problems can occur:

- Lock contention (due to excessively course granularity or inappropriate lock type).
- Deadlock (each thread is waiting for a lock held by another thread).
- Lost locks.
- Race conditions.
- Incomplete or buggy lock implementation.

Mutex Locks

A "**mutex lock**" is a "mutual exclusion lock." It is created by the LDSTUB (load-store-unsigned-byte) instruction, which is an atomic (indivisible) operation that reads a byte from memory and writes 0xFF into that location. (When the lock is cleared, 0x00 is written back to the memory location.)

If the value that was read from memory is already 0xFF, another processor has already set the lock. At that point, the processor can "spin" by sitting in a loop and testing to see if the lock has cleared (i.e., been written back to 0x00). This sort of **"spin lock"** is usually used when the wait time for the lock is expected to be short. (If the wait is expected to be longer, the process should sleep so that the CPU can be used by another process. This is known as a **"block."**)

Adaptive Locks

Solaris provides a type of locking known as **adaptive locks**. When one thread attempts to acquire one of these that is held by another thread, it checks to see if the second thread is active on a processor. If it is, the first thread spins. If the second thread is blocked, the first thread blocks as well.

Read/Write Locks

A **read/write** lock allows multiple concurrent reads, but prevents other accesses of the resource when writes are taking place.

Lock Contention Indicators

At the system level, one indicator of a lock contention problem is when **vmstat** reports that the system is not idle, but that cpu/sy dominates cpu/us. (Note: this observation is only true if the system is not running an NFS server or other major service that runs from inside the kernel.)

Another way to identify a problem is with **mpstat**. The smtx measurement shows the number of times a CPU failed to obtain a mutex immediately. The master CPU (the one taking the clock interrupt—usually CPU 0) will tend to have a high reading. Depending upon CPU speed, a reading of more than 500 may be an indication of a system in trouble. If the smtx is greater than 500 on a single CPU and sys dominates usr (ie, system time is larger than user time, and system time is greater than 20%), it is likely that mutex contention is occurring.

Similarly, the **mpstat**/srw value reports on the number of times that a CPU failed to obtain a read/write lock immediately.

The **lockstat** command can also help investigate a problem. With **lockstat**, look for large counts (indv), especially with long locking times (nsec).

> The kernel takes a performance hit while **lockstat** is running, so you probably only want to use this command while you are actually looking at the output.

An indicator of trouble for a particular process is when **prstat -m** reports that it is spending a large amount of time waiting for user locks in the LCK column. (Example 6-2 shows what **prstat -m** output looks like.) It may be useful to examine any problem process with **truss**.

The DTrace lockstat provider allows detailed direct monitoring of lock activity. See the "lockstat Provider" section of Chapter 5 for more details. The **lockstat** command is a DTrace consumer, but direct DTrace scripts will allow monitoring on a per-process or function basis. For example, the DTrace Toolkit contains the **lockbydist.d** and **lockbyproc.d** scripts to check lock distribution and lock times by process, respectively.

> In any case, extreme mutex contention problems should be reported to Sun. Changes have been implemented in current versions of the Solaris kernel to dramatically increase the scalability of the operating system over multiple processors. Unless additional issues are brought to the vendor's attention, they cannot be expected to correct them in future releases.

Resources

- Cockcroft, Adrian and Pettit, Richard. (April 1998) *Sun Performance and Tuning: Java and the Internet, 2nd Ed*. Prentice Hall.

- Cromar, Scott. (2007) *Solaris Troubleshooting and Performance Tuning at Princeton University*. Princeton, NJ. (http://www.princeton.edu/~unix/Solaris/troubleshoot/index.html)

- Galvin, Peter Baer. (Jan 2003) *Cool Commands*. SysAdmin Magazine. (http://www.samag.com/documents/s=7762/sam0301n/0301n.htm)

- Klauser, Werner. (June 1998) *The /proc File System*. SysAdmin Magazine. (http://www.samag.com/documents/s=1190/sam9806d/9806d.htm)

- McDougall, Richard and Mauro, Jim. (July 2006) *Solaris Internals*. Upper Saddle River, NJ: Prentice Hall & Sun Microsystems Press.

- McDougall, Richard, Mauro, Jim and Gregg, Brendan. (October 2006) *Solaris Performance and Tools*. Upper Saddle River, NJ: Prentice Hall & Sun Microsystems Press.

- OpenSolaris Community. (2007) Modular Debugger (*MDB)*. (http://www.opensolaris.org/os/community/mdb/)

- Sun Microsystems. (January 2005) *Solaris Modular Debugger Guide*. Palo Alto, CA: Sun Microsystems, Inc. (http://docs.sun.com/app/docs/doc/816-5041)

- Sun Microsystems. (May 2006) *System Administration Guide: Advanced Administration*. Palo Alto, CA: Sun Microsystems, Inc. (http://docs.sun.com/app/docs/doc/817-0403)

- Sun Microsystems. (2006) *proc.h*. Palo Alto, CA: Sun Microsystems, Inc. (http://src.opensolaris.org/source/xref/onnv/onnv-gate/usr/src/uts/common/sys/proc.h)

- Sun Microsystems. (2006) *user.h*. Palo Alto, CA: Sun Microsystems, Inc. (http://src.opensolaris.org/source/xref/onnv/onnv-gate/usr/src/uts/common/sys/user.h)

- Vahalia, Uresh. (October 1995) *Unix Internals: The New Frontiers*. Upper Saddle River, NJ: Prentice Hall.

5

Introduction to DTrace

DTrace is Solaris 10's new Dynamic Tracing facility. It allows us to peer into the innards of running processes, and even set breakpoints or force panics based on what we see. We can customize our view to span a variety of subsystems, exclude extraneous information and close in on the source of a problem.

A number of freely available scripts have been made available as the DTrace Toolkit. The Toolkit provides both programming examples and extremely useful tools for different types of system monitoring. The URL for the Toolkit is listed in the "Resources" section.

The DTrace facility provides data to a number of consumers, including commands such as **dtrace** and **lockstat**, as well as programs calling libraries that access DTrace through the **dtrace** kernel driver.

This chapter is designed to give enough of an introduction to DTrace for administrators to be able to perform some basic functions and learn more about DTrace on their own. The references at the end of the chapter may be helpful for people who are interested in learning more about this useful and exciting tool.

DTrace Probes

DTrace is built on a foundation of objects called **probes**. Probes are event handlers that **fire** when their particular event occurs. DTrace can bind a particular **action** to the probe to make use of the information.

Probes report on a variety of information about their event. For example, a probe for a kernel function may report on arguments, global variables, timestamps, stack traces, currently running processes or the thread that called the function.

Kernel modules that enable probes are packaged into sets known as **providers**. In a DTrace context, a **module** is a kernel module (for kernel probes) or a library name (for applications). A **function** in DTrace refers to the function associated with a probe, if it belongs to a program location.

Probes may be uniquely addressed by a combination of the provider, module, function and name. These are frequently organized into a 4-tuple when invoked by the **dtrace** command. Alternatively, each probe has a unique integer identifier, which can vary depending on Solaris patch level.

These numbers, as well as the provider, module, function and name, can be listed out through the **dtrace -l** command. The list will vary from system to system, depending on what is installed. It may even change based on

84

patch level. Probes can be listed by function, module, or name by specifying it with the `-f`, `-m`, or `-n` options, respectively.

Running a `dtrace` without a `-l`, but with a `-f`, `-m`, or `-n` option, enables all matching probes. All the probes in a provider can be enabled by using the `-P` option. An individual probe can be enabled by using its 4-tuple with the `-n` option.

> Do not enable more probes than necessary. If too many probes are enabled, it may adversely impact performance. In particular, be careful about how many `sched` probes are enabled at one time.

Some probes do not list a module or function. These are called "unanchored" probes. Their 4-tuple just omits the nonexistent information.

Providers

Providers are kernel modules that create related groups of probes. The most commonly referenced providers are:

- **fbt**: (Function Boundary Tracing) Implements probes at the entry and return points of almost all kernel functions.
- **io**: Implements probes for I/O-related events. Provides probes similar to what `iostat` provides.
- **lockstat**: Implements lock-related probes.
- **mib**: Implements probes corresponding to counters in the Solaris MIBs.
- **pid**: Implements probes for user-level processes at entry, return and instruction.
- **proc**: Implements probes for process creation and life-cycle events.
- **profile**: Implements timer-drive probes.
- **sched**: Implements probes for scheduling-related events.
- **sdt**: (Statistically Defined Tracing) Implements programmer-defined probes at arbitrary locations and names within code. Obviously, we hope that the programmer has chosen names whose meaning is clear.
- **syscall**: Implements entry and return probes for all system calls. Implements probes similar to what `truss` provides.
- **sysinfo**: Probes for updates to the `sys kstat` (including probes corresponding to `mpstat`).
- **vminfo**: Probes for updates to the `vm kstat` (including probes corresponding to `vmstat`).

Command Components

The dtrace command has several components:

- A **4-tuple identifier**:

  provider:module:function:name

  Leaving any of these blank is equivalent to using a wildcard match. (If left blank, the left-most members of the 4-tuple are optional.

- A **predicate** determines whether the action should be taken. They are enclosed in slashes: */predicate/*. The predicate is a C-style relational expression which must evaluate to an integer or pointer. If omitted, the action is executed when the probe fires. Some predicate examples are:

  Executable name matches xyz: `/execname == "xyz"/`

  Process ID does not match 1234: `/pid != 1234/`

arg0 is 1 and arg1 is not 2: `/arg0 == 1 && arg1 != 2/`

- An **action** (in the D scripting language) to be taken when the probe files and the predicate is satisfied. Typically, this is listed in curly brackets: {}

Example 5-1 demonstrates a simple command to display the system calls associated with process ID 123:

Example 5-1. DTrace: Display a Process's System Calls

```
dtrace -n 'syscall:::entry /pid==123/ {trace(execname)}'

# 'syscall:::entry /pid == 1286/ {trace(execname)}'
dtrace: description 'syscall:::entry ' matched 230 probes
^C
CPU    ID                   FUNCTION:NAME
  0  8248            lwp_sigmask:entry    sshd
  0  8248            lwp_sigmask:entry    sshd
  0  7966                   read:entry    sshd
  0  8278                pollsys:entry    sshd
  0  8248            lwp_sigmask:entry    sshd
  0  8248            lwp_sigmask:entry    sshd
  0  7968                  write:entry    sshd
  0  8278                pollsys:entry    sshd
  0  8248            lwp_sigmask:entry    sshd
  0  8248            lwp_sigmask:entry    sshd
  0  7966                   read:entry    sshd
  0  8278                pollsys:entry    sshd
  0  8248            lwp_sigmask:entry    sshd
  0  8248            lwp_sigmask:entry    sshd
  0  7968                  write:entry    sshd
  0  8278                pollsys:entry    sshd
```

Note that control-C was used to terminate the **dtrace** session and return the output. This is a common way for DTrace commands to run.

Aggregations

Aggregating functions allow multiple data points to be combined and reported. Aggregations take the form:
`@name[ keys ] = aggregating-function( arguments );`
Here, the **name** is a name assigned to the aggregation, the **keys** are a comma-separated list of D expressions which index the output, the **arguments** are a comma-separated list, and the **aggregating functions** may be one of the following:

- **avg**: Average of the expressions in the arguments.
- **count**: Number of times that the function is called.
- **lquantize**: The arguments are a scalar expression, a lower bound, an upper bound and a step value. This function increments the value in the highest linearly-sized bucket that is less than the expression.
- **max**: he largest value among the arguments.
- **min**: The smallest value among the arguments.
- **quantize**: Increments the value in the highest power of two bucket less than the expression in the argument.
- **sum**: Total value of the expressions in the arguments.

An example may make this clearer. Example 5-2 shows how to use count to see which processes are affected by involuntary context switches:

Example 5-2 Monitoring Involuntary Context Switches

```
# dtrace -n 'sysinfo:::inv_swtch /execname != "sched"/ {@icsw[execname]=count();}'
dtrace: description 'sysinfo:::inv_swtch ' matched 1 probe
^C

  inetd                                                         1
  sshd                                                          1
  svc.configd                                                   1
  nscd                                                          3
  svc.startd                                                    3
  dtrace                                                        4
```

D Scripting Language

In order to deal with operations that can become confusing on a single command line, a D script can be saved to a file and run as desired. A D script will have one or more **probe clauses**, which consist of one or more probe descriptions, along with the associated predicate and actions:

```
#!/usr/sbin/dtrace -s
probe-description[, probe-description...]
[/predicate/]
{
    action; [action; ...]
}
```

The **probe-description** section consists of one or more 4-tuple identifiers, separated by commas. If the predicate line is not present, it is the same as a predicate that is always true. The action(s) specified are to be run if the probe fires and the predicate is true.

Example 5-3 demonstrates a short script to count the number of times that each `libc` function is called by PID number 123.

Example 5-3. DTrace: Counting libc Functions

```
#!/usr/sbin/dtrace -s
pid123:libc::entry
{
    @function_count[probefunc]=count();
}
```

Each recording action dumps data to a trace buffer. By default, this is the **principal buffer**.

Environment Variables

DTrace provides several environment variables that are accessible from within D. They refer to characteristics of the D command itself.

- **$[0-9]**: Arguments to the D command.
- **$egid**: Effective Group ID (GID)
- **$euid**: Effective User ID (UID).
- **$gid**: Real GID.
- **$pid**: Process ID (PID).
- **$pgid**: Process group ID.
- **$ppid**: Parent process ID.

- **$projid**: Project ID.
- **$sid**: Session ID
- **$target**: Target process ID.
- **$taskid**: Task ID.
- **$uid**: Real UID.

Example 5-4 is a minor enhancement to Example 5-3 to allow us to put in the PID as an argument when the script is run. It counts the number of times that each libc function is called.

Example 5-4. DTrace: Counting libc Functions

```
#cat /usr/local/bin/libc-fn-cnt.d
#!/usr/sbin/dtrace -s
pid$1:libc::entry
{
    @function_count[probefunc]=count();
}

# /usr/local/bin/libc-fn-cnt.d
dtrace: script '/usr/local/bin/libc-fn-cnt.d' matched 2508 probes
^C

  __pollsys                                                      1
  _pollsys                                                       1
  mutex_lock                                                     1
  mutex_lock_impl                                                1
  mutex_unlock                                                   1
...
  lmutex_lock                                                   32
  lmutex_unlock                                                 32
  mutex_unlock_queue                                           32
```

Actions

The most commonly used built-in actions are:

- **breakpoint()**: System stops and transfers control to kernel debugger.
- **chill(*number-nanoseconds*)**: DTrace spins for the specified number of nanoseconds.
- **copyinstr(*pointer*)**: Returns null terminated string from address space referenced by pointer.
- **copyout(*buffer, address, number-bytes*)**: Copies number-bytes from the buffer to a memory address.
- **copyoutstr(*string, address, max-length*)**: Copies a string to a memory address.
- **normalize(*aggregation, normalization-factor*)**: Divides aggregation values by the normalization-factor.
- **panic()**: Panics the kernel; may be used to generate a core dump.
- **printf(*format, arguments*)**: Dumps the arguments to the buffer in the specified format.
  `printa(aggregation)` does the same thing for aggregation data.
- **raise(*signal*)**: Sends the signal to the current process.
- **stack(*number-frames*)**: Copies the specified number of frames of the kernel thread's stack to the buffer.
- **stop()**: Stops the process that fired the probe.
- **stringof()**: Converts values to DTrace string values.
- **system(*command*)**: Runs a program as if from the shell.
- **trace(*D-expression*)**: Dumps the output of *D-expression* to the trace buffer.
- **tracemem(*address*, size_t *number-bytes*)**: Dumps the contents from the memory address to the buffer.
- **trunc(*aggregation*)**: Truncates or removes the contents of the specified aggregation.

- **ustack(*number-frames*)**: Copies the specified number of frames of the user stack to the buffer.

Multiple actions in a probe clause can be combined using a semicolon between them inside the curly brackets.

Example 5-5 is a program to print out the name of every process that calls an exec() system call:

Example 5-5. DTrace: Processes Issuing exec-type Calls

```
#cat /usr/local/bin/count-exec.d
#!/usr/sbin/dtrace -s
syscall::exec*:entry
{
   trace(execname);
}
# /usr/local/bin/count-exec.d
dtrace: script '/usr/local/bin/count-exec.d' matched 2 probes
CPU    ID                    FUNCTION:NAME
  0   4074                    exece:entry    sshd
  0   4074                    exece:entry    sh
  0   4074                    exece:entry    sshd
  0   4074                    exece:entry    sshd
  0   4074                    exece:entry    ksh
  0   4074                    exece:entry    ksh
  0   4074                    exece:entry    hostname
  0   4074                    exece:entry    ksh
```

D Variables

D specifies both associative arrays and scalar variables. Storage for these variables is not pre-allocated. It is allocated when a non-zero value is assigned and deallocated when a zero value is assigned.

D defines several built-in variables, which are frequently used in creating predicates and actions. The most commonly used built-in variables for D are the following:

- **args[]**: The args [] array contains the arguments, specified from 0 to the number of arguments less one. These can also be specified by argn, for n between 0 and 9..
- **caller**: Program counter location of current thread just before entering current probe.
- **cpu**: Identifier for current CPU.
- **curcpu**: Pointer to the cpuinfo_t structure for the current CPU.
- **curpsinfo**: psinfo_t structure of current process.
- **curthread**: Pointer to the current thread's kthread_t
- **cwd**: Name of the current working directory of the process whose thread triggered the probe.
- **errno**: Error value returned by the last system call by this thread.
- **execname**: Current executable name.
- **ipl**: Interrupt Priority Level (IPL) on the current CPU when the probe fires.
- **pid**: Current process ID.
- **ppid**: Parent process ID.
- **probefunc**: Function name of the current probe.
- **probemod**: Module name of the current probe.
- **probename**: Name of the current probe.
- **root**: Root directory of the process associated with the current thread.
- **timestamp**: Time since boot (in nanoseconds).
- **uid**: Real User ID (UID) of the current process.

- **uregs[]**: Current thread's saved user-mode register values at the time the probe fires.

A variable's scope can be global, thread-local or clause-local. **Thread-local variables** allow separate storage for each thread's copy of that variable. They are referenced with names of the form:
`self->variable-name`

Clause-local variables are only defined for the particular clause in which they are referenced. At the end of the clause, the variable is deallocated and made available for the next clause. To define a variable as clause-local, it should be defined with a "this" statement. For example, the following two commands declare a clause-local integer and character variable.

`this int integer-variable;`

`this char char-variable;`

Associative arrays can be indexed by an arbitrary name. There is no pre-defined limit on the number of elements. **Scalar variables** hold a single data value. We can also access Solaris kernel symbols by specifying them in backquotes.

Providers define arguments based on their own requirements. Some of the more useful such arguments are listed in Table 5-1:

Table 5-1. Provider-Specific Variables for DTrace

Provider	Variable	Description
io	`arg[0]`	Pointer to a bufinfo structure.
	`arg[0]->b_bcount`	Byte count.
	`arg[0]->b_resid`	Bytes not transferred.
	`arg[0]->b_iodone`	I/O completion routine.
	`arg[0]->b_edev`	Extended device.
io	`arg[1]`	Pointer to a devinfo structure.
	`arg[1]->dev_major`	Major number.
	`arg[1]->dev_minor`	Minor number.
	`arg[1]->dev_instance`	Instance number.
	`arg[1]->dev_name`	Device name.
	`arg[1]->dev_pathname`	Device pathname.
io	`arg[2]`	Pointer to a `fileinfo` structure.
	`arg[2]->fi_name`	File name.
	`arg[2]->fi_dirname`	File directory location.
	`arg[2]->fi_pathname`	Full path to file.

Provider	Variable	Description
	`arg[2]->fi_offset`	Offset within a file.
	`arg[2]->fi_fs`	File system.
	`arg[2]->fi_mount`	File system mount point.
pid	`arg0-argn (entry)`	For entry probes, `arg0-argn` represent the arguments.
	`arg0-arg1 (return)`	For return probes, `arg0-arg1` represent return codes.
profile	`arg0`	Program counter if the current process is in the kernel or 0 if it is not.
	`arg1`	Program counter if the current process is user-level, 0 if it is not.
syscall	`arg0-argn (entry)`	For entry probes, `arg0-argn` represent the arguments.
	`arg0-arg1 (return)`	For return probes, `arg0-arg1` represent return codes.
sysinfo	`arg0`	Value of statistic increment.
	`arg1`	Pointer to the current value of the statistic before increment.
	`arg2`	Pointer to the `cpu_t` structure incrementing the statistic. (Defined in `sys/cpuvar.h`)
vminfo	`arg0`	Value of statistic increment.
	`arg1`	Pointer to the current value of the statistic before increment.

The full list for each provider can be found in the provider's chapter of the Solaris Dynamic Tracing Guide.

An obvious enhancement to Example 5-5 would be to print out the name of the program being executed by adding an action to **trace(copyinstr(arg0));**

While this would work most of the time, it would fail in the event that the `arg0` is written to disk as part of swapping activity. (`copyinstr` only knows how to read from memory. We can use a variable to store the parameter until a `return()` pulls any swapped-out information back into memory. (cf Bennett 10/2006)

In Example 5-6, a thread-local variable is used to store the pointer to the program filename and the executable name; these are reported upon a `return()`. Example 5-6 also uses an aggregator to count how many `exec`-type calls were attributed to each program.

Example 5-6. DTrace: Programs Issuing exec-type Calls

```
# cat /usr/local/bin/count-exec-file.d
#!/usr/sbin/dtrace -s
#pragma D option quiet
syscall::exec*:entry
{
    self->prog = copyinstr(arg0);
    self->exn = execname;
}
syscall::exec*:return
```

```
/ self->prog != NULL /
{
    printf("%-20s %s\n", self->exn, self->prog);
    @file[self->prog]=count();
    self->prog = 0;
    self->exn = 0;
}
# /usr/local/bin/count-exec-file.d
sshd                    /bin/sh
sh                      /usr/bin/locale
sshd                    /usr/lib/pt_chmod
sshd                    /bin/ksh
ksh                     /usr/bin/stty
ksh                     /usr/bin/hostname
hostname                /bin/uname
ksh                     /usr/bin/stty
^C

  /bin/ksh                                                                 1
  /bin/sh                                                                  1
  /bin/uname                                                               1
  /usr/bin/hostname                                                        1
  /usr/bin/locale                                                          1
  /usr/lib/pt_chmod                                                        1
  /usr/bin/stty                                                            2
```

The commands to set the local variables to zero (`self->prog =0`, for example) allows the space for these variables to be deallocated. There is no automatic garbage collection in D; we need to take out the trash ourselves.

Directives

Example 5-6 used the `quiet` directive to turn off default output. Directives provide options to a D script that can increase readability of the output. Each option is enabled by including a line like the following at the beginning of a D script:

`#pragma D option option-name`

The following are the most commonly-used directives.

- **cpu**: Specify CPU on which to enable tracing.
- **destructive**: Allow destructive actions (`breakpoint()`, `chill()`, `copyout()`, `copyoutstr()`, `panic()`, `raise()`, `stop()` or `system()`).
- **flowindent**: Indentation increased on function entry; decreased on function return.
- **quiet**: Don't print anything not explicitly specified.

DTrace Toolkit

The OpenSolaris community has created an extremely useful collection of pre-written DTrace scripts. (See the "References" section at the end of this chapter for the URL.) Table 5-2 includes information about several of the most useful programs, including references to examples where they are demonstrated.

Table 5-2. DTrace Toolkit Programs

Script Name	Description
anonpgpid.d	Attempts to identify which processes are suffering the most from a system that is hard swapping.
bitesize.d	Provides graphs of distributions of different I/O sizes. (Example 9-5)
connections	Displays server process that accepts each inbound TCP connection.
cputypes.d	Reports on types of CPUs on the system. (Example 7-1)
cpuwalk.d	Reports on which CPUs a process runs on. (Example 7-5)
cswstat.d	Reports on context switches and time consumed. (Example 7-5)
dapptrace	Traces user and library function usage. Similar to **apptrace**, but also gets elapsed and CPU times.
dispqlen.d	Measures dispatcher queue length (CPU saturation).
dnlcps.d	Measures DNLC hits and misses by process. (Example 9-10)
dnlcsnoop.d	Real time record of target, process and result of DNLC lookups. (Example 9-10)
dtruss	**truss** replacement without the performance hit.
filebyproc.d	Snoops files opened by process name.
fsrw.d	Traces I/O events at a system call level.
hotspot.d	Identifies disk "hot spots."
inttimes.d	Reports on time spent servicing interrupts for each device.
iofile.d	I/O wait times for each file by process.
iofileb.d	I/O size for each file by process.
iopattern	System-wide disk I/O usage patterns. (Example 9-4)
iosnoop	Tracks system I/O activity. (Example 5-7, 9-6)
iotop	Displays processes with highest I/O traffic. (Examples 9-2, 9-3)
lockbydist.d	Lock distribution by process.
lockbyproc.d	Lock times by process.
nfswizard.d	Identifies top NFS filename requests; reports on access and performance statistics.
opensnoop	Snoops open files. (Example 5-8)
pfilestat	I/O statistics for each file descriptor in a process.

Script Name	Description
priclass.d	Reports distribution of thread priorities by class. (Example 7-8)
pridist.d	Reports distribution of thread priorities by process. (Example 7-8)
procsystime	Process system call details: elapsed time, CPU time, counts, etc. (Example 9-2)
rfileio.d	Read size statistics from file systems and physical disks, along with a total miss rate for the file system cache. (Example 9-13)
rfsio	Read size statistics from file systems and physical disks, along with a total miss rate for the file system cache. (Example 9-13)
rwsnoop	Captures read/write activity, including identifying the source processes.
rwtop	Displays processes with top read/write activity.
sampleproc	Reports which process is on which CPU how much of the time.
seeksize.d	Directly measure seek lengths of I/Os. (Example 9-4)
swapinfo.d	Reports a summary of virtual memory use. (Example 8-2)
tcpstat.d	Reports TCP error and traffic statistics. (Example 11-7)
tcpsnoop.d	Snoops TCP packets and associates them with a port and a process.
tcptop	Displays top TCP packet-generating processes.
threaded.d	Measures effectiveness of thread utilization.
topsyscall	Reports on busiest system calls.
udpstat.d	Reports UDP error and traffic statistics. (Example 11-7)
vopstat	Function-level timings of I/Os. (Example 9-9)
xcallsbypid.d	Provides by-process cross-call information. (Example 7-6)
zvmstat	Zone-specific vmstat.

Some patch levels of Solaris 10 report that some DTrace Toolkit scripts are unable to run due to an "invalid type combination." This is due to bug ID 6468001; check for a fix to that bug to resolve the problem. A temporary workaround is to comment out the include lines for socket.h and socketvar.h in the script code.

The **iosnoop** program (Example 5-7) can be particularly useful in tracking I/O activity.

Example 5-7. iosnoop

```
# ./iosnoop -h
USAGE: iosnoop [-a|-A|-DeghiNostv] [-d device] [-f filename]
               [-m mount_point] [-n name] [-p PID]
       iosnoop              # default output
```

```
                        -a      # print all data (mostly)
                        -A      # dump all data, space delimited
                        -D      # print time delta, us (elapsed)
                        -e      # print device name
                        -g      # print command arguments
                        -i      # print device instance
                        -N      # print major and minor numbers
                        -o      # print disk delta time, us
                        -s      # print start time, us
                        -t      # print completion time, us
                        -v      # print completion time, string
                        -d device       # instance name to snoop
                        -f filename     # snoop this file only
                        -m mount_point  # this FS only
                        -n name         # this process name only
                        -p PID          # this PID only
        eg,
            iosnoop -v      # human readable timestamps
            iosnoop -N      # print major and minor numbers
            iosnoop -m /    # snoop events on filesystem / only
# more iosnoop
...
# FIELDS:
#             UID             user ID
#             PID             process ID
#             PPID            parennt process ID
#             COMM            command name for the process
#             ARGS            argument listing for the process
#             SIZE            size of operation, bytes
#             BLOCK           disk block for the operation (location)
#             STIME           timestamp for the disk request, us
#             TIME            timestamp for the disk completion, us
#             DELTA           elapsed time from request to completion, us
#             DTIME           time for disk to complete request, us
#             STRTIME         timestamp for the disk completion, string
#             DEVICE          device name
#             INS             device instance number
#             D               direction, Read or Write
#             MOUNT           mount point
#             FILE            filename (basename) for io operation
...
# ./iosnoop -D
DELTA       UID    PID D    BLOCK    SIZE       COMM PATHNAME
5618          0 15835 R     68912    8192       sshd /usr/lib/security/pam_authtok_get.so.1
6949          0 15835 R   4820800    8192       sshd /usr/lib/mps/libnss3.so
392           0 15835 R     69376    8192       sshd /usr/lib/security/pam_unix_account.so.1
6157          0 15835 W     18994    7168       sshd /var/adm/lastlog
3534          0 15835 W      6535     512       sshd <none>
3878       1029 15839 R   7479808    8192   pt_chmod /lib/libnsl.so.1
9511          0     3 W     56976    4096    fsflush /var/adm/messages
5211       1029 15840 W     99998    1024        ksh /export/home/scromar/.sh_history
2442       1029 15840 W     17813     512        ksh <none>
3403          0 15835 W     59312    8192       sshd /var/adm/wtmpx
```

The **opensnoop** program (Example 5-8) tracks open files and identifies the process that is opening them.

Example 5-8. opensnoop

```
# ./opensnoop
  UID    PID COMM            FD PATH
    0    124 picld            5 /devices/pci@1c,600000/scsi@2:devctl
    0    124 picld            5 /devices/pci@1c,600000/scsi@2:devctl
    0    124 picld            5 /devices/pci@1c,600000/scsi@2:devctl
    0    124 picld            5 /devices/pci@1c,600000/scsi@2:devctl
    0    337 xntpd            4 /var/run/syslog_door
```

Some of the scripts that use the `fbt` provider do not yield consistent results across patch sets. The DTrace Toolkit scripts provide fantastic functionality, but they should not be your front line of defense until the `fbt` provider stabilizes. If a script gives you problems, check the OpenSolaris.org discussion site; someone else is likely to have tripped over the same problem before.

DTrace Demo Programs

In addition to the DTrace Toolkit programs, there are several example D scripts in the */usr/demo/dtrace* directory. These programs will need to be specified with a **dtrace -s** command (or edited to have **#!/usr/bin/dtrace -s** on the first line). Of these commands, one of the most useful is the **iotime.d** program. It provides snoop-like output of disk I/Os, and includes the amount of time required for each operation. Example 5-8 runs **iotime.d** while an ssh login occurs:

Example 5-8. iotime.d

```
# cat iotime.d
/*
 * Copyright 2005 Sun Microsystems, Inc. All rights reserved.
 * Use is subject to license terms.
...
*/
...
#pragma D option quiet

BEGIN
{
        printf("%10s %58s %2s %7s\n", "DEVICE", "FILE", "RW", "MS");
}

io:::start
{
        start[args[0]->b_edev, args[0]->b_blkno] = timestamp;
}

io:::done
/start[args[0]->b_edev, args[0]->b_blkno]/
{
        this->elapsed = timestamp - start[args[0]->b_edev, args[0]->b_blkno];
        printf("%10s %58s %2s %3d.%03d\n", args[1]->dev_statname,
            args[2]->fi_pathname, args[0]->b_flags & B_READ ? "R" : "W",
            this->elapsed / 10000000, (this->elapsed / 1000) % 1000);
        start[args[0]->b_edev, args[0]->b_blkno] = 0;
}
cnjunixtest01/usr/demo/dtrace > dtrace -s iotime.d
    DEVICE                                                         FILE RW      MS
```

96

```
          sd0                                   /sbin/sh    R    0.187
          sd0                               /var/cron/log   W    0.149
          sd0                             /var/adm/lastlog  W    0.678
          sd0                                     <none>    W    0.438
          sd0                                /dev/pts/6      R    0.075
   ^C
```

Table 5-3 includes a listing of the most useful included demo programs, along with a brief description of what each one does.

Table 5-3. DTrace demo Programs

Script Name	Description
delay.d	Determine the amount of time spent in the delay() and drv_usecwait() functions. (Easily edited to go after the function of your choice.)
errorpath.d	Display function names with a non-zero return code.
find.d	Counts number of cross-calls attributed to each function called by **find**. Can be edited to perform the same task for any command name. Can be used in conjunction with the following 1-liner to identify and drill down to the source of excessive numbers of cross-calls: **dtrace -n xcalls'{@[execname]=count();}'**
intr.d	Distributions of how much time spent executing interrupt handlers by driver name.
iocpu.d	CPU time versus I/O waiting time for StarOffice. (Can be edited to work for other programs.)
iothrough.d	Distributions of throughputs of I/Os on different devices. Can be used to identify bottlenecks.
iotime.d	Snoop-like output of disk I/Os, and includes the amount of time required for each operation. See Example 5-7.
lwptime.d	Distributions of how long individual threads take to run.
pri.d	Distributions of how much priorities are raised and lowered.
progtime.d	Distributions of how long programs run from start to finish.
qlen.d	Distributions of how long each CPU's run queue is.
qtime.d	Distributions of which CPUs have threads waiting to run.
rwinfo.d	Read and write statistics for specified command.
rwtime.d	Shows times for reads and writes of specified program.
sig.d	Sending and receiving process associated with signals. (Example 3-2)
syscall.d	Counts number of each system call for target PID.

Script Name	Description
trussrw.d	Trace read and write system calls in **truss** format.
whatfor.d	Prints distributions of how much time threads spend sleeping for what reasons.
whatlock.d	Counts adaptive vs spin locks for **date**. Can be edited for use with other programs.
where.d	Which CPUs are running threads; displays distributions of how long threads run on each CPU.
whofor.d	Distributions of which applications are blocking on which applications, and for how long.
whoio.d	Displays device, application, PID and total bytes for I/Os.
whopreempt.d	Who is preempting whom, along with frequency counts.
whoqueue.d	Who is on the run queue when it is long?
whosteal.d	Distributions of which processor takes jobs from other CPUs.
whowrite.d	Number of times each application writes to each directory.
writesbycmdfd.d	Displays number of writes for each command as well as file descriptor numbers referenced.
writetime.d	Displays average amounts of wall clock time spent writing during each command.
writetimeq.d	Displays distributions of amounts of wall clock time spent writing during each command.

DTrace Probes

The next several tables list and describe most of the probes available from the different providers at the time of this writing. Since the list of providers is only expected to increase, this list should not be considered as complete.

It is also the case that not every probe is supported on every system or patch level. A complete list for a given system can be found by running **dtrace -l -P** *provider-name*

The dtrace provider itself supplies probes for BEGIN (fires before all other probes), END (fires after all other probes) and ERROR (fires upon run-time errors for DTrace probes). These probes can be used as part of clauses to initialize arrays or perform calculations before or after the rest of the script runs.

fbt Probes

The Function Boundary Tracing (fbt) provider has probes to monitor the entry to and return from most functions. The arguments for the entry probe are the same as were passed to the function. The argument for the return probe are the same as the function return value.

Table 5-4 contains descriptions of the fbt provider's probes.

Table 5-4. Probes for fbt

Probe	When It Fires
entry	When the function is entered.
return	When we return from the function.

io Probes

The `io` provider supplies probes related to disk I/O. Table 5-5 includes descriptions of the `io` provider's probes.

Table 5-5. Probes for io

Probe	When It Fires
done	After an I/O request has been fulfilled. `arg0` points at a `bufinfo_t` structure; `arg1` points at a `devinfo_t` structure and `arg2` points at a `fileinfo_t` structure.
start	Just before an I/O request is made to a peripheral or NFS server. `arg0` points at a `bufinfo_t` structure; `arg1` points at a `devinfo_t` structure and `arg2` points at a `fileinfo_t` structure.
wait-done	When a thread is done waiting for the completion of an I/O request. `arg0` points at a `bufinfo_t` structure; `arg1` points at a `devinfo_t` structure and `arg2` points at a `fileinfo_t` structure.
wait-start	Just before a thread begins to wait for the completion of an I/O request. `arg0` points at a `bufinfo_t` structure; `arg1` points at a `devinfo_t` structure and `arg2` points at a `fileinfo_t` structure.

lockstat Probes

lockstat ProbesThe `lockstat` provider makes contention-event probes available for dealing with lock contention. It also makes hold-event probes available for events associated with manipulating locks. Since hold-type events happen extremely frequently, enabling them may have a noticeable (but not pathological) performance impact. The upshot of this observation is that these probes should only be enabled when we are actually looking for something.

In the event that a thread wants a lock that is held by another thread, it can **spin** (continually check if the thread is released yet) or **block** (sleep and check back later).

The types of locks that are tracked by the `lockstat` provider are adaptive (spin if the lock is held by a running thread, block if held by a non-running thread), read-write (multiple reads or a single write may hold the lock at a time), spin (spin if the lock is held by another thread) or thread (spin locks that lock a thread for a state change).

Table 5-6 contains descriptions of the `lockstat` provider's probes.

Table 5-6. Probes for lockstat

Probe	When It Fires
adaptive-acquire	After an adaptive lock is acquired.
adaptive-block	After a blocked thread wakes up and acquires its lock.

99

Probe	When It Fires
adaptive-release	After an adaptive lock is released.
adaptive-spin	After a spinning thread acquires its lock.
rw-acquire	After a reader-writer lock is acquired.
rw-block	When an attempt to obtain a reader/writer lock fails.
rw-downgrade	After a thread downgrades from a writer lock to a reader lock.
rw-release	After a reader-writer lock is released.
rw-upgrade	After a thread upgrades from a reader lock to a writer lock.
spin-acquire	After a spin lock is acquired.
spin-release	After a spin lock is released.
spin-spin	After a spinning thread acquires its lock.
thread-spin	Just before a spinning thread acquires its lock.

pid Probes

The pid provider allows us to specify a particular Process ID (PID) within a 4-tuple. For example to specify process 123, our 4-tuple would start with pid123. The full set of probes for this PID would be specified with:

pid123:::

The pid provider will create a probe for every instruction in a function. The probe's name is a hexadecimal address of the offset of the instruction in the function. The module is the library name (not including numerical suffix) or a.out for the executable itself. The function is the function name from within the library.

Table 5-7 includes descriptions of the pid provider's boundary probes.

Table 5-7. pid Provider Boundary Probes

Probe	When It Fires
entry	When the function is entered. The arguments are the function arguments.
return	When we return from the function. arg0 is the return code.

proc Probes

The proc provider supplies probes about process and LWP creation and termination, program image execution and signal handling. Table 5-8 lists descriptions of the proc provider's probes.

Table 5-8. Probes for proc

Probe	When It Fires
create	When process created using fork-type call. arg0 points to child process proc_t

Probe	When It Fires
	structure.
exec	When process loads image with exec-type call. arg0 points to path of new process image.
exec-failure	When exec-type call fails.
exec-success	When exec-type call succeeds.
exit	When current process exiting. arg0 contains exit() code.
fault	When a thread experiences a machine fault. arg0 contains the fault code; arg1 contains a pointer to the siginfo_t structure.
lwp-create	When LWP created. arg0 points to the lwpsinfo_t structure; arg1 points to the process's psinfo_t structure.
lwp-exit	When LWP exiting.
lwp-start	Before any user-level instructions executed in new LWP.
signal-clear	When pending signal is cleared due to target in a sigwait-type state. arg0 contains the signal number.
signal-discard	When signal sent to single-threaded process, but signal unblocked and ignored. arg0 points to the lwpsinfo_t; arg1 points to the psinfo_t and arg2 contains the signal number.
signal-handle	Just before thread handles a signal. arg0 contains the signal number; arg1 points to the siginfo_t and arg2 contains the address of the signal handler.
signal-send	When signal sent to thread or process. arg0 points to the lwpsinfo_t; arg1 points to the psinfo_t and arg2 contains the signal number.
start	Before any user-level instructions executed in new process.

profile Probes

The profile provider gives us probes that fire at specified time intervals to allow us to sample behavior. Table 5-9 contains descriptions of the profile provider's probes.

Table 5-9. Probes for profile

Probe	When It Fires
profile-*n*	n times per second on all CPUs.
tick-*n*	n times per second, but only on one CPU.

n may have a time suffix, in which the probe fires as often as specified. Valid suffixes include ns (nanoseconds), us (microseconds), ms (milliseconds), s (seconds), m (minutes), h (hours), d (days) or hz (hertz—frequency per second). Hz is the default if no suffix is specified.

The profile provider is most useful when used with another provider to count an event's rate of occurrence.

sched Probes

The `sched` provider supplies probes to make visible CPU scheduling-related activity. Table 5-10 contains descriptions of several `sched` probes.

Table 5-10 Probes for sched

Probe	When It Fires
change-pri	Just before a thread's priority is changed. `arg0` points to a `lwpsinfo_t` structure; `arg1` points to a `psinfo_t` structure and `arg2` contains the thread's new priority.
dqueue	Just before a runnable thread is dequeued from a run queue. `arg0` points to a `lwpsinfo_t` structure; `arg1` points to a `psinfo_t` structure and `arg2` points to a `cpuinfo_t` structure.
enqueue	Just before a runnable thread is enqueued on a run queue. `arg0` points to a `lwpsinfo_t` structure; `arg1` points to a `psinfo_t` structure; `arg2` points to a `cpuinfo_t` structure and `arg3` indicates whether it was placed at the head of the queue.
off-cpu	Just before the current CPU ends execution of the thread. `arg0` points to a `lwpsinfo_t` structure and `arg1` points to a `psinfo_t` structure.
on-cpu	After a CPU has begun execution of a thread.
preempt	Just before the current thread is preempted.
remain-cpu	When a scheduling decision has been made, but the dispatcher continues running the current thread.
schedctl-nopreempt	When a thread is preempted and then re-queued at the front of the run queue due to preemption control. `arg0` points to a `lwpsinfo_t` structure and `arg1` points to a `psinfo_t` structure.
schedctl-preempt	When a thread using preemption control is preempted and re-queued at the back of the run queue. `arg0` points to a `lwpsinfo_t` structure and `arg1` points to a `psinfo_t` structure.
schedctl-yield	When a thread with preemption control enabled and its time slice extended yields CPU to other threads.
sleep	Before current thread sleeps on a synchronization object.
surrender	When CPU instructed by another CPU to make a scheduling decision.
tick	As part of clock tick-based accounting. `arg0` points to a `lwpsinfo_t` structure and `arg1` points to a `psinfo_t` structure.
wakeup	Before curren thread wakes a thread sleeping on a synchronization object. `arg0` points to a `lwpsinfo_t` structure and `arg1` points to a `psinfo_t` structure.

syscall Probes

The names of system calls used by the `syscall` provider are the versions found in the */etc/name_to_sysnum* file. These are usually (but not always) the same as the familiar system call names in section 2 of the man pages.

Some exceptions exist. In particular, the function name for exit() is rexit, the function name for time() is gtime and the function name for both execle() and execve() is exece.

In addition, large file probes have a 64 appended to the usual name. Examples include open64, mmap64, pread64, pwrite64 and stat64.

Table 5-11 contains a description of the syscall provider's probes.

Table 5-11. Probes for syscall

Probe	When It Fires
entry	When the call is entered.
return	When we return from the system call.

sysinfo Probes

The sysinfo provider has probes to access the kernel statistics with the name sys. Table 5-12 contains a list of probes available from the sysinfo provider.

Table 5-12. Probes for sysinfo

Probe	When It Fires
bawrite	Before a buffer is asynchronously written out to a device.
bread	When during a buffer read from a device.
bwrite	Just before a buffer is written out to a device.
cpu_ticks_idle	When a CPU is idle.
cpu_ticks_kernel	When a CPU is executing in the kernel.
cpu_ticks_user	When a CPU is executing in user mode.
cpu_ticks_wait	When a CPU is otherwise idle, but waiting for I/O.
idlethread	When a CPU enters an idle loop.
intrblk	When an interrupt thread blocks.
in_swtch	When an involuntary context switch occurs.
lread	When a buffer is logically read.
lwrite	When a buffer is logically written.
modload	When a module is loaded.
modunload	When a module is unloaded.
msg	When msgsnd() or msgrcv() call is made.

Probe	When It Fires
mutex_adenters	When a thread attempts to acquire an owned adaptive lock.
namei	When a name lookup is attempted in the file system.
nthreads	When a thread is created.
phread	Just before a raw I/O read is performed.
phwrite	Just before a raw I/O write is performed.
procovf	When a new process can't be created due to a lack of process table entries.
pswitch	When a CPU switches from executing one thread to another.
readch	After each successful read.
rw_rdfails	When a thread attempts to acquire a read lock when the lock is held or desired by a writer. (lockstat's rw-block probe fires at the same time.)
rw_wrfails	Thread attempts to acquire a write lock when the lock is held by either a reader or a writer. (lockstat's rw-block probe fires at the same time.)
sema	Just before a semaphore operation is performed.
sysexec	When an exec() call is made.
sysfork	When a fork() call is made.
sysread	When a read-type system call is made.
sysvfork	When a vfork() call is made.
syswrite	When a write-type system call is made.
trap	When a processor trap occurs. (Some lightweight traps are not caught by this probe.)
ufsdirblk	When a directory block is red from the UFS filesystem.
ufsiget	When an inode is retrieved.
ufsinopage	After an in-core inode with no associated data pages is made available for re-use.
ufsipage	After an in-core inode with associated data pages is made available for re-use.
wait_ticks_io	Same as cpu_ticks_wait.
writech	After each successful write.
xcalls	Just before a cross-call is made (ie, a CPU makes a request of another CPU).

vminfo Probes

The `vminfo` provider supplies probes corresponding to the `vm` kernel statistics. Table 5-13 contains a list of `vminfo` probes.

Table 5-13. Probes for vminfo

Probe	When It Fires
anonfree	When an unmodified anonymous (not associated with a file) page is freed.
anonpgin	When an anonymous page is paged in from swap.
anonpgout	When a modified anonymous page is paged out to swap.
as_fault	When a fault is taken on a page, where the fault is neither copy-on-write nor a protection fault.
cow_fault	When a copy-on-write fault is taken on a page.
dfree	When a page is freed.
execfree	When an unmodified executable page is freed.
execpgin	When an executable page is paged in from backing store.
execpgout	When a modified executable page is paged out to backing store.
fsfree	When an unmodified file system data page is freed.
fspgin	When a file system page is paged in from backing store.
fspgout	When a file system page is paged out to backing store.
kernel_asflt	When a page fault occurs in the kernel address space.
maj_fault	When a page fault results in I/O from backing store or swap.
pgfrec	When a page is reclaimed off the free page list.
pgin	When a page is paged in from backing store or swap, whether or not it is a result of a fault.
pgout	When page paged out to backing store or swap.
pgpgin	When page paged in from backing store or swap, whether or not it is a result of a fault.
pgpgout	When page paged out to backing store or swap.
pgrec	When a page is reclaimed.
pgrrun	When the pager is scheduled.
pgswapin	When pages from a swapped-out process are swapped in.

Probe	When It Fires
pgswapout	When pages swapped out as part of swapping out a process.
prot_fault	When a protection page fault is taken.
rev	When page daemon begins a new revolution.
scan	When page daemon examines a page.
softlock	When a page is faulted by placing software lock on page.
swapin	When swapped-out process swapped in.
swapout	When a process is swapped out.
zfod	When a zero-filled page is created.

Resources

- Bennett, Chip. Learning *DTrace; Parts 1-5*. (September 2006-January 2007) SysAdmin Magazine.
- Cromar, Scott. (2007) Solaris Troubleshooting and Performance Tuning at Princeton University. Princeton, NJ.
  (http://www.princeton.edu/~unix/Solaris/troubleshoot/index.html)
- McDougall, Richard, Mauro, Jim and Gregg, Brendan. (October 2006) *Solaris Performance and Tools*. Upper Saddle River, NJ: Prentice Hall & Sun Microsystems Press.
- OpenSolaris Project. (October 2006) DTrace Toolkit.
  (http://www.opensolaris.org/os/community/dtrace/dtracetoolkit/)
- Sun Microsystems. (May 2006) *DTrace User Guide*. Palo Alto, CA: Sun Microsystems, Inc.
  (http://docs.sun.com/app/docs/doc/819-5488)
- Sun Microsystems. (January 2005) Solaris Dynamic Tracing Guide. Palo Alto, CA: Sun Microsystems, Inc.
  (http://docs.sun.com/app/docs/doc/817-6223)

6

Performance Management

Performance Monitoring

Performance monitoring has gotten a reputation as a black art, understood by only a few gurus. In part, this is due to the lack of transparency of the standard performance monitoring commands. In part, it is due to misunderstandings about how the operating system actually works. Unfortunately, this lack of clarity and understanding is reinforced by several monitoring tool vendors, who focus on statistics that have little or no bearing on the actual health of the system.

Prime examples of this are the ways that most tools measure memory and CPU utilization. In Solaris, every megabyte of memory is presumed to be available for use as cache to improve disk I/O performance. That being the the case, it makes no sense to measure how much memory is being used. Instead, it makes much more sense to look at how frequently memory is requested that requires the page scanner to clear out old pages. (Current Solaris releases have enhanced the value of the page scanner rate as a memory shortage indicator by changing the way that buffer cache is managed, and some tools report memory usage without considering the amount in page buffer cache.)

CPU utilization is often reported in terms of an activity percentage. When this zips up to 100%, people are convinced that they have a problem. But the fact is that every time you run an fsflush (which happens regularly as part of normal operation), a CPU's utilization will pop up to 100% briefly. Monitoring solutions that do not take this effect into account are simply not providing useful information. Usually, load average is a much better measure of CPU utilization than an activity percentage.

Another common mistake with Solaris versions prior to 10 is to think that the %wio reported by **top** and **sar** actually refers to how long a process has to wait for I/O. In fact, %wio refers to the specific type of idle activity where the processor has nothing useful to do, so it allows a blocked process to sit on the processor rather than perform a context switch. A far better measurement of the performance of disk I/O on a multi-core system is provided by service time statistics. (This particular problem became acute enough that the Solaris 10 team chose to report %wio as zero.) Alternatively, the iofile.d script from the DTrace Toolkit reports on the amount of time spent by a process waiting for I/O, which is a useful statistic.

This section will not focus on setting up an enterprise-class SNMP reporting system to collect performance data. Instead, we will focus on a single-system view of performance in order to examine what these statistics actually mean—and which ones to look at in a given situation. (Understanding the various statistics will allow us to better understand what is actually being reported by a given enterprise performance monitoring tool.)

In Chapters 7-11, we examine each of the key system components that are examined by the monitoring commands. Usually, the most important performance statistics to gather are the ones listed in Table 6-1.

Table 6-1. Key Performance Metrics

Performance Metric	Monitoring Commands
CPU Saturation: Load Average or Run Queue Length	uptime sar -q vmstat
CPU Saturation: CPU Run Queue Latency	prstat -m
CPU Utilization by %sys and %usr	sar -u vmstat iostat mpstat
CPU Utilization: Multiple Processor Load Sharing	mpstat
Memory Saturation: Scan Rate	sar -g vmstat
Memory Saturation: Swap Space Usage and Paging Rates	vmstat sar -g sar -p sar -r sar -w
Disk Latency: Service Times per File System	iostat sar -d vxstat
Disk Latency: Traffic Levels per File System	iostat sar -d vxstat
Network Traffic Levels	netstat (router-based traffic statistics)
Network Error Levels	netstat -eE (router-based error statistics)
Disk Space Utilization	df -k df -h du -dsk
Context Switching Rages	mpstat sar -w vmstat
System Call Rates	mpstat sar -c
Lock Contention Rates	mpstat lockstat plockstat

Both throughput and latency contribute to the speed of the system, but there are cases where it makes sense to

108

optimize one at the expense of the other. For example, large file copies are more sensitive to throughput than latency, since throughput will have much more of an impact on the total amount of time spent to transfer the file. On the other hand, a database that performs several small writes to a data file will be much more sensitive to latency than throughput, since it has to wait for the write to be committed before proceeding to the next operation.

The particulars of a given case will dictate whether we want to optimize for one or the other or compromise between them. Depending on the answer to the question, it may make more sense to buy a "bigger pipe" or "more capacity" to improve throughput, or it may make more sense to move the data closer (eg through caching) to reduce latency.

Performance Data Collection

Solaris system components include structures to permit monitoring. kstat structures are created by system components to track historical information. These structures are implemented as counters that increment as specific events occur. The counters are queried by monitoring commands. The **kstat** command provides a listing of several kstat structures.

An increasing number of monitoring commands are using microstate accounting features built into the Solaris kernel. These features allow tracking of CPU statistics on a per-event basis rather than a sampling window basis. For example, load average (as reported by **uptime** and **prstat**) is calculated using microstate accounting. The **prstat -m** command reports several statistics that are measured using microstate accounting.

Example 6-1 demonstrates the sort of data that we collect with **prstat**. In this case, **prstat** is run with the **-s rss** options to sort the output by process **resident set size** (estimated memory usage). We can also sort the output by cpu usage (**cpu**), process priority (**pri**), process image size (**size**), or process execution time (**time**).

Example 6-1. prstat -s rss Output

```
soltest> prstat -s rss
   PID USERNAME  SIZE   RSS STATE  PRI NICE      TIME  CPU PROCESS/NLWP
   471 juser     125M   58M sleep   59    0   4:26:46 0.6% java/17
   200 daemon     62M   55M sleep   59    0   0:01:21 0.0% nfsmapid/4
 18296 juser     116M   39M sleep   26   11   0:05:36 0.1% java/23
...
   254 root     3968K 1016K sleep   59    0   0:00:03 0.0% sshd/1
Total: 47 processes, 221 lwps, load averages: 0.20, 0.21, 0.20
```

> In this output, memory usage is reported in both the SIZE and the RSS columns. SIZE refers to the total virtual memory size of the process, including all mapped files and devices. RSS reports the resident set size, which is an estimate of the actual memory usage provided by proc(4). In practice, the RSS column is the most useful for identifying a memory hog. When more precision is required, we can use **pmap -x**.

Example 6-2 shows the sorts of things that are reported by **prstat -m**. The first data columns report the time spent in usr mode (USR), sys mode (SYS), processing system traps (TRP), text page faults (TFL), data page faults (DFL), waiting for user locks (LCK), sleeping (SLP), and waiting for the CPU (LAT). Other columns report on the number of voluntary (VCX) and involuntary context switches (ICX), system calls (SCL) and signals received (SIG). (Context switching and locking are discussed in Chapter 4. Process memory usage will be discussed in Chapter 8. The discussion around Example 7-2 in Chapter 7 describes how to use **prstat** output to examine CPU saturation.)

Example 6-2. prstat -m Output

```
soltest> prstat -m
   PID USERNAME USR SYS TRP TFL DFL LCK SLP LAT VCX ICX SCL SIG PROCESS/NLWP
 19683 root      29  65 2.7 0.0 0.0 0.0 0.0 3.5   0 710 66K   0 prstat/1
   471 juser    0.0 0.0 0.0 0.0 0.0  53  47 0.2  68   0  81   0 java/17
 18910 root     0.0 0.0 0.0 0.0 0.0 0.0 100 0.0   1   0  17   0 sshd/1
```

```
 18296 juser      0.0 0.0 0.0 0.0 0.0  48  51 0.7  28   0  18   0 java/24
...
   203 daemon     0.0 0.0 0.0 0.0 0.0 0.0 100 0.0   0   0   0   0 lockd/2
   204 daemon     0.0 0.0 0.0 0.0 0.0 0.0 100 0.0   0   0   0   0 nfs4cbd/2
Total: 47 processes, 222 lwps, load averages: 0.22, 0.20, 0.19
```

Historical Data Collection with sar

The word "sar" is used to refer to two related items:

- The system activity report package.
- The system activity reporter.

This facility stores a great deal of performance data about a system. This historical information is invaluable when attempting to identify the source of a performance problem or how frequently it occurs.

The Report Package can be enabled by uncommenting the appropriate lines in the sys crontab. The **sa1** program stores performance data in the */var/adm/sa* directory. **sa2** writes reports from this data, and **sadc** is a more general version of **sa1**.

In practice, I do not find that the **sa2**-produced reports are terribly useful in most cases. I prefer to run **sa1** at regular intervals to collect the data and process it by running the output of the **sar** reporting commands through **awk**.

Alternatively, **sar** can be used on the command line to look at performance over different time slices or over a constricted period of time:

```
sar -A -o outfile 5 2000
```

(Here, "5" represents the time slice and "2000" represents the number of samples to be taken. "*outfile*" is the output file where the data will be stored.)

The data from this file can be read by using the "-**f**" option and specifying a particular file. For **sa1** run from the crontab, these files are named after the two-digit day-of-month:

```
sar -f /var/adm/sa/saday-of-month
```

sar has several options that allow it to process the data collected by **sa1** in different ways. Some of the more useful **sar** options are listed in Table 6-2:

Table 6-2. Useful sar Options

Option	Description	Data Reported
-b	Buffer activity.	**bread/s, bwrit/s**: Transfer rates (per second) between system buffers and block devices (such as disks). **lread/s, lwrit/s**: System buffer access rates (per second). **%rcache, %wcache**: Cache hit rates (%). **pread/s, pwrit/s**: Transfer rates between system buffers and character devices.
-c	System call reporter.	**scall/s**: System call rate (per second). **sread/s, swrit/s, fork/s, exec/s**: Call rate for these calls (per second). **rchar/s, wchar/s**: Transfer rate (characters per second).
-d	Block device (disk) activity.	**%busy**: % of time servicing a transfer request.

110

Option	Description	Data Reported
	.	**avque**: Average number of outstanding requests.
		r+w/s: Rate of reads+writes (transfers per second).
		blks/s: Rate of 512-byte blocks transferred (per second).
		avwait: Average wait time (ms).
		avserv: Average service time (ms). (For block devices, this includes seek rotation and data transfer times.)
-f *filename*	Use *filename* as the source for the binary **sar** data.	(Default locations for **sar** data files are in */var/adm/sa*.)
-g	Paging activity.	**pgout/s**: Page-outs (requests per second).
		ppgout/s: Page-outs (pages per second).
		pgfree/s: Pages freed by the page scanner (pages per second).
		pgscan/s: Scan rate (pages per second).
		%ufs_ipf: Percentage of UFS inodes removed from the free list while still pointing at reusable memory pages.
-k	Kernel memory allocations.	**sml_mem**: Amount of virtual memory available for the small pool (bytes). (Small requests are less than 256 bytes)
		lg_mem: Amount of virtual memory available for the large pool (bytes). (512 bytes-4 Kb)
		ovsz_alloc: Memory allocated to oversize requests (bytes). Oversize requests are dynamically allocated, so there is no pool. (Oversize requests are larger than 4 Kb)
		alloc: Amount of memory allocated to a pool (bytcs). The total KMA usage is the sum of these columns.
		fail: Number of requests that failed.
-m	Message and semaphore activity.	**msg/s, sema/s**: Message and semaphore statistics (operations per second).
-p	Paging activities.	**atch/s**: Attaches (per second). (This is the number of page faults that are filled by reclaiming a page already in memory.)
		pgin/s: Page-in requests (per second) to file systems.
		ppgin/s: Page-ins (per second). (Multiple pages may be affected by a single request.)
		pflt/s: Page faults from protection errors (per second).
		vflts/s: Address translation page faults (per second). (This happens when a valid page is not in memory. It is comparable to the vmstat-reported page/mf value.)
		slock/s: Faults caused by software lock requests that require physical I/O (per second).

Option	Description	Data Reported
-q	Run queue length and percentage of time the run queue is occupied.	
-r	Unused memory pages and disk blocks.	**freemem**: Pages available for use (Use pagesize to determine the size of the pages). **freeswap**: Disk blocks available in swap (512-byte blocks).
-u	CPU utilization.	**%usr**: User time. **%sys**: System time. **%wio**: Waiting for I/O (set to 0 in Solaris 10 due to confusion over its meaning). **%idle**: Idle time.
-w	System swapping and switching activity.	**swpin/s, swpot/s, bswin/s, bswot/s**: Number of LWP transfers or 512-byte blocks per second. **pswch/s**: Process switches (per second).

Data Collection with Custom Scripts

The most useful data may come as a result of comparisons or calculations based on the raw numbers. Nobody wants to spend tons of time doing meaningless comparisons or calculations. That is what computers are good for.

Custom scripts can be a wonderful labor-saving tool. They can become our eyes and ears in the machine room. They can notify us of impending disaster or provide us with historical trending reports.

The standard tools provide fantastic amounts of information, but it is almost never in the format or processed in the way that is most useful for a particular situation. Standard tools are like an ice cream shop that will serve you any flavor you want, as long as it's vanilla.

Every system administrator should become proficient in at least one scripting language. No mass-market tool will ever do things exactly the way we want things done. When we learn how to script, we free ourselves from the shackles of generic software.

Data Collection with SNMP

Open source and professional SNMP packages provide a useful framework for capturing system performance information. Of course, they are only as useful as the data that we collect with them. Too often, every alarm in the software is turned on, resulting in bleary-eyed admins and an unfair perception that things are falling apart.

Pages for the sake of pages are never a good idea. It will take a while before the software is tuned the way we need it. It helps to have an idea what information indicates a real problem and what information is just a normal fluctuation in traffic.

> I know of two sysadmins whose pager bill was in the thousands of dollars the month after an overzealous manager turned on all the alerts on the monitoring software. Once the manager paid the bill, he allowed them to tune it to something more reasonable.
>
> Make sure to set alerting levels appropriately. Besides running up the pager bill, overzealous paging will lead to important pages being ignored.

The information in this book will help identify the appropriate alerting levels for different items. We have to judge which items are worth a log entry, which are worth a little yellow icon on the monitoring software's display, which are worth an email report, and which are worth a midnight page.

Solaris 10 Resource Management

Solaris 10 Resource Management is a significant improvement over what was available in previous versions of Solaris. Resources can now be managed at a zone, project, task or process level.

- Several system parameters can be changed on the fly rather than requiring a reboot after changing */etc/system*.
- Workload resources can be managed on a very granular level. They can be aggregated and separated as required.

Projects and Tasks

Projects and tasks are administrative frameworks that allow for resource management of collections of processes. **Projects** are collections of related processes; each project has a unique integer ID. **Tasks** are collections of processes within the same project; each task also has a unique ID number.

Users and groups may be associated with one or more projects. When processes are started, they inherit their parent's project membership, unless another project is specified. Some commands (specifically, `login, cron, setproject,` and `su.`) may result in another project being assigned.

It is possible to have more than one policy in place for a particular object at a time. For example, a process may be assigned both a `task` and a `process` constraint. In this case, the smallest container's control is enforced first (process before task; task before project; project before zone).

The project database may be maintained in the */etc/project* file or in a NIS or LDAP mapping. The location of the database is specified in the */etc/nsswitch.conf* file. The default */etc/project* contains the following:

```
system:0::::(all system processes and daemons)
user.root:1::::(all root processes)
noproject:2::::(IPQOS)
default:3::::(default project assigned to every non-administrative user)
group.staff:10::::(project used for all users in the "staff" group)
```

The fields in a project database entry are:

`projname`: Name of the project.
`projid`: Unique numerical project identifier less than UID_MAX (2147483647).
`comment`: Project description.
`user-list`: Comma-separated list of usernames. (Wildcards allowed.)
`group-list`: Comma-separated list of groups. (Wildcards allowed.)
`attributes`: Semicolon-separated list of name-value pairs, such as resource controls, in a `name[=value]` format.

Resource constraints are set by adding them to the last field of the project entry. For example, to set the maximum number of LWPs per task to 100 for tasks within the project named `example`:
example:101::::task.max-lwps=(privileged,100,deny)

Changes to */etc/project* become available as new tasks are started in a project.

Managing A Project

Example 6-3 creates a project named "example" with appropriate user and group memberships, and with several resource controls set.

Example 6-3. Specifying Resource Limits for a New Project

```
projadd -p 111 -U username1,username2 -G groupname1,groupname2 -c \
"Example Project" -K "rcap.max-rss=10GB" \
-K "process.max-file-size=(priv,50MB,deny)" \
-K "task.max-lwps=(priv,100,deny)" example
```

This command would produce the following entry in */etc/project*:

```
example:111:Example Project:username1,username2:groupname1,groupname2:\
process.max-file-size=(priv,52428800,deny);\
rcap.max-rss=10737418240;task.max-lwps=(priv,100,deny)
```

Some common ways to use or monitor this new project are listed in the command examples below:

- We can start up a task under this project by running
  `newtask -p example command`
- To verify the project governing the current shell, we would run
  `id -p`
- All existing projects can be listed with
  `projects -l`
- A process's project id can be displayed with
  `ps -o projid -p PID`
- To match project or task ids for `pgrep`, `pkill` or `prstat` commands, use the `-T` or `-J` options:
  `pgrep -J project-IDs`
  `pkill -T task-IDs`
  `prstat -J`
- A running process can be associated with a new task:
  `newtask -v -p project-name -c PID`

Table 6-3 is a compilation of the most useful project-related commands.

Table 6-3. Resource Control Commands

Command	Description
projects	Displays project memberships for users, lists projects from the project database, prints information on given projects.
newtask	Executes the shell or command in a new task of the current project.
projadd	Adds a new project to /etc/project.
projmod	Modifies information for a project.
projdel	Deletes a project.
rctladm	Displays/modifies local active resource controls.
prctl	Displays/modifies local active resource controls.
ipcs	Identifies which IPC objects are being used in a project.

Command	Description
rcapadm	Manages rcapd memory capping daemon.
prstat -J	Displays resource consumption on a per-project basis.
priocntl -i *project-name*	Sets/displays scheduling parameters of the project.
poolbind -i *project-name*	Assigns a project to a resource pool.

System V IPC Tunables

In Solaris 10, most of the shared memory, semaphore and message queue parameters have been removed and the remaining controls moved to project-based resource controls (see "IPC Resource Controls" below).

In current versions of Solaris, many of the theoretical parameter limits have been increased significantly. These theoretical boundaries are based on the data types used to define the objects in the OS. We would never actually set many of these variables to their theoretical maxima; it would be a waste of system resources.

> Structures that are governed by these parameters do take up some memory space; it is important to take this into account when tuning.

Shared memory, semaphores and message queues are only enabled if the appropriate kernel modules are loaded. These are automatically loaded if certain IPC functions are called, but they can also be forced to load via */etc/system* forceload commands or root modload commands.

Each of these three facilities runs on top of the /kernel/misc/ipc module. Shared memory connects to the ipc module via /kernel/sys/shmsys, semaphores connect via /kernel/sys/semsys and message queues connect via /kernel/sys/msgsys. Solaris 10 sets the parameters for these facilities via the project interface. (Other IPC mechanisms exist (such as named pipes), but they are not tunable in the sense of this discussion.)

Each IPC resource has at least these attributes: key (identifies this instance of the resource), creator (UID/GID of the creating process), owner (UID/GID of the resource owner), and permissions (similar to file system read/write/execute owner/group/other permissions).

Each object is created by calling the appropriate *get function (shmget/semget/msgget) with the desired key. If no objects of that type with that key exist, it is created and a resource ID is passed back to the caller. Once created, the IPC objects can be controlled with the appropriate *ctl function (shmctl/semctl/msgctl).

The **ipcs** command presents information on IPC services that are currently loaded. It presents a "facility not in system" message if a given module has not been loaded yet. Example 6-4 shows the output of an **ipcs** command run on an Oracle server:

Example 6-4. ipcs -J Output

```
soltest> ipcs -J
IPC status from <running system> as of Thursday, May  3, 2007  7:41:02 PM EDT
T         ID      KEY         MODE        OWNER    GROUP         PROJECT
Message Queues:
Shared Memory:
m         1       0xe052fa34 --rw-r-----  oracle   oinstall      user.oracle
Semaphores:
s         3       0xc860ca8c --ra-r-----  oracle   oinstall      user.oracle
```

The Solaris 10 IPC resource management framework was designed to overcome several shortcomings of the older

SVR4-based system. Several parameters were converted to be dynamically resized, the defaults were increased, the names were changed to be more human-readable, the resource limits have been made more granular, and changes can now be made on the fly.

Shared Memory

Shared memory provides the fastest way for processes to pass large amounts of data to one another. As the name implies, **shared memory** refers to physical pages of memory that are shared by more than one process.

Of particular interest is the **"Intimate Shared Memory"** facility, where the translation tables are shared as well as the memory. This enhances the effectiveness of the TLB (**Translation Lookaside Buffer**), which is a CPU-based cache of translation table information. Since the same information is used for several processes, available buffer space can be used much more efficiently. In addition, ISM-designated memory cannot be paged out, which can be used to keep frequently-used data and binaries in memory.

Database applications are usually the heaviest users of shared memory. Vendor recommendations should be consulted when tuning the shared memory parameters.

Semaphores

Semaphores are a shareable resource that take on a non-negative integer value. They are manipulated by the P (wait) and V (signal) functions, which decrement and increment the semaphore, respectively. When a process needs a resource, a "wait" is issued and the semaphore is decremented. When the semaphore contains a value of zero, the resources are not available and the calling process spins or blocks (as appropriate) until resources are available. When a process releases a resource controlled by a semaphore, it increments the semaphore and the waiting processes are notified.

Message Queues

Unix uses **message queues** for asynchronous message passing between processes. Each message has a type field, which can be used for priority messaging or directing a message to a chosen recipient.

Message queues are implemented as FIFO (first-in first-out) mechanisms. They consist of a header pointing to a linked list.

IPC Resource Controls

The Solaris 10 IPC resource management framework was designed to overcome several shortcomings of the older SVR4-based system. Several parameters were converted to be dynamically resized, the defaults were increased, the names were changed to be more human-readable, the resource limits were system-wide (permitting potential conflicts) and reboots were required for even minor changes.

The Solaris 10 system allows changes to be associated with a `project` and monitored via **`prctl`**. Changes can be made on the fly and associated with separate projects and tasks on an individual basis.

For the purposes of IPC resource management, see Table 6-4 for the important parameters. The other parameters are either obsolete or size themselves dynamically.

Table 6-4. IPC Resource Management Controls

Control Name	Description	Replaces
`project.max-shm-ids`	Maximum shared memory IDs for a project.	`shmmni`
`project.max-sem-ids`	Maximum semaphore IDs for a project.	`semmni`

Control Name	Description	Replaces
project.max-msg-ids	Maximum message queue IDs for a project.	msgmni
project.max-shm-memory	Total shared memory allowed for a project.	shmmax
process.max-sem-nsems	Maximum number of semaphores per semaphore set.	semmsl
process.max-sem-ops	Maximum semaphore operations allowed per semop.	semopm
process.max-msg-messages	Maximum number of messages on a message queue.	msgtql
process.max-msg-qbytes	Maximum total size of message queue in bytes.	msgmnb

The Solaris 10 system allows changes to be associated with a project and monitored via **prctl**. Changes can be made on the fly and associated with separate processes, projects or tasks on an individual basis.

In addition to their new names, several parameters also had their defaults increased. In many cases, the new defaults may be large enough that old */etc/system* settings may no longer be necessary. Table 6-5 lists the new defaults, along with Oracle requirements. It is likely that max-shm-memory is the only parameter that will require adjustment.

Table 6-5. Solaris Defaults and Oracle Requirements

Parameter	Oracle Requirements	Solaris 10 Default
shmmax/max-shm-memory	varies	¼ Physical memory.
semmni/max-sem-ids	100	128
semmsl/max-sem-nsems	256	512
shmmni/max-shm-ids	100	128
semmns	1024	Obsolete.
shmmin	1	Obsolete.
shmseg	10	Obsolete.

Where there are multiple Oracle instances on a single system, we can use the flexibility of the new framework to set up a specific project and resource settings for each one. The following **projmod** command can be used to set the max-shm-memory to the desired level (*#gig*) for each project (*project-name*):

```
projmod -sK "project.max-shm-memory=(privileged,#gigGB,deny)" project-name
```

To ensure that each instance starts up in the desired project, the startup scripts will need to use something like the following **newtask** command to assign the project:

```
newtask -p project-name
```

We can check how a project's IPC objects are allocated against existing limits by running:

```
ipcs -J
```

(Example 6-4 above shows what the `ipcs -J` output looks like.)

If we only want to set up a single project for all jobs owned by a single user (say, oracle), we could set up a project with the special name `user.oracle`. The command to set up project ID 112 with a 4GB limit for shared memory used by processes owned by oracle would be something like:

```
projadd -p 112 -U oracle -G oinstall -c "Oracle" \
 -K "project.max-shm-memory=(privleged,4GB,deny)" user.oracle
```

(We can do something similar for group-specific projects by naming them `group.groupname`.)

Additional Resource Controls

The new Solaris 10 resource controls include compatibility interfaces to the old `rlimit`-style resource controls. Existing applications using the old interfaces can continue to run unchanged. Typically, the old interface would use a `limit` or `ulimit` command to check or set limits for the current session, and `plimit` to check or set limits for a running process. Example 6-5 shows the output of a typical `plimit` command:

Example 6-5. plimit Output

```
soltest> plimit 1017
1017:   ora_lgwr_orcl
   resource              current         maximum
  time(seconds)         unlimited       unlimited
  file(blocks)          unlimited       unlimited
  data(kbytes)          unlimited       unlimited
  stack(kbytes)         32768           unlimited
  coredump(blocks)      unlimited       unlimited
  nofiles(descriptors)  65536           65536
  vmemory(kbytes)       unlimited       unlimited
```

These limits can be adjusted using the `plimit` command, but it is best to adjust them with the new `project`-specific mechanisms.

The most commonly used resource controls are listed in Table 6-6. A full description (and a full list) of the new resource controls is available on the `resource_controls(5)` man page.

Table 6-6. Other Resource Controls

Control Name	Description
`[zone|project].cpu-shares`	Maximum CPU shares allowed (under Fair Share Scheduler).
`[process|task].max-cpu-time`	Maximum CPU time allowed for this process or task.
`project.max-contracts`	Maximum number of contracts allowed.
`project.max-crypto-memory`	Total kernel memory usable for hardware encryption acceleration by `libpkcs11`.
`project.max-device-locked-memory`	Total locked memory allowed.
`process.max-address-space`	Maximum address space.
`process.max-core-size`	Maximum core dump size allowed.

118

Control Name	Description
`process.max-data-size`	Maximum heap size.
`process.max-file-descriptor`	Maximum file descriptor index.
`process.max-file-size`	Maximum file offset allowed for writes.
`process.max-stack-size`	Maximum available stack memory segment.
`[zone|project|task].max-lwps`	Maximum LWPs available.
`process.max-port-events`	Maximum events per port.
`project.max-port-ids`	Maximum allowable event ports.
`project.max-tasks`	Maximum allowable tasks.
`rcap.max-rss`	Maximum physical memory consumption by processes in a project. (See `rcapd` below.)

To view resource constraints for a process, we would run something like the following:
prctl -n *resource-name* -i process *PID*

Example 6-6 shows the output of a **prctl** command to check the `process.max-stack-size` of the same process we saw in Example 6-5:

Example 6-6. Examining Process Constraints with prctl

```
soltest> prctl -n process.max-stack-size -i process 1017
process: 1017: ora_lgwr_orcl
NAME     PRIVILEGE       VALUE    FLAG    ACTION                  RECIPIENT
process.max-stack-size
         basic           32.0MB   -       deny                    1017
         privileged      8.00EB   max     deny                    -
         system          8.00EB   max     deny                    -
```

To check resource constraints for the current shell, we would run:

prctl $$

Or, to temporarily set resource constraints on a particular project, we could run something like:
prctl -n *resource-name* -t *priv-level* -v *value* -e *action* -i project *project-name*

Example 6-7 shows the results of an adjustment to the `process.max-stack-size` limit for the process from Example 6-6. The example demonstrates that either **plimit** or **prctl** can be used to adjust a process's limits:

Example 6-7. Changing a Process's Resource Constraints

```
soltest> prctl -n process.max-stack-size -i process 1017
process: 1017: ora_lgwr_orcl
NAME     PRIVILEGE       VALUE    FLAG    ACTION                  RECIPIENT
process.max-stack-size
         basic           32.0MB   -       deny                    1017
         privileged      8.00EB   max     deny                    -
         system          8.00EB   max     deny                    -
soltest> prctl -n process.max-stack-size -t basic -v 33.0MB -e deny -i process 1017
```

119

```
soltest> prctl -n process.max-stack-size -i process 1017
process: 1017: ora_lgwr_orcl
NAME       PRIVILEGE         VALUE    FLAG   ACTION                   RECIPIENT
process.max-stack-size
           basic             33.0MB     -    deny                         1017
           privileged        8.00EB   max    deny                            -
           system            8.00EB   max    deny                            -
soltest> plimit 1017 | grep stack
  stack(kbytes)             33792           unlimited
soltest> plimit -s 34816,unlimited 1017
soltest> prctl -n process.max-stack-size -i process 1017
process: 1017: ora_lgwr_orcl
NAME       PRIVILEGE         VALUE    FLAG   ACTION                   RECIPIENT
process.max-stack-size
           basic             34.0MB     -    deny                         1017
           privileged        8.00EB   max    deny                            -
           system            8.00EB   max    deny                            -
```

rcapd

rcapd is a user-level daemon that caps memory usage within a project. Where zones are used, rcapd is only able to manage projects within its own local zone.

In each zone, rcapd can be enabled via
rcapadm -E
which will start rcapd and enable it under SMF so that it will be restarted automatically. (Starting with the 11/06 release, we can also manage rcapd using **svcadm** for the rcap service. The "Service Management Facility" section in Chapter 12 discusses how to manage SMF services.)

projmod can be used to set the memory cap for a project:
projmod -s -K rcap.max-rss=*size*MB project-name
or the rcap.max-rss control can be set directly in */etc/project*.

Note that rcapd does not account for shared memory in an intuitive way, and Sun is reported to be changing their calculation algorithm. To be safe, allow enough room for shared memory to be included under your cap, and do not depend solely on rcapd to keep process memory usage under control.

Fair Share Scheduler

The default timesharing (TS) scheduling class in Solaris attempts to give relatively equal CPU access to all regular processes on the system. The **nice** command provides some limited ability to control process priorities, but it is at best a crude instrument. The Fair Share Scheduler (FSS) provides a more structured way to manage process priorities.

Each project is allocated a certain number of CPU shares via the project.§cpu-shares resource control. A project is allocated CPU time based on a weighted average of the active running projects with a non-zero §cpu-shares setting. The allocation formula for each project is its §cpu-shares value divided by the sum of the §cpu-shares values for all active processes.

> Anything with a zero cpu-shares value will not be granted any CPU time at all until every project with a non-zero cpu-shares value is totally done using the CPU. This can lead to odd and unexpected problems when FSS is implemented.

The maximum number of shares that can be assigned to any one project is 65535.

The Fair Share Scheduler can be assigned to processor sets. This allows more sensitive control of priorities on a server than processor sets allow on their own. The **dispadmin** command command controls the assignment of schedulers to processor sets, using a form like:
```
dispadmin -d FSS
```

To enable this change now, rather than after the next reboot, run a command like the following:
```
priocntl -s -C FSS
```

The shares assigned to an active project can be dynamically altered with the **priocntl** command. The command would have a form something like:
```
priocntl -r -n project.cpu-shares -v number-shares -i project project-name
```

The Fair Share Scheduler should not be combined with the TS, FX (fixed-priority) or IA (interactive) scheduling classes on the same CPU or processor set. All of these scheduling classes use priorities in the same range, so unexpected behavior can result from combining FSS with any of these. (There is no problem, however, with running TS and IA on the same processor set.)

> If the FSS is used on a system with zones, the global zone is given one zone.cpu-shares by default. This can only be changed by running **priocntl** against the global zone after each reboot, which may not be acceptable. Non-global zones can be assigned zone.cpu-shares values as in Example 6-8 below.
>
> In a system where zone.cpu-shares values are used to share CPU resources between zones, each zone's share is divided up based on project.cpu-shares within the zone's local project database.

Resource Control Parameter Attributes

Attributes are available to manage the behavior of resource controls. In particular, we can manage the logging level, modification privileges and enforcement actions associated with each control:

Logging

Global logging can be enabled by setting **syslog=level** with **rctladm**, where *level* is one of the usual syslog levels: debug, info, notice, warning, err, crit, alert or emerg.

To activate logging on a global resource control facility, run something like:
```
rctladm -e syslog=level resource-name
```

Privilege Levels

Each resource control threshold needs to be associated with one of the following privilege levels:

- **basic**: Can be modified by the owner of the calling process.
- **privileged**: Only modifiable by superuser.
- **system**: Fixed for the duration of the OS instance.

A given resource control can have an associated threshold for up to three privilege levels.

Actions

It is possible to use **rctladm** to specify one of the following actions on a process that violates the control:

- **none**: No action taken. (Useful for monitoring.)

- **deny**: Denies request.
- **signal**: Enable a signal. See the `rctladm` man page for a list of allowed signals.

Zones

Zones are containers to segregate services so that they do not interfere with each other. Sun provides two excellent downloadable books on zones (*The Sun Blueprints Guide to Solaris Containers* and *Solaris Containers—Resource Management and Solaris Zones*), which are listed in the "References" section.

One zone, the **global zone**, is the locus for system-wide administrative functions. **Non-global zones** are not able to interact with each other except through network interfaces. When using management commands that reference PIDs, only processes in the same zone will be visible from any non-global zone.

Zones requiring network connectivity have at least one dedicated IP address. Non-global zones cannot observe each other's network traffic.

Each zone is assigned a zone name and a unique numeric zone ID. The global zone always has the name *global* and ID 0. A node name is also assigned to each zone, including global. The node names are independent of the zone names. Each zone has a path to its root directory relative to the global zone's root directory.

A non-global zone's scheduling class is set to be the same as the system's scheduling class. If a zone is assigned to a resource pool, its scheduling class can be controlled by controlling the pool's scheduling class. Non-global zones can have their own zone administrators. Their authority is limited to their home zone.

The separation of the environments allows for better security, since the security for each zone is independent. Separation also allows for the installation of environments with distinct profiles on the same hardware. The virtualization of the environment makes it easier to duplicate an environment on different physical servers.

The system administrator configures new non-global zones via the `zonecfg` command, administers them via `zoneadm` and logs into them via `zlogin`.

Zone States

Non-global zones have one of the following states:

- **configured**: Configuration complete and in stable storage.
- **incomplete**: Installation or uninstallation underway
- **installed**: Configuration instantiated on system. Zone has no associated virtual platform.
- **ready**: Virtual platform established, `zsched` started, IPs plumbed, file systems mounted, zone ID assigned. No zone processes started yet.
- **running**: This state entered when zone `init` process starts.
- **shutting down**: Zone being halted.
- **down**: Transitional state during zone shutdown.

Control Commands

The following control commands can be used to manage and monitor transitions between states:

- `zlogin options zone-name`
- `zoneadm -z zone-name boot`
- `zoneadm -z zone-name halt`
- `zoneadm -z zone-name install`
- `zoneadm -z zone-name ready`
- `zoneadm -z zone-name reboot`

- **`zoneadm -z `*`zone-name`*` uninstall`**
- **`zoneadm -z `*`zone-name`*` verify`**
- **`zonecfg -z `*`zone-name`*`:`** Interactive mode; can be used to remove properties of the following types: `fs`, `device, rctl, net, attr`
- **`zonecfg -z `*`zone-name`*` commit`**
- **`zonecfg -z `*`zone-name`*` delete`**
- **`zonecfg -z `*`zone-name`*` verify`**

Zone Setup Example

Example 6-8 below demonstrates the setup process for a fairly standard zone.

Example 6-8. Zone Setup

```
global/ > zonecfg -z zonename
zonename: No such zone configured
Use 'create' to begin configuring a new zone.
zonecfg:zonename> create
zonecfg:zonename> set zonepath=/zonename
zonecfg:zonename> set autoboot=true
```

Setting up the file system as `lofs` in this way allows it to be both readable and writable from within the zone.

```
zonecfg:zonename> add fs
zonecfg:zonename:fs> set dir=/opt
zonecfg:zonename:fs> set special=/opt
zonecfg:zonename:fs> set type=lofs
zonecfg:zonename:fs> end
zonecfg:zonename> add net
zonecfg:zonename:net> set address=192.68.45.46
zonecfg:zonename:net> set physical=bge0
zonecfg:zonename:net> end
zonecfg:zonename> add rctl
zonecfg:zonename:rctl> set name=zone.cpu-shares
zonecfg:zonename:rctl> set value=(priv=privileged,limit=20,action=none)
zonecfg:zonename:rctl> end
zonecfg:zonename> add attr
zonecfg:zonename:attr> set name=comment
zonecfg:zonename:attr> set type=string
zonecfg:zonename:attr> set value="Zone Description"
zonecfg:zonename:attr> end
zonecfg:zonename> verify
zonecfg:zonename> commit
zonecfg:zonename> exit
global/ > zonecfg -z zonename info
zonename: zonename
zonepath: /zonename
autoboot: true
limitpriv:
inherit-pkg-dir:
        dir: /lib
inherit-pkg-dir:
        dir: /platform
inherit-pkg-dir:
        dir: /sbin
inherit-pkg-dir:
```

```
              dir: /usr
fs:
              dir: /opt
              special: /opt
              raw not specified
              type: lofs
              options: []
net:
              address: 192.68.45.46
              physical: bge0
rctl:
              name: zone.cpu-shares
              value: (priv=privileged,limit=20,action=none)
attr:
              name: comment
              type: string
              value: "Zone Description"
global/ > zoneadm -z zonename install
Preparing to install zone <zonename>.
Creating list of files to copy from the global zone.
Copying <2529> files to the zone.
Initializing zone product registry.
Determining zone package initialization order.
Preparing to initialize <1008> packages on the zone.
Initialized <1008> packages on zone.
Zone <zonename> is initialized.
Installation of these packages generated warnings: <SUNWkvm SUNWcsl
...
SUNWsshu SUNWocfd>
The file </zonename/root/var/sadm/system/logs/install_log> contains a log of the zone
installation.
```

In the event that the zone installation is interrupted, you can check the state with **zoneadm -z
zonename list -v** and uninstall it with **zoneadm -z *zonename* uninstall**. The latter
command also takes a **-F** option to force the uninstall, it it won't go quietly.

```
global/ > zoneadm -z zonename list -v
  ID NAME              STATUS          PATH
  - zonename           installed    /zonename
global/ > zlogin zonename
zlogin: login allowed only to running zones (zonename is 'installed').
global/ > zoneadm -z zonename ready
global/ > zoneadm -z zonename boot
global/ > zoneadm -z zonename list -v
  ID NAME              STATUS          PATH
  1 zonename           running      /zonename
global/ > zlogin zonename
[Connected to zone 'zonename' pts/5]
Sun Microsystems Inc.   SunOS 5.10      Generic January 2005
# exit
```

We can edit a zone's properties as well, using **zonecfg**.

```
global/usr/local/bin > zonecfg -z zonename
zonecfg:zonename> add dataset
zonecfg:zonename:dataset> set name=zfspoolname
zonecfg:zonename:dataset> end
```

124

Adding a pool as a dataset in this way (rather than mounting a file system) allows us to control the pool administratively.

```
zonecfg:zonename> verify
zonecfg:zonename> commit
zonecfg:zonename> exit
global/usr/local/bin > zlogin zonename
[Connected to zone 'zonename' pts/3]
Last login: Tue May 22 12:23:16 on pts/3
Sun Microsystems Inc.    SunOS 5.10      Generic January 2005
# zpool list
no pools available
# ls
bin       etc       home      mnt        platform  sbin      tmp       var
dev       export    lib       opt        proc      system    usr
# exit
```

Configuration changes (like the ZFS pool import) are not visible until after the zone is rebooted.

```
global/usr/local/bin > zoneadm -z zonename reboot
global/usr/local/bin > zlogin zonename
[Connected to zone 'zonename' pts/3]
Last login: Tue May 22 12:33:08 on pts/3
Sun Microsystems Inc.    SunOS 5.10      Generic January 2005
# zpool list
NAME                      SIZE    USED    AVAIL   CAP   HEALTH    ALTROOT
zfspoolname               712G    81K     712G    0%    ONLINE    -
```

From this point, zone setup can be finalized by using **zlogin -C *zonename*** to answer system setup questions.

Kernel Tuning

sysdef -i reports on several system resource limits. Other parameters can be checked or even changed on a running system using **mdb** −k or **ndd**.

```
mdb -k
parameter-name/D
$Q
```

Most parameters can be adjusted on a live system via **mdb**, though some will not take effect until the reboot after they are added to the */etc/system* file.

To set a parameter in the */etc/system* file, add a line like the following:

set nfssrv:nfs_portmon=1

The key parts of this command are the "set" command, the module name, the parameter name and the value that the parameter is set to. (This particular parameter checks whether an NFS client request comes from a reserved port.) */etc/system* changes do not take effect until the next reboot.

In the rest of the chapter, some of the more useful kernel tunables are listed. This is not a complete listing; see the *Solaris Tunable Parameters Reference Manaual* in the "References" section below for a more complete list.

In particular, paging, disk I/O-related and network-related parameters are addressed in Chapters 8, 9 and 10, respectively.

maxusers

maxusers is the most frequently tuned kernel parameter. Its original use (as an overall limit to the number of concurrent users on a system) is much less important than its role as a basis for calculating other kernel parameters.

The default value is set to either the number of MB of physical memory or 2048, whichever is lower. maxusers can be set explicitly in the */etc/system* file, but is limited to 4096.

Several key kernel parameters are calculated based on the value of maxusers at boot time (unless explicitly overridden in the */etc/system* file):

- **max_nprocs**: Maximum number of processes on the system. Defaults to: $10 + (16 \times maxusers)$. Requires an */etc/system* setting and a reboot to change.
- **ufs_ninode**: Inode cache size $= 4 \times (maxusers + max\_nprocs) + 320$. This setting can be changed on the fly in **mdb**.
- **ncsize**: Name lookup cache size $= (68 \times maxusers) + 360$. The efficiency of this cache can be examined with **kstat -n dnlcstats**. If it is adjusted, ufs_ninode and nfs:nrnode should also be set. Setting this value too high can negatively affect performance, so it should be tuned with care. Requires an */etc/system* setting and a reboot to change.
- **ndquot**: Quota table size $= (maxusers \times 40)/4 + max\_nprocs$. Should only be increased if "dquot table full" messages are noted in the log. Requires an */etc/system* setting and a reboot to change.
- **maxuprc**: User process limit $= max\_nprocs - 5$

ptys

Pseudo terminals (ptys) provide a resource to permit remote logins or the creation of additional X Windows command windows. These are managed differently in current versions of Solaris than was the case in earlier versions.

Previously, the number of ptys was limited by the parameter pt_cnt, which specified a default maximum number of ptys. We can still do things this way, by setting pt_cnt and pt_max_pty to the desired value in */etc/system* and performing a reconfiguration reboot (**boot -r**). By default, however, this facility is turned off by setting the values of pt_cnt and pt_max_pty to 0.

Instead, by default, ptys may be created up to a percentage of memory, which is specified by pt_pctofmem. This is an integer value 1-100, with a default of 5 (ie, 5% of available memory.) The number of ptys this represents can be calculated by allowing 176 bytes/pty for 64-bit kernels and 112 bytes/pty for 32-bit kernels.

Other related variables may or may not need to be set at the same time:

- **npty**: npty limits the number of BSD ptys. These are not usually used by applications, but may need to be increased on a system running a special service. In addition to setting npty in the */etc/system* file, the */etc/iu.ap* file will need to be edited to substitute the value npty-1 in the third field of the ptsl line. After both changes are made, a **boot -r** is required for the changes to take effect. Note that Solaris does not support any more than 176 BSD ptys in any case.
- **nautopush**: nautopush sets the number of STREAMS autopush entries. As such, it should be set to twice the value of sadcnt.
- **sadcnt**: sadcnt sets the number of STREAMS addressable devices.

File Descriptors

A **file descriptor** is a handle created by a process when a file is opened. A new descriptor is created each time the file is opened. It is associated with a file object which includes information such as the mode in which the file was opened and the **offset pointer** where the next operation will begin. This information is called the **context** of the file.

File descriptors are retired when the file is closed or the process terminates. Opens always choose the lowest-numbered file descriptor available. Available file descriptors are allocated based on the following system settings:

- **rlim_fd_cur**: Default file descriptor limit (per process). Also known as the "soft" limit, since it can be adjusted by the program or a non-root user (via `setrlimit()` or the **limit**/**ulimit** shell command). Defaults to 256.
- **rlim_fd_max**: Maximum number of file descriptors for each process. Also known as the "hard" limit, since only root can authorize increasing the number of file descriptors higher. Defaults to 65,536 in Solaris 9+.

There are a few gotchas to setting large file descriptor limits:

- 32-bit programs using standard I/O are limited to 256 file descriptors. (Similar 64-bit programs are limited to about 2 billion descriptors.)
- `select()` is limited to 1024 file descriptors by default. See the `select(3C)` man page for more information.

These limits can also be set via the `process.max-file-descriptor` resource control. This is more flexible than */etc/system* settings, since it can be done on a per-user or per-project basis.

Stack Size

The default thread stack size is set by `default_stksize`. This parameter replaces the older `lwp_default_stksize`, and overrides it when it is set.

The default setting of `default_stksize` is 3xPAGESIZE for SPARC systems, 2xPAGESIZE on x86 systems, and 5xPAGESIZE on x64 systems. The maximum setting is 32x the default setting. (The default page size is 8KB for SPARC and 4KB for x86 and x64 systems.)

Miscellaneous Tunables

There are a few additional kernel tunables that may be worth considering.

- **bufhwm**: Maximum memory allowed for caching metadata of referenced files. The default is 2% of physical memory; the maximum allowed value is 20% of physical memory. This parameter can only be set at boot time in the */etc/system* file. **sar -b** and **kstat -n biostats** provide some information on hit rates for the buffer cache.
- **bufhwm_pct**: Maximum percentage of memory allowed to cache metadata of referenced files. The defaults and limits are the numbers equivalent to those for `bufhwm`.
- **dump_cnt**: Size of dumps.
- **moddebug**: Sets debug levels for module operations. It is defaulted to 0 (off). Additional options include 0x80000000 (prints loading/unloading messages), 0x40000000 (prints detailed error messages) or 0x20000000 (even more detailed messages). When debugging is enabled, it can slow system boot because of the overhead to module loading/unloading operations.
- **ndquot**
- **ngroups_max**: Maximum number of supplementary groups per user (default=32).
- **rstchown**: Posix/restricted `chown` enabled (default=1). (Disabling this by setting it to 0 is not recommended, due to some security holes that are opened up. See the `chown(2)` man page for more details.)
- **ufs_HW**, ufs_LW: If more than ufs_HW bytes are queued for a write to a single file, additional writes are deferred (by sleeping their thread) until the queue drops to ufs_LW. The defaults are 16MB and 8MB, respectively. We can consider changing this value when we are attached to a high-speed disk subsystem

(striped disks or an array with a big front-end cache), but these settings are only available on a systemwide basis. We have to make sure not to kill other file systems that are not on the fast disks.

Resources

- Cockcroft, Adrian and Pettit, Richard. (April 1998) Sun Performance and Tuning: Java and the Internet, 2nd Ed. Prentice Hall.

- Cromar, Scott. (April 2007) *Solaris 10 Resource Management*. SysAdmin Magazine.

- Cromar, Scott. (2007) *Solaris Troubleshooting and Performance Tuning at Princeton University*. Princeton, NJ. (http://www.princeton.edu/~unix/Solaris/troubleshoot/index.html)

- Foxwell, Harry J; Lageman, Menno; van Hoogeveen, Joost Pronk; Rozenfeld, Isaac; Setty, Sreekanth and Victor, Jeff. The Sun Blueprints Guide to Solaris Containers. Santa Clara, CA: Sun Microsystems, Inc. (http://www.sun.com/blueprints/1006/820-0001.pdf)

- Galvin, Peter Baer. (April 2003) Solaris *Resource Management*. SysAdmin Magazine.

- McDougall, Richard and Mauro, Jim. (July 2006) *Solaris Internals*. Upper Saddle River, NJ: Prentice Hall & Sun Microsystems Press.

- McDougall, Richard; Mauro, Jim and Gregg, Brendan. (October 2006) *Solaris Performance and Tools*. Upper Saddle River, NJ: Prentice Hall & Sun Microsystems Press.

- Sun Microsystems. (June 2006) *man pages section 1: User Commands*. Palo Alto, CA: Sun Microsystems, Inc. (http://docs.sun.com/app/docs/doc/816-5165)

- Sun Microsystems. (June 2006) *man pages section 1M: System Administration Commands*. Palo Alto, CA: Sun Microsystems, Inc. (http://docs.sun.com/app/docs/doc/816-5166)

- Sun Microsystems. (June 2006) *man pages section 5: Standards, Environments and Macros*. Palo Alto, CA: Sun Microsystems, Inc. (http://docs.sun.com/app/docs/doc/816-5175)

- Sun Microsystems. (May 2006) *Solaris Tunable Parameters Reference Manual*. Santa Clara, CA: Sun Microsystems, Inc. (http://docs.sun.com/app/docs/doc/817-0404)

- Sun Microsystems. (May 2006) *System Administration Guide: Solaris Containers—Resource Management and Solaris Zones*. Santa Clara, CA: Sun Microsystems, Inc. (http://docs.sun.com/app/docs/doc/817-1592)

7

CPU Monitoring and Management

Most people know about the relationship between CPUs and performance—or at least they think they do. Unfortunately, this relationship is usually overstated. Usually, performance issues have more to do with memory and I/O bottlenecks than a lack of CPU capacity.

When performance expectations are not being met, we need to identify where the bottleneck is. Upgrading CPUs is not going to have a significant impact on a process that is throttled by disk I/O capacity. To see if our process is CPU-bound, we need to look at both CPU saturation and CPU utilization.

Table 7-1 reprises the most useful metrics for looking at CPU performance. These metrics will give us a solid answer in the vast majority of cases. Occasionally we will need to reach into our DTrace toolkit to look at things like concurrency, context switching or resource contention, but it is much more often the case that bulk saturation and utilization numbers will tell the tale.

Table 7-1. CPU Performance Metrics

Performance Metric	Monitoring Commands

CPU Saturation: Load Average or Run Queue Length	`uptime`
	`sar -q`
	`vmstat`

CPU Saturation: CPU Run Queue Latency	`prstat -mL`

CPU Utilization by %sys and %usr, as well as %idle	`sar -u`
	`vmstat`
	`iostat`
	`mpstat`

CPU Utilization: Multiple Processor Load Sharing	`mpstat`

Context Switching Rates	`mpstat`
	`sar -w`
	`vmstat`

Utilization vs Saturation

Utilization refers to the amount of the CPU resource that is being consumed at a point in time. It is measured directly by looking at the %idle reported by tools such as `sar -u`, `vmstat`, `iostat` or `mpstat`. High CPU utilization can degrade performance because new threads may not be able to get processor cycles immediately.

CPU utilization will vary widely over time, with steep spikes in utilization rates. It may be necessary to run a monitoring command with a short sampling window in order to get a real view of what is happening on short time scales. 5 seconds or even 1 second may show spikes that are not apparent in statistics resulting from longer sampling windows. DTrace allows even finer-grained statistics gathering, which can let us see very brief spikes in activity.

> Low CPU utilization does not necessarily mean that we don't have a problem. For example, multiple processor machines may show very low utilization rates while a poorly-threaded application beats on a single CPU core. The `mpstat` utility reports on each processor's utilization and can be useful in diagnosing this class of problem. Such an application (if it can't be re-written) might be better off on a system with fewer, faster cores.

CPU Saturation is much more likely to cause noticeable system performance problems. **Saturation** refers to a situation where there is not enough CPU capacity to adequately handle requests for processing resources. This can be measured directly by looking at the CPU latency time for each thread reported by `prstat -mL`. (LAT is reported as a percentage of the time that a thread is waiting to use a processor. See Example 7-2 below.) Other good indicators include load average and run queue length, as reported by `uptime` and `sar -q`, respectively. (The DTrace Toolkit's *dispqlen.d* program reports on dispatcher queue length as well.) High utilization can lead to CPU saturation if more threads continue to request resources.

Example 7-1 shows `sar -u` and `sar -q` output from a system that might benefit from additional CPU resources. The `sar -u` output shows a 0 %idle, indicating that the processor is always busy. The `sar -q` output shows a run queue length peaking over 25 with the run queue always being occupied.

Example 7-1. sar Output Indicating CPU Throttling

```
# sar -u

SunOS soltest 5.10 Generic_118822-30 sun4u    01/24/07

00:00:01    %usr    %sys    %wio    %idle
00:20:00      23      16       0       61
...
02:20:02      73      27       0        0
02:40:03      71      29       0        0
03:00:03      70      30       0        0
03:20:00      61      39       0        0
03:40:03      66      34       0        0
04:00:00      69      31       0        0
04:20:01      31      18       0       50
04:40:00       7       5       0       88
05:00:00       1       4       0       95
...

# sar -q
```

```
SunOS soltest 5.10 Generic_118822-30 sun4u     01/24/07

00:00:01 runq-sz %runocc swpq-sz %swpocc
00:20:00      7.5      11     0.0        0
...
02:20:02     22.1     100     0.0        0
02:40:03     20.5     100     0.0        0
03:00:03     20.3     100     0.0        0
03:20:00     25.7     100     0.0        0
03:40:03     19.7     100     0.0        0
04:00:00     12.5     100     0.0        0
04:20:01      3.0      16     0.0        0
04:40:00      1.0       0     0.0        0
05:00:00      1.0       0     0.0        0
...

# psrinfo -v
Status of virtual processor 0 as of: 01/24/2007 18:20:51
  on-line since 12/04/2006 08:35:13.
  The sparcv9 processor operates at 1280 MHz,
        and has a sparcv9 floating point processor.
Status of virtual processor 1 as of: 01/24/2007 18:20:51
  on-line since 12/04/2006 08:35:12.
  The sparcv9 processor operates at 1280 MHz,
        and has a sparcv9 floating point processor.
...
# /opt/DTT/Bin/cputypes.d
 CPU CHIP PSET LGRP   CLOCK  TYPE          FPU
   0    0    0    1    2400  i386          i387 compatible
   2    1    0    2    2400  i386          i387 compatible
   3    1    0    2    2400  i386          i387 compatible
   1    0    0    1    2400  i386          i387 compatible
```

The existing processors can be examined to see what their clock rate and processor types are with the **psrinfo -v** command or the DTrace Toolkit's **cputypes.d** (see the end of Example 7-1).

> A high run queue length (runq-sz) is only meaningful if the run queue is occupied (%runq-occ) for a significant percentage of the time. If the amount of time the run queue is occupied is too low, we can end up with the average run queue length being reported as excessively long due to rounding errors.

Example 7-2 shows the **prstat -mL** output from a single-CPU system that has been overloaded. Notice the load average and LAT numbers in particular.

Example 7-2. CPU Saturation Measured with prstat

```
 PID USERNAME USR SYS TRP TFL DFL LCK SLP LAT VCX ICX SCL SIG PROCESS/LWPID
2724 root      24 0.2 0.0 0.0 0.0 0.0 2.2  74 284 423 361   0 gzip/1
2729 root      21 0.3 0.0 0.0 0.0 0.0 3.3  75 396 564 518   0 gzip/1
2733 root      20 0.3 0.0 0.0 0.0 0.0 5.3  75 391 514 484   0 gzip/1
2737 root      14 0.2 0.0 0.0 0.0 0.0 4.1  81 176 415 383   0 gzip/1
2730 root     3.3 0.3 0.0 0.0 0.0 0.0  96 0.7 602 258 505   0 gunzip/1
2734 root     2.9 0.3 0.0 0.0 0.0 0.0  92 4.5 522 280 457   0 gunzip/1
2738 root     2.7 0.2 0.0 0.0 0.0 0.0  93 3.9 377 147 370   0 gunzip/1
2725 root     2.4 0.2 0.0 0.0 0.0 0.0  95 2.4 495 179 355   0 gunzip/1
2728 root     0.1 1.4 0.0 0.0 0.0 0.0  97 1.7 769  11  2K   0 tar/1
2732 root     0.1 1.3 0.0 0.0 0.0 0.0  99 0.2 762  14  2K   0 tar/1
2723 root     0.0 1.1 0.0 0.0 0.0 0.0  99 0.1 564   7  1K   0 tar/1
```

```
 2731 root      0.3 0.4 0.0 0.0 0.0 0.0  98 1.2 754    3  1K  0 tar/1
 2735 root      0.3 0.4 0.0 0.0 0.0 0.0  98 0.9 722    0  1K  0 tar/1
 2736 root      0.0 0.6 0.0 0.0 0.0 0.0  99 0.0 341    2  1K  0 tar/1
 2726 root      0.3 0.3 0.0 0.0 0.0 0.0  98 1.0 473  145  1K  0 tar/1
 2739 root      0.2 0.2 0.0 0.0 0.0 0.0  99 0.3 335    1 664 0 tar/1
 2749 scromar   0.0 0.1 0.0 0.0 0.0 0.0 100 0.0  23    0 194 0 prstat/1
  337 root      0.0 0.0 0.0 0.0 0.0 0.0 100 0.0   6    0  36  6 xntpd/1
 2716 scromar   0.0 0.0 0.0 0.0 0.0 0.0 100 0.0   3    1  21  0 sshd/1
  124 root      0.0 0.0 0.0 0.0 0.0 0.0 100 0.0   3    0  17  0 picld/4
  119 root      0.0 0.0 0.0 0.0 0.0 0.0 100 0.0  21    0  63  0 nscd/26
Total: 51 processes, 164 lwps, load averages: 4.12, 2.13, 0.88
```

The load average numbers show 1-, 5- and 10-minute averages. (See "Load Averages" below.) Based on this, we can see that we started to get into difficulty in the last 5 minutes or so. (**sar** historical data would back this up.) The LAT numbers show that the gzip threads are waiting for a significant amount of time to get CPU resources. Since LAT is reported in terms of percentage of the time that a thread spends waiting for time on a CPU, 70+% is clearly a problem. Example 7-2 is a classic example of a system whose CPU resources are saturated.

One of the most useful aspects of **prstat -mL** is that it allows us to estimate how much of a speedup could be anticipated if processor resources were not a constraint. For example, if the thread spends something like 50% of its time waiting for a CPU, we might be able to nearly double its performance with a CPU upgrade.

Solaris 10 allows us to directly monitor the amount of time threads wait for a processor via the **prstat -mL** command in the LAT category. This can provide a precise measurement of the percentage of the time a thread spends waiting for a CPU. If the load average is excessive, we can see which processes are being affected by looking at the LAT metrics (see Example 7-2 above).

For non-NFS servers, another danger sign is when the system consistently spends more time in sys than usr mode. (nfsd operates in the kernel in sys mode.) The usual rule of thumb is that a typical usr/sys ratio is in the neighborhood of 70/30 when the system is busy.

System Calls and Context Switching

Another issue to watch for is a high number of system calls per second per processor. With today's faster CPUs, 20,000 would represent a reasonable threshold, though it is higher for faster CPUs. System call rates can be monitored via **sar -c**, syscl in **mpstat** or via DTrace. In particular, large numbers of fork() or exec() calls may represent excessive context switching or process generation. Example 5-6 demonstrated a script to monitor which programs are generating exec() calls with DTrace:

```
#!/usr/sbin/dtrace -s
#pragma D option quiet
syscall::exec*:entry
{
   self->prog = copyinstr(arg0);
   self->exn = execname;
}
syscall::exec*:return
/ self->prog != NULL /
{
   printf ("%-20s %s\n", self->exn, self->prog);
   self->prog = 0;
   self->exn = 0;
}
```

We can also look within a particular process to see which particular functions are being called as in Example 7-3:

Example 7-3. Tracing Function Calls by a Process

```
# dtrace -n 'syscall:::entry /pid == 2926/ { @[probefunc] = count(); }'
dtrace: description 'syscall:::entry ' matched 226 probes
^C

    read                                                        454
    write                                                       559
```

Context switches occur when one thread's context is replaced by another's on a processor. This is a relatively expensive procedure, so it is best to minimize context switches as far as possible. **Voluntary context switches** occur when the thread releases the CPU in order to wait for something like an I/O to complete or a synchronization primitive. **Involuntary context switches** occur when the thread is kicked off of the processor by the scheduler to make way for another thread.

Context switching is monitored by faults/cs in **vmstat** or by csw and icsw in **mpstat**. Of these, the icsw measurement is the most useful, since it measures involuntary context switches. Obviously, if additional processors were available, the involuntary switch would not have been necessary. If our problem process is the victim of too many involuntary context switches, additional CPU resources may help.   Example 7-4 provides examples of **mpstat** output:

Example 7-4. mpstat Output Format

```
#  mpstat
CPU minf mjf xcal  intr ithr  csw icsw migr smtx  srw syscl  usr sys  wt idl
  0    4   4    0   244  142  116    2    0    1    0   163    1   1    0  98
```

DTrace can be tremendously helpful in identifying which specific processes are being context-switched. Example 5-2, for example, discusses using the following DTrace command to find the names of processes undergoing involuntary context switches:

```
dtrace -n 'sysinfo:::inv_swtch /execname != "sched"/ {@icsw[execname]=count();}'
```

We can also look at which particular processes are involved in context switching by using the **cpuwalk.d** program from the DTrace Toolkit. This program reports on how much of the time each process runs on each processor. To look at the actual impact of the context switches, the **cswstat.d** script reports on context switch statistics, along with time consumed and average time per switch.

Example 7-5. cpuwalk.d and cswstat.d Output

```
# ./cpuwalk.d
Sampling... Hit Ctrl-C to end.
^C
...

     PID: 9950      CMD: perl

          value ------------- Distribution ------------- count
            < 0 |                                         0
              0 |@@@@@@@@@@@@                             10
              1 |@@@@@@@@@@@@@@@@@@@@@@@@@@@@@@@@          26
              2 |                                         0
...
# ./cswstat.d
TIME                        NUM      CSWTIME      AVGTIME
2007 May  7 19:01:17        629         5496            8
2007 May  7 19:01:18        624         4668            7
2007 May  7 19:01:19        647         4985            7
```

In a similar vein, we need to look for high levels of migrations (reported by `migr` in **mpstat**). A **migration** occurs when a process's context is moved from one processor to another. Since this involves pulling data into the new processor's cache, it is good to avoid migrations where possible. Solaris has implemented processor affinity code to try to reduce the number of migrations where possible. Large numbers of migrations may help explain why a process runs more slowly than expected.

Cross calls are another thing to watch for in the **mpstat** output (`xcal`). A **cross call** takes place when one CPU requests an action by another CPU via an interrupt or trap. It can be tracked on a per-process basis through the DTrace Toolkit's **xcallsbypid.d** script. Example 7-6 shows what the **xcallsbypid.d** output looks like; it is very easy to see which process is responsible for cross calls.

Example 7-6. Xcallsbypid.d Output

```
# ./xcallsbypid.d
Tracing... Hit Ctrl-C to end.
^C
   PID CMD                  XCALLS
  9796 sshd                      1
 10048 dtrace                    9
     3 fsflush                  12
     0 sched                    27
```

We also need to watch for the number of processes that are blocked while waiting for I/O. `kthr/b` in **vmstat** provides a good window into this problem. Blocked processes often behave in ways that appear processor-bound. Chapter 9 has information on troubleshooting I/O problems.

It is nearly impossible to specify hard-and-fast thresholds for any of these values. The best way to deal with monitoring these measurements is to collect data when the system is functioning well to establish a benchmark for a well-functioning system when things are going well, then compare values when the system is misbehaving.

Processor sets may provide a way to limit migrations and cross calls by limiting the number of CPUs a given process may use. On the other hand, using processor sets in this way is likely to actually reduce performance. Things like context switches, migrations and cross calls are best viewed as an indicator of a problem rather than a statistic that needs to be adjusted directly.

Load Average

Intuitively, the **load average** is an average over time of the number of processes in the run queue. **uptime** reports load averages over 1-, 5-, and 15-minute intervals. Typically, load averages are divided by the number of CPU cores to find the load per CPU. Load averages above 1 per CPU core indicate that the CPUs are fully utilized. Depending on the type of load and the I/O requirements, user-visible performance may not be affected until levels of 2 per core are reached. A general rule of thumb is that load averages persistently more than 4 times the number of CPU cores will result in unacceptably sluggish performance.

Prior to Solaris 10, the calculation algorithm directly computed the load average by periodically sampling the length of the run queue (which is how many statistics are still measured). Since this measurement can be skewed by threads that enter and exit more quickly than the sampling interval, the new algorithm uses microstate accounting instead. Solaris 10 applies an exponential decay algorithm to a combination of high-resolution usr, sys and thread wait times. The numbers are comparable to a traditional load average.

Because the load averages are calculated using microstate accounting, they include all activity on the system. Statistics calculated based on the older `kstat`-style sampling are likely to only sample for very brief periods during each cycle, meaning that important activity may be missed. (In particular, the run queue lengths reported by **sar -q** and **vmstat** are based on periodic sampling, and may miss activity that occurs between sampling intervals.)

The load averages can be monitored intermittently via **uptime** or **prstat**. Over extended time periods, we can look

134

at run queue lengths and the amount of time that the run queue is occupied via `sar -q`. (See Examples 7-1 and 7-2 above.) If necessary, we can run `uptime` to a log file from a `cron` job in order to look at load averages over time.

Threading Effectiveness

Sometimes a multiple CPU system is not used effectively because application threading does not take advantage of the multiple CPUs. An 8-way box may show 12.5% utilization and still be CPU-bound if the application threading is so poor that it can't take advantage of the other seven CPUs.

We can look at `mpstat` output to get some understanding of how well or how poorly application threading is taking place. We can also look at the output of the DTrace Toolkit's `threaded.d` script to see how many concurrent threads the application is usually running.

If the application is poorly threaded, and if it is not locally maintained, there may not be much that we can do (aside from complaining to the vendor). On the other hand, if the application is not going to take advantage of that 8-way box, maybe we should consider replacing it with a single faster CPU and redeploying the big iron to an application that can take advantage of it. Or we can carve it into zones so that other applications can use the idle hardware.

CPU Cache Activity

Caches which may be used by a Solaris CPU include the following:

- **I-Cache**: Level 1 instruction cache.
- **D-Cache**: Level 1 data cache.
- **P-Cache**: Prefetch cache.
- **W-Cache**: Write cache.
- **E-Cache**: Level 2 cache. (The multiple cores on a T1 processor share level 2 cache.)
- **Level 3 Cache**: (Available on the UltraSPARC IV+ processors.)

Low cache hit ratios can be a drag on system performance. Solaris implements code to try to keep processes associated with the same CPU in order to try to maximize cache hits.

Cache hit ratios can be calculated by using the `cpustat` command to monitor the reference and hit rates of the different caches. (The `cputrack` command allows similar functionality on a per-process basis.) Cache monitoring statistics available on a particular CPU can be identified by running cpustat -h, as in Example 7-7:

Example 7-7. CPU Cache Hit Rates

```
# cpustat -h
Usage:
        cpustat [-c events] [-p period] [-nstD] [interval [count]]

        -c events specify processor events to be monitored
        -n        suppress titles
        -p period cycle through event list periodically
        -s        run user soaker thread for system-only events
        -t        include %tick register
        -D        enable debug mode
        -h        print extended usage information

        Use cputrack(1) to monitor per-process statistics.

        CPU performance counter interface: UltraSPARC IIIi & IIIi+

        event specification syntax:
```

```
            [picn=]<eventn>[,attr[n][=<val>]][,[picn=]<eventn>[,attr[n][=<val>]],...]

    event0:  Cycle_cnt Instr_cnt Dispatch0_IC_miss IC_ref DC_rd DC_wr
             EC_ref EC_snoop_inv Dispatch0_br_target Dispatch0_2nd_br
             Rstall_storeQ Rstall_IU_use EC_write_hit_RTO EC_rd_miss
             PC_port0_rd SI_snoop SI_ciq_flow SI_owned SW_count_0
             IU_Stat_Br_miss_taken IU_Stat_Br_count_taken
             Dispatch_rs_mispred FA_pipe_completion MC_read_dispatched
             MC_write_dispatched MC_read_returned_to_JBU
             MC_msl_busy_stall MC_mdb_overflow_stall
             MC_miu_spec_request

    event1:  Cycle_cnt Instr_cnt Dispatch0_mispred EC_wb EC_snoop_cb
             IC_miss_cancelled Re_FPU_bypass Re_DC_miss Re_EC_miss
             IC_miss DC_rd_miss DC_wr_miss Rstall_FP_use EC_misses
             EC_ic_miss Re_PC_miss ITLB_miss DTLB_miss WC_miss
             WC_snoop_cb WC_scrubbed WC_wb_wo_read PC_soft_hit
             PC_snoop_inv PC_hard_hit PC_port1_rd SW_count_1
             IU_Stat_Br_miss_untaken IU_Stat_Br_count_untaken
             PC_MS_misses Re_RAW_miss FM_pipe_completion
             MC_open_bank_cmds MC_reads MC_writes MC_page_close_stall
             Re_DC_missovhd

    attributes: nouser sys

    See the "UltraSPARC IIIi User's Manual" for descriptions of these
    events. Documentation for Sun processors can be found at:
    http://www.sun.com/processors/manuals
# cpustat -c pic0=EC_ref,pic1=EC_misses 5 1
   time cpu event      pic0      pic1
   5.009   0  tick     42650     4510
   5.009   1 total     42650     4510
```

In Example 7-7, we find the number of E-cache references and the number of E-cache misses over the sampling interval. From this, we can calculate the hit ratio:

hits/references = (references – misses)/references = 38140/42650 = .89 (89%)

Brendan Gregg's CacheKit (see "References" at the end of the chapter) includes scripts to automate data collection and processing for a broad variety of CPUs.

At the end of the day, there are few easy options for dealing with a poor cache hit rate on CPUs. We can try to pin a process to a particular processor using processor sets, or we can try to run less stuff on the server to reduce the amount of stuff that is being pulled into cache. We can also consider an upgrade to a CPU with larger cache.

Process Scheduling

In Solaris, highest priorities are scheduled first. Kernel thread scheduling information can be revealed with **ps -elcL**.

A process can exist in one of the following states: running, sleeping or ready.

The Solaris 10 kernel threads model consists of the following major objects:

- **kernel threads**: This is what is scheduled/executed on a processor
- **user threads**: The user-level thread state within a process.

136

- **process**: The object that tracks the execution environment of a program.
- **lightweight process (lwp)**: Execution context for a user thread. Associates a user thread with a kernel thread.

In the Solaris 10 kernel, kernel services and tasks are executed as kernel threads. When a user thread is created, the associated lwp and kernel threads are also created and linked to the user thread.

Solaris Priority Model

The Solaris kernel is fully preemptible. This means that all threads, including the threads that support the kernel's own activities, can be deferred to allow a higher- priority thread to run.

Solaris recognizes 170 different priorities, 0-169. Within these priorities fall a number of different scheduling classes:

- **TS (timeshare)**: This is the default class for processes and their associated kernel threads. Priorities within this class range 0-59, and are dynamically adjusted in an attempt to allocate processor resources evenly.
- **IA (interactive)**: This is an enhanced version of the TS class that applies to the in-focus window in the GUI. Its intent is to give extra resources to processes associated with that specific window. Like TS, IA's range is 0-59.
- **FSS (fair-share scheduler)**: This class is share-based rather than priority- based. Threads managed by FSS are scheduled based on their associated shares and the processor's utilization. FSS also has a range 0-59.
- **FX (fixed-priority)**: The priorities for threads associated with this class are fixed. (In other words, they do not vary dynamically over the lifetime of the thread.) FX also has a range 0-59.
- **SYS (system)**: The SYS class is used to schedule kernel threads. Threads in this class are "bound" threads, which means that they run until they block or complete. Priorities for SYS threads are in the 60-99 range.
- **RT (real-time)**: Threads in the RT class are fixed-priority, with a fixed time quantum. Their priorities range 100-159, so an RT thread will preempt a system thread.

The priority of a process can be adjusted with `priocntl` or `nice`, and the priority of an LWP can be controlled with `priocntl()`.

Fair Share Scheduler

The default user-level scheduling class in Solaris (TS, or "timesharing") attempts to give relatively equal CPU access to all regular processes running on the system. There is some limited ability to regulate process priority using the nice command. The Fair Share Scheduler (FSS) provides a more structured way to manage process priorities.

Each project is allocated a certain number of CPU shares via the `project.cpu-shares` resource control. Each project is allocated CPU time based on a weighted average of the active running projects with a non-zero `cpu-shares` setting. The allocation formula for each project is its `cpu-shares` value divided by the sum of the `cpu-shares` values for all active processes.

> This means that anything with a zero `cpu-shares` value will not be granted CPU time until all projects with non-zero `cpu-shares` are finished with the CPU.

The maximum number of shares that can be assigned to any one project is 65535.

The Fair Share Scheduler can be assigned to processor sets. This allows more sensitive control of priorities on a server than processor sets allow on their own. The `dispadmin` command command controls the assignment of schedulers to processor sets, using a form like:
```
dispadmin -d FSS
```
To enable this change now, rather than after the next reboot, run a command like the following:
```
priocntl -s -c FSS
```

The shares assigned to an active project can be dynamically altered with the **priocntl** command. The command would have a form something like:

```
priocntl -r -n project.cpu-shares -v number-shares -i project project-name
```

The Fair Share Scheduler should not be combined with the TS, FX (fixed-priority) or IA (interactive) scheduling classes on the same CPU or processor set. All of these scheduling classes use priorities in the same range, so unexpected behavior can result from combining FSS with any of these. (There is no problem, however, with running TS and IA on the same processor set.)

To move a specific project's processes into FSS, run something like:

```
priocntl -s -c FSS -i projid project-ID
```

All processes can be moved into FSS by first converting init, then the rest of the processes:

```
priocntl -s -c FSS -i pid 1
priocntl -s -c FSS -i all
```

Scheduler Implementation

The sched provider in DTrace allows us to look at the details of how processes are scheduled on our system. For example, the DTrace Toolkit's **priclass.d** script prints a distribution of thread priorities by scheduling class. Similarly, pridist.d prints a distribution of thread priorities by process. See Example 7-8.

Example 7-8. Scheduler Statistics

```
# /opt/DTT/Bin/priclass.d
Sampling... Hit Ctrl-C to end.
^C

  SYS
          value  ------------- Distribution ------------- count
            < 0 |@@@@@@@@@@@@@@@@@@@@@@@@@@@@@@@@@@@@@@@@@@ 2842
              0 |                                          0
             10 |                                          0
...

  RT
          value  ------------- Distribution ------------- count
             90 |                                          0
            100 |@@@@@@@@@@@@@@@@@@@@@@@@@@@@@@@@@@@@@@@@@@ 1
            110 |                                          0

  TS
          value  ------------- Distribution ------------- count
             20 |                                          0
             30 |@@@@@@@@@@@@@@@@@@@@@@@@@@@@@@@@@@@@@@@@    19
             40 |                                          0
             50 |@@@@                                      2
             60 |                                          0
# /opt/DTT/Bin/pridist.d
Sampling... Hit Ctrl-C to end.
^C
 CMD: sched            PID: 0

          value  ------------- Distribution ------------- count
            < 0 |@@@@@@@@@@@@@@@@@@@@@@@@@@@@@@@@@@@@@@@@@@ 1530
              0 |                                          0
...
```

```
CMD: dtrace          PID: 24211

          value  ------------- Distribution ------------- count
            < 0 |                                              0
              0 |@@@@@@@@@@@@@                                  6
              5 |                                              0
             10 |                                              0
             15 |                                              0
             20 |                                              0
             25 |                                              0
             30 |                                              0
             35 |                                              0
             40 |                                              0
             45 |                                              0
             50 |@@@@@@@@@@@@@@@@@@@@@@@@@@                     12
             55 |@@                                            1
             60 |                                              0
```

Time Slicing for TS and IA

TS and IA scheduling classes implement an adaptive time slicing scheme that increases the priority of I/O-bound processes at the expense of compute-bound processes. The exact values that are used to implement this can be found in the dispatch table. To examine the TS dispatch table, run the command:

```
dispadmin -c TS -g
```

(If units are not specified, **dispadmin** reports time values in ms.)

The following values are reported in the dispatch table:

- **ts_quantum**: This is the default length of time assigned to a process with the specified priority.
- **ts_tqexp**: This is the new priority that is assigned to a process that uses its entire time quantum.
- **ts_slpret**: The new priority assigned to a process that blocks before using its entire time quantum.
- **ts_maxwait**: If a thread does not receive CPU time during a time interval of ts_maxwait, its priority is raised to ts_lwait.
- **ts_lwait**:

The man page for ts_dptbl contains additional information about these parameters.

dispadmin can be used to edit the dispatch table to affect the decay of priority for compute-bound processes or the growth in priority for I/O-bound processes. Obviously, the importance of the different types of processing on different systems will make a difference in how these parameters are tweaked. In particular, ts_maxwait and ts_lwait can prevent CPU starvation, and raising ts_tqexp slightly can slow the decline in priority of CPU-bound processes.

In any case, the dispatch tables should only be altered slightly at each step in the tuning process, and should only be altered at all if you have a specific goal in mind.

The following are some of the sorts of changes that can be made:

- Decreasing ts_quantum favors IA class objects.
- Increasing ts_quantum favors compute-bound objects.
- ts_maxwait and ts_lwait control CPU starvation.
- ts_tqexp can cause compute-bound objects' priorities to decay more or less rapidly.
- ts_slpret can cause I/O-bound objects' priorities to rise more or less rapidly.

RT objects time slice differently in that `ts_tqexp` and `ts_slpret` do not increase or decrease the priority of the

IA objects add 10 to the regular TS priority of the process in the active window. This priority shifts with the focus on the active window.

Each RT thread will execute until its time slice is up or it is blocked while waiting for a resource.

Time Slicing for FSS

In FSS, the **time quantum** is the length of time that a thread is allowed to run before it has to release the processor. This can be checked using
`dispadmin -c FSS -g`

The QUANTUM is reported in ms. (The output of the above command displays the resolution in the RES parameter. The default is 1000 slices per second.) It can be adjusted using **dispadmin** as well. First, run the above command and capture the output to a text file (*filename.txt*). Then run the command:
`dispadmin -c FSS -s filename.txt`

Priority Inheritance

Each thread has two priorities: global priority and inherited priority. The inherited priority is normally zero unless the thread is sitting on a resource that is required by a higher priority thread.

When a thread blocks on a resource, it attempts to "will" or pass on its priority to all threads that are directly or indirectly blocking it. The `pi_willto()` function checks each thread that is blocking the resource or that is blocking a thread in the synchronization chain. When it sees threads that are a lower priority, those threads inherit the priority of the blocked thread. It stops traversing the synchronization chain when it hits an object that is not blocked or is higher priority than the willing thread.

This mechanism is of limited use when considering condition variable, semaphore or read/write locks. In the latter case, an **owner-of-record** is defined, and the inheritance works as above. If there are several threads sharing a read lock, however, the inheritance only works on one thread at a time.

When a resource is freed, all threads awaiting that resource are woken. This results in a footrace to obtain access to that object; one succeeds and the others return to sleep. This can lead to wasted overhead for context switches, as well as a problem with lower priority threads obtaining access to an object before a higher-priority thread. This is called a "**thundering herd**" problem.

Priority inheritance is an attempt to deal with this problem, but some types of synchronization do not use inheritance.

Each synchronization object (lock) contains a pointer to a structure known as a **turnstile**. These contain the data needed to manipulate the synchronization object, such as a queue of blocked threads and a pointer to the thread that is currently using the resource. Turnstiles are dynamically allocated based on the number of allocated threads on the system. A turnstile is allocated by the first thread that blocks on a resource and is freed when no more threads are blocked on the resource.

Turnstiles queue the blocked threads according to their priority. Turnstiles may issue a **signal** to wake up the highest-priority thread, or they may issue a **broadcast** to wake up all sleeping threads.

Real Time (RT) Issues

STREAMS processing is moved into its own kernel threads, which run at a lower priority than RT threads. If an RT thread places a STREAMS request, it may be serviced at a lower priority level than is merited.

Real time processes also lock all their pages in memory. This can cause problems on a system that is underconfigured for the amount of memory that is required.

Since real time processes run at such a high priority, system daemons may suffer if the real time process does not permit them to run.

When a real time process forks, the new process also inherits real time privileges. The programmer must take care to prevent unintended consequences. Loops can also be hard to stop, so the programmer also needs to make sure that the program does not get caught in an infinite loop.

Interrupts

Interrupt levels run between 0 and 15. Some typical interrupts include:

- soft interrupts
- SCSI/FC disks (3)
- Tape, Ethernet
- Video/graphics
- clock() (10)
- serial communications
- real-time CPU clock
- Nonmaskable interrupts (15)

Numbers of interrupts can be monitored using the `intr` and `ithr` columns of the *mpstat* output. `intr` indicates the number of interrupts taken by the associated CPU; `ithr` represents the number of interrupts converted into threads (usually related to incoming network packets, mutex blocking activity or synchronization events).

Resources

- Cockcroft, Adrian and Pettit, Richard. (April 1998) Sun Performance and Tuning: Java and the Internet, 2nd Ed. Prentice Hall.

- Cromar, Scott. (2007) Solaris Troubleshooting and Performance Tuning at Princeton University. Princeton, NJ. (http://www.princeton.edu/~unix/Solaris/troubleshoot/index.html)

- Gregg, Brendan. (March 2006) *CacheKit*. Http://www.brendangregg.com/cachekit.html

- McDougall, Richard and Mauro, Jim. (July 2006) *Solaris Internals*. Upper Saddle River, NJ: Prentice Hall & Sun Microsystems Press.

- McDougall, Richard, Mauro, Jim and Gregg, Brendan. (October 2006) *Solaris Performance and Tools*. Upper Saddle River, NJ: Prentice Hall & Sun Microsystems Press.

- OpenSolaris Project. (October 2006) DTrace Toolkit. (http://www.opensolaris.org/os/community/dtrace/dtracetoolkit/)

- Sun Microsystems. (June 2006) *man pages section 1: User Commands*. Palo Alto, CA: Sun Microsystems, Inc. (http://docs.sun.com/app/docs/doc/816-5165)

- Sun Microsystems. (June 2006) *man pages section 1M: System Administration Commands*. Palo Alto, CA: Sun Microsystems, Inc. (http://docs.sun.com/app/docs/doc/816-5166)

8

Memory and Paging

In the real world, memory shortfalls are much more devastating than having a CPU bottleneck. Two primary indicators of a RAM shortage are the scan rate and swap device activity. Table 8-1 shows some useful commands for monitoring both types of activity.

Table 8-1. Memory Monitoring Commands

Performance Metric	Monitoring Commands
Memory Saturation: Scan Rate	`sar -g` `vmstat`

Memory Saturation: Swap Space Usage and Paging Rates	`vmstat`
	`sar -g`
	`sar -p`
	`sar -r`
	`sar -w`

In both cases, the high activity rate can be due to something that does not have a consistently large impact on performance. The processes running on the system have to be examined to see how frequently they are run and what their impact is. It may be possible to re-work the program or run the process differently to reduce the amount of new data being read into memory.

(**Virtual memory** takes two shapes in a Unix system: physical memory and swap space. **Physical memory** usually comes in DIMM modules and is frequently called RAM. **Swap space** is a dedicated area of disk space that the operating system addresses almost as if it were physical memory. Since disk I/O is much slower than I/O to and from memory, we would prefer to use swap space as infrequently as possible. Memory **address space** refers to the range of addresses that can be assigned, or **mapped**, to virtual memory on the system. The bulk of an address space is not mapped at any given point in time.)

We have to weigh the costs and benefits of upgrading physical memory, especially to accommodate an infrequently scheduled process. If the cost is more important than the performance, we can use swap space to provide enough virtual memory space for the application to run. If adequate total virtual memory space is not provided, new processes will not be able to open. (The system may report "`Not enough space`" or "`WARNING: /tmp:`

142

```
File system full, swap space limit exceeded.")
```

Swap space is usually only used when physical memory is too small to accommodate the system's memory requirements. At that time, space is freed in physical memory by **paging** (moving) it out to swap space. (See "Paging" below for a more complete discussion of the process.)

If inadequate physical memory is provided, the system will be so busy paging to swap that it will be unable to keep up with demand. (This state is known as "thrashing" and is characterized by heavy I/O on the swap device and horrendous performance. In this state, the scanner can use up to 80% of CPU.)

When this happens, we can use the **vmstat -p** command to examine whether the stress on the system is coming from executables, application data or file system traffic. This command displays the number of paging operations for each type of data.

Scan Rate

When available memory falls below certain thresholds, the system attempts to reclaim memory that is being used for other purposes. The **page scanner** is the program that runs through memory to see which pages can be made available by placing them on the free list. The **scan rate** is the number of times per second that the page scanner makes a pass through memory. (The "Paging" section later in this chapter discusses some details of the page scanner's operation.) The page scanning rate is the main tipoff that a system does not have enough physical memory. We can use **sar -g** or **vmstat** to look at the scan rate.

vmstat 30 checks memory usage every 30 seconds. (Ignore the summary statistics on the first line.) If page/sr is much above zero for an extended time, your system may be running short of physical memory. (Shorter sampling periods may be used to get a feel for what is happening on a smaller time scale.)

A very low scan rate is a sure indicator that the system is not running short of physical memory. On the other hand, a high scan rate can be caused by transient issues, such as a process reading large amounts of uncached data. The processes on the system should be examined to see how much of a long-term impact they have on performance. Historical trends need to be examined with **sar -g** to make sure that the page scanner has not come on for a transient, non-recurring reason.

A nonzero scan rate is not necessarily an indication of a problem. Over time, memory is allocated for caching and other activities. Eventually, the amount of memory will reach the lotsfree memory level, and the pageout scanner will be invoked. For a more thorough discussion of the paging algorithm, see "Paging" below.

Swap Device Activity

The amount of disk activity on the swap device can be measured using **iostat**. **iostat -xPnce** provides information on disk activity on a partition-by-partition basis. **sar -d** provides similar information on a per-physical-device basis, and **vmstat** provides some usage information as well. Where Veritas Volume Manager is used, **vxstat** provides per-volume performance information.

If there are I/O's queued for the swap device, application paging is occurring. If there is significant, persistent, heavy I/O to the swap device, a RAM upgrade may be in order.

Process Memory Usage

The **/usr/proc/bin/pmap** command can help pin down which process is the memory hog. **/usr/proc/bin/pmap -x** *PID* prints out details of memory use by a process.

Summary statistics regarding process size can be found in the RSS column of **ps -ly** or **top**.

dbx, the debugging utility in the SunPro package, has extensive memory leak detection built in. The source code will need to be compiled with the -g flag by the appropriate SunPro compiler.

ipcs -mb shows memory statistics for shared memory. This may be useful when attempting to size memory to fit expected traffic.

Segmentation Violations

Segmentation violations occur when a process references a memory address not mapped by any segment. The resulting SIGSEGV signal originates as a major page fault hardware exception identified by the processor and is translated by as_fault() in the address space layer.

When a process overflows its stack, a segmentation violation fault results. The kernel recognizes the violation and can extend the stack size, up to a configurable limit. In a multithreaded environment, the kernel does not keep track of each user thread's stack, so it cannot perform this function. The thread itself is responsible for stack SIGSEGV (stack overflow signal) handling.

(The SIGSEGV signal is sent by the threads library when an attempt is made to write to a write-protected page just beyond the end of the stack. This page is allocated as part of the stack creation request.)

It is often the case that segmentation faults occur because of resource restrictions on the size of a process's stack. See "Resource Management" in Chapter 6 for information about how to increase these limits.

See "Process Virtual Memory" in Chapter 4 for a more detailed description of the structure of a process's address space.

Paging

Solaris uses both common types of paging in its virtual memory system. These types are **swapping** (swaps out all memory associated with a user process) and **demand paging** (swaps out the not recently used pages). Which method is used is determined by comparing the amount of available memory with several key parameters:

- **physmem**: physmem is the total page count of physical memory.

- **lotsfree**: The page scanner is woken up when available memory falls below lotsfree. The default value for this is physmem/64 (or 512 KB, whichever is greater); it can be tuned in the /etc/system file if necessary. The page scanner runs in demand paging mode by default. The initial scan rate is set by the kernel parameter slowscan (which is 100 by default).

- **minfree**: Between lotsfree and minfree, the scan rate increases linearly between slowscan and fastscan. (fastscan is determined experimentally by the system as the maximum scan rate that can be supported by the system hardware. minfree is set to desfree/2, and desfree is set to lotsfree/2 by default.) Each page scanner will run for desscan pages. This parameter is dynamically set based on the scan rate.

- **maxpgio**: maxpgio (default 40 or 60) limits the rate at which I/O is queued to the swap devices. It is set to 40 for x86 architectures and 60 for SPARC architectures. With modern hard drives, maxpgio can safely be set to 100 times the number of swap disks.

- **throttlefree**: When free memory falls below throttlefree (default minfree), the page_create routines force the calling process to wait until free pages are available.

- **pageout_reserve**: When free memory falls below this value (default `throttlefree/2`), only the page daemon and the scheduler are allowed memory allocations.

The **page scanner** operates by first freeing a usage flag on each page at a rate reported as "scan rate" in **vmstat** and **sar -g**. After `handspreadpages` additional pages have been read, the page scanner checks to see whether the usage flag has been reset. If not, the page is swapped out. (`handspreadpages` is set dynamically in current versions of Solaris. Its maximum value is `pageout_new_spread`.)

Solaris 8 introduced an improved algorithm for handling file system page caching (for file systems other than ZFS). This new architecture is known as the **cyclical page cache**. It is designed to remove most of the problems with virtual memory that were previously caused by the file system page cache.

In the new algorithm, the cache of unmapped/inactive file pages is located on a `cachelist` which functions as part of the `freelist`.

When a file page is mapped, it is mapped to the relevant page on the `cachelist` if it is already in memory. If the referenced page is not on the `cachelist`, it is mapped to a page on the `freelist` and the file page is read (or "paged") into memory. Either way, mapped pages are moved to the `segmap` file cache.

Once all other `freelist` pages are consumed, additional allocations are taken from the `cachelist` on a least recently accessed basis. With the new algorithm, file system cache only competes with itself for memory. It does not force applications to be swapped out of primary memory as sometimes happened with the earlier OS versions.

As a result of these changes, **vmstat** reports statistics that are more in line with our intuition. In particular, scan rates will be near zero unless there is a systemwide shortage of available memory. (In the past, scan rates would reflect file caching activity, which is not really relevant to memory shortfalls.)

Every active memory page in Solaris is associated with a **vnode** (which is a mapping to a file) and an **offset** (the location within that file). This references the **backing store** for the memory location, and may represent an area on the swap device, or it may represent a location in a file system. All pages that are associated with a valid `vnode` and offset are placed on the **global page hash list**.

vmstat -p reports paging activity details for applications (executables), data (anonymous) and file system activity.

The parameters listed above can be viewed and set dynamically via **mdb**, as in Example 8-1:

Example 8-1. Paging Parameters

```
# mdb -kw
Loading modules: [ unix krtld genunix specfs dtrace ufs sd ip sctp usba fcp fctl nca lofs
zfs random logindmux ptm cpc fcip sppp crypto nfs ]
> physmem/E
physmem:
physmem:        258887
> lotsfree/E
lotsfree:
lotsfree:       3984
> desfree/E
desfree:
desfree:        1992
> minfree/E
minfree:
minfree:        996
> throttlefree/E
throttlefree:
throttlefree:   996
> fastscan/E
```

```
fastscan:
fastscan:           127499
> slowscan/E
slowscan:
slowscan:           100
> handspreadpages/E
handspreadpages:
handspreadpages:127499
> pageout_new_spread/E
pageout_new_spread:
pageout_new_spread:              161760
> lotsfree/Z fa0
lotsfree:           0xf90              =         0xfa0
> lotsfree/E
lotsfree:
lotsfree:           4000
```

Swap Space

The Solaris virtual memory system combines physical memory with available swap space via swapfs. If insufficient total virtual memory space is provided, new processes will be unable to open.

Swap space can be added, deleted or examined with the **swap** command. **swap -l** reports total and free space for each of the swap partitions or files that are available to the system. Note that this number does not reflect total available virtual memory space, since physical memory is not reflected in the output. **swap -s** reports the total available amount of virtual memory, as does **sar -r**.

If swap is mounted on /tmp via tmpfs, **df -k /tmp** will report on total available virtual memory space, both swap and physical. As large memory allocations are made, the amount of space available to tmpfs will decrease, meaning that the utilization percentages reported by **df** will be of limited use.

The DTrace Toolkit's **swapinfo.d** program prints out a summary of how virtual memory is currently being used. See Example 8-2:

Example 8-2. Virtual Memory Summary

```
# /opt/DTT/Bin/swapinfo.d
RAM _____Total  2048 MB
RAM      Unusable    25 MB
RAM        Kernel   564 MB
RAM        Locked     2 MB
RAM          Used   189 MB
RAM          Free  1266 MB

Disk _____Total  4004 MB
Disk         Resv    69 MB
Disk        Avail  3935 MB

Swap _____Total  5207 MB
Swap         Resv    69 MB
Swap        Avail  5138 MB
Swap     (Minfree)  252 MB
```

Swapping

If the system is consistently below desfree of free memory (over a 30 second average), the **memory scheduler**

146

will start to swap out processes. (ie, if both `avefree` and `avefree30` are less than `desfree`, the swapper begins to look at processes.)

Initially, the scheduler will look for processes that have been idle for `maxslp` seconds. (`maxslp` defaults to 20 seconds and can be tuned in `/etc/system`.) This swapping mode is known as **soft swapping**.

Swapping priorities are calculated for an LWP by the following formula:
`epri = swapin_time - rss/(maxpgio/2) - pri`
where `swapin_time` is the time since the thread was last swapped, `rss` is the amount of memory used by the LWPs process, and `pri` is the thread's priority.

If, in addition to being below `desfree` of free memory, there are two processes in the run queue and paging activity exceeds `maxpgio`, the system will commence **hard swapping**. In this state, the kernel unloads all modules and cache memory that is not currently active and starts swapping out processes sequentially until `desfree` of free memory is available.

Processes are not eligible for swapping if they are:

- In the SYS or RT scheduling class.
- Being executed or stopped by a signal.
- Exiting.
- Zombie.
- A system thread.
- Blocking a higher priority thread.

The DTrace Toolkit provides the **anonpgpid.d** script to attempt to identify the processes which are suffering the most when the system is hard swapping. While this may be interesting, if we are hard-swapping, we need to kill the culprit, not identify the victims. We are better off identifying which processes are consuming how much memory. **prstat -s rss** does a nice job of ranking processes by memory usage. (**RSS** stands for "**resident set size**, " which is the amount of physical memory allocated to a process.)

Example 8-3. Ranking Processes by Memory Usage

```
# prstat -s rss
   PID USERNAME  SIZE   RSS STATE  PRI NICE      TIME  CPU PROCESS/NLWP
   213 daemon     19M   18M sleep   59    0   0:00:12 0.0% nfsmapid/4
     7 root     9336K 8328K sleep   59    0   0:00:04 0.0% svc.startd/14
     9 root     9248K 8188K sleep   59    0   0:00:07 0.0% svc.configd/15
   517 root     9020K 5916K sleep   59    0   0:00:02 0.0% snmpd/1
   321 root     9364K 5676K sleep   59    0   0:00:02 0.0% fmd/14
...
Total: 39 processes, 159 lwps, load averages: 0.00, 0.00, 0.00
```

We may also find ourselves swapping if we are running `tmpfs` and someone places a large file in */tmp*. It takes some effort, but we have to educate our user community that */tmp* is *not* scratch space. It is literally part of the virtual memory space. It may help matters to set up a directory called */scratch* to allow people to unpack files or manipulate data.

System Memory Usage

mdb can be used to provide significant information about system memory usage. In particular, the `::memstat` dcmd, and the **leak** and **leakbuf** walkers may be useful.

- **::memstat** displays a memory usage summary. (See Example 8-4.)

- **walk leak** finds leaks with the same stack trace as a leaked `bufctl` or `vmem_seg`.

- **walk leakbuf** walks buffers for leaks with the same stack trace as a leaked `bufctl` or `vmem_seg`.

Example 8-4. System Memory Usage

```
> ::memstat
Page Summary                Pages                MB  %Tot
------------        ----------------    ----------------  ----
Kernel                      31563               246   12%
Anon                         1523                11    1%
Exec and libs                 416                 3    0%
Page cache                     70                 0    0%
Free (cachelist)            78487               613   30%
Free (freelist)            146828              1147   57%

Total                      258887              2022
Physical                   254998              1992
```

In addition, there are several functions of interest that can be monitored by DTrace:

Table 8-2. Memory Functions

Function Name	Description
page_exists()	Tests for a page with a given vnode and offset.
page_find()	Searches the hash list for a locked page that is known to have a given vnode and offset.
page_first()	Finds the first page on the global page hash list.
page_free()	Frees a page. If it has a vnode and offset, sent to the cachelist, otherwise sent to the freelist.
page_ismod()	Checks whether a page has been modified.
page_isref()	Checks whether a page has been referenced.
page_lock()	Lock a page structure.
page_lookup()	Find a page with the specified vnode and offset. If found on a free list, it will be moved from the freelist.
page_lookup_nowait()	Finds a page representing the specified vnode and offset that is not locked and is not on the freelist.
page_needfree()	Notifies the VM system that pages need to be freed.
page_next()	Next page on the global hash list.
page_release()	Unlock a page structure after unmapping it. Place it back on the cachelist if appropriate.

Function Name	Description
`page_unlock()`	Unlock a page structure.

Kernel Memory UsageSolaris kernel memory is used to provide space for kernel text, data and data structures. Most of the kernel's memory is nailed down and cannot be swapped.

For UltraSPARC and x64 systems, Solaris locks a translation mapping into the MMU's translation lookaside buffer (TLB) for the first 4MB of the kernel's text and data segments. By using large pages in this way, the number of kernel-related TLB entries is reduced, leaving more buffer resources for user code. This has resulted in tremendously improved performance for these environments.

When memory is allocated by the kernel, it is typically not released to the `freelist` unless a severe system memory shortfall occurs. If this happens, the kernel relinquishes any unused memory.

The kernel allocates memory to itself via the `slab`/kmem and `vmem` allocators. (A discussion of the internals of the allocators is beyond the scope of this book, but Chapter 11 of McDougall and Mauro discusses the allocators in detail.)

The kernel memory statistics can be tracked using **sar -k**, and probed using **mdb**'s **::kmastat** dcmd for an overall view of kernel memory allocation. The **kstat** utility allows us to examine a particular cache. Truncated versions of **::kmastat** and **kstat** output are demonstrated in Example 8-5:

Example 8-5. Kernel Memory Allocation

```
# mdb -k
Loading modules: [ unix krtld genunix specfs dtrace ufs sd ip sctp usba fcp fctl nca lofs
zfs random logindmux ptm cpc fcip sppp crypto nfs ]
> ::kmastat
cache                    buf    buf    buf    memory      alloc alloc
name                    size in use  total   in use     succeed fail
----------------------  ------ ------ ------ ---------  --------- -----
kmem_magazine_1             16    274   1016     16384       4569     0
...
bp_map_131072           131072      0      0         0          0     0
memseg_cache               112      0      0         0          0     0
mod_hash_entries            24    187    678     16384     408634     0
...
thread_cache               792    157    170    139264      75907     0
lwp_cache                  904    157    171    155648      11537     0
turnstile_cache             64    299    381     24576      86758     0
cred_cache                 148     50    106     16384      42752     0
rctl_cache                  40    586    812     32768     541859     0
rctl_val_cache              64   1137   1651    106496    1148726     0
...
ufs_inode_cache            368  18526 102740  38256640     275296     0
...
process_cache             3040     38     56    172032      38758     0
...
zfs_znode_cache            192      0      0         0          0     0
----------------------  ------ ------ ------ ---------  --------- -----
Total [static]                                  221184     150707     0
Total [hat_memload]                            7397376    8417187     0
Total [kmem_msb]                               1236992     362278     0
Total [kmem_va]                               42991616       8893     0
Total [kmem_default]                         152576000  112494417     0
Total [bp_map]                                  524288       3387     0
```

149

```
Total  [kmem_tsb_default]                          319488      83391        0
Total  [hat_memload1]                              245760     229486        0
Total  [segkmem_ppa]                                16384        127        0
Total  [umem_np]                                  1048576      11204        0
Total  [segkp]                                   11010048      30423        0
Total  [pcisch2_dvma]                              458752    8891868        0
Total  [pcisch1_dvma]                               98304         11        0
Total  [ip_minor_arena]                               64      13299        0
Total  [spdsock]                                       64          1        0
Total  [namefs_inodes]                                 64         21        0
------------------------ ------ ------ ------ --------- --------- -----

vmem                     memory       memory     memory      alloc alloc
name                     in use        total     import    succeed  fail
------------------------ --------- ---------- --------- --------- -----
heap                   1099614298112 4398046511104          0     20207     0
    vmem_metadata         6619136     6815744   6815744       752     0
        vmem_seg          5578752     5578752   5578752       681     0
        vmem_hash          722560      729088    729088        46     0
        vmem_vmem          295800      346096    311296       106     0
...
ibcm_local_sid                  0  4294967295          0         0     0
------------------------ --------- ---------- --------- --------- -----
> $Q

# kstat -n process_cache
module: unix                          instance: 0
name:    process_cache                class:    kmem_cache
         align                8
         alloc                38785
         alloc_fail           0
         buf_avail            18
         buf_constructed      12
         buf_inuse            38
         buf_max              64
         buf_size             3040
         buf_total            56
         chunk_size           3040
         crtime               28.796560304
         depot_alloc          2955
         depot_contention     0
         depot_free           2965
         empty_magazines      0
         free                 38811
         full_magazines       3
         hash_lookup_depth    1
         hash_rescale         0
         hash_size            64
         magazine_size        3
         slab_alloc           104
         slab_create          9
         slab_destroy         2
         slab_free            54
         slab_size            24576
         snaptime             1233645.2648315
         vmem_source          23
```

Certain aspects of the kernel memory allocation only become possible if the debug flags are enabled in **kmdb** at boot

150

time, as in Example 8-6:

Example 8-6. Enabling Kernel Memory Allocator Debug Flag

```
ok boot kmdb -d
Loading kmdb...

Welcome to kmdb
[0]> kmem_flags/W 0x1f
kmem_flags:   0x0              =              0x1f
[0]> :c
```

If the system crashes while **kmdb** is loaded, it will drop to the **kmdb** prompt rather than the PROM monitor prompt. (This is intended to allow debugging to continue in the wake of a crash.) This is probably not the desired state for a production system, so it is recommended that **kmdb** be unloaded once debugging is complete.

0x1f sets all KMA flags. Individual flags can be set instead by using different values, but I have never run across a situation when it wasn't better to just have them all enabled.

Direct I/O

Large sequential I/O can cause performance problems due to excessive use of the memory page cache. One way to avoid this problem is to use direct I/O on file systems where large sequential I/Os are common.

Direct I/O is usually specified as a mount option in the *vfstab*. The specific file system option will vary based on file system type. For UFS, it is **forcedirectio**.

Resources

- Cockcroft, Adrian and Pettit, Richard. (April 1998) Sun Performance and Tuning: Java and the Internet, 2nd Ed. Prentice Hall.

- Cromar, Scott. (2007) *Solaris Troubleshooting and Performance Tuning at Princeton University*. Princeton, NJ. (http://www.princeton.edu/~unix/Solaris/troubleshoot/index.html)

- McDougall, Richard and Mauro, Jim. (July 2006) *Solaris Internals*. Upper Saddle River, NJ: Prentice Hall & Sun Microsystems Press.

- McDougall, Richard, Mauro, Jim and Gregg, Brendan. (October 2006) *Solaris Performance and Tools*. Upper Saddle River, NJ: Prentice Hall & Sun Microsystems Press.

- OpenSolaris Project. (October 2006) DTrace Toolkit. (http://www.opensolaris.org/os/community/dtrace/dtracetoolkit/)

- Sun Microsystems. (May 2006) *Solaris Tunable Parameters Reference Manual*. Santa Clara, CA: Sun Microsystems, Inc. (http://docs.sun.com/app/docs/doc/817-0404)

9

Disk and File System I/O

System vendors have us brainwashed. For years we have talked about system performance in terms of CPU clock speed. Those of us who are really in the know even understand that we need to look into memory capacity. And everyone understands network bandwidth.

The disk storage subsystem tends to be the poor relation when it comes time to purchase new and nifty hardware. Even Scott McNealy famously referred to enterprise storage as "just disks." (And he was trying to sell them to us!)

Disk storage can be a major contributor to poor system performance. No matter how fast your processors or network, or how much memory you have for temporary storage, if your disks are not up to snuff, your application will suffer.

This chapter takes a look at how to monitor the long-term storage subsystem as a whole to see if a disk performance problem exists. Chapter 10, *Disk Storage Management*, looks at different file system and disk storage options available, as well as providing some hints on how to troubleshoot problems with them.

Table 9-1 contains some of the most useful performance metrics to consider when identifying and troubleshooting disk I/O issues.

Table 9-1. Disk I/O Performance Metrics

Performance Metric	Monitoring Commands

Disk Latency: Service Times per File system	`iostat -xnP`
	`sar -d`
	`vxstat`

Disk Latency: Traffic Levels per File system	`iostat -xnP`
	`sar -d`
	`vxstat`

Disk Space Utilization	`df -k`
	`df -h`
	`du -dsk`

Disk I/O Troubleshooting

What we blithely call a "Disk I/O" is actually made up of several components, each of which may have an impact on overall performance. These layers may be broken down as follows for a typical I/O operation:

- **POSIX:** Application calls a POSIX library interface. (These frequently map directly to system calls, except for the asynchronous interfaces. These latter work via `pread()` and `pwrite()`.)

- **System Call:** The relevant **vnode** (unique file identifier) and **vfs** (virtual file system) calls are:

  vnode system calls: `close()`, `creat()`, `fsync()`, `ioctl()`, `link()`, `mkdir()`, `open()`, `read()`, `rename()`, `rmdir()`, `seek()`, `unlink()` and `write()`

  vfs system calls: `mount()`, `statfs()`, `sync()` and `umount()`

- **VOP:** The vnode operations interface is the architectural layer between the system calls and the file systems. DTrace provides the best way to examine this layer. Starting in version 0.96, the DTrace Toolkit's **vopstat** command allows direct monitoring at this level.

- **File systems:** This chapter includes some discussion of file system tuning and file system caching for UFS and NFS file systems. (ZFS will be discussed in Chapter 10.)

- **Physical Disk I/O:** This is the portion of the I/O that involves the transfer of data to or from the physical hardware. Traditionally, I/O troubleshooting focuses on this portion of the I/O process.

The best way to see if I/O is a problem is to examine the service times reported by **iostat** or **sar-d**. The **service time** is the amount of time from the issuing of the I/O request until its completion. In particular, use **iostat -xnP 30** during busy times to look at the I/O characteristics of your devices. Ignore the first bunch of output (the first group of output is summary statistics), and look at the output every 30 seconds. If you are seeing svc_t (service time) values of more than 20 ms on disks that are in use (more than, say, 10% busy), then the end user will see noticeably sluggish performance.

> Service times may be reported incorrectly if the disks are not busy. This is due to sampling error or to random I/Os from the `fsflush` routine. The service time numbers should only be taken seriously if there is a reasonable level of traffic on the disks.

Example 9-1 shows a system whose disks are being flooded with traffic. Note that the service times (`avserv` and `wsvc_t + asvc_t`, respectively) are showing numbers indicating a severe I/O bottleneck. Looking at the level of traffic (`blks/s` and `kw/s`, respectively), the culprit is clearly writing to slice 7 of disk 0.

Example 9-1. High Service Times

```
# sar -d 5 20

SunOS soltest 5.10 Generic_118833-17 sun4u    01/30/2007

19:51:06   device        %busy   avque   r+w/s   blks/s   avwait   avserv
19:51:11   nfs1              0     0.0       0        0      0.0      0.0
           sd0             100    40.2     101   136685      0.0    398.6
           sd0,a             0     0.0       0        1      0.0      8.2
           sd0,b             0     0.0       0        0      0.0      0.0
           sd0,c             0     0.0       0        0      0.0      0.0
           sd0,d             0     0.0       0        0      0.0      0.0
           sd0,g             0     0.0       0        0      0.0      0.0
           sd0,h           100    40.2     101   136684      0.0    399.4
...
# iostat -xnP 10
...
```

```
                 extended device statistics
    r/s    w/s   kr/s    kw/s wait actv wsvc_t asvc_t  %w  %b device
    0.3    0.0    1.9     0.0  0.0  0.3    0.0 1092.5   0  33 c1t0d0s0
    0.0    0.0    0.0     0.0  0.0  0.0    0.0    0.0   0   0 c1t0d0s1
    0.0    0.0    0.0     0.0  0.0  0.0    0.0    0.0   0   0 c1t0d0s2
    0.0    0.0    0.0     0.0  0.0  0.0    0.0    0.0   0   0 c1t0d0s3
    0.3    0.0    2.0     0.0  0.0  0.0    0.0   27.4   0   1 c1t0d0s6
    0.1   89.7    0.8 62467.8  0.0 49.1    0.0  546.8   0  99 c1t0d0s7
    0.0    0.0    0.0     0.0  0.0  0.0    0.0    0.0   0   0 c1t1d0s0
    0.0    0.0    0.0     0.0  0.0  0.0    0.0    0.0   0   0 c1t1d0s1
    0.0    0.0    0.0     0.0  0.0  0.0    0.0    0.0   0   0 c1t1d0s2
    0.0    0.0    0.0     0.0  0.0  0.0    0.0    0.0   0   0 c1t1d0s3
    0.0    0.0    0.0     0.0  0.0  0.0    0.0    0.0   0   0 c1t1d0s6
    0.0    0.0    0.0     0.0  0.0  0.0    0.0    0.0   0   0 c1t1d0s7
    0.0    0.0    0.0     0.0  0.0  0.0    0.0    0.0   0   0 soltest:vold(pid317)
```

The first batch of **iostat** data represents summary statistics since boot time. The second bunch is where **iostat** starts reporting on the current state of the system.

The items reported by **sar -d** are: device name, percentage of the time the device is busy, average I/O queue length (avque), numbers of I/Os (both reads and writes) per second (r+w/s), the number of blocks per second (blks/s), the average wait time (avwait) and the average service time (avserv).

The items reported by **iostat -xnP** are: reads and writes per second (r/s and w/s), kilobytes read and written per second (kr/s, kw/s), the average wait queue length (wait), the average number of requests actively being serviced (actv), the average time spent in the wait queue (wsvc_t), the average service time once the request begins to be processed (asvc_t), the percentage of time the wait queue is non-empty (%w), the percentage of the time that transactions are underway (%b), and the disk slice name.

Another way to see if I/O is a problem is to look at the amount of time spent on I/O-related library and system calls. There are advantages to this way of looking at things. It more closely mirrors what applications are actually seeing, rather than focusing too closely on what the OS sees.

For example, the DTrace Toolkit's **procsystime** utility tracks time spent on each system call, **iotop** can identify processes which are heavy I/O users, and the **dtruss -t _syscall_ -p _PID_** command can examine the time spent on a particular system call for a process. (The **truss -D -p _PID_** command also reveals the time spent by a process in I/O system calls, but it imposes a severe performance penalty.) The **pfilestat** utility in the current versions of the Toolkit also gives an indication of how much time a process spends on different I/O-related system calls. Example 9-2 shows a process which is spending most of its time processing I/O-related service calls. Based on the output, we can see that the **mkfile** on _/export/home/tempfile1_ is saturating the disk subsystem.

Example 9-2. Excessive Time on I/O Service Calls

```
# /opt/DTT/Bin/procsystime
Hit Ctrl-C to stop sampling...
^C

Elapsed Times for all processes,

          SYSCALL        TIME (ns)
            gtime             8916
        sigaction             9417
             pset            11416
            fstat            11833
             mmap            25083
            close            28334
```

```
            setcontext             35250
                   read            52834
               schedctl            53500
            lwp_sigmask            58334
               p_online            68001
               sysconfig           74416
                   open            90832
                   stat           110083
                    brk           308084
                  ioctl           594083
              sigsuspend        999838999
                  write         1941131414
               lwp_park         2172252498
                 pollsys         2176752997
# /opt/DTT/Bin/iotop -oC 10
Tracing... Please wait.
2007 Jan 30 20:15:14,  load: 3.11,  disk_r:       0 KB,  disk_w: 637121 KB

  UID     PID   PPID CMD                   DEVICE  MAJ MIN D      DISKTIME
    0       0      0                       sd0      32   0           3732
    0       0      0 sched                 sd0      32   0 W        28894
    0       0      0                       sd0      32   7         96410
    0       0      0 sched                 sd0      32   7 W       699216
    0   17659  15744 mkfile                sd0      32   7 W      8950257
# ./pfilestat 17659
     STATE   FDNUM      Time Filename
    waitcpu      0        1%
    running      0       21%
    sleep-w      0       28%
      write      3       47% /export/home/tempfile1

     STATE   FDNUM      KB/s Filename
      write      3      63289 /export/home/tempfile1


Total event time (ms): 4933   Total Mbytes/sec: 60
```

The **iotop -oC** command reports on the following information: 1-minute load average (load), kilobytes read (disk_r), kilobytes written (disk_w), UID, PID, PPID, process command name (CMD), device, major and minor numbers (MAJ and MIN), read vs write (D) and total time to complete disk requests (DISKTIME).

The **pfilestat** utility displays the STATE, file descriptor number (FDNUM), wall clock time in each state (Time) and Filename.

If the system call statistics reveal a persistent problem, we should look at ways of restructuring the I/O or increasing the speed of our disk channel. We can check the **sar -d** historical statistics to see if our current difficulties are due to a transient spike in usage or a long-term trend.

Disk I/O Utilization

If a disk is more than 60% busy over sustained periods of time, this can indicate overuse of that resource. The DTrace Toolkit provides a way to directly measure disk utilization via the **iotop -CP** command. This command shows UIDs, process IDs and device names, which can help identify a culprit. (The **-C** option provides a rolling output rather than having it clear at each time step. The **-P** option shows the %I/O utilization.)

The **iostat** statistic %b provides a reasonable measure for utilization of regular disk resources. (The same statistic can be viewed via **iostat -D** in Solaris 10.) Utilization measured by **iostat** may not take into account the usage pattern, the fact that disk array utilization numbers are almost impossible to interpret correctly, or whether application effects are adequately handled by I/O caching.

Examples 9-3 shows disks with high utilization, as measured with `iotop`. Example 9-1 above shows a disk with high utilization as measured by `iostat`.

Example 9-3. Measuring Disk Utilization with iotop -CP

```
# /opt/DTT/Bin/iotop -CP 10
Tracing... Please wait.

2007 Jan 30 20:30:31,  load: 0.19,  disk_r:    24 KB,  disk_w: 651580 KB

  UID    PID   PPID CMD            DEVICE  MAJ MIN D   %I/O
    0  17745  17744 dtrace         sd0      32   0 R      0
    0      0      0 sched          sd0      32   0 W      0
    0      0      0 sched          sd0      32   7 W      3
    0  17743  15744 mkfile         sd0      32   7 W     95
```

`iotop -CP` shows similar information to what we saw in Example 9-2. The main difference is that we see the amount of time each of these processes is spending on I/O requests (`%I/O`).

At the end of the day, service times are the keys to seeing whether a high utilization is actually causing a problem.

Disk I/O Saturation

A high disk saturation (as measured via `iostat`'s `%w`) always causes some level of performance impact, since I/Os are forced to queue up. Even if the disk is not saturated now, it is useful to look at throughput numbers and compare them to the expected maximums to make sure that there is adequate head room for unusually high activity. (We can measure the maximum directly by doing something like a `dd` or `mkfile` and looking at the reported throughput.)

If `iostat` consistently reports `%w` > 5, the disk subsystem is too busy. In this case, one thing that can be done is to reduce the size of the wait queue by setting `sd_max_throttle` to 64. (The `sd_max_throttle` parameter determines how many jobs can be queued up on a single HBA, and is set to 256 by default. If the `sd_max_throttle` threshold is exceeded, it will result in a `transport failure` error message.)

Reducing `sd_max_throttle` is a temporary quick fix. Its primary effect is to keep things from getting quite so backed up and spiraling out of control. A more permanent structural remedy needs to be implemented.

A possible cause for a persistently high `%w` is SCSI starvation, where low SCSI ID devices receive a lower precedence than a higher-numbered device (such as a tape drive). Where possible, tape drives should be segregated on their own SCSI channel.

Another indication of a saturated disk I/O subsystem is when the blocked threads (`kthr/b`) section of **vmstat** persistently reports a number that is comparable to the run queue (`kthr/r`).

The DTrace Toolkit's `iotop -o 10` command shows disk I/O time summaries. Each process's UID, process ID and device names are shown, along with the number of nanoseconds of disk time spent. This can help us to identify the heavy hitters on a saturated disk.

Example 9-2 (above) shows measurements of disk saturation with `iotop -o`.

Disk I/O Usage Pattern

It is useful to know whether our I/O is predominantly random or sequential. Sequential I/O is typical of large file reads and writes, and typically involves operating on one block immediately after its neighbor. With this type of

156

I/O, there is little penalty associated with the disk drive head having to move to a new location. Random I/O, on the other hand, involves large numbers of seeks and rotations, and is usually much slower.

Disk I/O can be investigated to find out whether it is primarily random or sequential. If `sar -d` reports that $(blks/s) / (r+w/s) < 16Kb$ (~32 blocks), the I/O is predominantly random. If the ratio is $> 128Kb$ (~256 blocks), it is predominantly sequential. This analysis may be useful when examining alternative disk configurations.

The DTrace Toolkit provides us a way to directly measure seek times using the `seeksize.d` script. If there are large numbers of large seeks, it indicates that our physical drives are spending a lot of time moving heads around rather than reading or writing data. The DTrace Toolkit's `iopattern` utility provides system-wide information about Disk I/O usage patterns. Example 9-4 shows samples of `seeksize.d` and `iopattern` output.

Example 9-4. Disk I/O Usage Patterns

```
# /opt/DTT/Bin/iopattern
%RAN %SEQ  COUNT    MIN     MAX      AVG      KR     KW
  76   24    316   1024  303104    23970   7397      0
  74   26    182   1024  647168    41168   7317      0
  81   19   1100   1024 1048576     6061   6511      0
  73   27     30   1024 1048576   205858   6031      0
# /opt/DTT/Bin/seeksize.d
Tracing... Hit Ctrl-C to end.
^C

     PID  CMD
   17937  tar cf - /\0

          value  ------------- Distribution ------------- count
             -1 |                                             0
              0 |@@@@@@@@@@@@@@@@@@@@@@@@@@@@@@@@@@@@@@@@@     13
              1 |                                             0
              2 |                                             0
              4 |                                             0
              8 |                                             0
             16 |                                             0
             32 |                                             0
             64 |@@@                                          1
            128 |                                             0
            256 |                                             0
            512 |                                             0
           1024 |                                             0
           2048 |                                             0
           4096 |                                             0
           8192 |                                             0
          16384 |                                             0
          32768 |                                             0
          65536 |                                             0
         131072 |@@@                                          1
         262144 |                                             0
```

`iopattern` provides the following output: percentage of I/O events that are random (`%RAN`), percentage of events that are sequential (`%SEQ`), number of I/O events (`COUNT`), minimum/maximum/average I/O event size (`MIN`, `MAX`, `AVG`) and kilobytes read and written (`KR`, `KW`). The `iopattern -m /filesystem` command only looks at I/Os on a particular file system.

To identify the culprit, the DTrace Toolkit contains a script called `bitesize.d`, which provides a graph of I/O sizes carried out by each process. If there are a large number of small I/Os, the pattern is predominantly random. If there are mostly large I/Os, the process is exhibiting sequential behavior. Example 9-5 shows how information is presented by **bitesize.d**

Example 9-5. I/O Sizes by Process

```
# /opt/DTT/Bin/bitesize.d
Tracing... Hit Ctrl-C to end.
^C

     PID  CMD
   15736  /usr/lib/ssh/sshd\0

          value  ------------- Distribution ------------- count
           4096 |                                         0
           8192 |@@@@@@@@@@@@@@@@@@@@@@@@@@@@@@@@@@@@@@@@@@ 1
          16384 |                                         0

   17937  tar cf - /\0

          value  ------------- Distribution ------------- count
           1024 |                                         0
           2048 |@@@@                                     14
           4096 |@@@@@@                                   22
           8192 |@@@@@@@@@@@@@@@@@                        57
          16384 |                                         1
          32768 |@@@                                      9
          65536 |@@@@@@                                   21
         131072 |                                         0
         262144 |@                                        3
         524288 |@@@@                                     16
        1048576 |                                         0
```

DTrace also provides a way to track which files are accessed how often. The "args2->fi_pathname" value from the io provider gives us a handle into this. For example, we could use a one-liner like:

**dtrace -n 'io:::start { printf("%6s %-12s %6s", pid, execname **

args[2]->fi_pathname); } '

to provide raw data for further processing, or we could use an aggregation to collect statistics. The DTrace Toolkit's **iosnoop** program provides a flexible way to collect this sort of information. The **-n** option provides information for a particular process name, as in Example 9-6. The **-D** option presents the elapsed (DELTA) time, and **-o** presents the disk start to completion time (DTIME). The **-m** option allows us to specify a file system of interest.

Example 9-6. Tracing I/Os by a Program

```
# /opt/DTT/Bin/iosnoop -Do -n sshd
DELTA      DTIME      UID    PID D    BLOCK     SIZE    COMM PATHNAME
8050       8078         0   1186 R  3396128     8192    sshd /usr/lib/ssh/sshd
7751       7767         0   1186 R    72736     8192    sshd <none>
2016       2031         0   1186 R    77296     8192    sshd <none>
5608       5631         0  17958 R   302606     1024    sshd /etc/hosts.allow
...
```

Disk Errors

iostat -eE reports on disk error counts since the last reboot. Keep in mind that several types of events (such as ejecting a CD or some volume manager operations) are counted in this output. Once these error messages rise above 10 in any category, further investigation is warranted. Example 9-7 shows what the disk error reports look like.

158

Node that `sd1` is reporting several different types of errors. The script in Example 9-8 gives a brief rundown of what these different errors mean.

Example 9-7. Disk Errors

```
# iostat -Ee
          ---- errors ---

md0         0    0    0    0
md1         0    0    0    0
md2         0    0    0    0
md10        0    0    0    0
md11        0    0    0    0
md12        0    0    0    0
md20        0    0    0    0
md21        0    0    0    0
md22        0    0    0    0
md30        0    0    0    0
md31        0    0    0    0
md32        0    0    0    0
md40        0    0    0    0
md41        0    0    0    0
md42        0    0    0    0
sd0         0    0    0    0
sd1       592   28    1  621
sd0      Soft Errors: 0 Hard Errors: 0 Transport Errors: 0
Vendor: SEAGATE  Product: ST373307LSUN72G  Revision: 0707 Serial No: 3HZ...
Size: 73.40GB <73400057856 bytes>
Media Error: 0 Device Not Ready: 0 No Device: 0 Recoverable: 0
Illegal Request: 0 Predictive Failure Analysis: 0
sd1      Soft Errors: 592 Hard Errors: 28 Transport Errors: 1
Vendor: SEAGATE  Product: ST373307LSUN72G  Revision: 0707 Serial No: 3HZ...
Size: 73.40GB <73400057856 bytes>
Media Error: 24 Device Not Ready: 0 No Device: 1 Recoverable: 592
Illegal Request: 0 Predictive Failure Analysis: 1
```

It is relatively straightforward to run a job out of `cron` to check the output of the `iostat` error checking and send out alerts when the error rate increments. Example 9-8 shows what such a script might look like.

Example 9-8. Disk Error Checking Script

```
#!/bin/sh
# Script to report on disk errors.
# Email notification sent to $NOTIFY.
#
DISKERRS=/usr/local/etc/tmp/diskerr
OUTFILE=/usr/local/etc/tmp/diskerrout
IOSTAT=/usr/local/etc/tmp/diskerriostat
LOGFILE=/var/adm/diskerr
NOTIFY=root; export NOTIFY

if [ ! -d /usr/local/etc/tmp ]; then
    echo "create scratch directory /usr/local/etc/tmp"
    exit 3
fi

# Remove old files if necessary; touch to prevent errors upon cleanup.
rm -f /usr/local/etc/diskerr*
touch ${DISKERRS} ${OUTFILE} ${IOSTAT}
```

```
# iostat -E output
if [ -s ${DISKERRS} ]; then
    /usr/bin/iostat -nE > ${IOSTAT}
    cat ${DISKERRS} | awk '{print $6}' | while read DISK
    do
        LINE=`cat ${IOSTAT} | grep -n ${DISK} | awk -F: '{print $1}'`
        PREVLINE=`expr ${LINE} - 1`
        cat ${IOSTAT} | sed -e 1,${PREVLINE}d | sed -e 7,\$d >> ${OUTFILE}
        echo >> ${OUTFILE}
    done
    echo "Recoverable Errors: Service time increased; no data lost." >> ${OUTFILE}
    echo "Predictive Failure: Drive failing; replace ASAP." >> ${OUTFILE}
    echo "Device not Ready: Device offline or dead." >> ${OUTFILE}
    echo "Media Error: Severe disk problems." >> ${OUTFILE}
    echo "Illegal Request: Possible driver or software failure." >> ${OUTFILE}
fi


# If the LOGFILE does not exist, create it.
if [ ! -f ${LOGFILE} ]; then
    rm -rf ${LOGFILE}
    touch ${LOGFILE}
fi

# See if the output has changed from the previous report.
# If it has, overwrite the log file and send another report.
DIFF=`diff ${LOGFILE} ${OUTFILE} | wc -l`

if [ ${DIFF} -lt 1 ]; then
#   echo "okay"
    exit 0
else
    /usr/ucb/Mail -s "`uname -n` Disk Errors" ${NOTIFY} < ${OUTFILE}
    cp ${OUTFILE} ${LOGFILE}
fi

# Clean up
rm ${DISKERRS} ${OUTFILE} ${IOSTAT}
```

This particular script is stripped down for illustration purposes. Among other things, it will send an alert whenever a CD is inserted or ejected, since such events will show up on the CD drive. It also typically shows a small number of recoverable soft errors on reboot when disk mirroring software is used.

Resolving I/O Performance Problems

The usual solutions to a disk I/O problem are:

- Check file system kernel tuning parameters to make sure that DNLC and inode caches are working appropriately. (See "File System Caching" below.)
- Spread out the I/O traffic across more disks. This can be done in hardware if the I/O subsystem includes a RAID controller, or in software by striping the file system (using Solaris Volume Manager/DiskSuite, Veritas Volume Manager or ZFS), by splitting up the data across additional file systems on other disks, or even splitting the data across other servers. (In extreme cases, you can even consider striping data over only the outermost cylinders of several otherwise empty disk drives in order to maximize throughput.) Cockroft and

Pettit recommend 128KB as a good stripe width for most applications. In an ideal world, the stripe width would be an integer divisor of the average I/O size to split the traffic over all disks in the stripe.

- Redesign the problematic process to reduce the number of disk I/Os. (Caching is one frequently-used strategy, either via `cachefs` or application-specific caching.)

- The **write throttle** can be adjusted to provide better performance if there are large amounts of sequential write activity. The parameters in question are `ufs:ufs_HW` and `ufs:ufs_LW`. These are very sensitive and should not be adjusted too far at one time. When `ufs_WRITES` is set to 1 (default), the write throttle is enabled. When the number of outstanding writes exceeds `ufs_HW`, writes are suspended until the number of outstanding writes drops below `ufs_LW`. Both can be increased where large numbers of sequential writes are occurring.

- `tune_t_fsflushr` sets the number of seconds after which `fsflush` will run `autoup` dictates how frequently each bit of memory is checked. Setting `fsflush` to run less frequently can also reduce disk activity, but it does run the risk of losing data that has been written to memory. These parameters can be adjusted using **mdb** while looking for an optimum value, then set the values in the */etc/system* file.

- Check for SCSI starvation; i.e., for busy high-numbered SCSI devices (such as tape drives) that have a higher priority than lower-numbered devices.

- Database I/O should be done to raw disk partitions or file systems mounted with direct I/O.

- In some cases, it may be worthwhile to move frequently-accessed data to the outer edge of a hard drive. In the outer cylinders, the read and write rates are higher.

- It may be worthwhile to match observed and configured I/O sizes by tuning `maxphys` and `maxcontig`.

Physical disk I/O is usually the focus of I/O troubleshooting sessions. McDougall, Mauro and Gregg suggest that it is more appropriate to focus on overall service times of I/O related system calls. (As noted above, the DTrace Toolkit's **procsystime** utility tracks time spent on each system call, the **dtruss -t *syscall* -p *PID*** command can examine the time spent on a particular system call for a process, and the **pfilestat** utility gives an indication of how much time a process spends on different I/O-related system calls.)

This approach allows end-to-end monitoring of the important portions of the I/O process. The traditional approach ignores performance problems introduced by the file system itself.

File system latency may come from any of the following:

- **Disk I/O wait**: This may be as short as zero, in the event of a read cache hit. For a synchronous I/O event, this can be reduced by restructuring disk storage or by altering caching parameters. Disk I/O wait can be monitored systemwide from **sar -d** or **iostat** (see Example 9-1) or directly through **dtrace**, including through the `wait-start` and `wait-done` probes in the `io` provider. The DTrace Toolkit traces wait time directly on a file-by-file basis with `iofile.d`.

- **File system cache misses**: These include block, buffer, metadata and name lookup caches. These may be adjustable by increasing the size of the relevant caches.

- **I/Os being broken into multiple pieces**, incurring the penalty of additional operations. This may be a result of the maximum cluster size for the file system or the OS.

- **File system locking**: Most file systems have per-file reader/writer locks. This can be most significant when there is a large file (like a database file) where reads have to wait for writes to a different portion of the file. Direct I/O is a mechanism for bypassing this limitation.

- **Metadata updating**: Creations, renames, deletions and some file extensions cause some extra latency to allow for updates to file system metadata.

The DTrace Toolkit's **vopstat** command allows monitoring of the number and duration of operations at the VOP level. (**VOP** is the architectural layer between the system calls and the file systems, so it is at a high enough level to provide interesting information.) Most of the functions are named in a way that makes it clear what they are doing; the output should at least make it clear where we are spending most of our time during I/Os. (*Solaris Internals*, by McDougall and Mauro, is an excellent resource for people who want to know exactly how these pieces fit together.)

161

Example 9-9 shows what the output of **vopstat** looks like.

Example 9-9. File System Latency Monitoring

```
# /opt/DTT/Bin/vopstat
VOP Physical IO                                              Count
fop_pageio                                                      1
fop_putpage                                                     1
fop_setsecattr                                                 1
fop_getpage                                                    29

VOP Count                                                    Count
fop_mkdir                                                       1
fop_pageio                                                      1
fop_setsecattr                                                 1
fop_fsync                                                       3
fop_putpage                                                     3
fop_setattr                                                     3
fop_readdir                                                     4
fop_pathconf                                                    5
fop_frlock                                                      7
fop_create                                                      8
fop_getsecattr                                                 10
fop_setfl                                                      11
fop_write                                                      76
fop_seek                                                       77
fop_poll                                                      103
fop_inactive                                                  105
fop_realvp                                                    105
fop_open                                                      151
fop_readlink                                                  166
fop_access                                                    167
fop_read                                                      216
fop_close                                                     225
fop_ioctl                                                     257
fop_rwunlock                                                  315
fop_rwlock                                                    316
fop_delmap                                                    328
fop_dispose                                                   407
fop_getattr                                                   419
fop_addmap                                                    571
fop_cmp                                                       755
fop_getpage                                                  1689
fop_lookup                                                   2596

VOP Wall Time                                             mSeconds
fop_poll                                                       0
fop_open                                                       0
fop_access                                                     0
fop_readlink                                                   1
fop_close                                                      1
fop_rwunlock                                                   1
fop_rwlock                                                     1
fop_delmap                                                     1
fop_getattr                                                    2
fop_dispose                                                    2
fop_write                                                      2
fop_addmap                                                     2
```

```
fop_ioctl                                              2
fop_cmp                                                3
fop_setsecattr                                         4
fop_putpage                                            9
fop_pageio                                            10
fop_lookup                                            14
fop_read                                             118
fop_getpage                                          119
```

File System Caching

The idea behind caching is that the most frequently accessed information should be located on the fastest available storage. There are several places where data can be stored. It can be stored in the CPU cache (which can be accessed extremely quickly), main system memory (still very fast), the system hard drive (not very fast) or the network (downright slow).

But if we are going to store stuff in cache, we need to make sure that our **hit ratio** (the percentage of the time that we find what we are looking for in cache) is high enough to make it worth the trouble. Every time we look for something in a cache and don't find it, it is called a **cache miss**. The miss actually costs us time, since we waste cycles looking for the data where it isn't rather than finding it where it is. The cache is only worth the effort if our hit ratio is high enough that we save more time than we waste on the cache misses.

There are several types of cache used by the Solaris file systems to cache name and attribute lookups. These are:

- **DNLC (Directory Name Lookup Cache)**: This cache stores vnode to path directory lookup information, preventing the need to perform directory lookups on the fly.
- **inode cache**: This cache stores logical metadata information about files (size, access time, etc). It is a linked list that stores the UFS inodes.
- **rnode cache**: This is maintained on NFS clients to store information about NFS-mounted nodes. In addition, an NFS attribute cache stores logical metadata information.
- **buffer cache**: The buffer cache stores inode, indirect block and cylinder group-related disk I/O. This references the physical metadata (eg block placement in the file system), as opposed to the logical metadata that is stored in other caches.

(Note that cache statistics will be skewed by things that walk the directory tree like `find`.)

The block cache provides performance enhancement by using otherwise idle memory in the page cache to keep copies of recently requested information. Cache hits in the block cache obviously have a huge performance advantage.

ZFS uses an adaptive replacement cache (ARC) rather than using the page cache for file data (like most other file systems do).

Directory Name Lookup Cache

The DNLC stores directory vnode/path translation information. It is managed as a least recently used cache to keep the hit rate as high as possible for frequently accessed objects.

For our purposes, the most important number is the `hits` and `misses` statistics in **kstat -n dnlcstats**, or the `name lookups/cache hits` line of **vmstat -s**. A good rule of thumb is that if the cache hit percentage ($hits/(hits + misses)$) is not above 90%, the DNLC should be resized. (Unless the activity profile is such that we would not expect a good hit ratio, as is the case with large numbers of file creations, or `find` commands combing the file systems.)

We can also look at the output of the DTrace Toolkit's **dnlcps.d** program to determine the effect of DNLC misses on each process or **dnlcsnoop.d** to look at the specific file lookups and whether or not they were cache hits.

DNLC size is determined by the ncsize kernel parameter. By default, this is set to (68x maxusers)+360. It is not recommended that it be set any higher than a value which corresponds to a maxusers value of 4096 . This can be viewed via mdb -k by querying ncsize/D

To set ncsize, add a line to the */etc/system* as follows:
set ncsize=10000

The DNLC can be disabled by setting ncsize to a non-positive number.

Example 9-10 shows how to check the DNLC hit rate. In this case, the DNLC cache hit percentage is 95%.

Example 9-10. DNLC Hit Rate

```
# kstat -n dnlcstats
module: unix                              instance: 0
name:   dnlcstats                         class:    misc
        ...
        hits                              146337352
        misses                            7407351
        negative_cache_hits               276030
        ...
# vmstat -s
  ...
153757566 total name lookups (cache hits 95%)
  ...
# /opt/DTT/Bin/dnlcps.d
Tracing... Hit Ctrl-C to end.
^C
 CMD: picld             PID: 124

           value  ------------- Distribution ------------- count
               0 |                                         0
             >= 1 |@@@@@@@@@@@@@@@@@@@@@@@@@@@@@@@@@@@@@@@@@@ 8
# /opt/DTT/Bin/dnlcsnoop.d
  PID CMD             TIME HIT PATH
  124 picld              7  Y  /devices
  124 picld              1  Y  /devices
  124 picld              2  Y  /devices
  124 picld              1  Y  /devices
  124 picld              2  Y  /devices
  124 picld              1  Y  /devices
  124 picld              1  Y  /devices
  124 picld              1  Y  /devices
```

Inode Cache

The inode cache is a linked list that stores the inodes that have been accessed.

sar -g reports %ufs_ipg, which is the percentage of inodes that were overwritten while still having active pages in memory. If this number is consistently nonzero, the inode cache should be increased.

By default, the inode cache size (ufs_ninode) is set to the same as ncsize, unless otherwise specified in the */etc/system* file. As with ncsize, it is not recommended that ufs_ninode be set any higher than a value which corresponds to a ncsize for a maxusers value of 4096.

`kstat -n ufs_inode_cache` reports on inode cache statistics.

While resizing the inode cache, it is important to remember that each inode will use about 300 bytes of kernel memory. Check your kernel memory size (perhaps with `sar -k`) when resizing the cache. Since `ufs_ninode` is just a limit, it can be resized on the fly with `mdb`. (Remember that any changes put in via `mdb` will need to be added to the */etc/system* in order to persist past a reboot.)

Example 9-11 demonstrates how to check the statistics for the inode cache.

Example 9-11. Inode Cache Statistics

```
# sar -g 5

SunOS cnjunixtest01 5.10 Generic_118833-17 sun4u    01/30/2007

20:13:46  pgout/s ppgout/s pgfree/s pgscan/s %ufs_ipf
20:13:51     0.00      0.00     0.00     0.00      0.00
# kstat -n ufs_inode_cache
module: unix                            instance: 0
name:    ufs_inode_cache                class:      kmem_cache
         align                8
         alloc                456468
         alloc_fail           0
         buf_avail            12
         buf_constructed      0
         buf_inuse            157794
         buf_max              157806
         buf_size             368
         buf_total            157806
...
```

Rnode Cache

The information in the rnode cache is similar to that from the inode cache, except that it is maintained for NFS-mounted files. The default rnode cache size is `2xncsize`, which is usually sufficient. Rnode cache statistics can be examined via the `kstat -n rnode_cache` command.

Buffer Cache

The buffer cache is used to store inode, indirect block and cylinder group-related disk I/O. This cache acts as a buffer between the inode cache and the physical disk devices.

Sun suggests tuning `bufhwm` in the */etc/system* file if `sar -b` reports less than 90% hit rate on reads (`%rcache`) or 65% on writes (`%wcache`).

Cockroft and Pettit note that performance problems can result from allowing the buffer cache to grow too large, resulting in kernel memory allocation starvation. The default setting for `bufhwm` allows the buffer to consume up to 2% of system memory, which may be excessive. The buffer cache can probably be limited to 8MB safely by setting `bufhwm` in the */etc/system* file:
```
set bufhwm=8000
```

Obviously, the effects of such a change should be examined by checking the buffer cache hit rate `sar -b`.

Example 9-12 displays an example of `sar -b` output.

Example 9-12. Buffer Cache Statistics

```
# sar -b 30
```

```
SunOS cnjunixtest01 5.10 Generic_118833-17 sun4u    01/30/2007

12:18:36 bread/s lread/s %rcache bwrit/s lwrit/s %wcache pread/s pwrit/s
12:19:06       0       2     100       0       0      17       0       0
```

Block Cache

The virtual memory is carved into 8KB chunks known as "pages." When a file is read, it is first loaded into memory, a process known as "paging in." These are recorded in the virtual memory statistics, such as the `pi` column in **vmstat**.

Items that are paged into memory are cached there for a time. Since the same files are frequently accessed repeatedly, this caching can dramatically improve I/O performance. We would expect the size of the page cache from read and write operations to be limited by `segmap_percent`, which has a default of 12% of physical memory.

The page scanner's job is to free up memory caching items that have not been accessed recently. Pages are made available by placing them on the free list.

The size of the page cache and its components can be viewed by running **mdb -k** and using the **::memstat** dcmd. The performance of the cache can be viewed with utilities available in the DTrace Toolkit; the **rfileio.d** and **rfsio.d** utilities provide cache hit rates on a file or file system basis.

The page cache is bypassed by using direct I/O. Direct I/O can improve performance on applications (such as databases) that wait for a write confirmation on **synchronous writes**.

For most applications, **asynchronous writes** (ones that do not require an immediate write confirmation) are perfectly acceptable. In those cases, direct I/O is not a good choice. In particular, utilities like **tar** that rely on block-based I/O may suffer severe performance penalties by not taking advantage of the caching inherent in the asynchronous writes.

Example 9-13 shows how to check the page buffer cache.

Example 9-13. Page Buffer Cache Statistics

```
# /opt/DTT/Bin/rfileio.d
Read IOPS, top 20 (count)
/devices/pseudo/clone@0:ptm        logical        1
/var/adm/wtmpx                     logical        1

Read Bandwidth, top 20 (bytes)
/var/adm/wtmpx                     logical        4
/devices/pseudo/clone@0:ptm        logical      261

Total File System miss-rate: 0%
^C
# /opt/DTT/Bin/rfsio.d
Read IOPS (count)
/                                  logical        1
/var                               logical        3
/proc                              logical        6

Read Bandwidth (bytes)
/                                  logical       52
/proc                              logical     2016
/var                               logical     4096
```

```
Total File System miss-rate: 0%
^C
```

Physical Disk I/O

The primary tool to use in troubleshooting disk I/O problems is `iostat`. `sar -d` provides useful historical context. `vmstat` can provide information about disk saturation. For Solaris 10 systems, `dtrace` can provide extremely fine-grained information about I/O performance and what is causing any utilization or saturation problems. The DTrace Toolkit provides a number of ready-to-use scripts to take advantage of DTrace's capabilities.

To start, use `iostat -xn 30` during busy times to look at the I/O characteristics of your devices. Ignore the first bunch of output (the first group of output is summary statistics), and look at the output every 30 seconds. If you are seeing `svc_t` (service time) values of more than 20 ms on disks that are in use (more than, say, 10% busy), then the end user will see noticeably sluggish performance.

(With modern disk arrays that contain significant amounts of cache, it may be more useful to compare to service times during periods when no performance problems are experienced. If the reads and writes are largely hitting the cache on a fiber-attached disk array, average service times in the 3-5 ms range can be achieved. If you are seeing a large increase in service time during the problem periods, you may need to look at your disk array's monitoring features to identify whether or not more disk array cache would be useful. The most useful measurements to be used with modern disk arrays are the throughput measurements, since large up-front caches mask any other issues.)

Physical I/O

Disk I/Os include the following components:

- **I/O bus access:** If the bus is busy, the request is queued by the driver. The information is reported by `sar -d` wait and %w and `iostat -x` avwait.
- **Bus transfer time**: Arbitration time (deciding which device gets to use the bus), time to transfer the command (usually ~ 1.5 ms), data transfer time (in the case of a write).
- **Seek time**: Time for the head to move to the proper cylinder. Average seek times are reported by hard drive manufacturers. Usage patterns and the layout of data on the disks will determine the number of seeks that are required.
- **Rotation time**: Time for the correct sector to rotate under the head. This is usually calculated as 1/2 the time for a disk rotation. Rotation speeds (in RPM) are reported by hard drive manufacturers.
- **ITR time**: Internal Throughput Rate. This is the amount of time required for a transfer between the hard drive's cache and the device media. The ITR time is the limiting factor for sequential I/O, and is reported by the hard drive manufacturer.
- **Reconnection time**: After the data has been moved to/from the hard drive's internal cache, a connection with the host adapter must be completed. This is similar to the arbitration/ command transfer time discussed above.
- **Interrupt time**: Time for the completion interrupt to be processed. This is very hard to measure, but high interrupt rates on the CPUs associated with this system board may be an indication of problems.

The disk's ITR rating and internal cache size can be critical when tuning `maxcontig` (maximum contiguous I/O size). Note: `maxphys` and `maxcontig` must be tuned at the same time. The unit of measurement for `maxphys` is bytes; `maxcontig` is in blocks.

`maxcontig` can be changed via the **mkfs**, **newfs** or **tunefs** commands.

By default, `maxphys` is set to 128KB for Sparc and 56KB for x86 systems. `maxcontig` should be set to the same size (but in blocks). We would tune these smaller for random I/O and larger for sequential I/O.

167

Bus I/O

When data moves between different parts of the system, it moves on data buses. Some of these are buses for peripherals (like PCI buses). Others of them are main system buses. In any case, these buses are potential bottlenecks, since they may be responsible for limitations on data throughput or latency within the system.

Specific bus capacities are usually reported on the fact sheets for a given hardware platform. If they aren't on the fact sheet, as the vendor. They can at least give you benchmark numbers that will be a good proxy for system capacity. One key to successful system sizing is to match expected traffic with system capacity. Bus size is a frequently overlooked but critical piece of this puzzle.

Keep in mind that bus bandwidth is not just a matter of the bus speed on the system bus itself. We also need to take into account the speed and capacity limitations of peripheral PCI or SCSI buses that the data must flow through, as well as the speed limitations of the hardware itself.

We also need to make sure to balance the total capacity of the hardware attached to any single bus. If we have objects attached to the bus which can collectively swamp the bus's capacity, we can expect to run into problems if they all start banging away at once.

It is almost always the case the the disk or tape drive is the speed bottleneck in any data path involving them. (This is why we get a performance boost by caching frequently accessed disk information in the page buffer cache in memory.) Similarly, the network is almost always the bottleneck in any channel involving network interaction. The bandwidth of the bottleneck is the bandwidth of that data path.

It doesn't matter if you have a huge system bus, an almost unpopulated PCI bus, fast processors and an amazing disk array if your application is dragging data across a slow connection to the Internet. Look at the whole data path, find the bottlenecks, and work on either increasing the capacity of the bottleneck, re-architecting your procedures to bypass it or adjusting expectations to live with it.

busstat

Buses which are instrumented for use with **busstat** can be listed with **busstat -1**. The events that can be viewed on each bus can be found with **busstat -e** *bus-name*. There is still very little documentation on this facility beyond the busstat(1M) man page, but most of the names are fairly self-evident. Hopefully Sun will produce some more documentation to allow us to fully use this facility.

The syntax for **busstat** is similar to that for **cpustat** (which we examined in Chapter 7). As with **cpustat**, the precise information available will vary from system to system. Example 9-14 shows what **busstat** output looks like:

Example 9-14. busstat Output

```
# busstat -1
Busstat Device(s):
saf2 pcis2 saf1 pcis1 pcis0 pcis3
# busstat -e saf1 | pr -t2
pic0                              pic1
saf_bus_cycles                    saf_bus_cycles
saf_pause_asserted_cycles         saf_pause_asserted_cycles
saf_frn_coherent_cmds             saf_frn_coherent_cmds
saf_frn_coherent_hits             saf_frn_coherent_hits
saf_my_coherent_cmds              saf_my_coherent_cmds
saf_my_coherent_hits              saf_my_coherent_hits
saf_frn_io_cmds                   saf_frn_io_cmds
saf_frn_io_hits                   saf_frn_io_hits
merge_buffer                      merge_buffer
interrupts                        interrupts
```

```
csr_pios                            csr_pios
upa_pios                            upa_pios
pcia_pios                           pcia_pios
pcib_pios                           pcib_pios
saf_pause_seen_cycles               saf_pause_seen_cycles
dvma_reads                          dvma_reads
dvma_writes                         dvma_writes
saf_orq_full_cycles                 saf_orq_full_cycles
saf_data_in_cycles                  saf_data_in_cycles
saf_data_out_cycles                 saf_data_out_cycles
# busstat -w saf1,pic0=dvma_reads,pic1=dvma_writes 1 5
time dev    event0          pic0        event1          pic1
1    saf1   dvma_reads      0           dvma_writes     0
2    saf1   dvma_reads      0           dvma_writes     0
3    saf1   dvma_reads      0           dvma_writes     0
4    saf1   dvma_reads      0           dvma_writes     0
5    saf1   dvma_reads      0           dvma_writes     0
# busstat -w saf1,pic0=interrupts,pic1=saf_frn_io_cmds 1 5
time dev    event0          pic0        event1          pic1
1    saf1   interrupts      20          saf_frn_io_cmds 604
2    saf1   interrupts      14          saf_frn_io_cmds 453
3    saf1   interrupts      8           saf_frn_io_cmds 326
4    saf1   interrupts      23          saf_frn_io_cmds 663
5    saf1   interrupts      11          saf_frn_io_cmds 388
```

PCI Bus

The PCI bus has replaced the Sbus as Sun's default expansion bus. PCI buses runs at 33 or 66MHz and may be 32 or 64 bit. The peak PCI bus bandwidth is 528 MB/s for 64-bit buses at 66MHz.

(For desktop PC hardware, 33MHz PCI buses are still common. 33 MHz buses have peak bandwidths of 264 MB/s for 64-bit and 132 MB/s for 32-bit.)

Newer PCI-x buses run at 133MHz and allow up to 1066 MB/s. PCI-x 2.0 defines clock rates of 266MHz and 533MHz, with peak bandwidths of 2.1 GB/s and 4.2 GB/s, respectively.

Low profile PCI buses are becoming more common, since their smaller form factor fits well with the increasing miniaturization of the system. Low profile PCI comes in MD1 and MD2 flavors, with the primary difference being the shorter length of the MD1 cards. Currently, they do not support 64-bit PCI extensions.

Mini PCI cards are also produced for use in portable and sealed case computers. They are small in size, do not support 64-bit extensions and have a different connector layout, but still otherwise follow the PCI standard.

SCSI Bus

The scsi_options parameter can be set in the */etc/system* file to limit bus speed or set other characteristics. Check device documentation to determine if these settings need to be specified.

SCSI chains may be made of single-ended or differential connections. They should not be mixed, as this may damage the equipment. (Differential connections permit longer chains, but the hardware is usually more expensive. Single-ended chains must be less than 6 m in length; differential chains must be less than 20 m for synchronous connections or 25 m for asynchronous connections.) Starting with the Ultra 2 standard, only differential connections are available.

SCSI buses can operate at one of these speeds:

- 4 MB/s (asynchronous)
- 5 MB/s (synchronous)

- 10 MB/s (fast)
- 20 MB/s (ultra, fast/wide or fast-20)
- 40 MB/s (ultra/wide or narrow ultra-2)
- 80MB/s (wide ultra-2)
- 160 MB/s (ultra-3 or ultra-160)
- 320 MB/s (ultra-320)

SCSI buses and devices negotiate speed between the controller and the devices on the chain. `prtconf` can report information that can be used to determine the speed of a particular device.

The SCSI target numbers represent attachment points on the SCSI chain. Each target number may include as many as 8 devices (**luns** or logical unit numbers) by default. Embedded SCSI devices only include one lun.

Higher target numbers receive better service. On a narrow bus, the target priorities run 7 -> 0. On a wide bus, they run 7 -> 0, then 15 -> 8. The host adapter is usually 7. This can cause problems where busy disks and tape devices share a SCSI bus, since tape devices are usually assigned target 6

format

The `analyze` option of **format** can be used to examine the hard drive for flaws in a nondestructive fashion. This particular function may be particularly useful as part of a burn-in or as a way to qualify refurbished or re-used parts.

Resources

- Cockcroft, Adrian and Pettit, Richard. (April 1998) Sun Performance and Tuning: Java and the Internet, 2nd Ed. Prentice Hall.
- Cromar, Scott. (2007) *Solaris Troubleshooting and Performance Tuning at Princeton University*. Princeton, NJ. (http://www.princeton.edu/~unix/Solaris/troubleshoot/index.html)
- Matteson, Ryan. (December 2005) *Observing I/O Behavior with the DTrace Toolkit*. SysAdmin Magazine. (http://www.samag.com/documents/s=9915/sam0512a/0512a.htm)
- McDougall, Richard and Mauro, Jim. (July 2006) *Solaris Internals*. Upper Saddle River, NJ: Prentice Hall & Sun Microsystems Press.
- McDougall, Richard, Mauro, Jim and Gregg, Brendan. (October 2006) *Solaris Performance and Tools*. Upper Saddle River, NJ: Prentice Hall & Sun Microsystems Press.
- OpenSolaris Project. (October 2006) DTrace Toolkit. (http://www.opensolaris.org/os/community/dtrace/dtracetoolkit/)
- Sun Microsystems. (November 2006) *System Administration Guide: Devices and File Systems*. Palo Alto, CA: Sun Microsystems, Inc. (http://docs.sun.com/app/docs/doc/817-5093)

10

Data Storage Management

This chapter continues where Chapter 9 left off. Chapter 9 dealt with monitoring the storage subsystem. This chapter discusses the components of the storage infrastructure, how to manage them and how to troubleshoot them.

Disk Space Management

Disk space exhaustion can hurt performance. More importantly, running out of disk space may stop some services from running altogether.

Every site needs a way to monitor and manage disk space. Quotas are one way to deal with this problem, but they are not always appropriate. Disk space tracking on a per-directory basis may be more appropriate to a site. Regardless, we need to have an alerting system in place to notify us when disk space exceeds acceptable limits.

There are several graphical and SNMP-based monitoring tools available, but we don't need to get that fancy. Example 10-1 is a simple script designed to be run from `cron`, check for disk space usage and send notifications via email when thresholds are exceeded.

Example 10-1. Disk Space Monitoring Script

```
#!/bin/sh
NOTIFY=root
WORKSPACE=/usr/local/etc/tmp/disk-space.$$
HOST=`/bin/hostname`

# Check for scratch directory, initialize work space
if [ ! -d /usr/local/etc/tmp ]; then
   mkdir -p /usr/local/etc/tmp
fi
/bin/rm -rf ${WORKSPACE}
touch ${WORKSPACE}

# Function to check if a file system is over capacity
check_space() {
  # Find the current file system capacity
  CAPACITY=`df -k ${1} | grep ${1} | awk '{print $5}' | awk -F% '{print $1}'`
  LIMIT=${2}
```

```
  if [ ${CAPACITY} -gt ${LIMIT} ]; then
    df -k ${1} | grep ${1} >> ${WORKSPACE}
  fi
}

# Run the check_space function for each file system.
check_space / 90
check_space /var 90
check_space /tmp 60

# If any thresholds were exceeded, send notification
if [ -s ${WORKSPACE} ]; then
    /usr/ucb/Mail -s "${HOST} Disk Space Warning" ${NOTIFY} < ${WORKSPACE}
fi

# Clean up
/bin/rm -f ${WORKSPACE}
```

df

df can be used to check a file system's available space (as in the script from Example 10-1). Of particular interest is **df -kl**, which checks available space for all local file systems and prints out the statistics in kilobytes. Solaris 10 also allows us to use **df -h**, which presents the statistics in a more human-friendly form (that doesn't require counting digits to decide whether a file system is 100M or 1G in size).

du

du can be used to check space used by a directory. In particular, **du -dsk** will report usage in kilobytes of a directory and its descendants, without including space totals from other file systems.

quotas

Many file systems (particularly UFS, NFS, and ZFS) support disk quotas. These are a way to keep one bad actor from exhausting the shared disk space.

Soft quotas provide a warning message to allow time to address a disk usage issue before it becomes critical. **Hard quotas** put a stop to any activity that would violate the disk space limit.

> ZFS quota management is handled on a file system level. To provide user-level quotas or group-level quotas, separate file systems will need to be created.
>
> NFS quotas are managed through the rquotad interface. Essentially, NFS enforces the quotas that are found on the NFS server.

UFS Quotas

In order to use quotas on a UFS file system, they need to be enabled at mount time. This is usually accomplished by adding a quota option to the file system's line of the */etc/vfstab*.

Quotas can be edited on the file system using the **edquota** command, checked on that file system with **quotacheck**, displayed with **quota**, activated with **quotaon**, and deactivated with **quotaoff**. Even if the quota option has been used at mount time, **quotacheck** should be run and **quotaon** must be run before quotas are actually enabled.

When quotas are first installed on a file system, we need to create a file named quotas at the root of the file system. (For obvious security reasons, this file should be set to root ownership and 600 permissions.)

Once this is done, `edquota username` allows us to edit the quotas for a particular username. They can be viewed with `quota -v username` and checked with `quotacheck -v filesystem-name`. They can be enabled with `quotaon -v filesystem-name`. A quota report for a file system can be generated with `repquota -v filesystem-name`.

In UFS quota parlance, a "**quota**" is a **soft quota** (which can be exceeded for a limited amount of time), while a "**limit**" is a **hard quota** (which cannot be exceeded).

UFS File Systems

File system corruption can be detected and often repaired by the `format` and `fsck` commands. If the file system corruption is not due to an improper system shutdown, the hard drive hardware may need to be replaced.

UFS file systems contain the following types of blocks:

- **Boot block:** This stores information used to boot the system.
- **superblock**: Much of the file system's internal information is stored in these.
- **inode**: Stores location information about a file—everything except for the file name. The number of inodes in a file system can be changed from the default if `newfs -i` is used to create the file system.
- **data block**: The file's data is stored in these.

fsck

The `fsck` command is run on each file system at boot time. This utility checks the internal consistency of the file system, and can make simple repairs on its own. More complex repairs require feedback from the root user, either in terms of a "y" keyboard response to queries, or invocation with the `-y` option.

If `fsck` cannot determine where a file belongs, the file may be renamed to its inode number and placed in the file system's `lost+found` directory. If a file is missing after a noisy `fsck` session, it may still be intact in the `lost+found` directory.

UFS file systems can carry "state flags" that have the value of `fsclean`, `fsstable`, `fsactive`, or `fsbad` (unknown). These can be used by `fsck` during boot time to skip past file systems that are believed to be okay.

Sometimes the `fsck` command complains that it cannot find the superblock. Alternative superblock locations were created by `newfs` at the time that the file system was created.

Solaris 10's 6/06 release includes enhancements to `fsck` to automatically find and repair bad superblocks. This option should only be used to repair file systems that were created with `mkfs` or `newfs`.

For older systems, we can often find an alternate superblock nondestructively by looking at the default superblock locations with:

`newfs -N /dev/rdsk/c#t#d#s#`

command while booted from a CD. (Note the `-N` option. Running this command without this option may mess things up beyond repair.) `fsck` can be run against an alternate superblock with

`fsck -o b=superblock /dev/rdsk/c#t#d#s#`

If there is a lot of output, it may be necessary to choose the `-y` option to avoid having to answer a ton of prompts. We may need to try several alternate superblocks before finding a working one. Once we are done, we need to re-install the bootblock:

```
cd /usr/platform/`arch -k`/lib/fs/ufs
/usr/sbin/installboot ./bootblk /dev/rdsk/c#t#d#s#
```

File System Tuning

File system performance can be improved by looking at file system caching issues. Several of these parameters were discussed in the "maxusers" section of Chapter 9. The following tuning parameters may be valuable in tuning file system performance with `tunefs` or `mkfs`/`newfs`:

- **inode count**: The default is based upon an assumption of average file sizes of 2 KB. This can be set with `mkfs`/`newfs` at the time of file system creation.
- **time/space optimization**: Optimization can be set to allow for fastest performance or most efficient space usage.
- **minfree**: The default percentage for `minfree` is (64 MB / file system size) x 100. This parameter specifies how much space is to be left empty in order to preserve file system performance.
- **maxbpg**: This is the maximum number of blocks a file can leave in a single cylinder group. Increasing this limit can improve large file performance, but may have a negative impact on small file performance.

Volume Management

Performance and reliability problems on the disk I/O system are best addressed by structuring the storage to be fast and reliable. This can be done by purchasing external disk arrays; Solaris supports SCSI, iSCSI and Fiber Channel arrays. But, especially on smaller systems, a disk array may not be cost-effective.

Software volume management can be a cost-effective solution (especially since Solaris Volume Manager comes bundled with Solaris). Software volume management allows us to spread I/Os across multiple disk spindles, provide redundancy to prevent data loss during a disk failure, or allow for disk replacement without re-creating the file system.

Software volume management allows us to stripe, mirror, concatenate and RAID our file systems. The software volume manager presents a **volume** or **metadevice** to the operating system that will be treated as a disk slice for the purposes of file system management. Each type of volume has different advantages and uses:

- **Concatenation**: This allows us to aggregate space from multiple slices and present them as a single volume. There is no reliability or performance advantage to concatenation; it is strictly a tool for growing the space beyond a single slice.
- **Mirroring**: A properly mirrored solution has two or more identical copies of the file system contents on multiple physical disks (and preferably on multiple disk controllers). Mirroring is primarily a reliability feature, since a single disk failure will not disrupt access to the file system data. Read performance will be improved, since any of the mirror devices can be accessed for the data. Write performance will be somewhat degraded, since every write needs to be placed on each of the mirror set members. Mirroring is sometimes known as RAID-1
- **Striping**: A striped solution allows us to improve performance by spreading I/O requests over multiple hard disk spindles. By itself, striping actually reduces the reliability of the file system, since now a failure of any of the devices in the volume will disrupt the volume's availability. Sometimes striping is combined with mirroring to give us the best of both worlds. Raw striping is sometimes known as RAID-0.
- **RAID-5**: RAID 5 configurations use striping to help improve performance, but each stripe reserves the space on one of the stripe elements for parity. (**Parity** refers to a calculation that is done that would allow us to reconstruct the information if any of the other disks is lost.) The bottom line is that RAID-5 sets allow us to lose a single disk without losing access to our data, but they keep a lot of the performance advantages of striping.

174

There are a few gotchas to RAID 5: Databases (such as Oracle) may not be supported on software RAID 5 volumes (though hardware RAID 5 volumes are okay), there is some overhead required to calculate the parity, and a two-disk failure in a single RAID set usually means that we have to restore from tape.

- **RAID-6:** RAID 6 sometimes refers to double-parity RAID. The advantage of RAID 6 over RAID 5 is that a two-component failure will not lead to data loss. (Since disks in a RAID set are usually manufactured and installed at the same time, the frequency of two-disk RAID failure are higher than we might expect.)
- **Striping + Mirroring**: Striping + mirroring potentially gives us the best of both worlds. In order to maximize reliability, it is important to make sure that we are striping across the mirror sets rather than mirroring across the stripe sets. Figure 10-1 illustrates a two-disk failure on two volume configurations. On the configuration where the disks were mirrored and then striped, data access is uninterrupted (copies of the data from both the M1 and M3 mirror sets are still available). On the configuration where the disks were striped and then mirrored, the two disk failure has resulted in the entire configuration being unavailable, since the two-disk failure has broken both of the mirrored stripe sets.

It would be nice if vendors would agree what to call these two types of RAID. It is usual to call one RAID 10 and one RAID 0+1, but vendors differ as to which one is labeled which way. The buyer must beware: when evaluating or architecting a solution, make sure that you get striping across the mirror sets rather than the other way around.

The standard is that the RAID 10 label belongs to solutions that stripe across mirror sets. But before you buy a RAID 10 solution, make sure that you are on the same page as the vendor.

Especially since Solaris Volume Manager is free, there is no good excuse for failing to protect disks containing the OS and critical data. Hard drives are one of the pieces of hardware that fails most frequently, and hard disk failures can be among the most difficult to recover from. By mirroring disks (especially OS disks), we can virtually eliminate unscheduled downtime due to hard disk failure. We won't keep the disks from failing, but we can postpone maintenance until the next convenient maintenance window, or we may even be able to replace the hardware on the fly, with no service interruption.

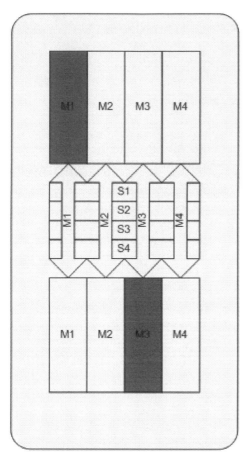
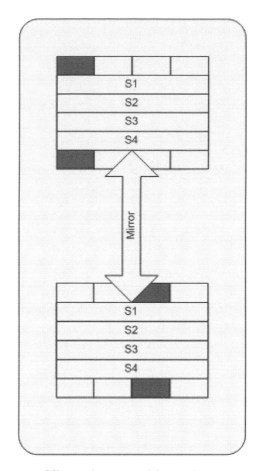

Striped across mirror sets   Mirrored across stripe sets

Figure 10-1. Striping and Mirroring

Solaris Volume Manager (DiskSuite)

Solaris Volume Manager (formerly known as DiskSuite) provides a way to mirror, stripe or RAID-5 local disks. New functionality is constantly being added to the base software. A full discussion is beyond the scope of this chapter or book, so we will focus on the most common cases, how to set them up, how to manage them and how to maintain them. Additional information is available in the *Solaris Volume Manager Administration Guide* (see the "References" section at the end of the chapter)

State Database

Solaris Volume Manager uses a **state database** to store its configuration and state information. (**State information** refers to the condition of the devices.) Multiple replicas are required for redundancy. At least four should be created on at least two different physical disk devices. It is much better to have at least six replicas on at least three different physical disks, spread across multiple controller channels, if possible.

In the event that the state databases disagree, a majority of configured state databases determines which version of reality is correct. This is why it is important to configure multiple replicas. A minimum of three database replicas must be available in order to boot without human assistance, so it makes sense to create database replicas liberally. They don't take up much space, and there is

176

very little overhead associated with their maintenance. On JBOD (Just a Bunch Of Disks) arrays, I recommend at least two replicas on each disk device.

State database replicas consume between 4 and 16 MB of space, and should ideally be placed on a partition specifically set aside for that purpose. In the event that state database information is lost, it is possible to lose the data stored on the managed disks, so the database replicas should be spread over as much of the disk infrastructure as possible.

State database locations are recorded in *etc/opt/SUNWmd/mddb.cf*. Depending on their condition, repair may or may not be possible.

Metadevices (the objects which Solaris Volume Manager manipulates) may be placed on a partition with a state database if the state database is there first.

The initial state databases can be created by specifying the slices on which they will live as follows:

```
metadb -a -f -c 2 slice-name1 slice-name2
```

Because pre-existing partitions are not usable for creating database replicas, it is frequently the case that we will steal space from swap to create a small partition for the replicas. To do so, we need to boot to single-user mode, use **swap -d** to unmount all swap, and **format** to re-partition the swap partition, freeing up space for a separate partition for the database replicas. Since the replicas are small, very few cylinders will be required.

Metadevice Management

The basic types of metadevices are:

- **Simple**: Stripes or concatenations--consist only of physical slices..
- **Mirror**: Multiple copies on simple metadevies (submirrors)
- **RAID5**: Composed of multiple slices; includes distributed parity.
- **Trans**: Master metadevice plus logging device.

Solaris Volume Manager can build metadevices either by using partitions as the basic building blocks, or by dividing a single large partition into soft partitions. **Soft partitions** are a way that SVM allows us to carve a single disk into more than 8 slices. We can either build soft partitions directly on a disk slice, or we can mirror (or RAID) slices, then carve up the resulting metadevice into soft partitions to build volumes.

Disksets are collections of disks that are managed together, in the same way that a Veritas Volume Manager (VxVM) disk group is managed together. Unlike in VxVM, SVM does not require us to explicitly specify a disk group. If Disksets are configured, we need to specify the set name for monitoring or management commands with a **-s setname** option. Disksets may be created as shared disksets, where multiple servers may be able to access them. (This is useful in an environment like Sun Cluster, for example.) In that case, we specify some hosts as **mediators** who determine who owns the diskset. (Note that disks added to shared disksets are re-partitioned in the expectation that we will use soft partitions.)

When metadevices need to be addressed by OS commands (like **mkfs**), we can reference them with device links of the form **/dev/md/rdsk/d#** or **/dev/md/disksetname/rdsk/d#**. (Note that the disksetname is in the opposite location of where it would be for a VxVM disk group.)

Table 10-1 contains the major command line utilities for managing metadevices.

Table 10-1. Metadevice Commands

Command	Description
metaclear	Deletes active metadevices and hot spare pools.

metadb	Manages state database replicas.
metadetach	Detaches a metadevice from a mirror or a logging device from a trans-metadevice.
metahs	Manages hot spares and hot spare pools.
metainit	Configures metadevices.
metaoffline	Takes submirrors offline.
metaonline	Places submirrors online.
metaparam	Modifies metadevice parameters.
metarename	Renames and switches metadevice names.
metareplace	Replaces slices of submirrors and RAID5 metadevices.
metaroot	Sets up system files for mirroring root.
metaset	Administers disksets.
metastat	Check metadevice health and state.
metattach	Attaches a metadevice to a mirror or a log to a trans-metadevice.

Table 10-2 outlines how to perform several common types of operations in Solaris Volume Manager.

Table 10-2. Common Solaris Volume Manager Operations

Operation	Procedure
Create state database replicas.	`metadb -a -f -c 2 c#t0d#s# c#t1d#s#`
Mirror the root partition.	
Create a metadevice for the root partition:	`metainit -f d0 1 1 c#t0d#s#`
Create a metadevice for the root mirror partition.	`metainit d1 1 1 c#t1d#s#`
Set up a 1-sided mirror	`metainit d2 -m d0`
Edit the *vfstab* and *system* files.	`metaroot d2; lockfs -fa; reboot`
Attach the root mirror.	`metattach d2 d1`
Mirror the swap partion.	
Create metadevices for the swap partition and mirror.	`metainit -f d5 1 1 c#t0d#s#` `metainit -f d6 1 1 c#t1d#s#`
Create a swap mirror metadevice.	`metainit d7 -m d5`
Attach submirror to mirror.	`metattach d7 d6`
Edit *vfstab* to mount swap mirror as a swap device.	Use root entry as a template.
Create a striped metadevice.	`metainit d# stripes slices c#t#d#s#...`

178

Operation	Procedure
Create a striped metadevice with a non-default interlace size.	`Add an -i interlacek option`
Concatenate slices.	`metainit d# #slices 1 c#t#d#s# 1 c#t#d#s#...`
Create a soft partition metadevice.	`metainit dsource# -p dnew# size`
Create a RAID5 metadevice.	`metainit d# -r c#t#d#s# c#t#d#s# c#t#d#s#...`
Manage Hot Spares	
Create a hot spare pool.	`metainit hsp001 c#t#d#s#...`
Associate a pool with a submirror.	`metaparam -h hsp### d##`
Add a slice to a pool.	`metahs -a hsp### /dev/dsk/c#t#d#s#`
Add a slice to all pools.	`metahs -a all /dev/dsk/c#t#d#s#`
Diskset Management	
Deport a diskset.	`metaset -s setname -r`
Import a diskset.	`metaset -s setname -t -f`
Add hosts to a shared diskset.	`metaset -s setname -a -h hostname1 hostname2`
Add mediators to a shared diskset.	`metaset -s setname -a -m hostname1 hostname2`
Add devices to a shared diskset.	`metaset -s setname -a /dev/did/rdsk/d# /dev/did/rdsk/d#`
Check diskset status.	`metaset`

Solaris Volume Manager Monitoring

Solaris Volume Manager provides facilities for monitoring its metadevices. In particular, the **metadb** command monitors the database replicas, and the **metastat** command monitors the metadevices and hot spares. (Output from both of these is included in Example 10-2 below.)

Status messages that may be reported by **metastat** for a disk mirror include:

- **Okay**: No errors, functioning correctly.
- **Resyncing**: Actively being resynced following error detection or maintenance.
- **Maintenance**: I/O or open error; all reads and writes have been discontinued.
- **Last Erred**: I/O or open errors encountered, but no other copies available.

Hot spare status messages reported by **metastat** are:

- **Available**: Ready to accept failover.
- **In-Use**: Other slices have failed onto this device.
- **Attention**: Problem with hot spare or pool.

Solaris Volume Manager Maintenance

Solaris Volume Manager is very reliable. As long as it is not misconfigured, there should be relatively little maintenance to be performed on Volume Manager itself. If the Volume Manager database is lost, however, it may need to be rebuilt in order to recover access to the data.

To recover a system configuration:

- Make a backup copy of */etc/opt/SUNWmd/md.cf*.
- Re-create the state databases:
  ```
  metadb -a -f -c 2 c#t#d#s# c#t#d#s#
  ```
- Copy *md.cf* to *md.tab*.
- Edit the *md.tab* so that all mirrors are one-way mirrors, RAID5 devices recreated with **-k** (to prevent re-initialization).
- Verify the md.tab configuration validity:
  ```
  metainit -n -a
  ```
- Re-create the configuration:
  ```
  metainit -a
  ```
- Re-attach any mirrors:
  ```
  metattach dmirror# dsubmirror#
  ```
- Verify that things are okay:
  ```
  metastat
  ```

More frequently, Solaris Volume Manager will be needed to deal with replacing a failed piece of hardware. To replace a disk which is spitting errors, but has not failed yet (as in Example 10-2):

- Add database replicas to unaffected disks until at least three exist outside of the failing disk.
- Remove any replicas from the failing disk:
  ```
  metadb
  metadb -d c#t#d#s#
  ```
- Detach and remove submirrors and hot spares on the failing disk from their mirrors and pools:
  ```
  metadetach dmirror# dsubmirror#
  metaclear -r dsubmirror#
  metahs -d hsp# c#t#d#s#
  ```
- [If the boot disk is being replaced, find the */devices* name of the boot disk mirror]:
  ```
  ls -l /dev/rdsk/c#t#d#s0
  ```
- [If the removed disk is a fibre channel disk, remove the */dev/dsk* and */dev/rdsk* links for the device.]
- Physically replace the disk. This may involve shutting down the system if the disk is not hot-swappable.
- Re-build any */dev* and */devices* links:
  ```
  drvconfig; disks
  ```
  or
  ```
  boot -r
  ```
- Format and re-partition the disk appropriately.
- Re-add any removed database replicas:
  ```
  metadb -a -c #databases c#t#d#s#
  ```
- Re-create and re-attach any removed submirrors:
  ```
  metainit dsubmirror# 1 1 c#t#d#s#
  metattach dmirror# dsubmirror#
  ```
- Re-create any removed hot spares.

Replacing a failed disk (as in Example 10-3) is a similar procedure. The differences are:

- Remove database replicas and hot spares as above; submirrors will not be removable.
- After replacing the disk as above, replace the submirrors with **metareplace**:
  ```
  metareplace -e dmirror# c#t#d#s#
  ```

Barring a misconfiguration, Solaris Volume Manager is a tremendous tool for increasing the reliability and redundancy of a server. More important, it allows us to postpone maintenance for a hard drive failure until the next maintenance window.

The `metastat` tool is quite useful for identifying and diagnosing problems. Along with `iostat -Ee`, we can often catch problems before they reach a point where the disk has actually failed. Example 10-2 shows how to replace a failing (but not yet failed) mirrored disk. (In this case, we were able to hot-swap the disk, so no reboot was necessary. Since the disks were SCSI, we also did not need to remove or rebuild any /dev links.)

Example 10-2. Replacing a Failing Disk with Solaris Volume Manager

```
# metastat
d0: Mirror
    Submirror 0: d1
      State: Okay
    Submirror 1: d2
      State: Okay
    Pass: 1
    Read option: roundrobin (default)
    Write option: parallel (default)
    Size: 20484288 blocks

d1: Submirror of d0
    State: Okay
    Size: 20484288 blocks
    Stripe 0:
        Device                   Start Block  Dbase State      Hot Spare
        c0t0d0s0                          0   No    Okay


d2: Submirror of d0
    State: Okay
    Size: 20484288 blocks
    Stripe 0:
        Device                   Start Block  Dbase State      Hot Spare
        c0t1d0s0                          0   No    Okay
...
# iostat -E
sd0      Soft Errors: 0 Hard Errors: 0 Transport Errors: 0
Vendor: SEAGATE  Product: ST373307LSUN72G  Revision: 0707 Serial No: 3HZ...
Size: 73.40GB <73400057856 bytes>
Media Error: 0 Device Not Ready: 0 No Device: 0 Recoverable: 0
Illegal Request: 0 Predictive Failure Analysis: 0
sd1      Soft Errors: 593 Hard Errors: 28 Transport Errors: 1
Vendor: SEAGATE  Product: ST373307LSUN72G  Revision: 0707 Serial No: 3HZ...
Size: 73.40GB <73400057856 bytes>
Media Error: 24 Device Not Ready: 0 No Device: 1 Recoverable: 593
Illegal Request: 0 Predictive Failure Analysis: 1
# metadb
        flags            first blk     block count
    a m p  luo           16            1034              /dev/dsk/c0t0d0s3
    a   p  luo           1050          1034              /dev/dsk/c0t0d0s3
    a   p  luo           2084          1034              /dev/dsk/c0t0d0s3
    a   p  luo           16            1034              /dev/dsk/c0t1d0s3
    a   p  luo           1050          1034              /dev/dsk/c0t1d0s3
    a   p  luo           2084          1034              /dev/dsk/c0t1d0s3

# metadb -d c0t1d0s3
# metadb
        flags            first blk     block count
    a m p  luo           16            1034              /dev/dsk/c0t0d0s3
    a   p  luo           1050          1034              /dev/dsk/c0t0d0s3
```

```
       a   p   luo          2084                1034                  /dev/dsk/c0t0d0s3
# metadetach d40 d42
d40: submirror d42 is detached
# metaclear -r d42
d42: Concat/Stripe is cleared
...
# metadetach d0 d2
d0: submirror d2 is detached
# metaclear -r d2
d2: Concat/Stripe is cleared
...
[Disk hot-swapped. No reboot or device reconfiguration necessary for this replacement]
...
# format
Searching for disks...done


AVAILABLE DISK SELECTIONS:
       0. c0t0d0 <SUN72G cyl 14087 alt 2 hd 24 sec 424>
          /pci@1c,600000/scsi@2/sd@0,0
       1. c0t1d0 <SUN72G cyl 14087 alt 2 hd 24 sec 424>
          /pci@1c,600000/scsi@2/sd@1,0
Specify disk (enter its number): 0
selecting c0t0d0
[disk formatted]


FORMAT MENU:
...
format> part


PARTITION MENU:
       0       - change `0' partition
...
       print  - display the current table
       label  - write partition map and label to the disk
       !<cmd> - execute <cmd>, then return
       quit
partition> pr
Current partition table (original):
Total disk cylinders available: 14087 + 2 (reserved cylinders)

Part    Tag     Flag    Cylinders       Size            Blocks
 0      root    wm       0 -  2012      9.77GB      (2013/0/0)    20484288
...
partition> q


FORMAT MENU:
...
format> di


AVAILABLE DISK SELECTIONS:
       0. c0t0d0 <SUN72G cyl 14087 alt 2 hd 24 sec 424>
          /pci@1c,600000/scsi@2/sd@0,0
```

```
        1. c0t1d0 <SUN72G cyl 14087 alt 2 hd 24 sec 424>
             /pci@1c,600000/scsi@2/sd@1,0
Specify disk (enter its number)[0]: 1
selecting c0t1d0
[disk formatted]
format> part
...
[sd1 partitioned to match sd0's layout]
...
partition> 7
Part      Tag     Flag   Cylinders       Size            Blocks
   7 unassigned   wm       0              0          (0/0/0)              0

Enter partition id tag[unassigned]:
Enter partition permission flags[wm]:
Enter new starting cyl[0]: 4835
Enter partition size[0b, 0c, 0.00mb, 0.00gb]: 9252c
partition> la
Ready to label disk, continue? y

partition> pr
Current partition table (unnamed):
Total disk cylinders available: 14087 + 2 (reserved cylinders)

Part      Tag     Flag   Cylinders       Size            Blocks
   0      root    wm      0 -  2012      9.77GB     (2013/0/0)    20484288
...
partition> q
...
# metadb -a -c 3 c0t1d0s3
# metadb
        flags            first blk       block count
    a m  p  luo          16              1034            /dev/dsk/c0t0d0s3
    a    p  luo          1050            1034            /dev/dsk/c0t0d0s3
    a    p  luo          2084            1034            /dev/dsk/c0t0d0s3
    a       u            16              1034            /dev/dsk/c0t1d0s3
    a       u            1050            1034            /dev/dsk/c0t1d0s3
    a       u            2084            1034            /dev/dsk/c0t1d0s3
# metainit d2 1 1 c0t1d0s0
d2: Concat/Stripe is setup
cnjcascade1#metattach d0 d2
d0: submirror d2 is attached
[Re-create and attach the remainder of the submirrors.]
...
# metastat
d0: Mirror
    Submirror 0: d1
      State: Okay
    Submirror 1: d2
      State: Resyncing
    Resync in progress: 10 % done
    Pass: 1
    Read option: roundrobin (default)
    Write option: parallel (default)
    Size: 20484288 blocks

d1: Submirror of d0
```

```
      State: Okay
      Size: 20484288 blocks
      Stripe 0:
         Device                  Start Block  Dbase State        Hot Spare
         c0t0d0s0                         0   No    Okay


d2: Submirror of d0
    State: Resyncing
    Size: 20484288 blocks
    Stripe 0:
       Device                    Start Block  Dbase State        Hot Spare
       c0t1d0s0                           0   No    Okay
```

It is important to format the replacement disk to match the cylinder layout of the disk that is being replaced. If this is not done, mirrors and stripes will not rebuild properly.

Example 10-3 demonstrates how to replace a disk that has already failed. In this case, there is no ability to remove the submirrors. Instead, the **metareplace -e** command is used to re-sync the mirror onto the new disk.

Example 10-3. Replacing a Failed Disk with Solaris Volume Manager

```
# iostat -E
...
sd1      Soft Errors: 0 Hard Errors: 0 Transport Errors: 5
Vendor: SEAGATE  Product: ST373307LSUN72G  Revision: 0507 Serial No: 3HZ7Z3CJ00007505
Size: 73.40GB <73400057856 bytes>
...
# metadb
        flags            first blk      block count
    a m  p  luo          16             1034                /dev/dsk/c1t0d0s3
    a    p  luo          1050           1034                /dev/dsk/c1t0d0s3
      W  p  l            16             1034                /dev/dsk/c1t1d0s3
      W  p  l            1050           1034                /dev/dsk/c1t1d0s3
    a    p  luo          16             1034                /dev/dsk/c1t2d0s3
    a    p  luo          1050           1034                /dev/dsk/c1t2d0s3
    a    p  luo          16             1034                /dev/dsk/c1t3d0s3
    a    p  luo          1050           1034                /dev/dsk/c1t3d0s3
# metadb -d /dev/dsk/c1t1d0s3
# format
Searching for disks...done



AVAILABLE DISK SELECTIONS:
       0. c1t0d0 <SUN72G cyl 14087 alt 2 hd 24 sec 424>
          /pci@1c,600000/scsi@2/sd@0,0
       1. c1t1d0 <SUN72G cyl 14087 alt 2 hd 24 sec 424>
          /pci@1c,600000/scsi@2/sd@1,0
       2. c1t2d0 <SUN72G cyl 14087 alt 2 hd 24 sec 424>
          /pci@1c,600000/scsi@2/sd@2,0
       3. c1t3d0 <SUN72G cyl 14087 alt 2 hd 24 sec 424>
          /pci@1c,600000/scsi@2/sd@3,0
Specify disk (enter its number): 0
selecting c1t0d0
[disk formatted]


FORMAT MENU:
```

184

```
...
        partition  - select (define) a partition table
...
format> part


PARTITION MENU:
...
        print  - display the current table
...
partition> pr
Current partition table (original):
Total disk cylinders available: 14087 + 2 (reserved cylinders)

Part      Tag    Flag     Cylinders        Size          Blocks
  0      root    wm       0 -  2012        9.77GB     (2013/0/0)  20484288
  1      swap    wu    2013 -  2214     1003.69MB     (202/0/0)    2055552
  2    backup    wm       0 - 14086       68.35GB   (14087/0/0) 143349312
  3 unassigned   wm    2215 -  2217       14.91MB       (3/0/0)      30528
  4 unassigned   wm    2218 -  5035       13.67GB    (2818/0/0)   28675968
  5 unassigned   wm    5036 - 12080       34.18GB    (7045/0/0)   71689920
  6       var    wm   12081 - 12684        2.93GB     (604/0/0)    6146304
  7      home    wm   12685 - 14086        6.80GB    (1402/0/0)   14266752

partition> q


FORMAT MENU:
        disk        - select a disk
...
format> di


AVAILABLE DISK SELECTIONS:
       0. c1t0d0 <SUN72G cyl 14087 alt 2 hd 24 sec 424>
          /pci@1c,600000/scsi@2/sd@0,0
       1. c1t1d0 <SUN72G cyl 14087 alt 2 hd 24 sec 424>
          /pci@1c,600000/scsi@2/sd@1,0
       2. c1t2d0 <SUN72G cyl 14087 alt 2 hd 24 sec 424>
          /pci@1c,600000/scsi@2/sd@2,0
       3. c1t3d0 <SUN72G cyl 14087 alt 2 hd 24 sec 424>
          /pci@1c,600000/scsi@2/sd@3,0
Specify disk (enter its number)[0]: 1
format> part


PARTITION MENU:
...
partition> pr
Current partition table (original):
Total disk cylinders available: 14087 + 2 (reserved cylinders)

Part      Tag    Flag     Cylinders        Size          Blocks
  0      root    wm       0 -    25      129.19MB      (26/0/0)     264576
  1      swap    wu      26 -    51      129.19MB      (26/0/0)     264576
  2    backup    wu       0 - 14086       68.35GB   (14087/0/0) 143349312
  3 unassigned   wm       0                    0       (0/0/0)          0
```

```
   4 unassigned    wm        0                  0         (0/0/0)              0
   5 unassigned    wm        0                  0         (0/0/0)              0
   6        usr    wm       52 - 14086      68.10GB       (14035/0/0) 142820160
   7 unassigned    wm        0                  0         (0/0/0)              0

...
partition> 7
Part        Tag    Flag    Cylinders        Size          Blocks
   7 unassigned    wm        0                  0         (0/0/0)              0

Enter partition id tag[unassigned]: home
Enter partition permission flags[wm]:
Enter new starting cyl[0]: 12685
Enter partition size[0b, 0c, 0.00mb, 0.00gb]: 1402c
partition> pr
Current partition table (unnamed):
Total disk cylinders available: 14087 + 2 (reserved cylinders)

Part        Tag    Flag    Cylinders        Size          Blocks
   0       root    wm        0 -  2012      9.77GB        (2013/0/0)   20484288
   1       swap    wu     2013 -  2214   1003.69MB        (202/0/0)     2055552
   2     backup    wu        0 - 14086     68.35GB        (14087/0/0) 143349312
   3 unassigned    wm     2215 -  2217     14.91MB        (3/0/0)         30528
   4 unassigned    wm     2218 -  5035     13.67GB        (2818/0/0)   28675968
   5 unassigned    wm     5036 - 12080     34.18GB        (7045/0/0)   71689920
   6        var    wm    12081 - 12684      2.93GB        (604/0/0)     6146304
   7       home    wm    12685 - 14086      6.80GB        (1402/0/0)   14266752

partition> la
Ready to label disk, continue? y

partition> q
...
# metastat
...
d19: Mirror
    Submirror 0: d17
      State: Okay
    Submirror 1: d18
      State: Needs maintenance
    Pass: 1
    Read option: roundrobin (default)
    Write option: parallel (default)
    Size: 14266752 blocks

d17: Submirror of d19
    State: Okay
    Size: 14266752 blocks
    Stripe 0:
        Device            Start Block  Dbase State        Hot Spare
        c1t0d0s7                    0  No    Okay


d18: Submirror of d19
    State: Needs maintenance
    Invoke: metareplace d19 c1t1d0s7 <new device>
    Size: 14266752 blocks
```

```
    Stripe 0:
        Device                  Start Block  Dbase State          Hot Spare
        c1t1d0s7                        0    No    Maintenance
...
# metareplace -e d19 c1t1d0s7
d19: device c1t1d0s7 is enabled
# metareplace -e d16 c1t1d0s6
d16: device c1t1d0s6 is enabled
# metareplace -e d13 c1t1d0s5
d13: device c1t1d0s5 is enabled
# metareplace -e d10 c1t1d0s4
d10: device c1t1d0s4 is enabled
# metareplace -e d2 c1t1d0s0
d2: device c1t1d0s0 is enabled
# metastat
...
d19: Mirror
    Submirror 0: d17
      State: Okay
    Submirror 1: d18
      State: Resyncing
    Resync in progress: 10 % done
    Pass: 1
    Read option: roundrobin (default)
    Write option: parallel (default)
    Size: 14266752 blocks

d17: Submirror of d19
    State: Okay
    Size: 14266752 blocks
    Stripe 0:
        Device                  Start Block  Dbase State          Hot Spare
        c1t0d0s7                        0    No    Okay


d18: Submirror of d19
    State: Resyncing
    Size: 14266752 blocks
    Stripe 0:
        Device                  Start Block  Dbase State          Hot Spare
        c1t1d0s7                        0    No    Resyncing
...
# metadb -a -c 2 c1t1d0s3
# metadb
        flags              first blk      block count
    a m p  luo            16             1034            /dev/dsk/c1t0d0s3
    a   p  luo            1050           1034            /dev/dsk/c1t0d0s3
    a      u              16             1034            /dev/dsk/c1t1d0s3
    a      u              1050           1034            /dev/dsk/c1t1d0s3
    a   p  luo            16             1034            /dev/dsk/c1t2d0s3
    a   p  luo            1050           1034            /dev/dsk/c1t2d0s3
    a   p  luo            16             1034            /dev/dsk/c1t3d0s3
    a   p  luo            1050           1034            /dev/dsk/c1t3d0s3
```

Veritas Volume Manager and File System

Veritas has long since been purchased by Symantec, but its products continue to be sold under the Veritas name. Over time, we can expect that some of the products will have name changes to reflect the new ownership.

Veritas produces volume and file system software that allows for extremely flexible and straightforward management of a system's disk storage resources. Now that ZFS is providing much of this same functionality from inside the OS, it will be interesting to see how well Veritas is able to hold on to its installed base.

In Veritas Volume Manager (**VxVM**) terminology, physical disks are assigned a **diskname** and imported into collections known as **disk groups**. Physical disks are divided into a potentially large number of arbitrarily sized, contiguous chunks of disk space known as **subdisks**. These subdisks are combined into **volumes**, which are presented to the operating system in the same way as a slice of a physical disk is.

Volumes can be striped, mirrored or RAID-5'ed. Mirrored volumes are made up of equally-sized collections of subdisks known as **plexes**. Each plex is a mirror copy of the data in the volume.

The Veritas File System (**VxFS**) is an extent-based file system with advanced logging, snapshotting, and performance features.

VxVM provides dynamic multipathing (DMP) support, which means that it takes care of path redundancy where it is available. If new paths or disk devices are added, one of the steps to be taken is to run **vxdctl enable** to scan the devices, update the VxVM device list, and update the DMP database. In cases where we need to override DMP support (usually in favor of an alternate multipathing software like EMC Powerpath), we can run **vxddladm addforeign**.

Table 10-3 contains procedures to carry out some common VxVM operations. VxVM has a Java-based GUI interface as well, but I always find it easiest to use the command line.

Table 10-3. Standard VxVM Operations

Operation	Procedure
Create a volume: (length specified in sectors, KB, MB or GB)	`vxassist -g dg-name make vol-name length(skmg)`
Create a striped volume (add options for a stripe layout):	`layout=stripe diskname1 diskname2 ...`

Remove a volume (after unmounting and removing from *vfstab*):	`vxstop vol-name`
	then
	`vxassist -g dg-name remove volume vol-name`
	or
	`vxedit -rf rm vol-name`

Create a VxFS file system:	`mkfs -F vxfs -o largefiles \` `    /dev/vx/rdsk/dg-name/vol-name`
Snapshot a VxFS file system to an empty volume:	`mount -F vxfs -o snapof=orig-vol \` `    empty-vol mount-point`

188

Operation	Procedure
Display disk group free space:	`vxdg -g dg-name free`
Display the maximum size volume that can be created:	`vxassist -g dg-name maxsize [attributes]`
List physical disks:	`vxdisk list`
Print VxVM configuration:	`vxprint -ht`

Add a disk to VxVM:	`vxdiskadm (follow menu prompts)`
	`or`
	`vxdiskadd disk-name`

Bring newly attached disks under VxVM control (it may be necessary to use **format** or **fmthard** to label the disk before the **vxdiskconfig**):	`drvconfig; disks`
	`vxdiskconfig`
	`vxdctl enable`

Scan devices, update VxVM device list, reconfigure DMP:	`vxdctl enable`
Scan devices on OS device tree, initiate dynamic reconfig of multipathed disks.	`vxdisk scandisks`
Reset a disabled vxconfigd daemon:	`vxconfigd -kr reset`
Manage hot spares:	`vxdiskadm (follow menu options and prompts)` `vxedit set spare=[off|on] vxvm-disk-name`
Rename disks:	`vxedit rename old-disk-name new-disk-name`
Rename subdisks:	`vxsd mv old-subdisk-name new-subdisk-name`
Monitor volume performance:	`vxstat`
Re-size a volume (but not the file system):	`vxassist growto|growby|shrinkto|shrinkby \` `  volume-name length[s|m|k|g]`
Resize a volume, including the file system:	`vxresize -F vxfs volume-name new-size[s|m|k|g]`
Change a volume's layout:	`vxassist relayout volume-name layout=layout`

The progress of many VxVM tasks can be tracked by setting the -t flag at the time the command is run: *utility* **-t** *taskflag*. If the task flag is set, we can use **vxtask** to list, monitor, pause, resume, abort or set the task labeled by the tasktag.

Physical disks which are added to VxVM control can either be **initialized** (made into a native VxVM disk) or **encapsulated** (disk slice/partition structure is preserved). In general, disks should only be encapsulated if there is data on the slices that needs to be preserved, or if it is the boot disk. (Boot disks must be encapsulated.) Even if there is data currently on a non-boot disk, it is best to back up the data, initialize the disk, create the file systems, and restore the data.

When a disk is initialized, the VxVM-specific information is placed in a reserved location on the disk known as a **private region**. The **public region** is the portion of the disk where the data will reside.

VxVM disks can be added as one of several different categories of disks:

- **sliced**: Public and private regions are on separate physical partitions. (Usually s3 is the private region and s4 is the public region, but encapsulated boot disks are the reverse.)
- **simple**: Public and private regions are on the same disk area.
- **cdsdisk**: (Cross-Platform Data Sharing) This is the default, and allows disks to be shared across OS platforms. This type is not suitable for boot, swap or root disks.

If there is a VxFS license for the system, as many file systems as possible should be created as VxFS file systems to take advantage of VxFS's logging, performance and reliability features.

> At the time of this writing, ZFS is not an appropriate file system for use on top of VxVM volumes. Sun warns that running ZFS on VxVM volumes can cause severe performance penalties, and that it is possible that ZFS mirrors and RAID sets would be laid out in a way that compromises reliability.

VxVM Maintenance

The first step in any VxVM maintenance session is to run **vxprint -ht** to check the state of the devices and configurations for all VxVM objects. (A specific volume can be specified with **vxprint -ht** *volume-name*.) This section includes a list of procedures for dealing with some of the most common problems. (Depending on the naming scheme of a VxVM installation, many of the below commands may require a **-g** *dg-name* option to specify the disk group.)

- Volumes which are not starting up properly will be listed as DISABLED or DETACHED. A volume recovery can be attempted with the **vxrecover -s** *volume-name* command.

- If all plexes of a mirror volume are listed as STALE, place the volume in maintenance mode, view the plexes and decide which plex to use for the recovery:

  vxvol maint *volume-name* (The volume state will be DETACHED.)
  vxprint -ht *volume-name*
  vxinfo *volume-name* (Display additional information about unstartable plexes.)
  vxmend off *plex-name* (Offline bad plexes.)
  vxmend on *plex-name* (Online a plex as STALE rather than DISABLED.)
  vxvol start *volume-name* (Revive stale plexes.)
  vxplex att *volume-name plex-name* (Recover a stale plex.)

- If, after the above procedure, the volume still is not started, we can force a plex to a "clean" state. If the plex is in a RECOVER state and the volume will not start, use a **-f** option on the **vxvol** command:

  vxmend fix clean *plex-name*
  vxvol start *volume-name*
  vxplex att *volume-name plex-name*

- If a subdisk status is listing as NDEV even when the disk is listed as available with **vxdisk list**

  the problem can sometimes be resolved by running
  vxdg deport *dgname;* **vxdg import** *dgname*
  to re-initialize the disk group.

- To remove a disk:

  Copy the data elsewhere if possible.

  Unmount file systems from the disk or unmirror plexes that use the disk.

  vxvol stop *volume-name* (Stop volumes on the disk.)
  vxdg -g *dg-name* **rmdisk** *disk-name* (Remove disk from its disk group.)
  vxdisk offline *disk-name* (Offline the disk.)
  vxdiskunsetup *c#t#d#* (Remove the disk from VxVM control.)

- To replace a failed disk other than the boot disk:

  In **vxdiskadm**, choose option 4: Remove a disk for replacement. When prompted, chose "none" for the disk to replace it.

  Physically remove and replace the disk. (A reboot may be necessary if the disk is not hot-swappable.) In the case of a fibre channel disk, it may be necessary to remove the /dev/dsk and /dev/rdsk links and rebuild them with **drvconfig; disks**, or a reconfiguration reboot.

  In **vxdiskadm**, choose option 5: Replace a failed or removed disk. Follow the prompts and replace the disk with the appropriate disk.

- To replace a failed boot disk:

  Use the **eeprom** command at the root prompt or the **printenv** command at the ok> prompt to make sure that the nvram=devalias and boot-device parameters are set to allow a boot from the mirror of the boot disk. If the boot paths are not set up properly for both mirrors of the boot disk, it may be necessary to move the mirror disk physically to the boot disk's location. Alternatively, the **devalias** command at the ok> prompt can set the mirror disk path correctly, then use **nvstore** to write the change to the nvram. (It is sometimes necessary to **nvunalias** *aliasname* to remove an alias from the nvramrc, then **nvalias** *aliasname* *devicepath* to set the new alias, then **nvstore** to write the changes to nvram.)

  In short, set up the system so that it will boot from the boot disk's mirror.

  Repeat the steps above to replace the failed disk.

- Clearing a "Failing" Flag from a Disk:

  First make sure that there really is not a hardware problem, or that the problem has been resolved. Then,

  vxedit set failing=off *disk-name*

- Clearing an IOFAIL state from a Plex:

  First make sure that the hardware problem with the plex has been resolved. Then,

  vxmend -g *dgname* **-o force off** *plexname*
  vxmend -g *dgname* **on** *plexname*
  vxmend -g *dgname* **fix clean** *plexname*
  vxrecover -s *volname*

Example 10-4. VxVM Resetting Plex State

```
soltest/etc/vx > vxprint -ht vol53
Disk group: testdg


V  NAME           RVG/VSET/CO   KSTATE    STATE    LENGTH    READPOL    PREFPLEX UTYPE
PL NAME           VOLUME        KSTATE    STATE    LENGTH    LAYOUT     NCOL/WID MODE
SD NAME           PLEX          DISK      DISKOFFS LENGTH    [COL/]OFF  DEVICE   MODE
SV NAME           PLEX          VOLNAME   NVOLLAYR LENGTH    [COL/]OFF  AM/NM    MODE
SC NAME           PLEX          CACHE     DISKOFFS LENGTH    [COL/]OFF  DEVICE   MODE
DC NAME           PARENTVOL     LOGVOL
SP NAME           SNAPVOL       DCO
```

191

```
EX NAME          ASSOC        VC                     PERMS    MODE      STATE
SR NAME          KSTATE

v  vol53         -                     DISABLED ACTIVE   20971520 SELECT    -          fsgen
pl vol53-01      vol53                 DISABLED IOFAIL   20971520 CONCAT    -          RW
sd disk141-21    vol53-01     disk141  423624704 20971520 0          EMC0_2    ENA
soltest/etc/vx > vxmend -g testdg -o force off vol53-01
soltest/etc/vx > vxprint -ht vol53
Disk group: testdg

V  NAME          RVG/VSET/CO  KSTATE   STATE    LENGTH    READPOL    PREFPLEX UTYPE
PL NAME          VOLUME       KSTATE   STATE    LENGTH    LAYOUT     NCOL/WID MODE
SD NAME          PLEX         DISK     DISKOFFS LENGTH    [COL/]OFF DEVICE    MODE

v  vol53         -                     DISABLED ACTIVE   20971520 SELECT    -          fsgen
pl vol53-01      vol53                 DISABLED OFFLINE  20971520 CONCAT    -          RW
sd disk141-21    vol53-01     disk141  423624704 20971520 0          EMC0_2    ENA
soltest/etc/vx > vxmend -g testdg on vol53-01
soltest/etc/vx > vxprint -ht vol53
Disk group: testdg

V  NAME          RVG/VSET/CO  KSTATE   STATE    LENGTH    READPOL    PREFPLEX UTYPE
PL NAME          VOLUME       KSTATE   STATE    LENGTH    LAYOUT     NCOL/WID MODE
SD NAME          PLEX         DISK     DISKOFFS LENGTH    [COL/]OFF DEVICE    MODE

v  vol53         -                     DISABLED ACTIVE   20971520 SELECT    -          fsgen
pl vol53-01      vol53                 DISABLED STALE    20971520 CONCAT    -          RW
sd disk141-21    vol53-01     disk141  423624704 20971520 0          EMC0_2    ENA
soltest/etc/vx > vxmend -g testdg fix clean vol53-01
soltest/etc/vx > !vxprint
vxprint -ht vol53
Disk group: testdg

V  NAME          RVG/VSET/CO  KSTATE   STATE    LENGTH    READPOL    PREFPLEX UTYPE
PL NAME          VOLUME       KSTATE   STATE    LENGTH    LAYOUT     NCOL/WID MODE
SD NAME          PLEX         DISK     DISKOFFS LENGTH    [COL/]OFF DEVICE    MODE

v  vol53         -                     DISABLED ACTIVE   20971520 SELECT    -          fsgen
pl vol53-01      vol53                 DISABLED CLEAN    20971520 CONCAT    -          RW
sd disk141-21    vol53-01     disk141  423624704 20971520 0          EMC0_2    ENA
soltest/etc/vx > vxrecover -s vol53
soltest/etc/vx > !vxprint
vxprint -ht vol53
Disk group: testdg

V  NAME          RVG/VSET/CO  KSTATE   STATE    LENGTH    READPOL    PREFPLEX UTYPE
PL NAME          VOLUME       KSTATE   STATE    LENGTH    LAYOUT     NCOL/WID MODE
SD NAME          PLEX         DISK     DISKOFFS LENGTH    [COL/]OFF DEVICE    MODE

v  vol53         -                     ENABLED  ACTIVE   20971520 SELECT    -          fsgen
pl vol53-01      vol53                 ENABLED  ACTIVE   20971520 CONCAT    -          RW
sd disk141-21    vol53-01     disk141  423624704 20971520 0          EMC0_2    ENA
```

VxVM Mirroring

Most volume manager availability configuration is centered around mirroring. While RAID-5 is a possible option, it is infrequently used due to the parity calculation overhead and the relatively low cost of hardware-based RAID-5 devices.

In particular, the boot device must be mirrored; it cannot be part of a RAID-5 configuration. To mirror the boot disk:

- `eeprom use-nvramrc?=true`

  > Before mirroring the boot disk, set `use-nvramrc?` to `true` in the EEPROM settings. If you forget, you will have to go in and manually set up the boot path for your boot mirror disk. (See "To replace a failed boot disk" in the "VxVM Maintenance" section for the procedure.) It is much easier if you set the parameter properly *before* mirroring the disk!

- The boot disk must be encapsulated, preferably in the bootdg disk group. (The `bootdg` disk group membership used to be required for the boot disk. It is still a standard, and there is no real reason to violate it.)

- If possible, the boot mirror should be **cylinder-aligned** with the boot disk. (This means that the partition layout should be the same as that for the boot disk.) It is preferred that 1-2MB of unpartitioned space be left at either the very beginning or the very end of the cylinder list for the VxVM private region. Ideally, slices 3 and 4 should be left unconfigured for VxVM's use as its public and private region. (If the cylinders are aligned, it will make OS and VxVM upgrades easier in the future.)

- (Before bringing the boot mirror into the bootdg disk group, I usually run an **installboot** command on that disk to install the boot block in slice 0. This should no longer be necessary; **vxrootmir** should take care of this for us. I have run into circumstances in the past where **vxrootmir** has not set up the boot block properly; Veritas reports that those bugs have long since been fixed.)

- Mirrors of the root disk must be configured with "sliced" format and should live in the bootdg disk group. They cannot be configured with cdsdisk format. If necessary, remove the disk and re-add it in **vxdiskadm**.

- In **vxdiskadm**, choose option 6: `Mirror Volumes on a Disk`. Follow the prompts from the utility. It will call **vxrootmir** under the covers to take care of the boot disk setup portion of the operation.

- When the process is done, attempt to boot from the boot mirror. (Check the EEPROM devalias settings to see which device alias has been assigned to the boot mirror, and run **boot *device-alias*** from the ok> prompt.

Procedure to create a Mirrored-Stripe Volume: (A mirrored-stripe volume mirrors several striped plexes—it is better to set up a Striped-Mirror Volume.)

- `vxassist -g dg-name make volume length layout=mirror-stripe`

Creating a Striped-Mirror Volume: (Striped-mirror volumes are layered volumes which stripes across underlaying mirror volumes.)

- `vxassist -g dg-name make volume length layout=stripe-mirror`

Removing a plex from a mirror:

- `vxplex -g dg-name -o rm dis plex-name`

Removing a mirror from a volume:

- `vxassist -g dg-name remove mirror volume-name`

Removing a mirror and all associated subdisks:

- `vxplex -o rm dis volume-name`

Dissociating a plex from a mirror (to provide a snapshot):

- `vxplex dis` *volume-name*
- `vxmake -U gen vol` *new-volume-name* `plex=`*plex-name* (Creating a new volume with a dissociated plex.)
- `vxvol start` *new-volume-name*
- `vxvol stop` *new-volume-name* (To re-associate this plex with the old volume.)
- `vxplex dis` *plex-name*
- `vxplex att` *old-volume-name* *plex-name*
- `vxedit rm` *new-volume-name*

Removing a Root Disk Mirror:

- `vxplex -o rm dis rootvol-02 swapvol-02 [other root disk volumes]`
- `/etc/vx/bin/vxunroot`

ZFS Management and Maintenance

Traditional file systems like UFS do not include the capability to manage disk space. Volume management packages (such as Veritas Volume Manager or Solaris Volume Manager/DiskSuite) have been used to manage tasks like aggregating disk devices, providing RAID data protection, or recovering from disk device failures.

ZFS is a next-generation file management system that can handle volume management tasks. It provides end-to-end management of disk storage. ZFS is a flexible, scalable and reliable POSIX-compliant file system. Key features include:

- Integrated storage pool management.
- Data protection and consistency, including RAID.
- Disk space quotas.
- Integrated management for mounts and NFS file sharing.
- Scrubbing and data integrity protection.
- Snapshots and clones.
- Advanced backup and restore features.
- Excellent scalability.
- Built-in compression.
- Maintenance and troubleshooting capabilities.
- Sharing of disk I/O bandwidth and space across file systems in a pool.
- Endian neutrality.

No separate file system creation step is required. The mount of the file system is automatic and does not require *vfstab* maintenance. (Instead, mounts are controlled by the `mountpoint` attribute on a file system. See Table 10-5 below.)

The expansion capacity of ZFS is astounding. It is a 128-bit file system. 256 quadrillion zetabytes of information is addressable. Directories can have up to 256 trillion entries. No limit exists on the number of file systems or files within a file system. For practical purposes, the limits in ZFS can be ignored.

ZFS includes measures to protect data and file system integrity. Each block is monitored via checksums, and mirrored or RAID-protected file systems self-heal data integrity faults from the valid copy of the data. File system writes are performed as copy-on-writes, so a file system check like `fsck` is not necessary.

> ZFS implements **copy-on-write** to prevent file system corruption during a crash. When a block is written to a ZFS file system, the write is applied to a fresh block. Once the write is completed, the

pointer to that block is switched from the old block to the new block.

Partial writes are not part of the file structure because the pointer has not been switched. The file system is never inconsistent as a result of a partial write, so `fsck` is not necessary to recover the file system.

Among other things, this mechanism allows a relatively easy implementation of snapshots. Snapshots just need to keep track of the original pointers and make sure that the original blocks don't get put on the free list.

ZFS was first publicly released in the 6/2006 distribution of Solaris 10. Previous versions of Solaris 10 did not include ZFS. The 11/2006 distribution of Solaris 10 included enhancements to ZFS to improve database performance and overall stability.

Endian refers to whether a particular system considers the left-most or right-most bit in a byte to be the most significant bit. SPARC and x86 systems have opposite orientations, so binary files may not be compatible between the two types of system.

ZFS uses **adaptive endianness** to allow a file system written by one type of system to be used by the other. Effectively, ZFS is **endian neutral**.

Since ZFS is endian neutral, disks can be moved between SPARC and x86 systems without requiring a file system re-format. At the time of this writing, no other Solaris-supported file system is endian neutral.

ZFS Pool Management

Storage pools should be composed of disk devices, though they can be composed of slices. Table 10-4 contains commands for performing several common pool management procedures.

While members of a storage pool may either be hard drives or slices of at least 128MB in size, Sun strongly recommends that pool members be whole hard drives. If slices are used as pool members, ZFS will not be able to spread the I/O traffic evenly over the pool's disk devices.

Table 10-4. ZFS Pool Management Commands

Operation	Procedure
To create a mirrored pool:	`zpool create -f pool-name mirror c#t#d# c#t#d#`
To check a pool's status:	`zpool status -v pool-name`
To list existing pools:	`zpool list`
To remove a pool and free its resources:	`zpool destroy pool-name`
A destroyed pool can sometimes be recovered:	`zpool import -D`
Additional disks can be added to an existing pool. When this happens in a mirrored or RAID pool, it is automatically re-silvered to redistribute the data:	`zpool add -f pool-name mirror c#t#d# c#t#d#`
Pools can be exported and imported to transfer them between hosts:	`zpool export pool-name` `zpool import pool-name`

Operation	Procedure
List pools available for import:	`zpool import`
Clear a pool's error count:	`zpool clear pool-name`

ZFS has volume management built in through its pools. It is not compatible with other volume management solutions.

Other volume management solutions (such as Solaris Volume Manager/DiskSuite and Veritas Volume Manager) should be used to support non-ZFS file systems such as UFS and Veritas File System (VxFS).

ZFS File System Management

Similar file systems should be grouped together in hierarchies to make management easier. Naming schemes should be thought out as well to make it easier to group administrative commands for similarly managed file systems.

When a new pool is created, a new file system is mounted at */pool-name*. ZFS has its own database for maintaining mount information; it does not use the */etc/vfstab*. Instead, a `zfs set` command is used to set the `mountpoint` attribute. Similarly, NFS shares are also managed through `zfs set`.

Table 10-5 contains procedures for several file system operations under ZFS.

Table 10-5. ZFS File System Operations

Operation	Procedure
Create a file system:	`zfs create pool-name/fs-name`
Delete a file system:	`zfs destroy fs-name`
Rename a file system:	`zfs rename old-name new-name`
Set properties:	`zfs set`
Turn on compression:	`zfs set compression=on pool-name/fs-name`
Share the file system with NFS:	`zfs set sharenfs=on pool-name/fs-name` `zfs set sharenfs="mountoption" pool-name/fs-name`
Mount file system persistently:	`zfs set mountpoint=mtptname pool-name/fs-name`
Set reservations (guaranteed minimum disk space):	`zfs set reservation=#gigG pool-name/fs-name`
Set quotas:	`zfs set quota=#gigG pool-name/fs-name`

Unlike UFS or VxFS file systems, ZFS maintains quotas on a file system basis rather than on user IDs within a file system. In a file server environment, this probably means that each user should be assigned a ZFS file system as a home directory. Since ZFS file systems automatically share the space in a pool, this is not as large a barrier as it would be in a traditional file system.

ZFS RAID Levels

ZFS file systems automatically stripe across all top-level disk devices. (Mirrors and RAID-Z devices are considered to be top-level devices.) It is not recommended that RAID types be mixed in a pool. (`zpool` tries to prevent this, but it can be forced with the `-f` flag.)

196

The following RAID levels are supported:

- RAID-0 (striping)
- RAID-1 (mirror)
- RAID-Z (parity RAID, but with variable-width stripes to avoid the RAID 5 write hole—see the note below)
- RAID-Z2 (double parity RAID)
- RAID-Z3 (triple parity RAID—available in Solaris 10 9/10 and later)

The `zfs(1m)` man page recommends 3-9 disks for RAID-Z pools.

> The **RAID-5 write hole** refers to the interval between when the data has been written to the stripe but before the parity has been re-calculated.
>
> RAID-Z uses **full stripe writes**, in which the entire stripe is written at the same time. ZFS implements full stripe writes by using a **variable stripe width**, in which each stripe is the size of a logical data block. ZFS automatically chooses a block size to match the performance characteristics of a particular workload.

ZFS Performance Monitoring

ZFS performance management is handled differently than with older generation file systems. In ZFS, I/Os are scheduled similarly to how jobs are scheduled on CPUs. The ZFS I/O scheduler tracks a priority and a deadline for each I/O. Within each deadline group, the I/Os are scheduled in order of logical block address.

Writes are assigned lower priorities than reads, which can help to avoid traffic jams where reads are unable to be serviced because they are queued behind writes. (If a read is issued for a write that is still underway, the read will be executed against the in-memory image and will not hit the hard drive.)

In addition to scheduling, ZFS attempts to intelligently prefetch information into memory. The algorithm tries to pick information that is likely to be needed. Any forward or backward linear access patterns are picked up and used to perform the prefetch.

The `zpool iostat` command can monitor performance on ZFS objects:

- **USED CAPACITY**: Data currently stored
- **AVAILABLE CAPACITY**: Space available
- **READ OPERATIONS**: Number of operations
- **WRITE OPERATIONS**: Number of operations
- **READ BANDWIDTH**: Bandwidth of all read operations
- **WRITE BANDWIDTH**: Bandwidth of all write operations

The health of an object can be monitored with
`zpool status`

Sun provides several recommendations related to running ZFS with adequate performance. Some of these are repeated elsewhere in this chapter:

- A minimum of 1GB of memory is required to run ZFS properly. Each mounted file system uses 64 KB. For systems with lots of mounted file systems or snapshots, Sun recommends an extra GB of memory per 10,000 file systems.

- Configure extra swap to allow for the fact that kernel sizes are larger on systems that use ZFS. (ZFS uses kernel-addressable memory for its cache.) The swap should be on disks other than those used by ZFS.

- Although ZFS can be configured on disk slices, this is not recommended for production systems.

- File systems that require better I/O dependability should be placed on a separate pool. Examples include database log or temp files.

- If the I/O consists of small writes being used to manage large files, it might make sense to reduce the `recordsize` setting. This is particularly true if I/O monitoring shows that we are approaching the maximum capacity of the channel.

- ZFS pool members should be made up of a single hard drive (or at worst, a small collection of hard drives). This way ZFS can make more intelligent I/O scheduling decisions.

- Starting with Solaris 10/08 the **ZFS Intent Log (ZIL)** can be separated onto a separate device, such as an NVRAM card. **Separate intent Logs (slogs)** may provide significant performance benefits, especially for applications like databases that require that writes be written to stable media.

- By default, the ZFS **Adaptive Replacement Cache (ARC)** will try to use all but 1G of available memory for ZFS caching. Memory will be released from the ARC as the OS demands it. It might be worthwhile to limit ARC's size if there are other applications that require large amounts of memory. If not, limiting ARC's size may hurt performance by reducing the cache hit rate for ZFS operations.

It is possible to limit the size of ARC by setting a kernel parameter, `zfs:zfs_arc_max`. This can be set in *etc/system* in current builds of OpenSolaris and Solaris 10 builds after 8/07, but it can only be set via **mdb** on older Solaris 10 builds. To set it to 30G in *etc/system*

```
    set zfs:zfs_arc_max = 0x780000000
```

or

```
    set zfs:zfs_arc_max = 32212254720
```

On a running kernel, it is recommended to set `arc.c` to the desired maximum value, and `arc.p` to half of that value. See Example 10-5 for a demonstration:

Example 10-5. Limiting the Size of ARC

```
# mdb -kw
Loading modules: [ unix krtld genunix specfs dtrace ufs ssd fcp fctl pcisch ip sctp usba
random nca md logindmux ptm sd cpc fcip sppp crypto zfs nfs ipc ]
> arc::print -a p c c_max
70546358 p = 0x5f38d400
70546360 c = 0xbe71a800
70546370 c_max = 0xbe71a800
> 5f38d400=E
                1597559808
> be71a800=E
                3195119616
> be71a800=E
                3195119616
> 70546358/W 0x40000000
arc+0x30:       0x3b9aca00      =       0x40000000
> 70546360/W 0x80000000
arc+0x38:       0x77359400      =       0x80000000
> 70546370/W 0x80000000
arc+0x48:       0x77359400      =       0x80000000
> 40000000=E
                1073741824
> 80000000=E
                2147483648
::formats
...
B - hexadecimal int (1 byte)
C - character using C character notation (1 byte)
```

```
D - decimal signed int (4 bytes)
E - decimal unsigned long long (8 bytes)
```

Example 10-5 shows a system with 4G of RAM. As expected, the ARC is set to consume up to 3G of it. Using **mdb**, we are able to reduce ARC's maximum size to 2G. As in Example 4-9, we use the = operator to display the values in long decimal format (E) rather than hexadecimal. We can use the **::formats** dcmd to display available formats so that we can pick the one that fits the situation.

- ZFS uses a file-level prefetching mechanism that tries to anticipate reads, increasing cache hit rates. For some loads, the additional CPU load can reduce scalability. On Solaris 10 8/07 and later, disabling file prefetching may improve performance for some loads by setting one of the following in */etc/system*

```
set zfs:zfs_prefetch_disable = 1
```

- ZFS can interact poorly with the cache on some storage arrays. Many of these problems were resolved in the Solaris 10 5/08 release. On some earlier versions we can experiment with turning on zfs_nocacheflush. Be prepared to validate this change on a workload test and back it out (with a CDROM or boot -a boot ifnecessary):

```
set zfs:zfs_nocacheflush = 1
```

ZFS Snapshots and Clones

ZFS supports a robust and easy-to-use snapshot and cloning facility. Table 10-6 lists the procedures for several common snapshot and cloning operations.

Table 10-6. ZFS Snapshot and Clone Operations

Operation	Procedure
Create a snapshot:	`zfs snapshot pool-name/fs-name@snap-name`
Clone a snapshot:	`zfs clone snap-name fs-name`
Roll back to a snapshot:	`zfs rollback pool-name/fs-name@snap-name`
Send a clone to another server:	`zfs send`
Import a clone from another server:	`zfs receive`

The difference between a snapshot and a clone is that a clone is a writable, mountable copy of the file system. This capability allows us to store multiple copies of mostly-shared data in a very space-efficient way.

Each snapshot is accessible through the *.zfs/snapshot* in the */pool-name* directory. This can allow end users to recover their files without system administrator intervention.

Zones and ZFS

A file system is created in the global zone and added to the local zone via **zonecfg**. It may be assigned to more than one zone unless the mount point is set to legacy.

zfs set mountpoint=legacy *pool-name/filesystem-name*

To import a ZFS file system within a zone:

```
zonecfg -z zone-name
add fs
set dir=mount-point
set special=pool-name/filesystem-name
set type=zfs
```

```
end
verify
commit
exit
```

Administrative rights for a file system can be granted to a local zone:

```
zonecfg -z zone-name
add dataset
set name=pool-name/filesystem-name
end
commit exit
```

ZFS Data Protection

ZFS is a transactional file system. Data consistency is protected via Copy-On-Write (COW). For each write request, a copy is made of the specified block. All changes are made to the copy. When the write is complete, all pointers are changed to point to the new block.

256-bit checksums are used to validate data during reads and writes. Unlike disk block checksums (which are stored with the data block), ZFS checksums are stored with the pointer. This can help detect disk problems that might result in a wrong (but consistent) disk block checksum. It also prevents bad data from being returned to an application from a mirror or RAID set that still has a good copy of the data available. And, if such a good copy exists, the bad data block is corrected automatically.

The checksum algorithm is user-selectable. Checksumming and data recovery is done at a file system level; it is not visible to applications.

RAID protections are also part of ZFS.

Scrubbing is an additional type of data protection available on ZFS. It performs regular validation of all data. Manual scrubbing can be performed by:
zpool scrub pool-name
The results can be viewed via:
zpool status
Any issues should be cleared with:
zpool clear pool-name

The scrubbing operation walks through the pool metadata to read each copy of each block. Each copy is validated against its checksum and corrected if it has become corrupted.

ZFS and Hardware Maintenance

To replace a hard drive with another device, run:
zpool replace pool-name old-disk new-disk

To offline a failing drive, run:
zpool offline pool-name disk-name
(A -t flag allows the disk to come back online after a reboot.)

Once the drive has been physically replaced, run the replace command against the device:
zpool replace pool-name device-name
After an offlined drive has been replaced, it can be brought back online:
zpool online pool-name disk-name

Firmware upgrades may cause the disk device ID to change. ZFS should be able to update the device ID automatically, assuming that the disk was not physically moved during the update. If necessary, the pool can be exported and re-imported to update the device IDs.

Troubleshooting ZFS

The three categories of errors experienced by ZFS are:

- **Missing devices:** Missing devices placed in a "faulted" state.
- **damaged devices**: Caused by things like transient errors from the disk or controller, driver bugs or accidental overwrites (usually on misconfigured devices).
- **data corruption**: Data damage to top-level devices; usually requires a restore. Since ZFS is transactional, this only happens as a result of driver bugs, hardware failure or file system misconfiguration.

It is important to check for all three categories of errors. One type of problem is often connected to a problem from a different family. Fixing a single problem is usually not sufficient.

Data integrity can be checked by running a manual scrubbing:
```
zpool scrub pool-name
zpool status -v pool-name
```
checks the status after the scrubbing is complete.

The `status` command also reports on recovery suggestions for any errors it finds. These are reported in the `action` section. To diagnose a problem, use the output of the `status` command and the `fmd` messages in */var/adm/messages*.

The `config` section of the `status` section reports the state of each device. The state can be:

- **ONLINE**: Normal
- **FAULTED**: Missing, damaged, or mis-seated device
- **DEGRADED**: Device being resilvered
- **UNAVAILABLE**: Device cannot be opened
- **OFFLINE**: Administrative action

The `status` command also reports READ, WRITE or CHKSUM errors.

To check if any problem pools exist, use
```
zpool status -x
```
This command only reports problem pools.

If a ZFS configuration becomes damaged, it can be fixed by running **export** and **import**.

Devices can fail for any of several reasons:

- **"Bit rot:"** Corruption caused by random environmental effects.
- **Misdirected Reads/Writes**: Firmware or hardware faults cause reads or writes to be addressed to the wrong part of the disk.
- **Administrative Error**
- **Intermittent, Sporadic or Temporary Outages**: Caused by flaky hardware or administrator error.
- **Device Offline**: Usually caused by administrative action.

Once the problems have been fixed, transient errors should be cleared:
```
zpool clear pool-name
```

In the event of a panic-reboot loop caused by a ZFS software bug, the system can be instructed to boot without the ZFS file systems:
```
boot -m milestone=none
```
When the system is up, remount / as `rw` and remove the file */etc/zfs/zpool.cache*. The remainder of the boot can proceed with the

svcadm milestone all command. At that point import the good pools. The damaged pools may need to be re-initialized.

ZFS Recommendations

Sun makes several recommendations for ZFS configurations to maximize reliability and performance:

- Because ZFS uses kernel addressable memory, we need to make sure to allow enough system resources to take advantage of its capabilities. We should run on a system with a 64-bit kernel, at least 1GB of physical memory, and adequate swap space.
- While slices are supported for creating storage pools, their performance will not be adequate for production uses.
- Mirrored configurations should be set up across multiple controllers where possible to maximize performance and redundancy.
- Scrubbing should be scheduled on a regular basis to identify problems before they become serious.
- When latency or other requirements are important, it makes sense to separate them onto different pools with distinct hard drives. For example, database log files should be on separate pools from the data files.
- Root pools are not yet supported in the Solaris 10 6/2006 or 11/2006 releases, though they are anticipated in a future release. When they are used, it is best to put them on separate pools from the other file systems.
- On file systems with many file creations and deletions, utilization should be kept under 80% to protect performance.
- The recordsize parameter can be tuned on ZFS file systems. When it is changed, it only affects new files. zfs set recordsize=*size* tuning can help where large files (like database files) are accessed via small, random reads and writes. The default is 128KB; it can be set to any power of two between 512B and 128KB. Where the database uses a fixed block or record size, the recordsize should be set to match. This should only be done for the file systems actually containing heavily-used database files.
- In general, recordsize should be reduced when **iostat** regularly shows a throughput near the maximum for the I/O channel. As with any tuning, make a minimal change to a working system, monitor it for long enough to understand the impact of the change, and repeat the process if the improvement was not good enough or reverse it if the effects were bad.
- To take advantage of ZFS's data integrity quality projections, Sun recommends using ZFS RAID even when the underlying storage array has RAID protections.

External SCSI Devices

External SCSI storage is typically the least expensive storage array option. Despite the large number of vendors and products in this marketplace, there are several general comments that can be made about all of these solutions.

Each vendor's hardware, driver and connectivity requirements will be different. Before purchasing a unit, it is critical to verify that our hardware, OS version and application software is certified for the unit.

PCI Expansion Bus

Since the death of the Sbus, the PCI bus is the main expansion bus for Sun systems. Almost all add-on SCSI adapters in current hardware use the PCI bus.

PCI buses runs at 33 or 66MHz and may be 32 or 64 bit. The peak PCI bus bandwidth is 528 MB/s for 64-bit buses at 66MHz. (For desktop PC hardware, 33MHz PCI buses are still common. 33 MHz buses have peak bandwidths of 264 MB/s for 64-bit and 132 MB/s for 32-bit.)

Newer PCI-x buses run at 133MHz and allow up to 1066 MB/s. PCI-x 2.0 defines clock rates of 266MHz and

533MHz, with peak bandwidths of 2.1 GB/s and 4.2 GB/s, respectively.

Low profile PCI buses are becoming more common, since their smaller form factor fits well with the increasing miniaturization of the system. Low profile PCI comes in MD1 and MD2 flavors, with the primary difference being the shorter length of the MD1 cards. Currently, they do not support 64-bit PCI extensions.

Mini PCI cards are also produced for use in portable and sealed case computers. They are small in size, do not support 64-bit extensions and have a different connector layout, but still otherwise follow the PCI standard.

SCSI Cabling and Termination

A lot of problems with SCSI chains are due to cables or terminators not being securely installed. Make sure that all connections are firmly in place, and use the little screw adapters to keep the cables from coming loose.

Once your cabling exercise is complete, and everything is working properly, take the time to label each cable and each device. Each cable should be labeled on each end to specify where it is supposed to be plugged in. Each server and each device should also be labeled so that it is clear what devices are being indicated. Where appropriate, each port may need to be labeled.

We need to make sure that the cable length and termination requirements are met as well; cable length and termination problems can be among the trickiest to diagnose. Table 10-7 includes maximum SCSI path lengths for each type of SCSI chain.

Table 10-7. SCSI Path Lengths

SCSI Connection Type	Number of Pins	Maximum Path Length (meters) (SE/LVD/HVD)			Maximum Number of Devices	Maximum Transfer Rate (MB/sec)
SCSI-1	25	6	12	25	8	5
SCSI-2	50	6	12	25	8	5
Fast SCSI	50	3	12	25	8	10
Wide/Fast Wide	68	3	12	25	16	20
Ultra SCSI	50	3			8	20
Ultra Wide	68		12	25	16	40
		1.5			8	40
		3			4	40
Ultra2	50		12	25	8	40
Ultra2 Wide	68		12	25	16	80
Ultra3/Ultra160	68		12		16	160
Ultra4/Ultra320	68		12		16	320

In Table 10-7, **SE**=single-ended, **LVD**=low voltage differential, and **HVD**=high voltage differential.

Note that the "Maximum Number of Devices" includes 1 device that needs to be usable by the host adapter.

The maximum path length includes the path internal to each device as well as the lengths of the different SCSI cables.

A SCSI chain may consist of SE, LVD, or HVD devices, but can not mix and match them. (We can mix and match device speeds, but using older, slower devices on a chain will slow down the following devices on the chain.)

Adapters exist that will allow interconnections of devices with different pin numbers, but we have to make sure that the "extra" paths are terminated properly. Problems on chains with different path widths are frequently problems with improper termination.

Do not use HVD cables for LVD chains or vice-versa. Doing so may damage your equipment. If you have a cable that is not labeled, it is almost certainly cheaper to throw it out and buy a new one rather than taking a chance on damaging the host adapter or external device.

If possible, new cables and terminators should be purchased as part of the array purchase. (Frequently, vendors can be persuaded to throw them in as part of the array purchase.) In any case, they should be included in the budget estimates and the quotations that are shown to management.

Don't go cheap on re-using old SCSI cables. A flaky cable will easily cost more grief than the cost of a new cable. Over time, cables will degrade as they get pinched, pulled, and stepped on. At a certain point, they need to be thrown out. And if a cable is removed as part of a troubleshooting exercise, it should be cut and discarded. (If you don't cut it, some helpful soul will put it back in inventory.)

It does make a performance difference where SCSI devices are placed on a chain. There are a few variables to keep in mind:

- Some SCSI device numbers receive better service than others. The top priority is given to SCSI address 7, which is almost always assigned to the host adapter. From there, priority is assigned in decreasing order from devices 6 to 0. On a wide bus, priorities are then assigned in decreasing order from 15 to 8.

  Tape devices are usually assigned SCSI ID 6 due to their performance requirements. This can cause problems where hard drives and tape drives share a chain. Where possible, tape devices and hard drives should be kept on separate SCSI chains, and hard drives should be assigned high ID numbers.

- Device buffer size can help determine an optimal ordering of devices on a SCSI chain. Devices with larger buffers (such as scanners and CD-ROM drives) should be closer to the beginning of the chain. Devices with smaller buffers (such as hard drives) should be near the end of the chain.

It may even be necessary to tweak system parameters to optimize transport through the SCSI bus. This can be done through the `scsi_options` variable in the */etc/system* file. These parameters should not usually be set, since the default settings allow the maximum possible utility for the driver. If we need to limit the capabilities of the SCSI driver, however, this is the place we would do it. The `scsi_hba_attach_setup(9F)` man page includes information on each of the options that can be enabled or disabled through this variable.

In particular, it may be necessary to turn off the tagged queuing option if we have a SCSI chain with obsolete devices which do not implement the option properly. To turn off tagged queuing, we would add the following line to */etc/system*:

```
set scsi_options & ~0x80
```

SCSI Storage Devices

Depending on how a particular piece of storage presents itself to the server, it is likely that the */kernel/drv/sd.conf* file will need to be edited. (By default, this file will only look for LUN 0 on SCSI targets 0-15.) We may need to add entries for the targets and LUNs presented by the storage, or we will not see them. (The syntax for the required edits is likely to be in your storage system documentation.) Lines may need to look like the following entry:

```
name="sd" class="scsi" target=15 lun=255;
```

If a SCSI device is attached to more than one server, make sure to follow the cabling diagrams carefully. It is way too easy to end up with a cabling scheme that causes the attached servers to interfere with each other.

Ideally, we would like to have as much front-end cache as possible. Writes to the storage device are reported as "committed" at the point in time when they are written to the cache. A larger cache is a great way to improve performance.

At the same time, we need to look at some of the technical details behind the storage device. We need to look at how efficiently cache is used; some vendors provide a huge amount of cache but use it so inefficiently that it doesn't matter. We need to look at bus "speeds and feeds" to identify where in the storage device any bottlenecks would lie, and whether the performance limitations are appropriate for our environment. And we need to look at part redundancy and how vulnerable the storage device is to any single point of failure.

In today's market, some vendors are providing solutions that are redundant down to the ground. Cache is mirrored (or at least RAID5-ed), battery backup is provided to prevent data loss from cache if the power fails, path redundancy is provided all the way to the disk, every power supply has a failover, and disk controller units are redundant.

Of course, all that extra hardware and engineering costs money. In every individual circumstance, we have to decide whether the cost savings of a cheaper unit is really enough to justify the additional risk of a failure. (And, given that failures usually happen under load, you can count on that failure happening at the worst possible time.) There is no easy answer, and answers will be different from situation to situation.

iSCSI Storage

iSCSI is a protocol that allows native SCSI commands to be sent over a regular IP network connection. It is a block-level storage protocol (as compared with NFS, which provides file-level access to storage.) This can simplify management of the storage network, since IP networking skills and hardware are commonly available in most enterprises.

When compared to SCSI and Fibre Channel, iSCSI is relatively immature. At this point in its development, iSCSI is stable and reliable enough for enterprise use, but it is still evolving quickly. This section attempts to provide a high-level overview of this emerging technology, with an emphasis on those aspects of the Solaris implementation that are expected to remain stable.

When iSCSI is deployed to an existing IP networking environment, care needs to be taken to segregate the storage traffic for performance and security reasons. Block-level transactions are very latency-sensitive. They will not tolerate networks that are saturated because of system backups or large file transfers.

When implemented properly, iSCSI solutions can provide an effective, fast and reliable storage infrastructure. But thought has to be given to providing a reliable and adequate level of network capacity to the storage traffic.

There are currently some restrictions on iSCSI in the Solaris environment. In particular, iSCSI devices should not be used as dump or swap devices, and they cannot be used as boot devices. Check the version of the *System Administrator's Guide: Devices and File Systems* appropriate for your OS version.

The **initiator** is the network adapter on the client system that initiates the SCSI requests to the storage device. The **target** is the file system on the storage device that is accessed by the initiator. **Discovery** is the process by which the initiator identifies available targets. Discovery may be via any of these three methods:

1. The Internet Storage Name Service (**iSNS**) is a server-based method of finding available targets.

2. **SendTargets** allows potential targets to be discovered by a discovery address.

3. **Static** configurations allow only a fixed list of targets to be discovered. Each target is specified by an entry of the form: `target,target-address[:port-number]`

The Solaris 10 1/06 release is the first one that allows iSCSI support, via the `SUNWiscsiu` and `SUNWiscsir` packages. Later OS releases will include enhancements to the Solaris iSCSI support. We have to check the support matrices for any iSCSI devices to make sure that the appropriate software and OS versions are in place.

iSCSI authentication is supported over the Challenge-Handshake Authentication Protocol (CHAP), which can be implemented in a third-party RADIUS server. CHAP can be set up to authenticate the initiator to the target (**unidirectional**), or to also authenticate the target to the storage client (**bidirectional**). The CHAP configuration is managed with the `iscsiadm` command. The syntax to perform several key authentication-related tasks is:

- **iscsiadm modify initiator-node --CHAP-secret**
  Initiate a dialog to define a CHAP secret key.
- **iscsiadm modify initiator-node --CHAP-name** *new-CHAP-name*
  Changes the initiator's name from the default of the node name.
- **iscsiadm modify initiator-node --authentication CHAP**
  Enable CHAP authentication once the secret has been set up.
- **iscsiadm modify target-param -B enable** *target-name*
  Enable authentication of the target to the storage client.
- **iscsiadm modify target-param --authentication CHAP** *target-name*
  Set the method to CHAP for target to client authentication.
- **iscsiadm modify target-param --CHAP-secret** *target-name*
  Initiate a dialog to define the CHAP secret key on the target.
- **iscsiadm modify target-param --CHAP-name** *target-CHAP-name*
  Change the target's CHAP name from the default of the target name.
- **iscsiadm modify initiator-node --radius-server** *ipaddr:port*
  Configure the initiator with the RADIUS IP address and port.
- **iscsiadm modify initiator-node --radius-shared-secret**
  Configure the initiator node with the RADIUS server's shared secret.
- **iscsiadm modify initiator-node --radius-access enable**
  Enable the RADIUS server.

The following commands manage target discovery:

- **iscsiadm add discovery-address** *ipaddr:port*

  iscsiadm modify discovery --sendtargets enable

  Configure SendTargets dynamic discovery.

- **iscsiadm add iSNS-server** *ipaddr:port*

  iscsiadm modify discovery --isns enable

  Configure iSNS dynamic discovery.

- **iscsiadm add static-config** *target-name,ipaddr*

  iscsiadm modify discovery --static enable

Configure static discovery for target.

- **devfsadm -i iscsi**

  Create iSCSI device links (on storage client).

Discovery methods can be disabled by using "`disable`" rather than "`enable`" and "`remove`" rather than "`add`" in the above commands.

The iSCSI configuration can be monitored with `iscsiadm` as well:

- **iscsiadm list initiator-node**
- **iscsiadm list discovery**
- **iscsiadm list discovery-address -v** *ipaddr*
- **iscsiadm list isns-server -v**
- **iscsiadm list target-param -v** *target-name*
- **iscsiadm list target -v** *target-name*

Fibre Channel Storage

Fibre channel storage provides a reliable and high-performing solution to data storage needs. Unfortunately, fibre channel storage is usually the most expensive disk storage option.

More people are migrating to iSCSI to save money on infrastructure and training costs associated with maintaining a fibre channel SAN (Storage Area Network). But at the high end, it is likely that fibre channel will be around for quite a bit longer.

Configuring and maintaining a SAN is a discipline all to itself. A full discussion is well beyond the scope of this book. Fortunately, fibre channel has matured significantly, to the point that most properly-configured fibre channel devices will work together.

Fibre Channel Connectivity

From the point of view of the OS, the most important thing to consider is the HBA that is installed (and the driver required to run it). Each driver is different, and will require changes to its own configuration to support our environment. Still, there are a lot of similarities.

With current releases of Solaris 10, the HBAs supporting the Leadville drivers allow us to find available storage easily, without directly editing configuration files. If we use the HBA vendor's driver, we will probably need to do some configuration file editing.

We will probably need to edit the *sd.conf* file to allow the kernel to set up the structures to deal with the new targets and LUNs that will be presented through the HBA. For example, the following is a line added to an *sd.conf* file for storage attached through an Emulex HBA:

```
name="sd" parent="lpfc" target=21 lun=247 hba="lpfc1";
```

In addition, the driver configuration file will need to be set up to look for the correct storage device address (known as a **World Wide Number** or **WWN**). For an Emulex HBA, the configuration file is at */kernel/drv/lpfc.conf*, and the driver is the `lpfc` driver. (As with most of these HBAs, the drivers are downloadable from the vendor web site.) The key line in the *lpfc.conf* file is:

```
fcp-bind-WWPN="50060482abcdabcd:lpfc1t21";
```

Each individual driver's configuration will need to be addressed according to the manufacturer's instructions. Most HBAs also come with a piece of monitoring software to identify when the HBA is connecting to the switch or array properly.

Aside from configuring the HBA, we need to configure the storage to be available to the server. This may mean zoning on the switch so that the server can talk to the disk storage unit, and it may also mean configuring the LUN masking on the storage array so that the LUN we want is permissioned to the server that needs it. The steps to perform the zoning and masking steps will depend on the particular hardware involved; consult the vendor documentation for your hardware.

Sometimes, it is necessary to "reset" an adapter that has become error-disabled. The method for doing this will depend on the driver in question. For example, Emulex HBAs use the `lputil` menu-based utility to allow an online driver reset (as opposed to a less convenient reboot.)

Multipathing

The "Solaris FC and Storage Multipathing Software" is included with the Solaris 10 license. (It is enabled by default with the Solaris 10x86 installation, but is optional in the Sparc installlation.) This software allows multiple path support for supported storage devices. Similar capabilities have been available for some time via third party software such as Veritas Volume Manager's `vxdmp` and EMC Powerpath, but the inclusion of free path management software is a major step forward for sites that want to use ZFS and Solaris Volume Manager for volume management tasks. Significant fixes were implemented in Solaris 10 5/09, so it is recommened to upgrade to at least that level, especially if multipathing will be used with ZFS.

As of this writing, the software supports multipathing for fibre channel connections using host bus adapters on the hardware compatibility list. It does not currently support multipathing for parallel SCSI devices or IP over FC. This may change with future releases of Solaris if there is customer demand for this capability.

For Sparc-based systems, multipathing support is enabled and disabled via the `stmsboot -e` and `stmsboot -d` commands. This command reboots the system to complete the process, so make sure that the right boot-device is included in the EEPROM settings before proceeding. When multipathing is enabled, copies of the */etc/vfstab* and */kernel/drv/fp.conf* files are preserved to allow the changes to be backed out if necessary.

For x86-based systems, directly edit the *fp.conf* to change the value of `mpxio-disable` to "no." (Disabling it will involve changing it to "`yes`.") After the change, run a reconfiguration reboot.

To enable or disable multipathing on a per-port basis, the `mpxio-disable` parameter may be set on a port-specific line in the *fp.conf*. (Syntax guidance is included in the comments of the *fp.conf* file.)

Multipathing is important because it allows continued access to storage even in the event of a component failure on one of the paths. In devices that support the T10 ALUA standard can even allow load balancing across all active paths.

> In the Solaris Multipathing Software, a **path** consists of an initiator port, a target port, and a logical unit. The **initiator port** is usually a host bus adapter port, a **target port** represents the port on the storage unit, and a **logical unit** is a virtual disk that is presented to the host. **Auto-Failback** allows us to specify one of the paths as being preferred, so that we will always fail back to it if it is available.

The `mpathadm` command is used to administer the multipathing facility. Table 10-8 lists several common activities and the command used to carry them out.

Table 10-8. mpathadm Command Support

Task	Command
List available multipathing support	`mpathadm list mpath-support`
View properties for supported multipathing facilities.	`mpathadm show mpath-support` *facilityname*
List initiator ports.	`mpathadm list initiator-port`
Get initiator port properties.	`mpathadm show initiator-port` *portname*
List available logical units.	`mpathadm list lu`
Get logical unit properties.	`mpathadm show lu` *lunname*
List logical units associated with a target port.	`mpatadm list lu -t` *portname*
Configure auto-failback.	`mpathadm modify mpath-support -a off \` *facilityname*
Disable a path.	`mpathadm disable path -i` *initportname* `\` `-t` *tgtportname* `-l` *lunname*

Example 10-6 illustrates what the output for some of these commands looks like:

Example 10-6. mpathadm Command Output

```
# mpathadm list mpath-support
mpath-support:  libmpscsi_vhci.so
# mpathadm show mpath-support libmpscsi_vhci.so
mpath-support:  libmpscsi_vhci.so
        Vendor:  Sun Microsystems
        Driver Name:  scsi_vhci
        Default Load Balance:  round-robin
        Supported Load Balance Types:
                round-robin
                logical-block
        Allows To Activate Target Port Group Access:  yes
        Allows Path Override:  no
        Supported Auto Failback Config:  1
        Auto Failback:  on
        Failback Polling Rate (current/max):  0/0
        Supported Auto Probing Config:  0
        Auto Probing:  NA
        Probing Polling Rate (current/max):  NA/NA
        Supported Devices:
                Vendor:  SUN
                Product:  T300
                Revision:
                Supported Load Balance Types:
                        round-robin
...
                Vendor:  EMC
                Product:  SYMMETRIX
                Revision:  5671
```

209

```
                    Supported Load Balance Types:
                            round-robin
# mpathadm list initiator-port
Initiator Port:   iqn.1986-03.com.sun:01:00144f2cabca.4651f73b,4000002a00ff
Initiator Port:   210100e08baa32ab
Initiator Port:   210100e08baa42ab
Initiator Port:   210000e08bdd42ab
Initiator Port:   210000e08bdd32ab
# mpathadm show initiator-port 210000e08bdd32ab
Initiator Port:   210000e08bdd32ab
        Transport Type:   Fibre Channel
        OS Device File:   /devices/pci@1e,600000/pci@0/pci@1/pci@0/pci@8/SUNW,qlc@2/fp@0,0
# mpathadm list lu
        /dev/rdsk/c6t60060480000038743014953652D343444d0s2
                Total Path Count: 2
                Operational Path Count: 2
...

# mpathadm show lu /dev/rdsk/c6t60060480000038743014953652D343444d0s2
Logical Unit:  /dev/rdsk/c6t60060480000038743014953652D343444d0s2
        mpath-support:  libmpscsi_vhci.so
        Vendor:  EMC
        Product:  SYMMETRIX
        Revision:  5671
        Name Type:  unknown type
        Name:  60060480000038743014953652D343444
        Asymmetric:  no
        Current Load Balance:  round-robin
        Logical Unit Group ID:  NA
        Auto Failback:  on
        Auto Probing:  NA

        Paths:
                Initiator Port Name:  210100e08baa42ab
                Target Port Name:  50060485c5edabcd
                Override Path:  NA
                Path State:  OK
                Disabled:  no

                Initiator Port Name:  210000e08bdd42ab
                Target Port Name:  50060485c5eddcba
                Override Path:  NA
                Path State:  OK
                Disabled:  no

        Target Ports:
                Name:  50060485c5edabcd
                Relative ID:  0

                Name:  50060485c5eddcba
                Relative ID:  0
```

Note that the **mpathadm show mpath-support** command above reported that the EMC Symmetrix was supported. This support is not contained in the default version of the configuration file at */kernel/drv/scsi_vhci.conf*. Example 10-7 shows the changes necessary to bring this support into the multipathing software:

Example 10-7. Adding Multipathing Device Support

```
# cat /kernel/drv/scsi_vhci.conf
#
# Copyright 2004 Sun Microsystems, Inc. All rights reserved.
# Use is subject to license terms.
#
#pragma ident    "@(#)scsi_vhci.conf    1.9    04/08/26 SMI"
#
name="scsi_vhci" class="root";
...
# symmetric-option = 0x1000000;
device-type-scsi-options-list =
"EMC      SYMMETRIX        5671", "symmetric-option";

symmetric-option = 0x1000000;
```

Unfortunately, the syntax on the *scsi_vhci.conf* file is incredibly picky. The vendor name must be exactly eight characters long, even if you have to pad it with spaces. The product ID can be "up to" 16 characters long, but most recommendations I've seen say to pad the product ID with spaces as well.

Resources

- Ault, Mike. (April 2004) *Oracle Disk I/O Tuning: Disk I/O Performance & Optimization for Oracle Databases*. Rampant Press.
- Cockcroft, Adrian and Pettit, Richard. (April 1998) *Sun Performance and Tuning: Java and the Internet, 2ⁿᵈ Ed*. Upper Saddle River, NJ: Prentice Hall.
- Cromar, Scott. (2007) *Solaris Troubleshooting and Performance Tuning at Princeton University*. Princeton, NJ. (http://www.princeton.edu/~unix/Solaris/troubleshoot/index.html)
- EMC. (April 2007) *EMC Host Connectivity Guide for Sun Solaris*. Hopkinton, MA: EMC Corporation.
- Farley, Marc. (2000) *Building Storage Networks*. Berkeley, CA: Osborne.
- Matteson, Ryan. (December 2005) *Observing I/O Behavior with the DTrace Toolkit*. SysAdmin Magazine. (http://www.samag.com/documents/s=9915/sam0512a/0512a.htm)
- McDougall, Richard and Mauro, Jim. (July 2006) *Solaris Internals*. Upper Saddle River, NJ: Prentice Hall & Sun Microsystems Press.
- McDougall, Richard; Mauro, Jim and Gregg, Brendan. (October 2006) *Solaris Performance and Tools*. Upper Saddle River, NJ: Prentice Hall & Sun Microsystems Press.
- Nadgir, Neelakanth. (September 2006) *Databases and ZFS*. (http://blogs.sun.com/realneel/entry/zfs_and_databases)
- OpenSolaris Community (July 2007) *ZFS Best Practices Guide*. (http://www.solarisinternals.com/wiki/index.php/ZFS_Best_Practices_Guide)
- Sun Microsystems. (December 2006) *Solaris Fibre Channel and Storage Multipathing Administration Guide*. Palo Alto, CA: Sun Microsystems, Inc. (http://docs.sun.com/app/docs/doc/819-0139)
- Sun Microsystems. (May 2006) *Solaris Volume Manager Administration Guide*. Palo Alto, CA: Sun Microsystems, Inc. (http://docs.sun.com/app/docs/doc/816-4520)
- Sun Microsystems. (November 2006) *Solaris ZFS Administration Guide*. Palo Alto, CA: Sun Microsystems, Inc. (http://docs.sun.com/app/docs/doc/819-5461)
- Sun Microsystems. (November 2006) *System Administration Guide: Devices and File Systems*. Palo Alto, CA: Sun Microsystems, Inc. (http://docs.sun.com/app/docs/doc/817-5093)

- Symantec. (2004) *Veritas Volume Manager 4.0 Administrator's Guide, Solaris*. Mountain View, CA: Veritas Software Corporation.

.

11

Network Troubleshooting

Network Models

Network models provide excellent frameworks for troubleshooting network problems. They allow us to carve up network connectivity into discrete layers, each of which can be investigated independently. Table 11-1 lists the layers of the OSI network model. Table 11-2 lists the layers of the TCP/IP Protocol Architecture.

> This chapter will focus on IPv4. IPv6 is an extension of IPv4 that includes secure transmission capabilities and an extended address space. We can expect to see IPv6 installations increase over the next several years as a result of government mandates and increased support for IPv6 by vendors. IPv6 may be coming, but it is not here yet in the vast majority of production networks. Unless otherwise specified, "IP" in this chapter means "IPv4."
>
> Several key concepts of IPv6 are presented in the "IPv6 Considerations" section at the end of the chapter.

For the purposes of this book, we will focus on using the TCP/IP Protocol Architecture to construct our network troubleshooting methodology. In general, this model matches up better with the types of tools and techniques available to us from the server side. (Many methodologies suggested by manufacturers of network equipment use the OSI model as their jumping-off point, but this book has a definite server-side bias.)

The advantage to doing things this way is that the symptoms may tell you which layer is most likely to be the problem. For example, if some network services work, but others don't, it makes the most sense to start with the Application Layer rather than the Network Access Layer.

Both the OSI model and the TCP/IP model describe the same sorts of activity. The fact that the TCP/IP model has fewer layers reflects the implementation details and history of TCP/IP. Some functions described as separate layers in the OSI model (such as the Data Link Layer, for example) are folded into other layers in the TCP/IP architecture.

In both models, data is sent from the application down the stack to the network. On the receiving side, the data is sent up the stack to the application.

OSI Model

Table 11-1. OSI Network Reference Model

Layer Name	Description
Application Layer	Application programs using the network.
Presentation Layer	Data presentation to the applications.
Session Layer	Manages sessions between cooperating applications.
Transport Layer	End-to-end error detection and correction.
Network Layer	Manages connections and addressing on the network.
Data Link Layer	Reliable data delivery across physical network components.
Physical Layer	Network media characteristics.

The OSI model is intended to describe a generic computer networking implementation. In actual implementations, such as TCP/IP, some of the layers may be combined. This does not mean that the particular layers are unimportant; it just means that the implementation details are hidden from us, the end user of the implementation.

TCP/IP Protocol Architecture

Table 11-2. TCP/IP Protocol Architecture

Layer Name	Description	Objects
Application Layer	Applications and processes that use the network.	Stream (TCP). Message (UDP).
Transport Layer	End-to-end data delivery services.	Segment (TCP). Packet (UDP).
Internet Layer	Routes and delivers data.	Datagrams
Network Access Layer	Access to physical networks.	Packets or frames, depending on underlying network technology.

As each piece of network-transmitted data is passed down the stack, each layer adds a header to the chunk of data. (This is known as **encapsulation**.) This header tells the corresponding layer on the receiving system how to deliver the data to the next layer. On the receiving system, each layer removes the corresponding header before passing the message on to the next layer.

Figure 11-1 shows encapsulation and de-encapsulation during network communication.

The vast majority of TCP/IP traffic consists of either TCP (Transmission Control Protocol) or UDP (User Datagram Protocol) packets or frames. (In order to avoid confusion, we will refer to the Network Access Layer objects as "frames" in the following discussion.) The "Transport Layer" section below discusses TCP and UDP in more detail.

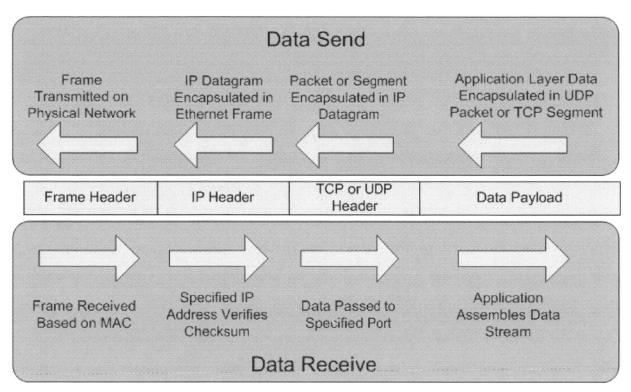

Figure 11-1. Encapsulation

Connectivity and Capacity

The two types of problems that appear on the network have to do with capacity and connectivity.

Connectivity problems occur when two objects in our network cannot communicate properly on the physical network. These can occur anywhere along the network path between the two network objects. Problems may appear as a result of a poorly seated host bus adapter or cable, a flaky cable, or a bad network port or misconfigured router anywhere along the path.

The **ping** command is a primary tool to use when looking at apparent connectivity problems. If ping works, it is a pretty good bet that we should start by looking at application and service issues first. If it fails, it will usually fail in one of three ways:

1. "Unknown Host" types of errors usually indicate a name lookup problem of some sort. Check the *ipnodes* and *hosts* files to make sure that no incorrect entries have crept in. Check the *nsswitch.conf* to make sure that we are going after the right naming service. Check the naming service configuration files on the client. Finally, tools like DNS's **dig** and **nslookup** can be used to make sure that the correct information is stored in the name service repository.

2. "Network Unreachable" sorts of errors indicate a routing problem of some sort. It may be worth **ping**ing the IP address directly to make sure we don't have a name lookup problem. If not, **netstat -r** will report on the routing table for the system. Make sure that the route to the target system leads to the correct gateway.

3. "No Answer" messages (including "100% Packet Loss" and "Connection Timed Out")

215

indicate that a route exists, but that no answer is received from the target system. As above, try `ping`ing the IP address to eliminate the name service as the source of the problem. Make sure that the target system is online and communicating to the network at its end. See if there are any firewalls or network security settings on intermediate devices that are preventing us from `ping`ing the target. `traceroute` may be useful in telling us at what point the ball gets dropped.

Packet loss messages where the percentage is less than 100% are frequently caused by network congestion. **Capacity bottlenecks** are situations where an increase in network capacity would result in better performance. These bottlenecks can occur at any of several places along the network path. They can occur at the host bus adapter, the router, hub or switch attached to the host, at any of the intervening network devices, or at the host bus adapter of the target system. Each of these needs to be investigated separately.

Capacity problems may manifest themselves as utilization or saturation problems. Heavy **utilization** occurs when network traffic starts to approach the theoretical maximum for the network link. Network **saturation** occurs when network traffic starts to build up in the buffers because it cannot be transmitted quickly enough. Saturation can result in unacceptable application performance.

> It is possible to have high utilization without there being a problem. For example, large file transfers or backups would be expected to push as much data through the pipe as quickly as possible. As long as the resulting full pipe is infrequent and does not cause unacceptable application delays, this may not be an issue.
>
> On the other hand, high utilization should always be examined to see whether or not it represents a problem.

Network Access Layer[2]

The TCP/IP **Network Access Layer** specifies how the system may deliver data to other systems on a directly connected network. Among other things, the network access layer is responsible for translating IP addresses into physical addresses (ethernet addresses on an ethernet network, for example) which can be transmitted on the physical network. To this end the Network Access Layer attaches a header to the datagram to create a frame of the proper format to be transmitted on the network.

Problems at the Network Access Layer may include physical connectivity problems with network hardware or cables, driver configuration problems, or Address Resolution Protocol (ARP) problems. (**ARP** maps IP addresses to ethernet addresses.)

Connectivity and Configuration

To check for connectivity problems at the port level, there are a number of different actions that we can take:

- Check the link lights on the host network adapter and the network port to which it is attached.
- Check the network device logs to see if there are errors reported on our port.
- Use a cable tester to check the cable attached to the host.
- Use `ndd` or `kstat` to check the connection status (Example 11-2).
- `ifconfig` can report whether the interface is currently configured correctly, plumbed, and up. Check the IP address, mask and broadcast settings on the interface. (Example 11-1).

---

2 In some Solaris documentation, the Network Access Layer is split into a Physical Network Layer and a Data Link Layer. For our purposes, it makes more sense to follow Hunt (2002) and consider them to be combined in a Network Access Layer.

- **ping** the default gateway on the network device. (**netstat -r** specifies the default route.) Check that the default gateway is set properly (see "Routing" in the "Internet Layer" section below).
- Check **netstat -i** for high network error levels, especially input and output errors (Example 11-1).
- Use **ndd** to check the autonegotiation settings (Example 11-2).
- Check any VLAN settings on the switch port.

Example 11-1 demonstrates the use of **ifconfig** and **netstat** to investigate the error rates of a network interface. **ifconfig** output should also be examined to make sure that the IP address and netmask settings are correct.

Example 11-1. Interface Configuration and Error Rates

```
# netstat -i -I ce0
Name Mtu  Net/Dest   Address       Ipkts   Ierrs Opkts  Oerrs Collis Queue
ce0  1500 soltest    soltest       691654249 0    332180836 80091 205287 0

# ifconfig -a
lo0: flags=1000849<UP,LOOPBACK,RUNNING,MULTICAST,IPv4> mtu 8232 index 1
        inet 127.0.0.1 netmask ff000000
ce0: flags=1000843<UP,BROADCAST,RUNNING,MULTICAST,IPv4> mtu 1500 index 2
        inet 192.168.10.163 netmask ffffff00 broadcast 192.168.10.255
        ether ab:cd:ef:12:34:56
```

netstat -i reports three types of error conditions:

- **Collis**: Collisions. These occur when the interface attempts to send a packet while another packet is being sent. On hubs, this is part of normal activity and is not a cause for concern unless collision counts get above 5% of total packets. On a switch, however, collisions may indicate a problem.

- **Ierrs**: Input errors. Caused when a frame failed its frame check sequence.

- **Oerrs**: Output errors. A collision occurred after the first 64 bytes were sent. (Also known as a "late collision.")

Possible causes for Ierrs and Oerrs include hardware problems with cards, cables or ports as well as autonegotiation problems or interference. Example 11-1 shows a large number of Oerrs and Collis in its **netstat -i** output, which is troubling because it is attached to a high-capacity switch. (In this case, the problem was an autonegotiation problem. The "Autonegotiation and Port Settings" section below describes how to deal with this sort of problem.)

> Since the **netstat** output reports on the number of errors since boot time, it makes sense to add an interval to check for increasing numbers of errors rather than looking at the raw numbers.

The **ifconfig -a** command reports on a number of interface configuration parameters for each of the interfaces on the system, including the loopback interface. (**lo0** is called the **loopback interface**, and is the virtual device through which the host talks to itself.) Among other things, the **ifconfig** output reveals the state of the interface (whether it is plumbed and in an UP state, for example), the Maximum Transmission Unit (**mtu**) size (which must match or be smaller than what your network device expects), the internet address, the network mask, the broadcast address, and the ethernet address.

All of these settings need to be checked. They can be corrected temporarily via the **ifconfig** command, but any fixes must be made permanent by putting them in the *ipnodes*, *hosts*, or *netmasks* file or adding them to an **rc** script.

(We will revisit network masks and broadcasts in "Network Masks and Broadcasts" in the "Internet Layer" section. For now, make sure they are appropriate for your network. In practice, the easiest way to do this is to compare the settings to another working system on the same subnet.)

Autonegotiation and Port Settings

When the interface and the network port first speak to each other, they have to agree on how fast to send data (**link speed**) and whether it can be sent bidirectionally (**link mode** or **link_duplex**). Sometimes the network interface may be improperly autonegotiating the link speed and mode. A quick way to check the speed and duplex settings on a machine is to use **dladm show-dev**. Or it can be checked by using **ndd** to check the link_speed and link_mode or link_duplex values and comparing them to the settings expected by the network device.

It is often useful to prohibit the interface from autonegotiating to the wrong setting. For example, we can nail down the speed and mode setting on the switch side to be 1000/full, then do the same for the driver. Depending on the particular driver (and even on the driver version), it may also be necessary to turn off autonegotiation on the driver.

Individual types of interfaces use different settings to specify different speeds and modes. (The documentation for different types of interfaces may be found on the docs.sun.com site.) The most common settings are that 10mbs links have link_speed of 0 or 10, 100mbs links have link_speed of 1 or 100, and gigabit links have a link_speed of 1000. Half duplex links have link_mode or link_duplex of 0 and full duplex links have a link_mode or link_duplex of 1.

To check the names of parameters for a particular driver, the **ndd /dev/module \?** command can be used. In some cases (such as hme, eri and ce), the interface module name does not include the instance number. In other cases, (such as nge and bge), it does. Running the above **ndd** command is a good way to check which is the case for a particular interface type. Or we can check the manual.

Example 11-2. Checking and Setting Interface Driver Settings

```
# ndd /dev/nge \?
operation failed: Invalid argument
# ndd /dev/nge0 \?
?                             (read only)
autoneg_cap                   (read only)
...
1000fdx_cap                   (read only)
1000hdx_cap                   (read only)
100T4_cap                     (read only)
100fdx_cap                    (read only)
100hdx_cap                    (read only)
10fdx_cap                     (read only)
10hdx_cap                     (read only)
adv_autoneg_cap               (read and write)
...
link_status                   (read only)
link_speed                    (read only)
link_duplex                   (read only)
link_autoneg                  (read only)
...
# ndd /dev/eri0 \?
open of /dev/eri0 failed: No such file or directory
# ndd /dev/eri \?
?                             (read only)
transceiver_inuse             (read only)
link_status                   (read only)
link_speed                    (read only)
link_mode                     (read only)
...
#  ndd /dev/ce \?
?                             (read only)
instance                      (read and write)
```

```
adv_autoneg_cap              (read and write)
adv_1000fdx_cap              (read and write)
adv_1000hdx_cap              (read and write)
adv_100T4_cap                (read and write)
adv_100fdx_cap               (read and write)
adv_100hdx_cap               (read and write)
adv_10fdx_cap                (read and write)
adv_10hdx_cap                (read and write)
...
link_status                  (read only)
link_mode                    (read only)
link_speed                   (read only)
# ndd -set /dev/ce instance 0
# ndd -get /dev/ce link_status
1
# ndd -get /dev/ce link_speed
1000
# ndd -get /dev/ce link_mode
1
...
# dladm show-dev
bge0         link: up        speed: 1000  Mbps      duplex: full
bge1         link: up        speed: 1000  Mbps      duplex: full
nxge0        link: up        speed: 1000  Mbps      duplex: full
nxge1        link: unknown   speed: 0     Mbps      duplex: unknown
nxge2        link: unknown   speed: 0     Mbps      duplex: unknown
nxge3        link: unknown   speed: 0     Mbps      duplex: unknown
nxge4        link: up        speed: 1000  Mbps      duplex: full
nxge5        link: up        speed: 1000  Mbps      duplex: full
nxge6        link: unknown   speed: 0     Mbps      duplex: unknown
nxge7        link: unknown   speed: 0     Mbps      duplex: unknown
clprivnet0        link: unknown    speed: 0    Mbps       duplex: unknown
```

Example 11-2 shows output from different servers with different types of network drivers. (Note that clprivnet0 is a virtual network interface used by Sun Cluster, not a physical network interface.)

For drivers (such as hme, eri and ce) that do not specify the instance number in the name of the module, we need to set the instance manually in order to know which particular interface is being referenced. This was done in Example 11-2 with

ndd -set /dev/ce instance 0

to specify that we wanted to look at ce0.

With the exception of the oddity about whether or not **ndd** wants the instance number as part of the module name, most of the syntax and parameter names are the same across network drivers. (The usual meanings of the link_speed and link_mode or link_duplex parameters are discussed above.)

link_status is very straightforward. A link_status of 1 indicates that the link is up, 0 indicates that it is down.

The parameters with names like adv_1000fdx_cap or 1000fdx_cap indicate the values that the interface is allowed to autonegotiate to. The name indicates the speed in megabits/second as well as whether it is full duplex (fdx) or half duplex (hdx). (Both of the above parameter names refer to gigabit/second speeds at full duplex.) Each of these parameters will be set to 1 (meaning that autonegotiation to that speed and mode is permitted) or 0 (meaning that the interface cannot autonegotiate to that value.)

To nail an interface down to a particular level, we would set all but one of these variables to zero (forbidding autonegotiation to that speed/mode setting). For example,

```
ndd -set /dev/ce instance 0
```

```
ndd -set /dev/ce adv_10hdx_cap 0
```

would have the effect of forbidding the ce0 interface from autonegotiating to 10mbs/hdx.

> Manual settings via **ndd** are only in effect for this boot session. Upon a reboot, everything reverts to the default. These settings can be nailed down in the */etc/system* file or via a rc script containing **ndd** commands. I prefer the latter method because it allows us to change the values by running additional **ndd** commands rather than requiring a reboot to make further changes.

ARP Problems[2]

The **Address Resolution Protocol** (ARP) is the translation mechanism between the IP address and the hardware address for a network node. ARP problems can manifest themselves in some odd ways. In particular, an ARP problem may lead to the "wrong" host responding to a request. In cases where two hosts have accidentally been configured to share the same IP address, we may see intermittent problems where the hosts respond to requests based on who gets the packet first.

The **arp -a** command can be used to dump the contents of the ARP cache for a system that is local to the subnet where we are observing the problem. If we see two different mappings for the same IP address, we have two systems who have shared an IP address. After we make sure that only one system is using the IP address, we can remove the extra ARP table entry with the **arp -d** command. If necessary, we can use the **arp -s** command to add a correct entry to the ARP cache.

Network Capacity

The network interface may simply not have the capacity for our traffic. To see if this is the case, we want to look at utilization statistics, where we are looking at the utilization as a percentage of the theoretical capacity on the network adapter. (We need to keep in mind that there is approximately 10% overhead on IP traffic, so our limit should be about 90% of the theoretical limit.)

Unfortunately, most of the utilization statistics reported by the server are reported in terms of packets per second. This is only helpful when looking at error levels; different-sized packets mean that a packets-per-second measurement does not help us measure utilization.

The most easily available measurement for the number of bytes of traffic may be found as in Example 11-3 with the command:

```
kstat -p 'mod:ins:modins:*bytes64' 1
```

Example 11-3. Network Traffic Levels with kstat

```
# kstat -p 'bge:0:bge0:*bytes64' 1
bge:0:bge0:obytes64      395875047
bge:0:bge0:rbytes64      690929588

bge:0:bge0:obytes64      395875569
bge:0:bge0:rbytes64      690930352
^C
```

---

2 I am following Hunt in including the discussion of the Address Resolution Protocol (ARP) in the Network Access Layer rather than the Internet Layer. ARP problems are more likely to manifest like a physical network problem than a software problem.

```
# /usr/local/bin/nicstat.pl
    Time      Int   rKB/s   wKB/s   rPk/s   wPk/s    rAvs    wAvs   %Util    Sat
14:33:50   bge0/0    1.58    0.91    9.97    0.69   162.5  1349.3    0.02   0.00
14:33:50   bge3/0    0.00    0.00    0.00    0.00    0.00    0.00    0.00   0.00
14:33:50   bge1/0    0.00    0.00    0.00    0.00    0.00    0.00    0.00   0.00
14:33:50   bge2/0    0.00    0.00    0.00    0.00    0.00    0.00    0.00   0.00
14:33:50     bge0    1.58    0.91    9.97    0.69   162.5  1349.3    0.02   0.00
14:33:50      lo0    0.00    0.00    0.00    0.00    0.00    0.00    0.00   0.00
# cat /usr/local/bin/traffic.sh
#!/bin/sh
OBYTESOLD=0
RBYTESOLD=0
kstat -p 'bge:0:bge0:*bytes64' 1 | while read DATA
do
  if [ `echo ${DATA} | /bin/grep obytes | wc -l` -gt 0 ]; then
    if [ ${OBYTESOLD} -eq 0 ]; then
      OBYTESOLD=`echo ${DATA} | awk '{print $2}'`
    else
      OBYTES=`echo ${DATA} | awk '{print $2}'`
      echo `expr ${OBYTES} - ${OBYTESOLD}` " output bytes/sec"
      OBYTESOLD=${OBYTES}
    fi
  fi
  if [ `echo ${DATA} | /bin/grep rbytes | wc -l` -gt 0 ]; then
    if [ ${RBYTESOLD} -eq 0 ]; then
      RBYTESOLD=`echo ${DATA} | awk '{print $2}'`
    else
      RBYTES=`echo ${DATA} | awk '{print $2}'`
      echo `expr ${RBYTES} - ${RBYTESOLD}` " read bytes/sec"
      RBYTESOLD=${RBYTES}
    fi
  fi
done
# /usr/local/bin/traffic.sh
538  output bytes/sec
2203 read bytes/sec
316  output bytes/sec
1699 read bytes/sec
```

The output from these `kstat` commands (as in Example 11-3) can be processed to get a traffic rate of bytes per second on each interface. The sample `traffic.sh` script in the example shows one way of doing this.

The `kstat` information is processed in a nice form via the `nicstat` program, which is provided as part of the free K9Toolkit (see the "References" section). Example 11-3 includes an example of `nicstat` output. `nicstat` can also be run with a specified interval, which can be useful in examining transient problems.

The information is also available via the SNMP MIB-II interface, but only in a form that is sampled every 30 seconds. The following command reports input and output octets (bytes):

/usr/sfw/bin/snmpnetstat -v1 -c public -o localhost

Unfortunately, this command does not currently allow us to run it with an interval without reverting to packet counts. (We can hope that this is fixed in future versions. In any case, intervals of less than 30 seconds will not be accurate for this command.)

Ultimately, the easiest way to track the utilization from a server network connection may be to track the statistics on the network device port via `mrtg` or another network monitoring tool.

Link Aggregations

Versions of Solaris 10 after 1/06 support link aggregations to combine the network bandwidth of several network ports into a single channel. (Similar functionality can be achieved in earlier versions of Solaris with the Sun Trunking software.)

We also need to have the right kind of network hardware to support link aggregation. Specifically, we need to check that the ports are of the GLDv3/non-vlan type. We can check this using the **dladm show-link** command. Compatible port types (such as xge, e1000g, and bge) will show a "type: non-vlan" entry in the **dladm** output.

Before we proceed, the switch ports will need to be configured to be used as an aggregation (ie, they need to be trunked together). LACP may also need to be set on the switch.

Once we have identified some compatible interfaces, we can create an aggregation with a command like the following:

```
dladm create-aggr -d bge0 -d bge1 1
```

(In this command, each interface is listed after a "-d" flag, and a unique identifying number is assigned to each aggregation on the server.)

To plumb the new aggregation and bring it up, we would use **ifconfig** and specify the aggregation as aggr#, where # is the number assigned to the aggregation:

```
ifconfig aggr1 plumb 192.168.0.5 up
```

We can verify that the aggregation is online with:

```
dladm show-aggr
```

To make the aggregation persist across reboots, we would create an */etc/hostname.aggr.#* file (or */etc/hostname6.aggr.#* for an IPv6 aggregation).

It may be necessary to set the aggregation to the appropriate LACP settings. If the switch runs LACP in passive mode, we would need to set active mode on the aggregation, and we should match the timer value on the switch (short or long).

```
dladm modify-aggr -l active -t short 1
```

Interfaces can be removed from an aggregation using the **dladm remove-aggr** command and specifying the device to be removed with the **-d** flag. Make sure to configure the switch appropriately. An entire aggregation can be removed using **dladm remove-aggr** by specifying the aggregation's ID number.

The **dladm** command can also be useful in looking at all attached network ports, whether or not they are plumbed yet:

```
dladm show-dev
```

Internet Layer

The **Internet Layer** defines the basic datagram delivery infrastructure on which everything else in TCP/IP is built. This layer takes the responsibility for addressing and routing datagrams to remote locations, breaking up and reassembling datagrams (to comply with frame size restrictions on the physical network) and translating data between the Network Access Layer and the Transport Layer.

The **Internet Protocol** (IP) is the protocol that implements these functions. It is a **connectionless protocol**, meaning that it sends the datagrams on their way and does not check on their arrival at the remote end.

222

(Connection-oriented features are implemented in other related protocols, such as TCP.)

Through `kstat`, we can check the values of several parameters and counters associated with key protocols and drivers:

```
kstat -m tcp
kstat -m ip
kstat -m bge
```

report on all available `kstat` statistics for these modules. `no can puts` per second and `defers per second` may be indications of network saturation.

ICMP[3]

The `ping` program implements the Internet Control Message Protocol (**ICMP**) to see whether a target IP address is responding. ICMP has other uses, such as sending a "source quench" message back to a sender which is sending datagrams too quickly for the target to process, sending a "redirect message" to tell a host to use a different gateway to reach the target or to send a "destination unreachable" message back to the source system if the target cannot be reached.

The `traceroute` program also implements ICMP to attempt to trace a route between our system and a target on the network. Each successive iteration sends an ICMP packet with a slightly longer TTL (Time To Live) so that each line of output represents a step further along the network path. Since there may be more than one way to travel between two IP addresses, it is possible that the reported paths will be inconsistent, but this is less common than one might think. (Example 11-4 below shows an example of `traceroute`'s output.)

Name Service

The name service is implemented by identifying the primary host lookup mechanism in the */etc/nsswitch.conf*'s `hosts` line. Usually more than one mechanism is specified so that if a lookup is not found in one place, we can check another.

One common scheme is to have the name lookups check the local *hosts* and *ipnodes* files first, then fall back to another name lookup scheme. Sometimes the backup scheme is DNS (Domain Name Service), which is the principal name lookup mechanism for the Internet. Sometimes the secondary mechanism is another service (eg NIS) which checks its own database first before checking with DNS.

When a `files` option is set on the *nsswitch.conf*'s `hosts` line, Solaris 10 looks first in the *ipnodes* file, then in the *hosts* file. Since *ipnodes* is a new file that has been added to support IPv6, a lot of experienced admins will forget that they need to check there as well as *hosts*. For that matter, it makes sense to put critical hostnames in *ipnodes* to save the time required to switch to the hosts file before finding the hostname translation. Sun recommends keeping the two files in sync for all IPv4 addresses. (*hosts* does not allow IPv6 addresses.)

DNS is configured using the */etc/resolv.conf* file. This file allows us to set the default lookup zone as well as the IP addresses of servers that can be queried for name lookup information. The `nslookup` and `dig` commands can be used to query a DNS server to make sure that accurate information is being returned.

The */etc/nodename* file is a critical part of making sure that the right hostname and IP address are assigned to a server on its reboot. If no */etc/nodename* file exists, Solaris's `hostconfig` program will attempt to find the host name, domain name, and router addresses from network configuration servers. Generally speaking, a server's */etc/nodename* file should contain the same hostname as exists in the *ipnodes/hosts* files and the */etc/hostname.interface* file associated with the primary interface.

---

3 Hunt includes ICMP in his discussion of the Network Access Layer. From a troubleshooting perspective, I feel that it is more logically included in the Internet Layer, as is the case in the Solaris *IP Services* manual.

Similarly, */etc/domainname* should contain the domain name if a NIS domain is being assigned, and the */etc/defaultrouter* needs to contain the address of the default gateway. (An empty *defaultrouter* file forces the client to use dynamic routing, which may or may not work out, depending on your network configuration.)

Network Masks and Broadcast Addresses

Network masks (or **netmasks**) are how a range of IP addresses is partitioned into a physical network or VLAN (Virtual LAN). In order for a subnet to work properly, every node on the subnet must have the same mask and broadcast address.

The mask defines which addresses are directly accessible to a given node (the local network), and which ones will need to pass their packets to a gateway for further delivery.

To understand how masks and broadcast addresses are selected, we need to understand how IP addresses are put together. The usual decimal representation of an IPv4 IP address contains four decimal numbers 0-255, separated by periods, each representing an 8-bit value. Masks are easier to understand when the address is represented by binary numbers, each 8 bits long.

The leftmost group of bits represents the network address (the address of the network as a whole). The rightmost group of bits represents the address of a specific node within the network. The mask defines where the dividing line between "leftmost" and "rightmost" occurs.

For example, the standard class-C mask is usually written as 255.255.255.0, which translates to 11111111.11111111.11111111.00000000 in binary. This means that the first 24 bits of the address (the part represented by ones in the mask) is the network address, and the last 8 (the part represented by zeros in the mask) is the host address.

The **broadcast address** is generated by taking the network address and rounding out the rest of the address with ones. Assuming that the above mask is for the network at 128.128.128.0 (aka 10000000.10000000.10000000.00000000), the broadcast address would be at 10000000.10000000.10000000.11111111, which translates to 128.128.128.255.

The netmask and broadcast addresses are reported by the `ifconfig` command, as in Example 11-1 above.

Sometimes networks are defined by specifying the network address and the number of bits. The number of bits refers to the number of "1" bits at the beginning of the mask. This type of address notation is called CIDR format. Many configuration files (such as /etc/netmasks) require the dotted decimal notation. Table 11-3 includes translations between the two conventions.

Table 11-3. CIDR Netmask Address Translations

CIDR Network Bits	Dotted Decimal Netmask	IP Addresses Per Subnet
/19	255.255.224.0	8192
/20	255.255.240.0	4096
/21	255.255.248.0	2048
/22	255.255.252.0	1024
/23	255.255.254.0	512
/24	255.255.255.0	256
/25	255.255.255.128	128
/26	255.255.255.192	64

/27	255.255.255.224	32
/28	255.255.255.240	16
/29	255.255.255.248	8
/30	255.255.255.252	4
/31	255.255.255.254	2

RoutingNetwork addresses on the local network do not need to be routed. Packets to those systems can be sent directly. Everything else needs to be routed through a gateway.

One way to set a default gateway is to put the IP address in */etc/defaultrouter*. Upon reboot, the OS checks this file and sets the contents to be the default route. Alternatively, if no default route exists, the default route can be set with the command:

```
route add default ip-address
```

The `netstat -r` command displays all routes defined on the system, including the default route. (`-rn` displays the same thing, but without doing name lookups.) To change the default route, we first need to delete and re-add the default route:

```
route del default ip-address
```

Routes can also be added and deleted to particular addresses and networks.

`traceroute` can be used to see if the route to a particular address is working properly. `traceroute` also measures the latency between hops in the path. The `pathchar` command, which was written by Van Jacobson, takes the extra step of measuring the network bandwidth between hops. (This measurement is done via sampling and some fancy mathematics, not by saturating the link like some other tools do.) While `traceroute` is part of the standard Solaris distribution, `pathchar` is not. The URL to download `pathchar` is in the "References" section at the end of the chapter. Example 11-4 shows examples of `netstat -rn`, `traceroute` and `pathchar` output.

Example 11-4. Displaying Current Routes

```
#  traceroute soltest2
traceroute to soltest2 (192.168.64.104), 30 hops max, 40 byte packets
 1  192.168.128.2 (192.168.128.2)  0.473 ms  0.312 ms  0.216 ms
 2  192.168.129.73 (192.168.129.73)  0.574 ms  0.541 ms  0.602 ms
 3  192.168.255.73 (192.168.255.73)  2.400 ms  2.168 ms  2.346 ms
 4  192.168.254.17 (192.168.254.17)  2.334 ms  2.418 ms  2.725 ms
 5  soltest2 (192.168.64.104)  2.457 ms  2.239 ms  2.384 ms
# netstat -rn

Routing Table: IPv4
  Destination          Gateway              Flags  Ref   Use    Interface
-------------------- -------------------- ----- ----- ------ ---------
192.168.128.0        192.168.128.26       U      1    1036   bge0
224.0.0.0            192.168.128.26       U      1     0     bge0
default              192.168.128.1        UG     1    503
127.0.0.1            127.0.0.1            UH     4    502    lo0
# ./pathchar soltest2
pathchar to soltest2 (192.168.64.104)
 doing 32 probes at each of 64 to 1500 by 32
 0 localhost
 |    49 Mb/s,   105 us (457 us)
 1 192.168.128.2 (192.168.128.2)
 |   245 Mb/s,    70 us (645 us)
```

225

```
 2 192.168.129.73 (192.168.129.73)
 |    46 Mb/s,   865 us (2.64 ms)
 3 192.168.255.73 (192.168.255.73)
 |    42 Mb/s,    34 us (2.99 ms)
 4 192.168.254.17 (192.168.254.17)
 |   229 Mb/s,    27 us (3.10 ms)
 5 soltest2 (192.168.64.104)
 5 hops, rtt 2.20 ms (3.10 ms), bottleneck  42 Mb/s, pipe 16217 bytes
```

The great thing about **traceroute** is that when it fails, it indicates where in the path we may have a problem. The *pathchar* readings are not entirely accurate, especially on the other side of the bottleneck. The reported bandwidths should not be accepted as gospel. There is a lot of noise for the program to filter out. Still, in this example, it correctly identified the bottleneck as being a T3 link, and 42 Mb/s is not an unreasonable estimate of the bandwidth limitations. **pathchar**'s greatest usefulness is as a bottleneck-finder that does not require saturating the link to estimate the bandwidth of the bottleneck.

Network Security Settings

Some network problems are caused by different sorts of attacks that can be launched against our network. Part of recovering from this class of problem will involve hardening our systems against network attacks. Sun has published a series of recommendations for hardening the network stack.

While the Solaris 10 installation has tightened up some of the default settings, other settings need to be adjusted to improve the network security posture of our systems. Example 11-4 and Table 11-4 define some of these settings and show how to change them. They can be added to the */etc/system* file or as an rc script to be run at boot time. I usually prefer the latter approach, since some settings cannot be changed once they have been nailed down in */etc/system*.

Example 11-4. Setting TCP Security Settings

```
ndd -set /dev/ip ip_forwarding 0
ndd -set /dev/ip ip6_forwarding 0
ndd -set /dev/ip ip_strict_dst_multihoming 1
ndd -set /dev/ip ip6_strict_dst_multihoming 1
ndd -set /dev/ip ip_send_redirects 0
ndd -set /dev/ip ip6_send_redirects 0
ndd -set /dev/ip ip_ignore_redirect 1
ndd -set /dev/ip ip6_ignore_redirect 1
ndd -set /dev/ip ip_forward_src_routed 0
ndd -set /dev/ip ip6_forward_src_routed 0
ndd -set /dev/ip ip_forward_directed_broadcasts 0
ndd -set /dev/tcp tcp_conn_req_max_q0 4096
ndd -set /dev/tcp tcp_ip_abort_cinterval 60000
ndd -set /dev/ip ip_respond_to_timestamp 0
ndd -set /dev/ip ip_respond_to_timestamp_broadcast 0
ndd -set /dev/ip ip_respond_to_address_mask_broadcast 0
ndd -set /dev/arp arp_cleanup_interval 60000
ndd -set /dev/ip ip_ire_arp_interval 60000
```

While I can think of scenarios where we might want to adjust some of the above parameters on a running system, there are some parameters I can't imagine changing. For example, I recommend the following setting in */etc/system*:

```
set nfssrv:nfs_portmon=1
```

(This setting requires that NFS client requests come from the privileged range of ports. While this is extremely weak protection, I can't conceive of any legitimate reason to set it any other way.)

226

Table 11-4. Network Parameter Security Settings; Default/Recommended

Parameter	Default /Recommend	Description
arp_cleanup_interval	300000 /60000	How frequently arp cache flushed. (60000=1 min)
ip[6]_forwarding[4]	0/0	Whether IP forwarding is enabled.
ip[6]_strict_dst_multihoming	0/1	Whether a packet can be received on an interface not configured with that IP address.
ip[6]_send_redirects	1/0	Whether interfaces send out ICMP redirect messages.
ip[6]_ignore_redirect	0/1	Whether interfaces should ignore redirect messages.
ip[6]_forward_src_routed	1/0	Controls whether packets forwarded with source routing.
ip_forward_directed_broadcasts	0/0	Whether system forwards directed broadcasts.
ip_respond_to_timestamp[_broadcast]	0/0	Whether system responds to timestamp queries/broadcasts (not related to NTP).
ip_respond_to_address_mask_broadcast	0/0	Whether system responds to address mask broadcasts.
ip_ire_arp_interval	1200000 /60000	How frequently IP routing table refreshed. (60000=1 min)
tcp_conn_req_max_q	128 /1024	Maximum number of pending TCP connections waiting for socket accept(3S).
tcp_conn_req_max_q0	1024 /4096	Number of incomplete 3-way handshakes allowed.
tcp_ip_abort_cinterval	180000 /60000	Amount of time a connection can stay in a half-open state.
tcp_rev_src_routes	0/0	Whether to forward source-routed packets.

---

4   I'm using the [6] in brackets to indicate that this parameter should be set for both IPv4 (without the "6") and IPv6 (with the "6").

Parameter	Default /Recommend	Description
`tcp_strong_iss`	1/2	Strength of sequence-number choosing routine.

Sometimes an improperly configured network or a poorly configured host may result in overloading the network with broadcasts of different types. Overwhelming levels of broadcast traffic are known as **broadcast storms**. Excessive levels of ARP requests can be detected by looking at the statistics reported by `netstat -s`.

Some common causes of broadcast storms include:
- Hosts configured to use the broadcast address as their own IP address.
- Improperly configured broadcast forwarding on a network device.
- Use of mixed 0s and 1s styles of broadcast addresses.
- ARP requests for broadcast addresses.
- Improperly formatted ARP requests.

To detect improper levels of broadcast traffic, it is important to have a baseline to compare against. We can compare to similarly configured networks, or we can periodically log the traffic profiles to create a historical record.

A lot of performance-related measurements really require a historical context before they can be well-understood. Set up some `cron`-driven scripts to collect baseline information over time so that it is available when we need it for troubleshooting.

Non-Routable IP Addresses

There are three blocks of IPv4 address space reserved for use on **private networks** (networks which do not route to the Internet). These private network addresses are sometimes referred to as "**Non-Routable IP Addresses**." Routing may be enabled for networks using these addresses by using **Network Address Translation** (NAT), which effectively routes the private network's addresses through a single routable IP address. Without using something like NAT, it will not be possible to use private network addresses on Internet-connected hosts. Even without NAT, it is very handy to be able to use these addresses to set up test networks which should not talk to the outside.

Table 11-5 lists the reserved private address ranges:

Table 11-5. Private (Non-Routable) IPv4 Addresses

Beginning Address	Ending Address
10.0.0.0	10.255.255.255
172.16.0.0	172.31.255.255
192.168.0.0	192.168.255.255

Transport LayerThe two most important protocols in the Transport Layer are TCP and UDP. They serve different purposes and supply different needs within the TCP/IP protocol. **TCP** provides reliable data delivery and end-to-end error detection and correction. **UDP**, on the other hand, provides low-overhead, connectionless delivery.[5]

The connectionless nature of UDP is sometimes referred to as "unreliability." By this, we mean that the datagram is sent on its way, and no further effort is made to determine whether or not it arrived. Sometimes applications that

---

5 Solaris also supports the SCTP protocol at the Transport Layer. The SCTP protocol supports connections (called "associations") between multi-homed hosts that allow traffic to flow over all available interfaces. This is much less frequently used, so it is outside the scope of this chapter. See the `sctp(7P)` man page for more information.

involve a "query-response" model of operation use UDP under the theory that the response itself is evidence that the original query arrived.

A common analogy is to compare UDP to mailing a letter. We address the letter, slap a stamp on it, drop it at the post office, and take no further thought. Typically, we do not take direct action to track the letter or verify its arrival.

TCP, on the other hand, is used for applications that require a persistent connection or "guaranteed" delivery and error correction. This is accomplished by having TCP repeatedly re-send the packet until it receives a positive acknowledgment that it was received. An essential part of the protocol, then, is that the recipient needs to send a positive acknowledgment if the segment arrived undamaged.

The information required to keep track of a TCP session is included in the segment headers. These include information about the sending and receiving ports, segment ordering information, and checksum information to allow us to verify that the data package is undamaged.

TCP connections with the remote host are initialized by using a "**three-way handshake.**" For example, the initiating host sends a **SYN** packet (Synchronize sequence numbers). This packet includes a **sequence number**, which will be used by the sending host to keep track of the packets sent to the target host. The receiving host acknowledges receipt of the SYN packet by sending a **SYN-ACK** (Synchronize/Acknowledgment) packet. This packet includes a sequence number, which will be used to keep track of packets sent from the target to the source. Upon receipt of the SYN-ACK, the source system sends an **ACK** segment to acknowledge receipt of the SYN-ACK, and starts sending data. Figure 11-2 depicts a three-way handshake.

TCP uses the sequence number and acknowledgment number fields to track the status of a stream of data segments. If necessary, a segment can be re-sent until its receipt is acknowledged by the target system.

Not every segment is acknowledged. Instead, the acknowledgment number verifies receipt of all bytes up to the specified number. The Acknowledgment Segment includes a Window field which specifies the number of bytes the target system can receive. This enforces flow control on the stream so that it does not flow faster than the remote system can handle.

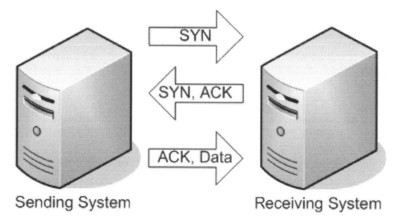

Figure 11-2. Three-Way Handshake

At the end of a session, a **FIN** packet is sent to close the connection.

snoop is a command that shows all the packets seen by a network interface. The following snoop output includes examples of SYN, SYN-ACK and ACK packets. Note how the sequence numbers increment over the course of the conversation, and note that port 22 (ssh) is indicated:

Example 11-5 shows snoop used to record the beginning of an ssh session.

Example 11-5. Network Traffic with snoop

```
#  snoop | grep soltest2
Using device /dev/bge0 (promiscuous mode)
soltest2.composers.caxton.com -> soltest TCP D=22 S=37430 Syn Seq=3802861805 Len=0 Win=49640
Options=<mss 1460,nop,nop,sackOK>
soltest -> soltest2.composers.caxton.com TCP D=37430 S=22 Syn Ack=3802861806 Seq=2059584060
Len=0 Win=49640 Options=<mss 1460,nop,nop,sackOK>
soltest2.composers.caxton.com -> soltest TCP D=22 S=37430 Ack=2059584061 Seq=3802861806
Len=0 Win=49640
soltest -> soltest2.composers.caxton.com AUTH C port=32858
soltest2.composers.caxton.com -> soltest AUTH R port=32858
soltest -> soltest2.composers.caxton.com TCP D=37430 S=22 Push Ack=3802861806 Seq=2059584061
Len=20 Win=49640
soltest2.composers.caxton.com -> soltest TCP D=22 S=37430 Ack=2059584081 Seq=3802861806
Len=0 Win=49640
soltest2.composers.caxton.com -> soltest TCP D=22 S=37430 Push Ack=2059584081 Seq=3802861806
Len=20 Win=49640
soltest -> soltest2.composers.caxton.com TCP D=37430 S=22 Ack=3802861826 Seq=2059584081
Len=0 Win=49640
soltest2.composers.caxton.com -> soltest TCP D=22 S=37430 Push Ack=2059584081 Seq=3802861826
Len=256 Win=49640
soltest -> soltest2.composers.caxton.com TCP D=37430 S=22 Ack=3802862082 Seq=2059584081
Len=0 Win=49640
soltest -> soltest2.composers.caxton.com TCP D=37430 S=22 Push Ack=3802862082 Seq=2059584081
Len=712 Win=49640
soltest2.composers.caxton.com -> soltest TCP D=22 S=37430 Ack=2059584793 Seq=3802862082
Len=0 Win=49640
soltest2.composers.caxton.com -> soltest TCP D=22 S=37430 Push Ack=2059584793 Seq=3802862082
Len=144 Win=49640
soltest -> soltest2.composers.caxton.com TCP D=37430 S=22 Push Ack=3802862226 Seq=2059584793
Len=464 Win=49640
soltest2.composers.caxton.com -> soltest TCP D=22 S=37430 Ack=2059585257 Seq=3802862226
Len=0 Win=49640
```

The real utility of a **snoop** command is that we can literally follow the progress of a network session. (By **snoop**ing the interface of a Jumpstart server, for example, I was able to discover that the tftp file had been misnamed. Finding the problem by any other method I can think of would have been extremely difficult; **snoop** made it almost trivial.)

Transmission Errors

Transmission errors are logged, and should be checked if we are seeing intermittent network problems. The DTrace Toolkit offers **tcpstat.d** and **udpstat.d** to check for TCP and UDP errors, respectively. Example 11-6 includes samples of output from both.

Example 11-6. Checking Port Error Rates

```
# ./udpstat.d
   UDP_out  UDP_outErr      UDP_in  UDP_inErr  UDP_noPort
        0           0           0          0          15
# ./tcpstat.d
   TCP_out   TCP_outRe      TCP_in  TCP_inDup    TCP_inUn
        0           0           0          0           0
      200           0         104          0           0
```

230

Open Port Connections

The OSI session layer is represented by sockets and ports in the TCP/IP model. We can view which connections are currently open by using **netstat -a** (**netstat -an** provides the same information, but without name lookups). Example 11-7 prints out a list of open ports and who is connected to them.

Example 11-7. Checking Open Ports

```
# netstat -an

UDP: IPv4
   Local Address         Remote Address        State
------------------    --------------------  -------
      *.123                                  Idle
127.0.0.1.123                                Idle
192.168.128.26.123                           Idle
      *.111                                  Idle
      *.*                                    Unbound
      *.32777                                Idle
      *.*                                    Unbound
      *.32778                                Idle
      *.4045                                 Idle
      *.32779                                Idle
      *.514                                  Idle
      *.32780                                Idle
      *.32783                                Idle
      *.32802                                Idle
      *.*                                    Unbound
      *.161                                  Idle
      *.33362                                Idle

TCP: IPv4
   Local Address         Remote Address       Swind Send-Q Rwind Recv-Q  State
------------------    --------------------  ----- ------ ----- ------  -------
      *.*                  *.*                 0      0 49152      0  IDLE
      *.111                *.*                 0      0 49152      0  LISTEN
      *.*                  *.*                 0      0 49152      0  IDLE
      *.32771              *.*                 0      0 49152      0  LISTEN
      *.4045               *.*                 0      0 49152      0  LISTEN
      *.7100               *.*                 0      0 49152      0  LISTEN
      *.32772              *.*                 0      0 49152      0  LISTEN
      *.22                 *.*                 0      0 49152      0  LISTEN
      *.23                 *.*                 0      0 49152      0  LISTEN
      *.21                 *.*                 0      0 49152      0  LISTEN
      *.79                 *.*                 0      0 49152      0  LISTEN
      *.513                *.*                 0      0 49152      0  LISTEN
      *.514                *.*                 0      0 49152      0  LISTEN
      *.21                 *.*                 0      0 49152      0  LISTEN
      *.23                 *.*                 0      0 49152      0  LISTEN
      *.25                 *.*                 0      0 49152      0  LISTEN
192.168.128.26.22    192.168.131.49.37430 49640     51 49640      0  ESTABLISHED
      *.25                 *.*                 0      0 49152      0  LISTEN
      *.587                *.*                 0      0 49152      0  LISTEN
192.168.128.26.22    192.168.131.90.4083  64375      0 49640      0  ESTABLISHED
192.168.128.26.22    192.168.131.90.4199  65535      0 49640      0  ESTABLISHED
```

```
192.168.128.26.22     192.168.131.90.4560    64631       0 49640       0 ESTABLISHED

TCP: IPv6
   Local Address                    Remote Address               Swind Send-Q Rwind Recv-
Q   State       If
-------------------------------- -------------------------------- ----- ------ -----
------ ----------- -----
     *.*                              *.*                             0      0 49152
0 IDLE
     *.7100                           *.*                             0      0 49152
0 LISTEN
     *.22                             *.*                             0      0 49152
0 LISTEN
     *.23                             *.*                             0      0 49152
0 LISTEN
     *.21                             *.*                             0      0 49152
0 LISTEN
     *.79                             *.*                             0      0 49152
0 LISTEN
     *.513                            *.*                             0      0 49152
0 LISTEN
     *.514                            *.*                             0      0 49152
0 LISTEN
     *.25                             *.*                             0      0 49152
0 LISTEN

SCTP:
        Local Address                   Remote Address          Swind  Send-Q Rwind  Recv-Q
StrsI/O  State
-------------------------------- -------------------------------- ------ ------ ------ ------
------- -----------
0.0.0.0                          0.0.0.0                          0      0 102400      0
32/32  CLOSED

Active UNIX domain sockets
Address    Type         Vnode      Conn    Local Addr      Remote Addr
600012f57f0 stream-ord 300074a6980 00000000 /tmp/ssh-zmq21118/agent.21118
600012f5988 stream-ord 60001caabc0 00000000 /var/run/.inetd.uds
600012f5b20 stream-ord 6000a8d0540 00000000 /tmp/ssh-vHy20920/agent.20920
600012f5cb8 stream-ord 300074a7b80 00000000 /tmp/ssh-Rpx20974/agent.20974
```

The output shows several ssh connections established with 192.168.131.90 and 192.168.131.49.

The DTrace Toolkit's connections program provides similar information in a nicer format, as in Example 11-8:

Example 11-8. Connections

```
# /opt/DTT/Bin/connections
  UID    PID CMD           TYPE  PORT IP_SOURCE
    0    441 sshd           tcp 65535 192.168.131.90
```

The pfiles command also provides information about the ports associated with different processes. The **procsnports.sh** script in Example 11-9 identifies processes and their associated ports.

Example 11-9. procsnports.sh

```
# cat procsnports.sh
#!/bin/sh

for PID in `ps -ef -o pid | tail +2`
```

```
do
        FOUNDPORT=`pfiles ${PID} 2>&1 | grep "sockname:" | grep "port:" | awk
'{ print $NF }'`
        if [ X"${FOUNDPORT}" != "X" ]; then
                FOUNDPROC=`pfiles ${PID} 2>&1 | grep "^${PID}:"`
                echo "${FOUNDPROC}, ${FOUNDPORT}" | tr "\012" " "
                echo
        fi
done
# procsnports.sh
421:    /usr/lib/inet/inetd start, 21 513 514 514 32778 13782 13724
13783 13722
268:    /usr/lib/nfs/statd, 0
330:    /usr/lib/ssh/sshd, 22
8352:   /usr/apache2/bin/httpd -k start, 80
8353:   /usr/apache2/bin/httpd -k start, 80
13418:  /usr/apache2/bin/httpd -k start, 80
8355:   /usr/apache2/bin/httpd -k start, 80
8351:   /usr/apache2/bin/httpd -k start, 80
5929:   /usr/lib/ssh/sshd, 22
5918:   /usr/lib/ssh/sshd, 22
8455:   /usr/apache2/bin/httpd -k start, 80
8354:   /usr/apache2/bin/httpd -k start, 80
8472:   /usr/apache2/bin/httpd -k start, 80
24377:  /usr/lib/sendmail -bd -q5s, 25 25 587
8382:   /usr/apache2/bin/httpd -k start, 80
8350:   /usr/apache2/bin/httpd -k start, 80
```

Security Settings

An important issue to keep in mind is the sorts of security settings that we have in place on the network as well as the OS level. Network-level security may take the form of firewall our router settings. OS-level security may be handled by things like the TCP wrappers and their *hosts.allow* and *hosts.deny* files. TCP Wrappers can be enabled with the following command:

`inetadm -M tcp_wrappers=TRUE`

Networks are usually partitioned into one or more internal networks, which may be separated by "Demilitarized Zones" (DMZs), which contain servers needing to communicate to more than one network partition. In between the network partitions, a limited number of ports are left open to allow for necessary communications. It is usually the case that more "outgoing" than "incoming" connections are allowed from internal partitions to external networks like the Internet.

The *hosts.deny* file identifies which types of connections are denied by default. A common setting for this file is ALL@*.*, which forbids all connections by default. H*osts.deny* settings can be overridden by *hosts.allow* settings, which can allow settings for particular services from particular hostnames or address ranges.

Application Layer

The Application Layer includes almost all of the programs that come to mind when we think about the "computer network." It includes built-in facilities like telnet or the r-commands, and it includes things like apache web servers and NFS or Samba file shares. Entire books are written about many of these facilities; detailed debugging hints for each of them are well outside the scope of this book. Instead, we will focus on several common troubleshooting methods that can be used over a range of network services.

The DTrace Toolkit's **tcptop** and **tcpsnoop.d** programs provide a way to look at the processes that are the top network consumers and trace the traffic associated with given PIDs.

Example 11-9. Network Traffic

```
# /opt/DTT/Bin/tcptop
2007 Feb  8 16:24:01,  load: 0.04,  TCPin:       0 KB,  TCPout:       1 KB

 UID    PID LADDR             LPORT RADDR            RPORT     SIZE NAME
   0  21480 0.0.0.0           65535 0.0.0.0              0      108 sshd
   0    441 0.0.0.0           65535 0.0.0.0              0     3404 sshd
# /opt/DTT/Bin/tcpsnoop.d
 UID    PID LADDR             LPORT DR RADDR           RPORT SIZE CMD
   0    441 0.0.0.0           65535 <- 0.0.0.0             0   54 sshd
   0    441 0.0.0.0           65535 -> 0.0.0.0             0   54 sshd
   0    441 0.0.0.0           65535 <- 0.0.0.0             0   54 sshd
   0  21493 0.0.0.0           65535 -> 0.0.0.0             0   54 sshd
   0  21493 0.0.0.0           65535 <- 0.0.0.0             0   54 sshd
...
```

NFS and RPC Services

One common network application is the Network File Service (NFS). To function properly, an NFS server must be running an nfsd, rpc.mountd and rpc.lockd daemon. RPC services can be detected with **rpcinfo**. To find the registered program numbers on a system, we use **rpcinfo -p** *hostname*. To ping the services themselves, we can use **rpcinfo -T tcp** and **rpcinfo -T udp**.

Other Services

sshd, telnetd, ftpd, Apache and Samba are examples of services that live at the Application Level. Most services at the Application Level will need to be debugged based on the documents for the particular service.

Many services are managed through the Service Management Facility (SMF). These services can be diagnosed as per the suggestions in the "Service Management Facility" section in Chapter 12.

IPv6 Considerations

IPv6 was created to deal with an impending shortage of IPv4 addresses. Rather than the 32 bits of address space in IPv4, IPv6 has 128 bits. A lot of the impetus for IPv6 has died down, since NAT-ing of private networks has become a way to multiply the available IP addresses. But with government mandates for conversions to IPv6 looming, it seems likely that we will start to see more migrations to IPv6.

The Solaris implementations of IPv6 and IPv4 coexist on the system. Systems may well have both IPv6 and IPv4 addresses defined. Where this is the case, operations may take place using either addressing scheme.

Several key Solaris services may be configured to use IPv6, including the naming services of DNS, LDAP, and NIS. In addition, the Solaris implementation of IPv6 supports IP Security Architecture (IPSEC), Internet Key Exchange (IKE), IP Quality of Service (IPQoS), and IP network Multi-Pathing (IPMP).

Some typical network services that are IPv6-ready include sendmail, NFS, apache, DNS, and LDAP. Since the IPv4 and IPv6 protocols co-exist on the stack, services which are not IPv6-ready will continue to work in IPv4 mode if an IPv4 address has been configured. Some additional configuration may be needed as well. For example, the DNS server will need to be populated with the relevant IPv6 AAAA records and their associated PTR records.

This section is intended to be a brief introduction to IPv6. The Solaris *IP Services* manual listed in the "References" section provides a more in-depth discussion.

IPv6 Terminology

Some familiar terms have a particular definition when used in an IPv6 context. A **router** forwards IPv6 packets and advertises the site prefix over the internal network. **Hosts** have an IPv6 address, but do not forward packets. **Nodes** may be either hosts or routers. A link is a contiguous stretch of network medium with a router bounding either end. **Neighbors** are nodes that are on the same IPv6 link. A **subnet** is an administrative segment of an IPv6 network; **multilink subnets** (with nodes on more than one link being part of a single subnet) are supported. A **tunnel** provides a virtual point-to-point path between node endpoints. **Boundary routers** are at the edge of an IPv6 network and are endpoints of tunnels to other systems outside of the local network.

IPv6 networks do not have a concept of a netmask. While IPv4 networks are defined by a combination of a network address and a netmask, IPv6 networks are defined by the **site prefix** and the **subnet prefix**.

IPv6 Addresses

The 128 bits of an IPv6 address are divided into 8 fields of 16 bits each. These are expressed as hexadecimal numbers separated by semicolons.

The first 3 fields (48 bits) are the **site prefix**, which defines how the public would connect to your network (the **public topology**). The next field (16 bits) is the **subnet prefix**, which defines how the network is laid out (the **private topology**). The rightmost four fields (64 bits) are the **interface ID** or **token**.

Since most addresses contain several fields that contain nothing but zero, the standard notation allows adjacent fields of all zeros to be replaced by two colons. For example, the IPv6 address `2001:0db8:abcd:0015:0000:0000:ab12:cd34` is equivalent to `2001:db8:abcd:15::ab12cd34`.

In the above example, the site prefix is `2001:db8:abcd`, the subnet prefix is `15`, and the interface ID is defined by `0:0:ab12:cd34`

We can use CIDR notation to specify a network and subnet length. As with IPv4 addresses, the number after the slash represents the number of bits in the prefix. Of particular interest for our purposes is `2001:db8::/32`, which is a 32-bit prefix associated with network addresses that have been reserved for documentation examples. Other reserved addresses include `2002::/16` (IPv6-IPv4 routing), `fe80::/10` (link local), and `ff00::/8` (multicast).

Neighbor Discovery

The IPv6 **Neighbor Discovery** (ND) protocol might be considered to be a replacment mechanism for services that were previously provided by a combination of ARP, ICMP, Router Discovery (RDISC), and ICMP Redirect. IPv6 routers advertise the network prefix, which facilitates the ability of IPv6 hosts to autoconfigure their own IP addresses. Usually, this will be configured based on the 48-bit MAC address.

(We probably want servers to have stable addresses even when interfaces are swapped out. We should assign an address rather than allowing ND to assign one. One common scheme is to nail the node address down to the IPv4 address, which saves time and confusion when designing and implementing the new scheme.)

Address autoconfiguration can be turned off by creating an appropriate */etc/inet/ndpd.conf* file. Adding the line

```
if-variable-name StatelessAddrConf false
```

will turn off autoconfiguration on all interfaces. An appropriate prefix can be assigned for each interface, and other settings can also be altered.

ND allows automatic determination of next-hop and redirection for routing. It also detects duplicate addresses and identifies when neighbors disappear from the network.

Tunnels

Solaris supports a few types of tunnels to allow easier migration involving IPv4 networks. A connection between two IPv6 networks over an IPv4 network can be configured manually. Similarly, we can manually configure a tunnel between two IPv4 networks over an IPv6 network. And a 6to4 tunnel can be dynamically configured between two IPv6 networks over an IPv4 network.

IPv6 Name Resolution

The local translation table for an IPv6 address is the *ipnodes* file. The hosts file is not able to handle IPv6 addresses. The */etc/nsswitch.conf* file has an `ipnodes` line to define which facilities should be used for IPv6 address lookups.

The local interface should be set to configure IPv6 at reboot via an */etc/hostname6.interface* file. During the reboot, the interface will be brought online via an

```
ifconfig inet6 interface plumb up
```

command, the */usr/lib/inet/in.ndpd* IPv6 daemon will be started, and ND will assign an address if none is specified in the `token` line of the *hostname6.interface* file.

As mentioned above, the DNS server will need to be configured with a dual stack, and the relevant IPv6 AAAA records and PTRs will need to be loaded in the database.

IPv6 Security Considerations

Since IPv6 packets may be tunneled through IPv4, we need to take care not to accidentally bypass our firewall protections. In particular, we need to make sure that both ends of the tunnel are protected by firewalls with matching rule sets, the firewalls need to do content inspection inside the tunnel, and stateful inspection may be required to make sure that public access to the internal network is not accidentally created by a dynamically configured tunnel.

The IPSEC and IKE features of IPv6 allows us to implement encrypted communication and public key authentication for our IPv6 traffic.

Resources

- Cromar, Scott. (2007) *Solaris Troubleshooting and Performance Tuning at Princeton University*. Princeton, NJ. (http://www.princeton.edu/~unix/Solaris/troubleshoot/index.html)

- Gregg, Brendan. (March 2006) *K9Toolkit*. (http://www.brendangregg.com/k9toolkit.html)

- Henry-Stocker, Sandra. (April, 2004) *What process owns this port?* Southborough, MA: Unix Insider, April 15, 2004.

- Hunt, Craig. (April 2002). *TCP/IP Network Administration, 3rd Edition*. Sebastopol, CA: O'Reilly.

- Jacobson, Van. (April 1997) *pathchar—a tool to infer characteristics of Internet paths*. Berkeley, CA: Lawrence Berkeley National Laboratory; Network Research Group. (ftp://ftp.ee.lbl.gov/pathchar/)

- McDougall, Richard; Mauro, Jim and Gregg, Brendan. (October 2006) *Solaris Performance and Tools*. Upper Saddle River, NJ: Prentice Hall & Sun Microsystems Press.

- Noordergraaf, Alex. (June 2003) *Solaris Operating Environment Network Settings for Security: Updated for Solaris 9 Operating Environment*. Santa Clara, CA: Sun Microsystems, Inc. (http://www.sun.com/blueprints/0603/816-5240.pdf)

- OpenSolaris Project. (October 2006) *DTrace Toolkit*. (http://www.opensolaris.org/os/community/dtrace/dtracetoolkit/)

- Sun Microsystems. (November 2006) System Administration Guide: IP Services. Santa Clara, CA: Sun Microsystems, Inc. (http://docs.sun.com/app/docs/doc/816-4554)

12

Availability Management

A service's **availability** is a measurement of whether an end user can use the service. This means that availability is defined in terms of the end-to-end functioning of the service. Each component of the service contributes to the availability of the service; the failure of any single component may mean a failure of the entire service.

By this definition, sub-standard performance may also cause availability problems. If the service is non-responsive or slow, it can get in the way of the end user. Adequate capacity needs to be provisioned, and the application may need to be tuned to provide adequate performance.

Several common components that may contribute to the availability of the service are:

- **The network.** You can't use an application you can't reach.
- **Shared disk or file storage**. Most applications use some sort of shared storage, whether it be directly from a storage array or indirectly through a file server.
- **Database repositories**. Database access can fail in a number of ways, including index corruption, database server hardware or OS failures, a lack of log or storage space, resource or lock contention, bugs in the database management software, poor data structure layout, data inconsistency or corruption, and poorly designed queries from the application.
- **Application and web servers**. These can be misconfigured, or they can suffer crashes due to hardware or software problems.
- **The end-user application used to access the service**. Software bugs in the application can cause service outages or poor performance.
- **The integration between the service components**. Even if each individual component is working as advertised, it isn't good enough unless all the components are working together.

Software, hardware, testing methodology, change procedures and the computing environment can all have an enormous impact on the availability of the service.

Availability is not a category of hardware or software or even services that can be purchased. A good availability record requires a commitment to architecture, process, hardware and software that will support the desired level of availability. Some of the issues that contribute to good availability, including recovery planning, system security and system management procedures, are discussed in the next few chapters.

A system is **highly available** only if we understand and have controlled the failure modes of the system. For each failure mode, we must know how to recover and how long the recovery will take. The upper bound on the recovery times is known as the **Maximum Time To Recover** (MTTR). In other words, **high availability** means that each failure mode is recoverable in a known and acceptable amount of time. (Highly available systems are also called **resilient**.)

> Marcus and Stern argue for a less mechanistic view of high availability. Their definition states that **high availability** is "A level of system availability implied by a design that is expected to meet or exceed the business requirements for which the system is implemented."

Some failure modes are difficult to recover from. A fried network core or a machine room fire are not *easily* recoverable, but they are recoverable. (We discuss approaches to business continuity management in Chapter 13.)

Availability is frequently reported as a percentage, defined in terms of the **Mean Time Between Failures** (MTBF) and the Maximum Time To Recover (MTTR). Specifically, `Availability = MTBF / (MTBF + MTTR)`. The standard measurement of availability is in terms of the **number of nines** in the availability percentage. For example, a system with 99% availability (3.65 days of downtime per year) has two nines. 99.9% (8 hours, 45 minutes of downtime per year) has three nines. Table 12-1 lists a translation of availability percentages in terms of the amount of downtime allowed per year or month.

Table 12-1. Nines of Availability

Nines	% Uptime	Downtime/Year	Downtime/Month
2	99%	3.65 days	7 hours, 18 minutes
3	99.9%	8 hours, 45 minutes	43 minutes, 45 seconds
4	99.99%	52 minutes, 30 seconds	4 minutes, 22.5 seconds
5	99.999%	5 minutes, 15 seconds	5.25 seconds
6	99.9999%	31.5 seconds	2.625 seconds

Marcus and Stern report that each additional 9 of uptime may cost upwards of 5 or 10 times as much as the previous level of availability.

> A service consists of several components, so the overall service availability combines the availabilities of the components. (It is *not* just a measurement of the least available component.)
>
> Consider a service that includes a network, database, application server, file server and client component, each with an availability of 99.9%. We can estimate the overall availability by multiplying the availabilities of the components: 0.999 x 0.999 x 0.999 x 0.999 x 0.999 = .995 = 99.5%.
>
> This works out to 43 hours and 45 minutes of downtime per year, not the 8 hours and 45 minutes our intuition might have expected.

Approaches to Availability

There are several general approaches to system availability:

- **Backups Only**: No special measures are taken except for backups. Support personnel will attempt a recovery at the time of an incident
- **Data Redundancy**: Data is protected by disk mirroring or parity RAID in addition to backups. This allows much faster recovery in the event of a disk failure. Data redundancy may even permit the system to continue to provide services until a scheduled maintenance window.
- **Failover Clustering**: A standby machine is available to pick up services in the event of a system failure. Such a solution may involve shared storage or at least data replication. Ideally, this failover should be automatic.

(Manual "failovers" require the constant presence of trained support staff and will take longer than automatic failovers. The downtime and support costs will be higher than the costs for failover software such as Veritas Cluster Server or Sun Cluster.)

- **Active-Active Clustering**: Some applications allow us to have two or more independent servers offering the same services at the same time. Examples of such applications include things like DNS servers, application servers and even some database servers (such as Oracle's RAC). Active-active clusters frequently implement some form of load balancing to spread the load over the available servers; the best load balancing solutions also take care of automatic, instantaneous failovers. When we absolutely must have 100% availability during certain times, active-active clustering may be the best way to accomplish this.
- **Remote Standby Systems**: Standby systems at a backup site allow easier recovery from a disaster. These systems may be owned by a service provider like SunGard, or they may be owned by the company itself. Recovery at this level will involve something like a restore from offsite tape backups.
- **Remote Standby Systems and Data Replication**: In addition to having system hardware at a backup site, data is replicated as well. The recovery time is dramatically reduced, since a tape recovery is not required.

Each of these approaches costs more than the one before it. Whether or not this cost is worthwhile depends on the cost of a service outage. The last two solutions cross the line into Continuity Management and will be considered in Chapter 13.

Cost of Availability

Higher levels of availability cost more money. The very highest levels of availability can cost millions of dollars to achieve. Whether or not the availability is worth the cost depends on how much downtime on the service costs the company.

Downtime costs include the time of the people who are unable to work, the value of the work that they would have accomplished during that time, the costs of delayed project completion, lost sales, and the direct costs associated with recovering from the outage. Some of these costs are easier to estimate than others, and the value of each of these costs will vary from industry to industry and even company to company. The cost of an outage that prevents a brokerage company from making a profitable trade may be in the millions.

Identifying the required level of availability is something of an art. Almost every project manager ever born will insist that *this* project requires absolute, unfaltering availability. When management gets an estimate of the cost, however, they are more likely to take a hard look at business requirements.

We have a responsibility to explain what levels of availability to expect from different architectures. And we have a responsibility to provide good estimates of the costs of the different options.

> It is human nature for us to want to please our co-workers and managers by providing "optimistic" cost and availability estimates, but it would not be honest. Our job is to provide a conservative, complete estimate. People cannot make informed decisions if we have not fully informed them of the costs and benefits of each approach.

Risk management offers a rule of thumb for determining how much to spend to mitigate a risk, based on the probable cost if the problem occurs, the cost if the mitigation measure is taken, and the likelihood of the problem occurring:

```
(cost if problem occurs - cost after mitigation) x likelihood of problem
```

The resulting risk scores provide us a way to prioritize our efforts. It may make sense to mitigate a likely risk with a low per-incident cost before tackling a less likely risk with a higher cost. And some risks may be deemed so unlikely that the business decides to gamble on their never occurring.

Three ways to deal with a risk are:

240

- **mitigation**: Implement changes to reduce the likelihood or impact of a risk. An example would be implementing disk mirroring on server boot disks. Boot disks would still be expected to fail at the same rate, but the impact would be much reduced. Insurance policies and service contracts are also mitigation measures, since they reduce the financial impact of an event.
- **avoidance**: Sometimes we can avoid a risk by doing things differently. If we are concerned about a developer typing commands as root on a production server, for example, we can provide a mechanism (like `sudo`) to limit root access to a few acceptable commands.
- **acceptance**: Some risks are deemed so unlikely that the business is willing to gamble on them never happening. Other risks may carry a low enough cost that they can be ignored.

Risk mitigation should be a global rather than a case-by-case exercise. Measures that reduce one risk may also help mitigate other risks. Network upgrades taken to reduce one kind of risk are going to improve performance and reliability for everything else, too. And setting up a remote recovery location would mitigate the risk of several different types of site loss disasters, including fires, earthquakes, bombs, hurricanes, or power outages.

When we discuss which effort to fund, we need to consider the global impact of each proposal. The benefits of each change for the overall environment need to be into account. We can't just focus on the local benefits for a particular service.

Cost of Inaction

There is also a cost associated with inaction. A University of Minnesota study showed that 87% of companies who suffer a major disaster without a disaster recovery plan will be out of business within two years. The same study reported that 20% of the Fortune 500 would have been put out of business by an outage of 48 hours.

The bottom line is that the business bought these systems to make money. If the systems are offline or not working properly, that money is not being made. Besides these direct costs, there are indirect costs to be considered in terms of loss of time, project slippage, damage to reputation, reductions in stock price, potential legal liability, reduced employee morale, and lost opportunity.

Service Level Agreements

At the end of the negotiating process, we will arrive at a service level agreement with the project owner. A **service level agreement** (SLA) defines what level of service can be expected for the architecture that is being constructed. SLAs typically specify acceptable maintenance windows, maintenance notification procedures, uptime expectations and periods of time when availability is particularly important. SLAs may also specify penalties if targets are not met.

Some of the things an SLA should specify are:

- **Availability Level**: What percentage of the time should the service be up?
- **Critical Time Periods**: Which days and times is it especially important for the service to be available?
- **Maintenance Windows**: During which days and times can we schedule system maintenance and software upgrades and deployments?
- **Locations of Service**: At which physical locations should this service be available? Are some of them more important than others?
- **Priorities**: What is the priority of this service relative to other services? Are there parts of it that are especially important? In the event of a service outage, what parts of it should be brought back first?
- **Contacts**: Who should be contacted in the event of a problem or to schedule system maintenance?
- **Escalation Procedures**: If problems cannot be resolved, who should be called? After how long? What format should escalation requests take?

- **Agreement Renegotiation**: SLAs should be revisited from time to time. Who on the IT and customer teams will be responsible for reviewing and updating the SLA? Who needs to be informed when an update occurs? Who needs to approve any proposed updates?

Too many system administrators cave in to pressure to agree to unrealistic service level agreements for unrealistic costs. Doing so is irresponsible and unprofessional.

On the other hand, it is also irresponsible to get too emotional about the negotiation process. It is our job to present reality and (if necessary) to be able to support what we are saying with facts and figures. Consistency, accuracy, and a businesslike demeanor are the keys to negotiating an SLA that faithfully represents the business needs and available resources.

Architecting for Availability

Table 2-2 lists the results of three different studies of the frequency of different causes of downtime. The differences may well be due to different definitions of what downtime is and how to classify the causes of a particular incident.

Table 12-2. Causes of Downtime

Cause of Downtime	Percentage
Source: IEEE Computer, 1995	
Server Software	30%
Planned Downtime	30%
People	15%
Hardware	10%
Client Software	5%
Network Software	5%
Environment	5%
Source: Gartner/Dataquest	
System Software	27%
Hardware	23%
Human Error	18%
Network Failure	17%
Natural Disaster	8%
Unknown	7%
Source: CNT	
Hardware Malfunction	44%
Human Error	32%
Software Corruption or Bug	14%
Viruses	7%
Natural Disaster	3%

When considering how best to spend the company's money on availability, we should focus on those areas with the highest failure rates, most involved recovery, and the highest cost associated with failures.

Where possible, buy quality rather than features. The maturity of a product and the commitment of the vendor to quality will result in better availability. Measuring this commitment to quality is not easy, but we can:

- Read articles and reviews.
- Search related newsgroups, web sites and blogs for references.
- Interview fellow users of the product.
- Talk to disinterested experts.
- Test the solution in a vendor test lab or with a loaner unit.

Word of mouth is an important way for system administrators to get the low-down on whether or not a product performs as expected. Due to legal restrictions, most shops will not publish details of their experience with a particular vendor or solution. On the other hand, most admins are more than happy to swap war stories in an informal setting. User groups and system administrator communities like LOPSA and SAGE provide a great setting for meeting people doing similar things in other environments. The chance to learn from other peoples' mistakes and successes is well worth the annual membership dues.

Approaches for Improved Availability

As we discussed above, availability is defined as `MTBF / (MTBF + MTTR)`. This means that there are two ways to increase availability: increase the Mean Time Between Failures (MTBF) or reduce the Mean Time To Recover (MTTR).

There are several strategies to increase the MTBF:

- Server and storage hardware with redundant parts.
- Monitor hardware for early warning signs of part failure.
- Implement parity RAID or mirroring for data protection.
- Structure databases properly.
- Choose high-quality software vendors.
- Use reliable software and system architectures.
- Thoroughly test and coordinate environment changes.
- Implement reliable power and HVAC systems.
- Keep the machine room clean and well-organized.
- Implement network redundancy and best network engineering practices.

MTTR can be reduced in several ways:

- Improve service contracts
- Keep parts inventories onsite for parts that fail frequently
- Improve recovery mechanisms.
- Train staff in troubleshooting and recovery procedures.
- Postmortem analyses to identify ways to avoid problems or recover from them better.

Hardware Availability

Hardware failures are most often the result of failures of components with moving parts. In particular, power supply fans and disk drives are the server components that fail most frequently. These components are particularly problematic because power supplies are not usually monitored very well, and disk drives contain the personality of the computer.

Power supply fan problems can cause problems with heat-sensitive elements like memory and CPUs. Most modern systems come with redundant power supplies and fans to help work around this problem. Redundant power supplies are only useful if we check that we do not have a failed unit.

Someone should check for system warning lights every day. As with every other daily task, the responsible person should sign off on a checklist every day. (Human nature being what it is, these tasks will be overlooked if there is not some sort of enforcement mechanism.) It may also make sense to rotate some of these daily duties so that no one person gets stuck with it.

Some systems provide temperature monitoring capabilities; it makes sense to take advantage of these facilities. Custom written scripts or SNMP-based monitoring can use these facilities to look for dangerously high temperatures and send out notifications.

System logs may also report power supply problems; system logs should be monitored regularly. The `logcheck` and `logwatch` programs provide a way to parse message logs and send out email reports on critical messages.

The Fault Management Facility (discussed below) provides some capabilities to automatically offline failed components without taking the system down.

Environmental Availability

Environmental problems include problems with the physical facility and the general computing environment. Typical environmental issues include problems with the electrical feed, HVAC systems, fire suppression systems, and the data network.

We can protect against power failures by running redundant power paths through different circuit breakers. Where there are redundant power supplies on a piece of equipment, each power cord should come from a different power distribution unit (PDU) plugged into a different circuit breaker.

Machine room UPS and generator units protect against utility failures. In some cases, it may even be worth the expense of running separate power feeds in from outside. Power systems need to be bought with enough extra capacity for growth; upgrading power capability is an expensive and time-consuming process.

Power systems have the potential to cause widespread problems. It is well worth the money to make sure that power systems consist of high-quality equipment from manufacturers with a commitment to effective support. Planning, architecture and installation of power and UPS equipment is a specialized discipline. Experienced professionals should be brought in if necessary; this is not something that should be done by an unqualified person. It costs much more to repair a bad installation than to design and install it correctly in the first place.

Cooling and dehumidification systems (commonly known as HVAC systems) are another potential point of failure. Redundancy and extra capacity needs to be designed in. This is another area that is a specialized discipline that is outside of the expertise of most system administration staff. Reliable, experienced and responsible professionals should oversee the design and implementation of the HVAC system.

Fire suppression systems need to be reviewed and regularly inspected by an expert. Unreliable or hazardous fire suppression systems can cause unnecessary outages or even physical injury.

Network infrastructure is a critical part of overall system availability. Physical components such as cables, ports or network devices may fail. Routing, network or broadcast addresses may be misconfigured. Firewall, VPN, or WAN settings may prevent proper application access. Or we may be the target of network denial of service (DOS) or penetration problems. Network management is beyond the scope of this book, but a well-designed and properly maintained network will dramatically improve service availability.

Even cable management is a key piece of system availability. Poorly managed "rats nests" of cables can result in downtime due to interference, cable stretching or accidental disconnections. It costs almost no additional time to organize and label cables, but the payback is huge.

244

The cabinets in a machine room can also affect availability. Well-designed, sturdy and properly installed racks and rack-mounted equipment can reduce the risk of servers being damaged during service. Some racks even offer earthquake mitigation to reduce damage during an earthquake.

Database and Application Structure

Improper database or application architecture can have a huge impact on availability. Fully 35% of system downtime is related to software faults. Proper project management, application development and testing procedures can dramatically reduce downtime due to poorly architected software solutions.

Database table layout can have a dramatic impact on performance and data quality. The layout can affect the impact of locking behaviors by the database engine, and it can help eliminate data redundancies that contribute to data becoming stale. Database management is beyond the scope of this book, but the architecture and health of our databases needs to be examined by someone who understands them.

An ideal database client application will recognize a broken connection to the database server and quietly rebuild it. Less well-behaved database client apps may sullenly sit idle and disconnected from the database, force a user to re-enter login credentials, or not report back an error when a transaction is aborted.

Chapter 14 discusses project management and change control issues.

Storage Architecture

Storage should be the first thing we think about when designing a high availability environment. The storage is where the critical data is kept, and the data is the reason that they pay us the big bucks to play with all this nifty hardware. The storage should be the centerpiece of our environment, and we should make sure to invest in well-performing, reliable, redundant and expandable storage hardware.

Storage area networks (SANs) are environments where many servers can share access to many storage solutions. Usually, SANs are connected to the hosts through a network of some sort, almost always either via the SCSI protocol over a fiber channel network or an IP network.

SANs can be difficult to set up and may involve a lot of issues that are not apparent to a non-expert. If there is no SAN expert on staff, we need to bring in a storage expert with expertise covering the equipment we are installing. Ideally, someone on our staff should do the actual installation with a consultant nearby to lend support and double-check that things have gone right. Errors in a SAN installation are very difficult and expensive to clear up later. We will save money in the long run by making sure that the installation is done right. Figure 12-1 shows a typical SAN. Note that the solution has been architected to reduce reliance on any single point of failure.

Network attached storage (NAS) is another approach for providing high-availability storage. NAS is based on file-sharing protocols such as CIFS/SMB and NFS, rather than being based on block-level protocols like SCSI. Typically, performance and locking granularity is not as good as is available on a SAN, but the setup is much easier and the maintenance is more straightforward. If a NAS can handle the capacity, performance and functionality requirements of a given environment, it might be the way to go. Database applications are usually not able to function properly on a NAS solution; tread very carefully before deciding to put a database on a NAS.

Some storage virtualization devices can be attached to a SAN to allow NAS access to the storage. Where the budget can bear the cost of such a device, it may be worth the money.

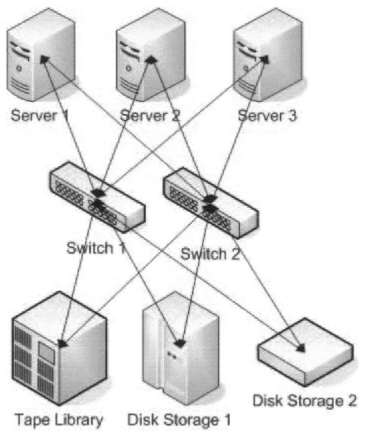

Figure 12-1. Typical SAN

Storage Performance

Vendors love to talk about speeds and feeds. Being humans, sales reps will focus on the fastest components in their solution. As system administrators, we need to focus on the bottlenecks. Our performance will only be as good as the performance of the bottleneck.

Sizing our storage environment is something that has to be done right the first time. Extra time doing our homework here will save us time, money, aggravation and downtime down the road. It may even save us from making a mistake that costs us our job.

There are several places that bottlenecks may occur. Each of these need to be considered when sizing a storage solution. Figure 12-2 diagrams the locations of "typical" storage system bottlenecks.

246

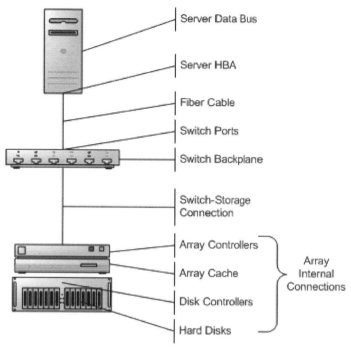

Figure 12-2. Typical Storage Bottlenecks

Consider each of these areas as a potential bottleneck.

- The server data bus.
- The host bus adapter (or network adapter, for iSCSI) on the server.
- The cabling (especially for iSCSI).
- The switch ports (for either fiber channel or iSCSI).
- The switch backplane. Can the backplane handle the traffic of all the ports banging away a the same time?
- The data connection between the switch and the storage device, including the array controllers, ports and cabling. Can this connection handle the expected traffic from all the servers at once? Can it be expanded if necessary? (And, if so, what will it cost?)
- When there are redundant data paths, is the data connection to the storage device an active-active connection, or a failover connection? Many vendors report the total aggregate speed, even if multiple paths operate in active-passive mode. Also pin down what the vendor means by active-active. Some vendors mean that each data connection is only active on one link, but the connections can be divided between the available paths.
- The size of the cache and how efficiently it is used. (Some vendors provide more cache, but use it less efficiently. The best way to get to the bottom of this issue is to invite several vendors to present on this issue and question them closely.)
- Interconnect buses between the access ports, the cache, the storage unit processors and the hard drives. Make sure to understand the speed of the actual data path, and whether there is contention with control information on the same bus. Most vendors report on the total aggregate speed, including the speed of channels that are dedicated to control information. It may take some work, but keep asking questions until we understand how much data can flow at the same time over different channels, and what the channels are used for.
- Connections to the disks themselves. How many disks are associated with each disk controller. Can the controllers handle the bandwidth required to service all the disks at the same time? Ask the same questions about failover situations. Some storage units have controllers take on double duties when a fellow controller goes offline. Does the controller have enough capacity to handle all the disks at once? And is its data connection in the event of a failover big enough to keep performance at a reasonable level?

When asking these questions, we will almost always run into problems with the fact that each vendor refers to their component parts by different names.

Storage Reliability

Vendors don't usually like to divulge mean time between failure (MTBF) statistics. When they do volunteer these numbers, they typically reveal them only for the components that fail very infrequently. Push the vendor to get the best numbers possible.

Ask about whether reboots are required for firmware upgrades, and how frequently firmware upgrades have occurred over the last 12 months. If reboots of the storage hardware are required on a weekly basis to resolve a critical issue, we should be looking at different storage.

The best storage solutions have redundancy built in for every component. Any single component in the array can fail without service being interrupted. Ideally, the parts can even be replaced on the fly with no service interruption. Some performance degradation may occur during certain failure modes, but service availability is almost always more important than performance.

If the sales engineer is being evasive about single points of failure, start running down the list of components on the architecture diagram to make sure that the array can withstand the failure of any single component. Make sure that there are no fuses, batteries or data paths that represent a single point of failure for any piece of data. Common single points of failure in storage systems include:

- Array cache.
- Battery backup for the array cache.
- Power supplies, power cords and fuses.
- Cooling fans.
- Array disk controllers.
- Array backplane and interconnect buses.

In particular, array cache needs to be protected on several levels. It needs to be mirrored or at least protected by parity RAID to prevent data loss in the event of a component failure. Array cache will also need to have its own battery backup or other provisions for when the array loses power; otherwise the databases or other data may end up in an inconsistent state. Consider what will happen to the cached data in the event of a power failure. Make sure that the batteries allow enough time to either de-stage the data (write it to the disks) or preserve it in cache until power is restored.

Maintainability of key components is also important. The best storage arrays allow hot-swapping of key components. This means that downtime can be eliminated for a part failure, not just postponed to a maintenance window.

Beyond the hardware and software of the storage solution itself, we need to think about data protection and path redundancy.

We discussed data protection in a slightly different context in Chapter 10's section on "Volume Management." The general approaches are:

- Mirroring (RAID-1):
- Parity RAID (eg RAID-5 or RAID-Z):
- Striping and Mirroring (preferably striping the mirror sets): Figure 12-3 demonstrates why we want to stripe the mirrors.

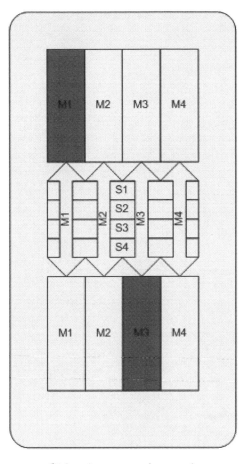 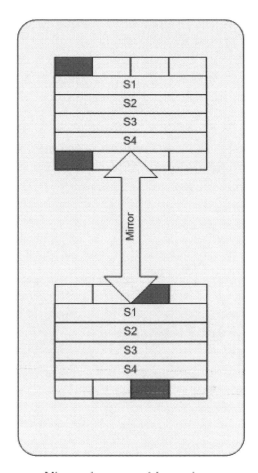

Striped across mirror sets   Mirrored across stripe sets

Figure 12-3. Combining Stripes and Mirrors

In addition, we can protect data via checkpointing, snapshotting, or replication software which is built into the arrays. These features are usually extra-cost options, but they may be well worth the money. If these features can be offloaded onto the storage array, there will be that much more headroom for server-side processes.

High-quality storage devices monitor their own health and provide alerts to staff and support vendors when components and software configurations fail.

Sizing Storage

A good rule of thumb is that we should purchase storage that can be expanded to at least double the maximum capacity represented by our projections. This may seem like overkill, but long experience has shown that data expands to fit the space allotted.

One of the advantages of a SAN is that it permits us to expand storage relatively easily, simply by adding more devices. Even then, adding devices costs us ports on our switch infrastructure. The same rule of thumb applies to switches; purchase switches with the capacity to expand to double the expected maximum number of ports.

The real key to storage management is to monitor, budget and control the amount of storage allocated to different uses. Even where chargebacks are not used to enforce discipline, a storage administrator has to moderate storage consumption and make sure that the company's money is not wasted storing, managing, backing up, indexing and archiving files with no legitimate business use. If people want to store their mp3s, they should buy a thumb drive. Work storage space is for business files.

Extra Features

Modern disk array and storage software vendors offer a broad selection of additional features. Some of these features are very useful in making it easier to manage storage. Most of these features will cost extra money, but it is well worth sitting through the vendor's sales presentation on features and extra cost options. We can't let them push us into options that we won't use, but maybe they'll give us something that will solve a problem we're having. Some typical features are:

- Snapshots
- Checkpoints
- Replication
- Migration
- Performance monitoring and optimization
- SAN management options
- Storage virtualizaton

Server Hardware

Server hardware is becoming more reliable with each new generation. Not only are the individual components becoming more reliable, but it is becoming easier to diagnose and replace them. Advanced operating systems like Solaris 10 have built-in capacities to identify and offline damaged hardware without service interruptions. Systems have phone-home or email-home capabilities to notify service providers so that by the time we know we have a problem, the service tech is already on the way with a replacement part.

While these advances are exciting, we still have to plan our server configurations and architecture to cut unexpected downtime to an absolute minimum.

Power Supplies

Most modern servers come with redundant power supplies. These should be plugged into separate power feeds. The ideal situation would be to have totally redundant power systems feeding different panels in the machine room. If this is not in the cards, at least try to keep the redundant power supplies plugged into different power paths as far back the infrastructure as they exist. If nothing else, plug them into separate panels or at least separate circuit breakers.

System logs need to be inspected on a daily basis for evidence of failing power supplies (or other components, for that matter. Modern equipment is getting better at logging part failures to the OS rather than waiting for someone to notice that the power supply fan sounds like a 747 on the runway at O'Hare.

Power supplies sometimes fail without notice, with the only indication of failure being a warning light. Someone should be assigned the task of walking the machine room every day looking for amber or red warning lights on equipment. At the end of the inspection, this person should initial a checklist or otherwise indicate that this task is done. (Without the discipline of a checklist, this "trivial" task will get lost in the shuffle.) While this task is simple and can be safely assigned to an intern or junior member of the team, it is an important part to catching problems before they spiral out of control.

Virtualization

Some higher-end server solutions allow large servers to be carved up into domains. **Domains** are collections of processors, memory and I/O resources that act as if they were a physical server. Domain management can be done on live systems on the fly.

Domains are a distinct technology from zones or virtual machines (VMs). **Zones** are independent execution environments within the same OS instance. **Virtual machines**, like those offered by VMWare or Xen, are collections of system resources where an multiple independent OS instances can be installed on a single server.

Domains are different from both zones and VMs because a domain has its own dedicated hardware in addition to its own execution environment and OS instance. (For that matter, VMs and Zones can be installed inside of a domain.)

The advantages of domains are the flexibility of changing hardware resource allocations as well as the management advantages of a more consolidated server environment.

Network Redundancy

Solaris allows us to set up a second network interface to be used in the event that the first one becomes unavailable. Ideally, this second interface should be connected to a separate network switch or at least a separate blade on a large switch in order to reduce our dependence on a single piece of networking equipment.

Typically, network failover is implemented by setting up a virtual IP address on a physical interface. This can be done by a command like:

```
ifconfig interface-typeinstance:virtual-instance-number hostname up
ifconfig bge0:1 newname up
```

Clustering

No matter how good the self-healing capabilities built into the hardware and software of the server, sometimes servers will crash. If the service is not a critical one, it may be okay to wait for our service provider to fix the problem. For critical services, we need something better.

Clustering can provide protection in the event of a server failure. Either failover or active-active clustering can keep a service online even when the server has failed.

When designing a cluster, one decision to make is whether to go with a few large servers or a group of small servers. Each configuration has its advantages. A particular concern is whether **state** needs to be maintained (ie, if there is information about the condition of the session or process that needs to be preserved). Large server clusters do better with applications that need to maintain state, since it is difficult to replicate state across a large number of small servers. If state is not important, and if clients don't care which server they connect to, a large number of cheaper, smaller servers may be a better solution. And if state is not an issue, but the OS itself may be a limiting factor (due to resource limitations of some sort), a large number of smaller servers may be a better fit in order to spread out the load.

Failover

Failover clustering involves a standby server which can pick up a service when it fails on the primary server. Services are usually associated with a **service group** which includes the network identity associated with the service, shared storage for the service and the group of processes which provide the service. The service group is the object that is transferred to the new server when the service fails on the old one.

Failover clusters can come in many flavors. **Active-passive clusters** involve one server actively providing a service while the other one waits for the active server to fail. **Active-active failover clusters** or **symmetric failover**

clusters involve two servers which each provide a service, and where each can run its companion's services when it fails. Variations on these themes can be expanded out to large numbers of servers, including so-called **n+1 clusters**, where one idle machine is the standby for several other servers in the cluster. Figure 12-4 illustrates the difference between Active-Passive and Symmetric Failover Clustering.

The two most popular cluster management software packages for Solaris are Veritas Cluster Server (from Symantec) and Sun Cluster. Both of these are solid, mature packages with support for several third-party software packages. EMC's Legato subsidiary also provides a mature clustering solution that plays in this space.

Ping-pong failures are when a resource (like shared disk storage) prevents a service group from coming online on any members of the cluster. This can result in the service group bouncing around the cluster, which in turn may result in data corruption as the process crashes repeatedly. Good clustering solutions allow us to configure the service group to only attempt a certain number of restarts before sending a page and waiting for human intervention.

Professional clustering solutions also pay a lot of attention to avoiding a **split-brain** scenario. This occurs when two or more servers in a failover cluster are both trying to write data to the same location at the same time, resulting in data corruption. If professional cluster management solutions detect a problem where split-brain may be occurring, they will shut the whole service down and wait for human intervention.

A typical measure to avoid split-brain issues is a **heartbeat network**. This is a communications method by which members of a failover cluster monitor one another's health. Heartbeat networks take a number of forms, including crossover cables between network ports, dedicated LANs on a switch or hub, special-purpose communication interfaces, or even disk-based lock and status files on shared storage.

> Heartbeat networks can fail if they lose all pathways a once. For this reason, heartbeat connections should be set up on different network adapters, preferably on separate expansion buses, and they should not be plugged in to the same piece of network equipment. Components of different heartbeat networks should not share the same power source. Single points of failure must be avoided.
>
> It even makes sense to use two different mechanisms, such as a combination of network and disk heartbeats.

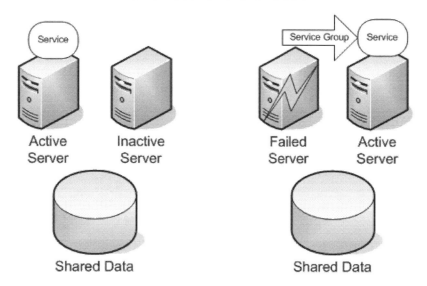

Active-Passive Failover Cluster

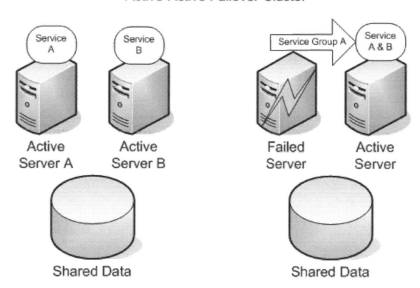

Active-Active Failover Cluster

Figure 12-4. Failover Clustering Approaches

The other major cause of split-brain problems is when a computer's operation is stopped and restarted. This can be done on an UltraSPARC system, for example, by entering a break or L1-A, then resume by typing "go" at the console prompt. System console access needs to be closely controlled, and administrators have to be told that if they accidentally send a break on a clustered system, they need to reboot rather than resume.

Another method for limiting the damage of a split-brain scenario is to have volume management software which only allows one server at a time to "own" the disks associated with the service group. This can be implemented, for example, by having an internal flag on the disks which indicates which server is allowed to write to them. (Symantec's Veritas Volume Manager implements this protection members by having disk groups which must be

253

imported before they can be mounted.)

We *can* custom-write failover software, but it is not usually a good idea. If we have invested the money to set up a failover cluster, it is likely that the cost of a failure of the clustering software would be very high. Even worse, if we mess up on monitoring for split-brain (which is easy to do), the cost could involve the cost of lost data. Given that we do not have anywhere near the resources of Sun or Symantec, it is likely that our software will be less reliable.

> Split-brain is a real danger with misconfigured or home-grown clustering solutions. Remember that the worst thing that could happen to most services is not a service outage; it is data corruption.

It is very difficult to leave the failover system idle. Businesses feel that an investment the size of a failover server ought to be "doing something." There are some activities that are better than others. For example, application development should not be done on the failover system. If buggy, untested code causes a system problem or resource shortfall, it may be the case that the production service will not be able to run properly when a failover occurs.

If the standby server must be used for something, it is best that it be used to support another production service, perhaps one that fails onto the other server in the cluster. That way, the load profile on both servers will be predictable. We do need to make sure that the total load of all services will be able to run on either server in the event of a failover. Assuming that we are disciplined enough to monitor usage and keep capacity at the proper level, this can be a solution that keeps management and IT happy.

Active-Active Clustering

Active-active clustering is distinct from active-active failover clustering, though some vendors will try to muddy the waters. **Active-active clustering** is when two or more servers are offering the same service simultaneously.

The hardest thing to deal with in an active-active cluster is the state information. Some solutions provide a multicast of state information to keep other nodes in the cluster up to date on the status of a request. Due to latency concerns, most stateful active-active clusters need to be on the same physical network.

Typically, a load balancer distributes the load between these servers. (Some solutions include an integrated load balancer, others require an external load balancer.) In a well-designed solution, the load balancer will also mediate a failover.

Load balancers can come in a number of different shapes, including high-availability appliances like those offered by F5 or software-based DNS load balancers. The type of load balancer used will depend on the requirements, but we have to be sure that the load balancer itself has an appropriate level of availability.

The F5 Big-IP appliance even maintains information to protect session-based traffic. This can avoid the problem of a session being opened on one device, then subsequent packets in the session being sent to another device that doesn't know what to do with them.

There are also high-quality free software-based DNS load balancers like lbnamed. These even provide a built-in layer of failover functionality.

Where a load balancer is deployed, we need to set it up to provide high availability for services behind it (by monitoring the availability of those hosts) as well as providing high availability and continuity services for the load balancing service itself.

A related way to deal with a multiple host solution is to distribute jobs via a job scheduler like BMC Control-M or IBM's Tivoli Workload Scheduler. These products can be configured to submit a job to one of a collection of systems, track the job to completion, or send notifications in the event of a failure. The real advantage of such a solution is that they allow us to organize dependencies between jobs across our environment into job streams, which can then be managed as objects.

Some active-active clustering solutions (such as Oracle RAC) have shared storage with a clustering file system. **Cluster file systems** are specifically designed to allow multiple servers to use the file system simultaneously. Sophisticated locking mechanisms are necessary to make this work properly.

Other active-active clusters use shared storage that is provided by a file server. File servers use the CIFS/SMB or NFS protocols to provide the locking necessary for concurrent application access.

Some active-active clusters do not have shared storage. This type of cluster is called a **shared nothing cluster**.

Some active-active clusters can even run at remote locations, which can provide both an availability solution and a business continuity solution. Such solutions will be discussed in Chapter 13.

> Round-robin DNS does *not* provide for failover, so it is *not* a good load balancing solution for high availability services. It effectively multiplies our exposure to server problems by almost the number of servers involved.

Server Consolidation

Server consolidation refers to the practice of combining multiple compatible services on a single piece of server hardware. Sometimes this involves some level of server virtualization (like Xen or Zones), but the end result is a reduced number of pieces of equipment to be maintained.

Consolidation helps improve availability by reducing system management overhead and allowing us to focus our attention and resources on a smaller number of systems. This frequently has the result of allowing us to purchase higher-quality hardware than would be permitted if we had to purchase large numbers of smaller servers.

System Health Monitoring

Several professional SNMP-based packages exist to monitor system health. Some of the best known are IBM's Tivoli Global Enterprise Manager, HP OpenView, BMC Patrol and CA Unicenter. Freeware packages also exist, such as Nagios and Net SNMP. Sun provides Sun Management Center as part of its no-cost N1 Management Portfolio.

Fault Management

With Solaris 10, Sun has implemented a daemon, `fmd`, to track and react to fault management. In addition to sending traditional `syslog` messages, the system sends binary telemetry events to `fmd` for correlation and analysis. Solaris 10 implements default fault management operations for several pieces of hardware in Sparc systems, including CPU, memory, and I/O bus events. Similar capabilities are being implemented for x64 systems.

Once the problem is defined, failing components may be offlined automatically without a system crash, or other corrective action may be taken by `fmd`. If a service dies as a result of the fault, the Service Management Facility (SMF) will attempt to restart it and any dependent processes.

The Fault Management Facility reports error messages in a well-defined and explicit format. Each error code is uniquely specified by a Universal Unique Identifier (UUID) related to a document on the Sun web site at http://www.sun.com/msg/ .

Resources are uniquely identified by a Fault Managed Resource Identifier (FMRI). Each Field Replaceable Unit (FRU) has its own FMRI. FMRIs are associated with one of the following conditions:

- **ok**: Present and available for use.
- **unknown**: Not present or not usable, perhaps because it has been offlined or unconfigured.

- **degraded**: Present and usable, but one or more problems have been identified.
- **faulted**: Present but not usable; unrecoverable problems have been diagnosed and the resource has been disabled to prevent damage to the system.

The `fmdump -V -u eventid` command can be used to pull information on the type and location of the event. (The eventid is included in the text of the error message provided to syslog.) The `-e` option can be used to pull error log information rather than fault log information.

Statistical information on the performance of fmd can be viewed via the `fmstat` command. In particular, `fmstat -m modulename` provides information for a given module.

The `fmadm` command provides administrative support for the Fault Management Facility. It allows us to load and upload modules and view and update the resource cache. The most useful capabilities of `fmadm` are provided through the following subcommands:

- **config**: Display the configuration of component modules.
- **faulty**: Display faulted resources. With the `-a` option, list cached resource information. With the `-i` option, list persistent cache identifier information, instead of most recent state and UUID.
- **load** */path*/*module*: Load the module.
- **unload module**: Unload module; the module name is the same as reported by `fmadm config`.
- **rotate logfile**: Schedule rotation for the specified log file. Used with the logadm configuration file.

Process Monitoring

Individual processes can be monitored to make sure that they are running properly and that their resource utilization is within bounds. Professional packages such as Foglight provide monitoring for several different application packages, but an adept scripter can write custom scripts that focus on a site's particular requirements.

At the very least processes can easily be monitored to make sure that they are running. It is not much harder to determine that they are not exceeding thresholds of memory or CPU use.

Services that have been adapter for the Service Management Facility are monitored to see if the process is running.

Service Management Facility

The Service Management Facility (SMF) was introduced in Solaris 9 as an alternative way to manage services. In Solaris 10, SMF has been made the default way to manage most services. The SMF framework has significant advantages over the legacy SVR4 mechanisms, primarily in terms of service monitoring and integration with the Fault Management Facility.

The SMF allows us to specify chains of dependencies in a more flexible way than is allowed by the traditional SVR4 rc scripts. When services are down, SMF knows the order to restart them.

Together with the Fault Management Facility, SMF is a part of Solaris 10's self-healing capability. If a service crashes out as part of a recovery operation, the system is smart enough to start up the service again as well as services that depend on it.

Basic Commands

The basic commands for managing services under SMF (Service Management Facility) control are **svcs**, **svccfg** and **svcadm**. The man pages for these commands are a good source of detailed information. For services under inetd control, we can use the **inetadm** command.

Many commands require referencing the service identifier, also known as a Fault Managed Resource Identifier

(FMRI). An example FMRI is:

`svc:/system/system-log:default`

Some commands do not require the full FMRI if there is no ambiguity. Instead, only the tail part without the "default" string would be adequate in most cases. Here, the abbreviated version of the FMRI "`system-log`" would be adequate, since there is no other service with that name.

Legacy init scripts have FMRIs starting with `lrc`. For example:

`lrc:/etc/rcS_d/S35cacheos_sh`

Converted `inetd` services have a syntax like one of the following, depending on whether or not they are `rpc` services:

`svc:network/`*`service-name`*`/`*`protocol`*

`svc:network/`*`rpc-service-name`*`/`*`rpc_protocol`*

Table 12-3 lists some of the most useful commands:

Table 12-3. SMF Adminstrative Commands

Command	Description
`inetadm -l` *`FMRI`*	Displays FMRI properties.
`inetadm -m` *`FMRI property=value`*	Set FMRI property.
`svcadm clear` *`FMRI`*	Clears FMRI faults.
`svcadm disable` *`FMRI`*	Disables FMRI (persists through reboots).
`svcadm enable` *`FMRI`*	Enables FMRI (persists through reboots).
`svcadm refresh` *`FMRI`*	Forces FMRI to re-read configuration file.
`svcadm restart` *`FMRI`*	Restarts FMRI.
`svccfg`	Enter interactive mode.
`svccfg -s` *`FMRI`* `setenv` *`VAR value`*	Sets an environment variable for FMRI. The service should be refreshed and/or restarted.
`svcprop -p start` *`FMRI`*	Shows the start properties for FMRI.
`svcs -a`	Lists all currently installed services, including state.
`svcs -d` *`FMRI`*	Lists dependencies for FMRI.
`svcs -D` *`FMRI`*	Lists dependents for FMRI.
`svcs -l` *`FMRI`*	Long listing of information about FMRI including detailed dependency information.
`svcs -p` *`FMRI`*	Shows relationships between services and processes.
`svcs -t`	Temporary change; not persistent past a reboot.

Command	Description
svcs -x	Explains why a service is not available.
svcs -xv	Verbose debugging information.

To make configuration changes to a non-`inetd` service, edit the configuration file, then enter the **svcadm restart** command. In particular, the "exec" value for an `inetd`-controlled service is the command line executed for that service by SMF. It may be desirable, for

SMF Service Maintenance

The `svc.startd` daemon is the master process starter and restarter f example, to change this value to add logging or other command-line flags.

To convert an `inetd.conf` file to SMF format, run the command:
inetconv -i /etc/inet/inetd.conf or SMF. It tracks service state and manages dependencies. The `svc.configd` daemon is started by `svc.startd` to read in the service configuration information from the repository in /etc/svc/repository.db

Services that are managed through `init` scripts can be added to SMF via the `inetconv` command. Such additions are only monitored for status, but other SMF capabilities may not work.

If a service is in the maintenance state, first make sure that all associated processes have died (with **svcs -p FMRI**). If necessary, kill off any remaining processes. Check for errors in the appropriate logs in /var/svc/log or /etc/svc/volatile and perform any needed maintenance. (A particular service's log file can be located using the **svcadm -l FMRI | grep logfile** command. The /etc/svc/volatile directory covers services that are started prior to single-user mode.) When the maintenance is complete, clear service faults with **svcadm clear FMRI**

Boot messages are much less verbose than with the old `init` scripts. To get verbose output, boot with the **boot -v** or **boot -m verbose** commands. Svcadm can be used to change the run levels. The FMRIs associated with the different run levels are:

- **S**: `milestone/single-user:default`
- **2**: `milestone/multi-user:default`
- **3**: `milestone/multi-user-server:default`

The current run level can be displayed with **who -r** To step through the run levels, use the following series of commands:

```
boot -m none
svcadm milestone svc:/milestone/single-user:default
svcadm milestone svc:/milestone/multi-user:default
svcadm milestone svc:/milestone/multi-user-server:default
```

SMF Profiles

SMF profiles are XML files in /var/svc/profile which list sets of service instances which are enabled and disabled. Different SMF profiles can be used. To use a different one, use the following command:
svccfg apply /var/svc/profile/*desired_profile.xml*

To make a copy of the current profile for editing, run:
svccfg extract> *profile-file.xml*

Service Configuration Repository

The Service Configuration Repository stores persistent configuration information and SMF runtime data for services. Each service's manifest is in an XML-formatted text file located in `/var/svc/manifest`. The information from the manifests is imported into the repository through **svccfg import** or during a reboot.

If the repository is corrupted, it can be restored from an automatic backup using the `/lib/svc/bin/restore_repository` command. The **svcadm refresh; svc adm restart** command will make a snapshot active. Automatic snapshots are taken for `initial` (import of the manifest), `running` (when service methods are executed) and `start` (last successful start).

To revert to a snapshot, run **svccfg** in interactive mode, list the available snapshots, and revert t one of them:

```
# svccfg
svc:> select FMRI
svc:> listsnap
svc:> revert desired_snapshot_label
svc:> quit
# svcadm refresh FMRI; svcadm restart FMRI
```

syslog Monitoring

Chapter 3 discusses how to configure the `syslog` service to record log messages. As we discussed there, these log messages should be summarized and reports sent to responsible administrators on at least a daily basis.

We can configure custom log messages through the `syslog` facility by using the **logger** command. The contents of a file can be logged to a particular facility and log level, along with the associated process ID:

logger -i -f *filename* -p *facility.level*

Or, to log a specific message text to a facility and log level:

logger -p *facility.level* *message-text*

Network Service Monitoring

Network services can be monitored for availability and responsiveness. Nagios is a good freeware monitor. Mercury Interactive provides a software package for monitoring real-world application response.

As always, we can use open source tools such as `expect` and `wget` to design our own monitors for individual applications.

Resources

* Limoncelli, Thomas and Hogan, Christine. (2002) *The Practice of System and Network Administration*. New York City, NY: Addison Wesley.
* Marcus, Evan and Stern, Hal. (2000) *Blueprints for High Availability*. New York, NY: John Wiley & Sons.
* Rich, Amy. (November, 2004) Predictive Self-Healing. (http://www.sun.com/bigadmin/features/articles/selfheal.html)
* Schulz, Greg. (2004) *Resilient Storage Networks*. Burlington, MA: Elsevier Digital Press.
* Sun Microsystems. (November, 2006) *System Administration Guide: Basic Administration*. Santa Clara, CA: Sun Microsystems, Inc. (http://docs.sun.com/app/docs/doc/817-1985)

13

Continuity Management

Continuity Planning

Gartner reports that two out of five companies go out of business within five years of suffering a major disaster. Business continuity planning can be the difference between being a survivor or being roadkill.

Continuity management deals with preparing architectures and plans to deal with disasters. In the past, this discipline was called **Disaster Recovery**, but the industry has recognized that the focus should be on business continuity, not the techniques required to recover the service. Some companies owe their continued existence to their continuity plans; see the "Lehman Loses IT Headquarters" sidebar.

Lehman Loses IT Headquarters

In the wake of the September 11, 2001 attacks on the World Trade Center, some companies found that they had lost data, people and capabilities that they needed to support critical business activities. Some of those companies never recovered.

Lehman Brothers could have found themselves among that number. Fortunately, all but one of their 625 IT workers (from the 38th-40th floors of Tower One) were able to make it out of the building alive.

Unfortunately, Lehman had lost a data center and facilities in three other nearby buildings.

Lehman's staff immediately implemented their disaster recovery plan. On the day of the attack, the treasury department was able to move to the disaster recovery facility and carry out its cash management functions.

Lehman CTO Bob Schwartz told reporters that Lehman's IT staff was able to use their disaster recovery plans to keep critical business functions going. "No information was lost," he said. "I'm sure there were a couple of little things here and there, but nothing that interfered with our ability to provide service to our customers."

(Source: Network World, 11/26/2001)

Fortunately, not every disaster is as life-threatening or heart-wrenching as the September 11, 2001 attacks, Hurricane Katrina, or the Oklahoma City bombing. Fires, power outages, storms, floods and morons driving backhoes are also varieties of disasters.

And I certainly do not mean to imply that an IT environment recovery is the most important element in a disaster recovery; memories of frantic phone calls to track down family members and friends on September 11, and the memories of funerals in the weeks afterward are still much too close to the surface for me to ever say such a thing.

People come first. I've heard too many stories about my colleagues making their way into structurally unsound buildings to rescue vital hard drives or backup tapes. There is no excuse for endangering employees. If the data was that important, it should have had offsite replication or storage in the first place.

On the other hand, we have a responsibility as IT professionals to help our company prepare to be one of the survivors the next time a disaster strikes. I hope these suggestions help.

Recovery Objectives

Besides cost, the key business continuity drivers for a recovery solution are the Recovery Point Objective and the Recovery Time Objective. Figure 13-1 illustrates a typical disaster timeline to help explain these two concepts.

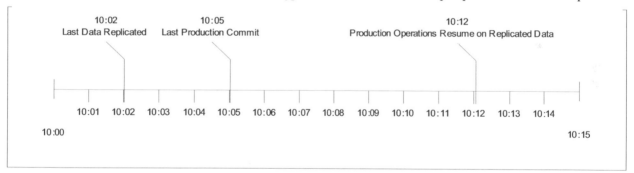

Figure 13-1. Disaster Timeline

The **Recovery Point Objective** (RPO) refers to the recovery point in time. Another way to think of this is that the RPO specifies the maximum allowable time delay between a data commit on the production side and the replication of this data to the recovery site.

It is probably easiest to think of RPO in terms of the amount of allowable data loss. The RPO is frequently expressed in terms of its relation to the time at which replication stops, as in "less than 5 minutes of data loss."

In Figure 13-1, three minutes of data loss would be expected, since production commits continued until 10:05, but were not replicated after 10:02.

The second major business driver is the **Recovery Time Objective** (RTO). This is the amount of time it will take us to recover from a disaster. Depending on the context, this may refer only to the technical steps required to bring up services on the recovery system. Usually, however, it refers to the amount of time that the service will be unavailable, including time to discover that an outage has occurred, the time required to decide to fail over, the time to get staff in place to perform the recovery, and then the amount of time to bring up services at the recovery site.

The costs associated with different RPO and RTO values will be determined by the type of application and its business purpose. Some applications may be able to tolerate unplanned outages of up to days without incurring substantial costs. Other applications may cause significant business-side problems with even minor amounts of unscheduled downtime.

In figure 13-1, the recovery time would usually be calculated to be 10 minutes. Effectively, the business has been without a working production system since 10:02, since any transactions between 10:02 and 10:12 will not have been applied properly to the new production environment that came online at 10:12. In some cases (where data loss is not an issue), the recovery time would be calculated as 7 minutes, since the system would have been functioning until 10:05. It is important to discuss which definition is being used when a Service Level Agreement (SLA) is specified for a system.

In some applications in regulated industries, the RPO must allow no data loss. For example, once a bank accepts a transaction, it is potentially disastrous for that transaction to be lost due to an excessive RPO. In such cases, a technology such as synchronous replication will be necessary to guarantee zero data loss.

Other types of applications are architected in a way that permits a minor amount of data loss, but where the recovery time is as close to zero as possible. (In other words, the service is almost always available.) An example of such an application might be an LDAP server cluster, where replication between the servers is infrequent because the data is largely static. It is possible for a data update to be lost if the server that accepted the update becomes unavailable before being able to pass it on. On the other hand, an actual outage of the LDAP service could have far-ranging implications throughout the enterprise.

Start Planning Early

Continuity planning should be done during the initial architecture and design phases for each service. If the service is not deployed to accommodate a natural recovery, it will be expensive and difficult to retrofit a recovery mechanism.

The type of recovery that is appropriate for each service will depend on the importance of the service and what the tolerance for downtime is for that service.

There are five generally-recognized approaches to recovery architecture:

- **Server Replacement**: Some services are run on standard server images with very little local customization. Such servers may most easily be recovered by replacing them with standard hardware and standard server images.
- **Backup and Restore**: Where there is a fair amount of tolerance for downtime on a service, it may be acceptable to rely on hardware replacement combined with restores from backups.
- **Shared Nothing Failover**: Some services are largely data-independent and do not require frequent data replication. In such cases, it might make sense to have an appropriately configured replacement at a recovery site. (One example may be an application server that pulls its data from a database. Aside from copying configuration changes, replication of the main server may not be necessary.)
- **Replication and Failover**: Several different replication technologies exist, each with different strengths and weaknesses. Array-based, SAN-based, file system-based or file-based technologies allow replication of data on a targeted basis. Synchronous replication techniques prevent data loss at the cost of performance and geographic dispersion. Asynchronous replication techniques permit relatively small amounts of data loss in order to preserve performance or allow replication across large distances. Failover techniques range from nearly instantaneous automated solutions to administrator-invoked scripts to involved manual checklists.

- **Live Active-Active Stretch Clusters**: Some services can be provided by active servers in multiple locations, where failover happens by client configurations. Some examples include DNS services (failover by *resolv.conf* lists), SMTP gateway servers (failover by MX record), web servers (failover by DNS load balancing), and some market data services (failover by client configuration). Such services should almost never be down. (**Stretch clusters** are **clusters where the members are located at geographically dispersed locations.**)

Which of these recovery approaches is appropriate to a given situation will depend on the cost of downtime on the service, as well as the particular characteristics of the service's architecture.

The cost of downtime on the service should be considered when designing, architecting and deploying the service. Continuity requirements are a key consideration when making choices about platforms, products, configurations and approaches during application development and deployment.

Replication Strategies

Different applications and environments have different tolerances for RPO and RTO. Some applications might be able to tolerate a potential data loss of days or even weeks; some may not be able to tolerate any data loss at all. Some applications can remain unavailable long enough for us to purchase a new system and restore from tape; some cannot.

There are several different strategies for recovering an application. Choosing a strategy will almost always involve an investment in hardware, software, and implementation time. If a strategy is chosen that does not support the business RPO and RTO requirements, an expensive re-tooling may be necessary.

Many types of replication solutions can be implemented at a server, disk storage, or storage network level. Each has unique advantages and disadvantages. Server replication tends to be cheapest, but also involves using server cycles to manage the replication. Storage network replication is extremely flexible, but can be more difficult to configure. Disk storage replication tends to be rock solid, but is usually limited in terms of supported hardware for the replication target.

Regardless where we choose to implement our data replication solution, we will still face a lot of the same issues.

One issue that needs to be addressed is re-silvering of a replication solution that has been partitioned for some amount of time. Ideally, only the changed sections of the disks will need to be re-replicated. Some less sophisticated solutions require a re-silvering of the entire storage area, which can take a long time and soak up a lot of bandwidth. Re-silvering is an issue that needs to be addressed with the vendor during the product evaluation.

Tape Recovery

Tape recovery remains the most common recovery mechanism. It has the advantages of cheapness and simplicity. It has some strong disadvantages in terms of both RPO and RTO.

In particular, protection from a site-loss disaster will require off-site storage of tape media. The time to recover tapes from the storage location, set up the recovery server, configure the backup server and restore the tapes must all be considered when a tape backup/recovery mechanism is selected as the primary recovery solution.

Tape backups may be used in conjunction with a service provider like SunGard or IBM, who will provide recovery services and machine room space for tape restores. For companies with a single location, this may allow a level of recoverability for a relatively low cost.

Periodic Replication

Some applications do not require anything like real-time data updates. Instead, periodic file copies of key directories or files will be enough to keep the remote system in sync with the local one. Rcp and scp can automate these copies, alone or in combination with `rdist`, `rsync` or backup and restore functions such as `ufsdump`/`ufsrestore`, `tar` and `cpio`. If large files or directories are being copied, it might make sense to compress a copy of the file with `compress` or `gzip` before shipping them; the time spent on the compression will probably more than pay for itself in reduced transmission time.

Periodic replication can also be performed on a block basis, which can reduce network requirements (as compared to synchronous or asynchronous replication), but which also leaves a bigger window for potential data loss.

Transaction Log Replication

Some database management systems providers allow remote databases to be kept in sync by periodically shipping transaction logs via a **transfer manager** to the remote site and applying them to an identical database there. (Oracle Data Guard is an example of this sort of recovery mechanism.) This scheme has the advantage of always knowing that the remote database is in a runnable state, since it must be running to apply the logs.

It is also possible to schedule the log updates in such a way that the effect of the changes on production is validated before the logs are rolled into the standby database. This would allow us to keep a valid copy of the database for recovery purposes in the event that somebody submits a disastrous command that truncates an entire table or submits a request that corrupts the database.

One downside with Oracle Data Guard in particular is the fact that Oracle charges for the CPUs on the recovery system as if they were in production. Another is that the RPO may allow a greater amount of potential data loss than most storage-based replication solutions.

An alternative approach to providing a similar type of functionality is provided by **transaction processing monitors** (TPMs) like BEA Tuxedo or IBM CICS or **asynchronous queuing systems** like IBM MQ Series or BEA Tuxedo/Q. These queuing solutions sit in front of the database and take care of submitting them to multiple instances at once. The queuing approach has some obvious advantages, in that performance on the client application is not held hostage to long-distance replication. The queuing software maintains the transactions in a disk-based queue to ensure that once the transaction is accepted, it will be written to all of the databases being front-ended. On the other hand, it is not a good solution where a solid confirmation of a database write is required by the application.

Figure 13-2 illustrates a Log File Replay sort of replication.

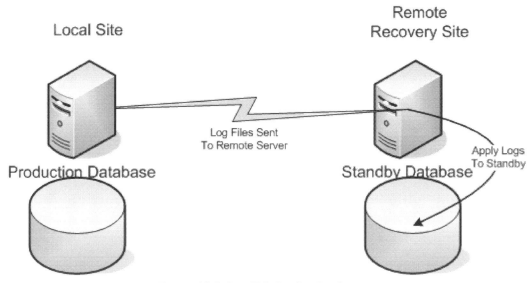

Figure 13-2. Log File Replay Replication

Synchronous vs Asynchronous Replication

Synchronous replication refers to a type of replication where the `commit` for a write is not returned until both replicas have been updated. The primary advantage to this sort of replication is that there is never any risk of data loss.

There are a few disadvantages to synchronous replication, however. One is that the loss of either copy of the data (or the network between them) results in a service outage. This can cause problems, since anything we're spending money to replicate is likely something that requires the best availability we can provide.

Another problem is that the latency of the network link is added to the usual latency for the write operation. Even with the best, most expensive extenders, dark fiber and fancy fiber gear, the outer limits for synchronous replication is about 100 km. Even then, the added latency may be too much to meet performance expectations.

Synchronous replication is the only choice where the RPO is zero. But then every "commit" will only be valid after it is written to the remote storage.   Two times the latency of the link needs to be added to every write transaction, which may be an unacceptable performance penalty. The only way to mitigate this problem is to reduce the link latency, either by moving the recovery location closer or by improving the network. The problem with reducing the physical separation of the two images is that both sites may be affected by a region-wide problem, like a storm or an earthquake. And long-distance low-latency networks can be very expensive.

Synchronous replication keeps both images of the data strictly in lock-step, as illustrated in Figure 13-3:

In **asynchronous replication**, on the other hand, writes are reported as complete as soon as they have been committed to local disk. The writes are then passed to the remote replica on a best effort basis. "Best effort" is defined differently for different implementations, but it usually involves an RPO with a relatively short window for data loss.

Since asynchronous replication allows the `commit` message to be sent back to the host operating system once the write has taken place on the primary array, the service can move on to the next thing while the replication of the data write is completed.

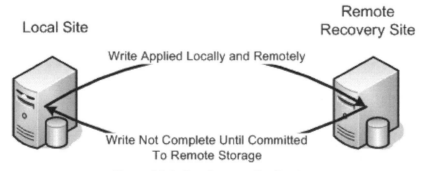

Figure 13-3. Synchronous Replication

There are several general approaches to asynchronous replication. Some solutions attempt to send the information about the data change immediately; others batch several writes together and send them off as a group. Either way, some sort of error checking is required to make sure that every write on the original storage is replicated to the remote storage.

Figure 13-4 illustrates asynchronous replication.

Figure 13-4. Asynchronous Replication

Asynchronous replication provides a compromise, where the data loss is limited to a few minutes or seconds. The upside is that commits are now reported from local rather than remote storage.

Write Order Consistency

Some applications, particularly database applications, are very sensitive to the order in which writes are made. In order to have a runnable image at the target location, we need to make some sort of provision so that image consistency is maintained.

With synchronous replication, write order consistency is managed by the application itself, since `commit` messages are only received once both sides have been updated. The application's native locking mechanisms will preserve file consistency.

For asynchronous replication, things get more complicated. There are two primary approaches to addressing this problem:

- Sequentially number each data change and apply the changes to the remote disks in the same order that they were applied on the local disks. (Hitachi TrueCopy uses this scheme, for example.)
- Batch the changes together, and only apply changes in complete batches. (EMC SRDF uses this method for its asynchronous replication.)

Each of these approaches has advantages relative to the other one. The sequential numbering scheme ensures that data changes are sent to the remote storage as soon as possible, reducing the window of potential data loss in the event of an outage. The batch scheme allows some optimization of write traffic and transmission bandwidth by allowing the replication engine to process the batch of changes before sending them.

Hybrid Replication

It is possible to combine the advantages of both synchronous and asynchronous replication using a hybrid replication technique. Figure 13-5 illustrates such an installation:

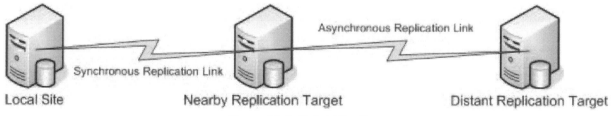

Figure 13-5. Hybrid Replication

Sometimes we need the assurance of synchronous replication but the long-distance capabilities of asynchronous replication. In a **hybrid replication** solution, the database is replicated synchronously to a nearby site, perhaps at a colocation or "colo" facility. From there, the data is replicated asynchronously to a recovery site located in another geographic region.

This arrangement has the advantage of limiting the performance hit of the synchronous replication while also allowing us to place our recovery distance at a large enough distance from our primary site.

This avoids most of the latency penalty associated with synchronous replication. And it also provides enough distance separation to allow for a recovery in the event of a regional disaster (like a hurricane, earthquake or large-scale blackout).

The major downside to such a solution is its cost, since it requires obtaining computer room space at a nearby location for the first leg in the replication. There is also a performance penalty associated with the synchronous leg of the replication.

Replication to Improve Data Access

Replication may be used to move data storage closer to data consumers, especially when the data access is mostly reads. Good examples of this sort of replication include replication of NFS servers providing reference data or replication of LDAP servers.

This sort of replication is especially valuable where WAN latency or throughput amounts to a significant proportion of the time required to return an answer to a query.

Recovery Planning

Successful recoveries do not just happen; they are architected, planned, and tested. Recovery plans should have several characteristics:

- **Clear**: Plans should be understandable by the people who would carry out a recovery. Depending on the nature of the disaster, the document's author may not be available to explain the document.
- **Current**: A procedure needs to be in place for periodic review and updates to these documents. The person or group reviewing the document needs to sign off on the review, and the quality of documentation reviews should be a standard section in annual employee evaluations.
- **Complete**: Nothing is worse than a plan that leaves out critical steps. Completeness of the document should be a focus of document reviews and recovery testing. Documents should also mention alternative recovery mechanisms when necessary.
- **Comprehensive**: All key services need to be identified and documented.
- **Available**: Okay, there is something worse than an incomplete document: a missing one. Up-to-date paper and electronic copies of the documents should be located in well-known, standard locations in multiple sites. These documents should be organized in a standard way, with a version-numbering system and a procedure for pushing updates out to all copies of the document.

It is much easier to identify key recovery issues and organize them properly *before* a recovery is necessary. Prioritize services and get signoffs on what gets done first. Let the stake holders slug it out *before* the disaster happens.

When disaster strikes, it is a virtual lock that the boss will be leaning over your shoulder asking "Is it done yet? How much longer?" That is not the time to be making decisions about whether email or file service comes up first.

Recovery Testing

If a plan has not been tested, it is not valid. No recovery plan that works exactly as documented. Thinking through a plan is a valuable exercise all by itself, but the plan is just words on paper until a full test has been carried out.

Testing should be done at multiple levels. **Unit tests** are carried out on each individual service or system. Frequent unit testing demonstrates that each individual piece of the recovery plan is conceptually sound. Unit testing also guarantees that focused attention will be paid to the recovery plans for each individual service.

Integration testing demonstrates that the recovered versions of several interrelated services or systems will work well together. Integration tests typically involve more resources and people than unit tests, and will take place less frequently.

Full scale or **site-loss tests** demonstrate that our plans allow us to recover from major disasters which disable or destroy entire business sites. These tests require significant resources and people from across the enterprise, and will need to be scheduled months in advance. The fact that they are difficult to organize, coordinate and carry out cannot distract us from performing them.

Typical recommendations are that full scale tests be carried out at least once and preferably twice each year. Integration and unit tests should be scheduled as frequently as necessary to assure successful full scale tests.

The frequency of testing will depend largely on the criticality of the services involved. Services that are absolutely critical for business functioning should be tested as frequently as possible, even if only as unit tests.

Different scenarios should be tested each time; it makes no sense to keep running through the same script time after time. During each test, each participant needs to keep a log of issues faced and how they were overcome (or suggestions to restructure the plan so that they can be overcome during the next test).

Test the Documentation

At the end of the test, these logs should be collected and reviewed. The test coordinator needs to produce a "lessons learned" document. After the test, the coordinator should identify issues to be addressed, make sure that responsibility for each issue is assigned and follow up to make sure that the issues are addressed.

Issues that were not resolved successfully during the test need to be revisited in future tests so that we can make sure that our plans, procedures and architecture have been fixed.

One particular type of document should be tested. Each service should have a dependency graph. **Dependency graphs** are a way to organize the dependency relationships between services. Each service is represented by an oval, and the dependency relationship is represented by an arrow pointing toward the dependent service. Figure 13-6 shows a fairly standard dependency graph for a web service.

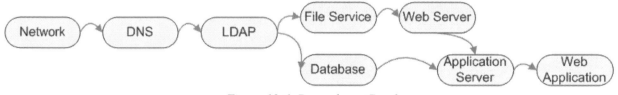

Figure 13-6. Dependency Graph

Real problems can be indicated by an area of the dependency graph where the arrows can be followed around in a **cycle** or **circle tour**. In that case, we have a conflict where services rely on each other to function properly. This can result in a **deadly embrace**, which is a deadlock condition preventing services from initializing properly while they wait for each other.

Test the People

A common mistake in recovery testing is to use the same staff for day-to-day support and continuity testing. The people who should run the test are the people who would be available in the recovery site in the event of a disaster. It might be a good idea to have the usual support staff standing by to provide advice or answer questions, but the recovery staff's fingers should be on the keyboards.

If questions do need to be addressed to the usual support staff, it is an indication that the documentation is unclear. Keep logs of the questions asked and figure out how to improve the recovery documents.

Backups and Restores

Most shops have a plan to back up their servers. Fewer have thought about what is involved in running restores from those backups. Backup windows are a standard part of planning, perhaps because they happen so frequently. Restore windows need to be determined by seeing what the costs of downtime are.

There are new techniques and technologies that allow us to cut restore times to a few minutes for even a large amount of data. Checkpointing and snapshotting software is available on storage units, volume managers and file systems. Log rollbacks on databases take only a little longer. Where the cost of downtime is extreme, the cost of these solutions makes a lot of sense.

Checkpoints and Snapshots

Checkpoints are operations in which all memory-resident or outstanding transaction data is written to disk and the resulting consistent state is given an identifier. S**napshots** are readable images of a file system state at a particular point in time. F**ull snapshots** are mirror image copies of the file system at a particular time; **block-level snapshots** only keep copies of blocks that have changed since the snapshot was taken. Figure 13-7 illustrates how a block-based snapshot reads the original data while the file system reads the current copy of each data block.

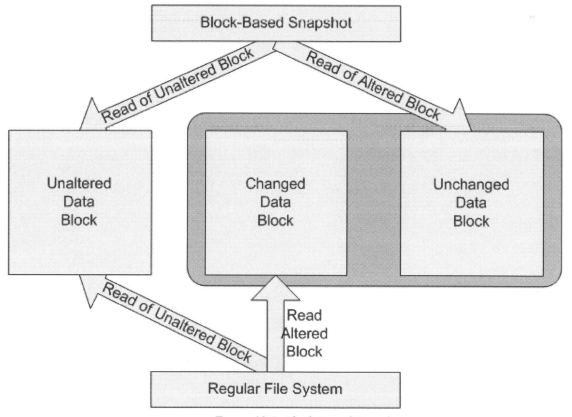

Figure 13-7. Block-Based Snapshot

(When a block-level snapshot is read, any unchanged blocks are read directly from the file system disk storage. If a changed block is read, the "old" version of that block is mapped by the snapshot. This means that block-level snapshots consume only as much space as has been written since the snapshot was taken.)

Some snapshotting software offers the option to "roll back" the file system to the state at the time of the snapshot. This can provide an extremely flexible way to run a "restore" to a specified point in time without the overhead of a traditional recovery from disk or tape media.

Checkpoints and snapshots can be combined to capture the system state at a particular point in time; in particular, they can be used to capture an image of a consistent database state. Snapshotting software provides a way to take consistent backups without having to take databases or file systems offline for extended periods. The fact that it takes hours to drain that multi-terabyte database to tape does not mean that the database itself needs to be offline.

Backup and Restore Verification

Backups need to be verified. Every day. This does not mean that someone has to parse thousands of lines of backup logs every day; that is what scripts are for.

Most professional backup software programs produce reports that pop errors and timeouts in a way that can be examined at a glance. Someone needs to sign their initials every day that the reports have been examined and problems have been resolved.

Check the amount of time required for a restore. If you don't test it, you will never know for sure. It might be good enough to restore a measured portion of the total and extrapolate, but we need to make sure that we can still hit our restore windows.

Off-site Backups

Copies of backups need to be kept both off-site and on-site. On-site copies are needed to facilitate restore requests as part of normal operations. Off-site copies are required as part of our business continuity plan.

If the building burns down and the backup tapes were all on the table next to the server, we are toast. Off-site backups may be made over a network link to a remote disk or tape storage, or data cartridges may be sent off-site with a storage company like Iron Mountain or one of its competitors.

The off-site storage facility needs to be secure, climate-controlled, organized, and available 24x7. (If our building burns down in the middle of the night, we need those tapes as soon as they can put them in a truck, not sometime tomorrow.)

From time to time, we should test the ability of the storage facility to deliver a specified tape to the recovery site in the time specified in the contract. This should be part of our disaster testing, but it should be done at odd times and without prior notification to the storage company. Tape recovery testing is one thing that should probably be scheduled separately from the rest of the full DR test.

A common practice among smaller companies is to take backup tapes to an employee's home. While this may be better than nothing, the level of security, climate control, and organization in a residence is probably not something we want to stake the company's future on.

Critical data on off-site tapes should be encrypted. Every month there is a new report of tapes that have gone missing from an off-site facility, and thousands of customers have been exposed to the risk of identity theft. Tape encryption is a good way to keep our company's name off the front pages.

At the same time, we need to make sure that we can decrypt the data at the recovery site. Decrypting these tapes should be a part of our disaster recovery drill.

Disk vs Tape

Disk-based backup systems provide a reasonable alternative to tape backups in many cases. Current disk-based systems allow random access, flexible space management and rapid access to backup data. When located at a remote location, they provide a reasonable way to organize off-site backups.

Even with all these advantages, tape still has its place in today's data center. Tapes are portable, durable, flexible and easily archived. Several companies exist which provide services for archiving tapes off-site in climate-controlled, secure locations. Performance on newer tape units is good enough for most backup environments.

Tapes provide an unbeatable way to archive and transport large amounts of data in the event of a site-loss disaster. Sure, your new WAN architecture boasts much better latency, but it will never beat the throughput of a delivery van full of high-density tapes.

Several vendors are offering hybrid backup systems under the flag of **disk-to-disk-to-tape**. The idea of such solutions is that the initial backup is made to a low-cost disk storage unit, then drained off to tape. This concept has several advantages:

- The initial backup takes place at high speeds, especially if the initial backup is taken within the same storage array or SAN.
- The tape backup window can be expanded to impinge on business hours without causing problems for the production systems.
- If the initial disk backup is kept as the "local" copy for a reasonable period of time, restores can take place much more quickly than from tape.

Watch the Basics

When backup systems fail, it is usually for the dumbest reasons imaginable. Tapes wear out, backups fail unnoticed for long periods of time, or servers are not scheduled for backup appropriately. Just for completeness sake, here are a few things to keep in mind:

- Test restores regularly: Perform test restores of arbitrary files from different locations in the environment. Compare the checksums of the restored files against the checksums of the original.
- Keep the tape heads clean: Vendors recommend a number of service hours between tape head cleanings. Clean the heads at least that frequently.
- Get rid of dirty and damaged tapes: Don't risk your data to a questionable cartridge. De-gauss it, destroy it, and discard it.
- Get rid of old tapes: When the tape has reached the manufacturer-recommended number of mounts, destroy it.
- Tapes only retain data for a certain shelf life: Test restores from old tapes. Depending on the retention requirements, the data will need to be migrated onto new tapes.
- Tapes require a drive to read them: Retain at least one or two tape drives capable of restoring from old tapes. At some point, data should be migrated to new media.
- Critical tapes need two copies: Otherwise, when tapes fail, our data will be gone. One copy of the tape should be kept off-site.

Media Relations

A frequently overlooked aspect of disaster recovery planning is public and media relations. Part of a business continuity plan should be a decision about who will (and who will not) be responsible for providing information and the "company line" to customers, shareholders and the media. And it makes sense to think through what types of information should and should not be released.

It may be worthwhile to develop a relationship with a public relations firm with disaster recovery experience. Effective communication in the wake of a disaster is a specialized discipline. It does not make sense to be handing out information by whoever picks up the phone. Disasters can be disruptive enough without having to deal with the effects of improper or inaccurate releases of information.

Resources

- Ferelli, Mark; et al. (2003) *Disaster Recovery and Business Continuance*. Beverly Hills, CA: WestWorld Productions, Inc.
- Gaudin, Sharon. (November 26, 2001) *Lehman Brothers' Network Survives*. Network World Magazine, 11/26/2001 pp 36-37.
- Limoncelli, Thomas and Hogan, Christine. (2002) *The Practice of System and Network Administration*. New York City, NY: Addison Wesley.
- Marcus, Evan and Stern, Hal. (2000) *Blueprints for High Availability*. New York, NY: John Wiley & Sons.
- Schulz, Greg. (2004) *Resilient Storage Networks*. Burlington, MA: Elsevier Digital Press.

14

Procedures and People

Change Management

The sidebar "Upgrade Gone Bad" tells the story of a software upgrade on the Australian Stock Exchange (ASX) trading system. It resulted in a major outage during trading hours. This was a huge failure, with repercussions throughout the entire financial community.

There are some positive aspects of the story; in particular, the upgrade did happen during a maintenance window, and the disaster recovery site proved capable of handling production traffic. Still, the positive aspects of the story are far outweighed by what went wrong.

Upgrade Gone Bad

In 1995, the Australian Stock Exchange (ASX) suffered a massive failure of their share trading system. The failure occurred on a Monday, only two days after a federal election. Due largely to the 2-hour outage during prime trading hours, only $550 million (Australian) was traded, instead of the expected $1 billion (Australian).

A major software upgrade the previous weekend was responsible for the failure. The ASX's IT team attempted to roll back to the previous version, but the attempt resulted in a corrupted production database. Disaster recovery procedures were implemented, and trading was able to resume two hours later from the recovery site. (Source: Gartner)

Every production environment will need to be changed over time. Capacity needs to be increased, bug fixes and functionality enhancements need to be implemented, and new services need to be rolled out. An appropriate change management procedure avoids problems where possible and recovers from them where necessary.

273

A change management system needs to include the following for each change:

- **Executive Summary**: Brief description of the change.
- **Change Request**: Tracking of problem reports/change requests, including who requested the fix/change, who approved it, and who was assigned to it.
- **Impact Analysis**: The impact of the change, and which other systems will be affected.
- **Risk Analysis**: What bad things might happen as a result of the change, including their costs, probabilities, and mitigation actions taken or proposed.
- **Justification**: Why does the change need to be made?
- **Version Control**: Tracking the files and objects that are to be changed.
- **Back-out Plan**: How to roll back to the system state prior to the change.
- **Quality Management**: Architecture and code reviews; testing methodology and reporting.
- **Distribution Plan**: Specifies who is responsible for doing what.
- **Change Schedule**: The time estimates and schedule to execute the change.

Besides managing the information about the changes, we need to enforce a discipline about when and how changes may occur. Multiple groups should not be changing the same thing at the same time; rollbacks and testing will become much more complicated. If two changes *must* go in at the same time, the testing and rollback procedures for both changes need to be coordinated, and there needs to be a single decision maker who decides whether to stay with the change or roll the whole thing back. The sidebar "One at a Time" demonstrates what can happen when we try to bite off too much at once.

A change control committee needs to include members from each of the different customer and IT organizational groups that are affected by changes. These members need to take responsibility for communicating information about changes to their respective groups, as well as taking information to the committee about upcoming changes planned by their groups. Changes need to be coordinated, and people from the organizational groups need to make themselves available to do post-change testing.

One at a Time

A large medical group in Canada needed to make a large number of changes, including a datacenter move, software upgrades of the medical records tracker and the practice management software, a scanner software implementation, a SAN migration, and an authentication server upgrade.

Nobody likes multiple-weekend deployments, so the CIO scheduled all the upgrades for the same weekend.

The upgrade started on Friday evening. On Saturday morning, the only functional services were the staff time-clock software and an old Exchange server. While the plan called for testing to take place on Saturday, nothing was working well enough to test.

Over the next week, the company shoveled money to vendors and outside consultants to try to untangle the chaos. By Thursday evening, many important services were working, and by Friday the staff was no longer in fear of killing a patient due to an IT malfunction.

The final price tag for the installation is estimated to be about double what had been budgeted. (Source: InfoWorld 2/5/2007)

Postmortem

After a change is complete, the team should undertake a "postmortem" process to analyze what went right and wrong with the deployment. This postmortem process should be appropriate to the change; it may be a note appended to the change log for a small change, or it may be a series of meetings and a final report examining the results of the change.

In retrospect, I suspect that every member of the ASX IT team would confess that more testing should have been done before and after the deployment of the upgrade. Maybe additional testing methods and targets would have occurred to the recovery staff. Insights like these need to be captured and added to the testing methodology.

If we do not capture these insights in the immediate aftermath of the deployment, they will be lost in the jumble of day-to-day concerns. Whatever level and form of postmortem is appropriate for a particular deployment, it needs to be done before the deployment is considered to be complete. Like all other documentation tasks, postmortems require discipline and a commitment to process improvement.

Process Automation

When we automate processes, the environment becomes more reliable and easier to manage. Automation can reduce the complexity of documentation and training, and it can reduce the effects of errors while typing in commands. It can also reduce the probability of an error by less experienced administrators.

It does not make sense to repeat the same job over and over. Do it once, do it right and move on. And if someone else on your team already did it, leverage their work rather than repeating it your self.

Automated Installations

Installation automation creates standardized configurations that are easier to maintain. Sun Jumpstart and Solaris Flash mechanisms standardize and automate installations. It requires some work to structure and script an appropriate installation for your site, but the effort is paid back in terms of improved installation and recovery time as well as increased efficiency due to consistent system standards.

Software Architecture and Development

Software should be architected with several key goals in mind:

- **Keep it Simple**: Unnecessary features provide additional ways for the software to fail and additional code to maintain and test. If the feature isn't actually needed by the business customer, don't put it in.
- **Plan for Failure**: Redundancy and reliability have to be designed into software from the beginning. What will happen when a failure occurs? How will we recover from a disaster? How do we back it up? How do we monitor its behavior, and how do we recover from misbehavior?
- **Coordinate Hardware and Software Architecture**: This seems like it shouldn't need to be said, but it is amazing how often hardware and software requirements are not communicated clearly and completely.
- **Get Good Requirements**: A surprising number of projects fail because nobody ever decides exactly what the software is supposed to do. The only way to make sure that the project is successful is to define what success is.

Development Environment

Development activity should not occur on production systems once they go live. A separate development environment is a key aspect of a well-run, reliable IT infrastructure. There are several different types of development and testing environments that should be considered:

- **Production Mirror**: A production mirror environment is typically used to look at production as it looked in the recent past. This environment can be used for testing change rollouts or rollbacks, and it can be useful for duplicating problems that are observed in production.
- **Quality Assurance (QA)**: This environment is the last testing environment before a change is deployed to production. Changes to the QA environment should be controlled the same way that production changes are controlled.
- **Development**: This environment is where code is created and tried out. It needs to be strictly separated from production so that buggy code does not affect any production services.
- **Test/Sandbox**: These environments are valuable for trying to work out procedures or duplicate problems in an environment where it will not affect many people. A sandbox is distinct from development in that it is not typically a permanent or shared environment.
- **Disaster Recovery**: This is where production services would be recovered in the event of a disaster.

Project Management

Project management is a key discipline in any successful IT department. Without the focus imposed by an organized project manager, projects will meander through time, blown hither and yon by the opinion of the last person to make a request of the project team. The result will be over budget and late, and it is a virtual lock that the end users will not be happy.

A project manager's job has several key components:

- Identify requirements by negotiating with the stake holders.
- Establish a project schedule, including milestones and timelines.
- Create a project budget.
- Assemble and schedule needed resources.
- Track and document the progress of various phases of the project.
- Deal with proposed changes to requirements, budget, or schedule.
- Balance the natural tension between quality, cost, and speed. Negotiate competing demands by the stakeholders.
- Supervise the testing of the project; verify with the stake holders that requirements are being met.
- When a project is in danger, propose alternatives, including the costs and benefits of each. When a project is in deep trouble, it may even fall on the project manager to propose terminating the project.

Project management is well beyond the scope of this book. There are several excellent books, courses, and web sites to teach the basics of project management. A few such sources are listed in the "Resources" section below.

Capacity Management

We need to understand how our computing resources are being used, and we need to be periodically examine utilization data to see what trends exist. We should be able to forecast resource requirements into the future. This will allow us to purchase more effectively, rather than reacting to the emergency of the moment.

As part of this process, project managers need to provide projections of how much and what type of resources will be required for upcoming projects. The budget for capacity should be included as part of the overall project planning and budgeting process.

Protecting People from Themselves

Ultimately, the purpose of a good policy is to notify people about actions that might cause harm to themselves or the company. The first step to protecting people from themselves is to carefully draw up policies to protect the company's assets, including its data and its employees.

Policies are only as good as the enforcement mechanisms that we use to make sure that they are followed. Human nature leads people to take "shortcuts" if there are no obvious consequences.

The two main approaches to protecting people from them are:

- Use authorizations and permissions to keep people from doing things that are contrary to the policies.
- Use auditing and reporting to identify violations of policies and the people who perpetrated them.

Depending on the nature of the policy, the consequences of a violation may range from a friendly email to firing or even criminal prosecution. But if we haven't taken the time to set up appropriate security precautions or identify policy violations, it is a lock that the policies are just words on paper.

Testing Procedures

Several different levels of testing should be done:

- **Unit Testing**: Testing of each system component.
- **Assembly** or **Integration Testing**: Testing as components are added to the overall system.
- **End-to-End Testing**: Testing of the full system, including all components.

Simulation software can be helpful for designing a test suite for quality assurance testing. If the same test suite can be applied automatically, and if the test suite is grown to cover each failure mode as it is discovered, the test suite will make sure that base functionality is achieved and that old errors are not re-introduced. By automating the test suite, we can make sure that tests are not forgotten or ignored as the deployment day draws near.

Before the system is released to production, the end users need to test the system in as real-life a scenario as possible. The end user or customer representative should sign of on each change before it is released to production. The representative should also sign off on the change after it has been released to production.

Problem Tracking and Resolution

Problems should be documented and tracked. The resolutions of the problems should be verified and documented as well. Having a record of problems allows us to apply previous fixes to current problems, and it allows us to look for problematic trends.

There should also be a clearly stated and understood ranking of which problems are the most important and will receive priority attention. If large portions of a company's business is done via email, email problems need to take precedence over setting up a PC for the CEO's granddaughter. It will be easiest to get people to agree to priorities in advance. Get management signoff on a memo stating the priorities of the different services we provide, then stick to it.

Senior IT staff needs to look over problem reports and make sure that the proper root cause analysis is being done. A junior admin will "fix" a disk space problem over and over, but may not check into *why* the error logs are growing so darn fast.

We noted in Chapter 1 the importance of getting a sign-off from a service owner verifying that the fix is effective.

Standardization

If we standardize on a few hardware and software configurations, we will reduce the amount of time required to train staff, increase our ability to stay on top of important patches and service announcements, and consolidate our spare parts pool.

There are additional advantages when it comes time to negotiate purchasing and maintenance agreements. Vendors will go farther to keep happy a customer who has a commitment to their products.

Where possible, we should keep our standard configurations as simple as possible. Simplicity reduces the number of possible adverse interactions between components, and it makes it easier to narrow down the list of the possible causes of the problem.

Best Practices

In addition to standardizing within our environment, we should work to keep our environments within the usual industry standards, or at least keep them within areas with active user communities.

Conferences, user groups, mailing lists, blogs, and web sites can all be important sources of advice and assistance while designing and maintaining a high-quality IT environment.

Whatever we are trying to do is likely to have been attempted before. If we are using components with an active user community, we are likely to be able to tap into that experience and expertise and save ourselves time rather than re-inventing the wheel.

Some best practices are universal:

- Eliminate unneeded hardware or software.
- Minimize the points of control and the sources of change.
- Reduce application contention where possible.
- Only allow network or application access where needed.
- Automate routine tasks.
- Test, document, track and control changes completely.
- Document systems clearly and completely.
- Identify a service owner and/or customer representative for each service.

Documentation

Solid documentation is an essential part of a solid environment. A project or task should not be considered complete until the documentation has been written or updated appropriately. This documentation includes comments in the code and configuration files as well as operational documentation and architectural descriptions.

We should also make it clear that high-quality documentation makes it less likely that people will be interrupted during vacation days or after hours when they are not on support.

Documentation is worthless if it is outdated. All documentation needs to be reviewed periodically. Nobody likes to write or review documentation. To help enforce documentation review, the reviewers name and the date of the review should be recorded. This may be as simple as typing initials and dates at the end of the document after the review, or it may involve a separate log.

The quality of documentation should be made a part of the standard employee annual review process. Long experience has shown that people are most likely to do a good job on the tasks where their contributions are measured and recognized. As unglamorous as it is, documentation is one of the key ingredients of a well-run IT department.

Configuration Management

We need to track which systems are using which software, for what purposes, and who is responsible for it. Without this information, performing an impact analysis during change control becomes very difficult.

Building a configuration management database is a chore and will cost staff and monetary resources. But the first time the company goes through a software audit, the database will probably pay for itself.

Some software solutions exist to help track the software automatically so that not everything has to be done by hand. Cfengine and puppet are two free software projects that have packages in this space. The major ITIL tool vendors (such as BMC, IBM, and HP) include configuration management offerings in their suites.

Training

Unfortunately, a lot of companies view training as an employee perk that brings no value back to the company. In fact, a well-designed training program can save a company money, both in terms of making sure that things get done correctly the first time and also in saving direct costs that would otherwise go to outside contractors to implement or repair facilities that are beyond the capabilities of our staff.

A well-designed training program will fill gaps in the staff's knowledge, introduce them to new technologies and techniques, allow them to find out how other companies handle the same problems we have, and raise staff morale. People are smart enough to realize that they are valued if the company thinks enough of them to invest in their training. Failure to provide training sends the opposite message.

Training programs should have some important characteristics:

- **Relevance**: It should be relevant to the goals and operations of the company.
- **Promote Growth**: Training courses should require staff members to stretch a little outside of their comfort zone.
- **Time Efficiency**: Boot camp classes will frequently cover several 1-week courses worth of material in a single course. Even though these may be more expensive, they may provide a better value.
- **Hands On**: The content of technical courses is more likely to stick with staff members if the classes have a significant lab component. Students need a chance to practice what they are learning, and it is a great opportunity to practice in a lab where no production systems will be affected.
- **Fair**: Nothing turns off a staff faster than an environment where the manager's chosen few get to go to the good conferences and training while everyone else slogs away in the trenches. Everyone should have a chance to get training appropriate to his or her level of expertise.

Resources

- Anonymous. (February 5, 2007) *Rush to Disaster*. InfoWorld, p 68. (http://www.infoworld.com/article/07/01/30/06OPrecord_1.html)
- Cfengine. http://www.cfengine.org/pages/manual_guides
- Cromar, Scott. (January 2003) *Configuration and Patch Verification on Solaris Systems*. Bethesda, MD: SANS. (http://www.sans.org/reading_room/whitepapers/solaris/921.php)
- Duvall, Mel and Bartholomew, Doug. (February 2007) *The Promise and Peril of PLM*. Baseline Magazine, pp 34-47.
- Ferris, Karen. (2000) *Answering the ITIL Sceptics*. (http://www.itilpeople.com/articles/Answering%20the%20ITIL%20sceptics.htm)

- Limoncelli, Thomas and Hogan, Christine. (2002) *The Practice of System and Network Administration*. New York City, NY: Addison-Wesley.
- Project Management Institute. (2007) (http://www.pmi.org/info/PIR_KWCOverview.asp?nav=0603)
- Puppet. http://projects.puppetlabs.com/projects/puppet
- Schwalbe, Kathy. (2006) *Information Technology Project Management*. Boston, MA: Thompson.
- Shelford, Thomas J. and Remillard, Gregory A. (October 2002) *Real Web Project Management*. Boston, MA: Addison-Wesley.
- Sun Microsystems. (November 2006) *Solaris 10 Installation Guide: Custom Jumpstart and Advanced Installations*. Santa Clara, CA: Sun Microsystems, Inc. (http://docs.sun.com/app/docs/doc/819-6397)
- Sun Microsystems. (November 2006) *Solaris 10 11/06 Installation Guide: Planning for Installation and Upgrade*. Santa Clara, CA: Sun Microsystems, Inc. (http://docs.sun.com/app/docs/doc/819-6764)

15

Security

Security is more a philosophy than a policy or set of technologies. Information security encompasses a number of technologies, skills, and practices. But more important than that, information security is based on an attitude. Security is impossible unless everyone in the organization shares a commitment to protecting its information assets.

Solaris 10 includes a number of features to improve system security. In this chapter, we will discuss both general concepts and some Solaris-specific implementation details.

The CIA Triad

The three key elements of information security are confidentiality, integrity, and availability. These three elements together are frequently called the **CIA Triad**.

Confidentiality may be defined in terms of preventing the unauthorized disclosure of confidential information. Such disclosures may be accidental or intentional. A key part of this definition is that we need to define which information is deemed confidential, and we need to have a system in place to specify how confidential a piece of information is. It would be prohibitively expensive to provide top levels of protection for all data. Instead, we need to identify which information is most sensitive.

Information **integrity** means that the data are consistent and protected from unauthorized modifications. Key parts of information integrity include rules to validate input, compare related data from different sources, and checks to make sure that any data modifications are both correct and authorized.

Availability means that the information can be accessed by authorized people in a timely and reliable way. Chapters 12 and 13 deal with several important aspects of availability.

Information systems are only secure if all three conditions of the CIA Triad have been satisfied. An attack on our information's security may be made against any or all of these conditions.

Least Privilege Model

Good security practice dictates that we limit access to data and computing facilities to people who require them to pursue legitimate company business. If someone does not need access to information to carry out a legitimate job for the organization, that person should not have access.

Beyond this, the people authorized to use company computing resources must be vetted properly to make sure that they are honest, responsible and understand how to use the resources in a way that protects the company and its customers.

It is certainly easiest to set things up to allow everyone access to everything, but setting things up that way increases the number and variety of security risks that we have to consider. Information security can only be achieved by limiting data access to the people who really need it.

Later in this chapter, we discuss Solaris's Role-Based Access Control (RBAC), which includes a powerful mechanism for restricting privileges to the bare minimum necessary.

Authentication

Authentication is how a user identifies himself or herself to the system. Passwords are a frequent authentication mechanism. Where passwords are used, they should be audited frequently to make sure that they are secure enough.

Where possible, access to the system or application should be controlled by something more secure than passwords. Two-factor authentication schemes and digital certificates are additional mechanisms that can provide an extra layer of security.

Solaris comes bundled with tools to enable several different types of authentication, including smart cards, kerberos, SASL, and digital certificates. There are simply too many different authentication schemes to allow us to do full coverage of this topic in a book of this size. Instead, we'll take a high-level overview of a few of the most important topics. Additional information is located in the *System Administration Guide: Security Services* manual listed in the References for this chapter.

This list is far from complete. Third-party authentication mechanisms may be provided through PAM by packages within Samba and SSH, as well as by vendors of token or RADIUS-based authentication packages.

PAM

The **Pluggable Authentication Module** (PAM) is a framework that makes it easier to plug different authentication technologies into the OS without requiring a reboot or recompilation of the service. PAM also permits using different authentication mechanisms for different services.

PAM is controlled through the */etc/pam.conf* configuration file. Each service includes a collection of lines which are applied in order to any authentication requests. The entries in each section are lines containing the following fields:

- Service Name: The name of the system entry service. Examples include login, ftp, telnet, and ssh.
- Module Type: The service's module type. The valid types are:
- `account`: Deal with password aging, account expiration, and access restriction. After authentication, these determine if the user should be given access to the system.
- `auth`: Account authentication.
- `password`: Allow for changes to a user passwords.
- `session`: Manage opening and closing of login sessions.
- Control Flag: Determines the behavior for this module upon success or failure. Each operation may return a success, failure, or ignore state. The result of the operation is determined by one of the following flags:
- `binding`: If this module is successful, and no previous "required" modules have failed, the result is success. No further modules are checked.

- `required`: If the module is successful, additional modules are checked. If it fails and is the first required module failure, PAM saves the error message and continues checking the stack. The request will only succeed if all of the required, requisite, and binding entries succeed.

- `requisite`: This behaves like the required flag, except that no further checking is performed after a failure is returned. The request will only succeed if all of the required, requisite, and binding entries succeed.

- `optional`: Success or failure is logged, but does not affect the success or failure of the request.

- `sufficient`. If this is successful, and no previous required modules have failed, PAM skips any remaining lines and returns a success. Failure is equivalent to an optional failure.

- Module Path: Path to the library objects implementing the security policy.

- Module Options: Options passed to the service module.

PAM errors are logged based on the configuration in the */etc/syslog.conf.*

Kerberos

The **Kerberos** service was created by MIT to provide a secure but flexible authentication framework with bundled encryption for network communications. An implementation of Kerberos V5 is included in Solaris 10. A full discussion of Kerberos is outside the scope of this book, but there is a substantial section on Kerberos in Solaris 10's *Security Services* manual, including a chapter on troubleshooting.

LDAP

LDAP is a directory service protocol allowing us to store all kinds of information, including security and login information. There are several different types of LDAP servers available, including Sun One, OpenLDAP, and Microsoft. A full discussion of LDAP is outside the scope of this book, but additional information is available in Solaris 10's *Naming and Directory Services (DNS, NIS, and LDAP)* manual.

Key advantages of LDAP include:

- Allows us to centralize directory information, rather than having a separate database for each type of environment.

- Allows data to be shared across naming services.

- Provides a central repository that can easily be replicated and distributed.

- Broad compatibility across environments and applications.

Smart Cards

Smart cards are plastic cards that contain a processor and memory. They can be used in conjunction with a card reader to authenticate to systems.

Password Management

Since most systems still rely on passwords for authentication, it is important to think about how best to protect them. Fields in the */etc/shadow* file or `passwd/shadow` database +allow us to set password expirations or to lock accounts.

In general, passwords should be at least 8 characters long, and should include a mixture of upper and lower case letters, numerals, and special characters. Passwords should not be kept forever; a common recommendation is that passwords should be changed at least every 90 days or so.

Password cracking programs, such as John the Ripper or Crack, should be run against the password database periodically to verify that people are not choosing easily guessable passwords.

Solaris 10 includes features to allow us to check password strength. In */etc/default/passwd*, we can set a comma-separated list of dictionaries that can be used to exclude potential passwords, a minimum number of changes between new and old passwords, minimum numbers of alphabetic and nonalphabetic characters in a password, minimum numbers of upper and lower case characters in the password, and the maximum allowable number of consecutive repeating characters.

The location of the encrypted passwords is specified in the */etc/nsswitch.conf* file in the `passwd` line. Entries may include some combination of the following:

- `files`: User login information located in */etc/passwd* and */etc/shadow*.

- `ldap`: Located on the LDAP directory service.

- `nis`: Located in the NIS database.

- `nisplus`: Located in the NIS+ database.

- `compat`: Understands the + and – tokens to specify which users' passwords are specified locally on */etc/shadow* and which are in the NIS database. This mode is used to provide backwards compatibility and is deprecated. If you are still using `compat`, consider switching to a "`files nis`" configuration instead; odd bugs have been known to inhabit the `compat` functionality.

Password encryption is done by using the password to generate a one-way hash. Authentication takes place by generating a hash with the submitted password and comparing the generated hash to the one stored in the password database.

Solaris 10 allows several choices for generating default password hashes and using them to perform authentications. In the */etc/security/policy.conf* file, the `CRYPT_ALGORITHMS_ALLOW` line specifies which algorithms may be used to perform authentication, the `CRYPT_ALGORITHMS_DEPRECATE` line specifies which algorithms may not be used, and `CRYPT_DEFAULT` specifies the default. The algorithms available in Solaris 10 are:

- `1`: The same MD5 algorithm used by Linux and BSD systems.

- `2a`: The same Blowfish algorithm used by BSD systems.

- `md5`: An improved MD5 algorithm that may not be compatible with other system types.

- `__unix__`: The standard Unix `crypt` algorithm. This algorithm is considered to be least robust of the four options.

System accounts (such as `daemon`, `bin`, `sys`, `adm`, `lp`, `uucp`, and `nuucp`) are not intended for use as login accounts. They should be locked by the following means:

- No valid shells should be provided in the last field of their `passwd` entry.

- An illegal password hash should be placed in the encrypted password field of their `shadow` entry. Such illegal hashes might include strings like "NP" or "*LK*" which cannot be the hash for any legal password.

Though it becomes less common with each passing year, Solaris does support dialup logins. The files that support the dialup login mechanism are */etc/dialups* (which contains a list of ports through which a dialup login attempt may be made) and */etc/d_passwd* (which contains a list of passwords associated with potential login shells).

Authorization

Authorization refers to controls put into place to make sure that only appropriate people are permitted to view or change information. People who do not require access to a system or application should not have that access. Lists of people with access need to be reviewed periodically, and people who do not need access should be removed.

Solaris 10 allows fine-grained control over access to devices on the OS. Devices may be restricted to certain users or certain zones.

Sometimes people require administrative privileges to perform a limited set of functions. There are a few different ways to handle this without giving out the root password.

One of the most flexible methods for dealing with this is the sudo command.

Another is through an enterprise scheduling program, where individual users can be given permission to order and execute jobs which would then run with administrative privileges. Any such jobs need to be writable only by root.

Solaris implements another way to handle this issue with RBAC.

sudo

sudo is a third-party utility that allows us to specify which users can run a command as which other users. By default, someone invoking a command through sudo needs to authenticate with their user password. The configuration for sudo is located in */etc/sudoers*.

When unauthorized users attempt to run a command through sudo, email can be set to alert root or some other specified address. Both successful and unsuccessful attempts are logged.

While sudo is not as powerful as RBAC, it does have the advantage of being available on most Unix and Linux environments. It provides the majority of features that most people want in a easily-used and portable package.

RBAC

Role Based Access Control (RBAC) provides a way to grant groups of privileges to individual users. One advantage of this approach is that as these roles are granted directly to administrators, they can be removed from the root account. This has the effect of limiting the exposure of traditional Unix systems to the "system god" powers of root.

A key advantage of RBAC over a traditional rights model is that it provides an audit trail for important accounts. People perform administrative actions from their own accounts, and the results are audited and tracked.

Another advantage of the current security model is that extra privileges for a process can be limited to those actually required for proper functioning. If a privilege is not strictly required, it can be excluded from the process. This can reduce the amount of damage caused by an exploit as well as limiting the types of exploits that may work.

The RBAC model involves several key concepts. The RBAC-centered definitions of these concepts follow:

- **Authorization**: Permissions to perform a class of action. An example would be the solaris.device.cdrw authorization, which allows read and write capability to a CD device. Authorizations are stored in the */etc/security/auth_attr* file.

- **Privilege**: A discrete right that can be granted. Process rights management is implemented through privileges; without a needed privilege, the kernel will forbid the process from performing a privileged action. A user can view his or her basic privileges by running **ppriv -vl basic**. If a user does not have the proper authorizations, he or she will be prevented from performing security-sensitive operations within a privileged application.

- **Security attribute**: These allow a process to perform an operation. Authorizations and privileges are types of attributes.

- **Privileged application**: An application that requires privileges or authorizations to succeed. Within RBAC, we can specify the privileges required for specific commands. An example (in a traditional Unix setting) would be a SUID program, which requires a given Effective User ID (EUID) to succeed.

- **Rights profile**: Collection of assignable administrative capabilities. These may include authorizations, privileges, and even other rights profiles. These are defined locally in */etc/security/prof_attr* and */etc/security/exec_attr*. The `prof_attr` contains the profile name and authorizations. The `exec_attr` contains the privileged applications assigned to rights profiles.

- **Role**: Identity for running privileged applications. Only specified users may assume a given role. A role may be assigned rights profiles.

Figure 15-1 demonstrates the way that rights should be propagated within an RBAC framework. Authorizations and the rights to use commands with security attributes are granted to rights profiles. Rights profiles are frequently aggregated into more comprehensive rights profiles. These rights profiles are granted to roles. Roles are assumed by users who wish to perform a security-controlled function. Example 15-1 below examines this particular scenario in more detail.

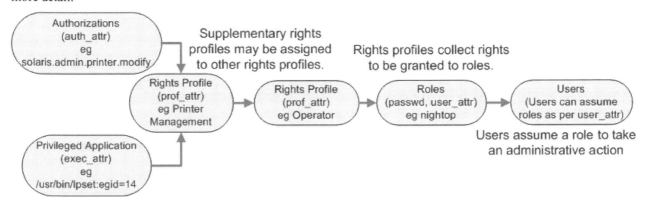

Figure 15-1. RBAC Rights Assignments

While it is possible to assign privileges and authorizations directly to users, it is not a good practice. Especially with privileges with large ramifications, it is best to require a user to assume a role in order to use the privilege. Since attack vectors are not always straightforward, it is hard to distinguish between important and unimportant privileges. It is best to assign privileges in the recommended way.

Users who wish to run a privileged application would do so through a **profile shell**. These shells (**pfsh**, **pfcsh**, and **pfksh**) verify that the user has the rights to use the rights profile in question, then run the privileged application. All activities performed in a profile shell are logged.

The most frequent use of RBAC is to replace an existing user account. Three key characteristics of a role that may be useful as a login account replacement are:

- No direct logins for roles. Root or application service accounts are usually not appropriate for use as direct login accounts.

- All actions taken after assuming a role may be logged easily. Since su is required to enter the protected account, there is no ambiguity about who performed which action.

- A special shell (pfksh, pfsh, or pfcsh) is required to execute commands within a role. These shells allow for careful privilege checking by the OS.

Table 15-1 describes the key databases and configuration files associated with RBAC:

Table 15-1. RBAC Databases and Configuration Files

Database	Name	Description
user_attr	Extended user attributes.	Associates users and roles with authorizations and rights.
prof_attr	Rights profile attributes.	Defines rights profiles, along with assigned authorizations and help file name.
auth_attr	Authorization attributes.	Authorizations and their attributes.
exec_attr	Execution attributes.	Relates commands to security attributes; assigns them to rights profiles.
policy.conf	Default rights.	Authorizations, privileges, and rights profiles applied to all users.

The name service scope for each of these databases is set in the */etc/nsswitch.conf* file. In this file, the auth_attr line specifies where to look for the auth_attr database. The passwd line specifies where to look for user_attr. The prof_attr entry sets the location for the prof_attr and exec_attr databases.

The information fields in each of these databases are laid out as in the following sections.

auth_attr

Authorizations in this database can be assigned to users, roles, or rights profiles. Usually, it is best to assign an authorization to a rights profile, assign the profile to a role, and grant the role to one or more users.

The format for auth_attr entries is:

```
authname:res1:res2:short-description:long-description:attr
```

The definitions for these fields are:

- authname: Unique character string identifying the authorization. Solaris OS authorization names have the form solaris.name. Other authorizations start with the reverse-order domain name of the organization, ie com.companyname.name.

  When the authname ends in a period, it is a heading indicating a group of authorizations.

  When the authname ends with the string "grant," it refers to the ability to grant to other users authorizations with a matching prefix.

- res1:res2: Not currently used.

- short-description: A short name suitable for display in a management GUI.

- long-description: A long name suitable for display in a management GUI's help function.

- attr: Semicolon-separated *key=value* pairs describing the attributes of an authorization. In particular, the help=*helpfile*.html pair allows us to specify a help file in */usr/lib/help/auths/locale/C* directory.

exec_attr

Defines commands that need special permissions to run; these commands are assigned to a rights profile in prof_attr. The format for exec_attr entries is:

```
profname:policy:type:res1:res2:id:attr
```

- profname: Rights profile name from prof_attr.

- policy: Security policy associated with this entry. The "solaris" policy recognizes permissions, but the "suser" policy does not.
- type: Currently, the only recognized type is "cmd."
- res1:res2: Not currently used.
- id: String identifying the entry. Normally, this would consist of the full path of the command, or a full path indicating several commands with a wildcard (*). If options need to be specified, we should create a script in the profile shell that specifies the options.
- attr: Semicolon-separated list of key=value pairs of attributes. For an suser policy, these can set the effective UID and GID with euid and egid; or they can set the real and effective UID and GID with uid and gid. For a solaris policy, we can use the privs keyword to specify a comma-separated list of the required privileges.

prof_attr

This database defines rights profiles and the authorizations assigned to them. The format for entries in this database is:

profname:res1:res2:desc:attr

- profname: Rights profile name as assigned to users and/or roles in user_attr.
- res1:res2: Not yet in use.
- desc: A long description of the profile, suitable for use in a management GUI's help screen. In particular, specify the purpose of the rights profile and the type of user to which it should be assigned.
- attr: Semicolon-separated list of *key=value* pairs describing the attributes that apply on execution. The valid entries are:
- help=*helpfile*.html: Specify a help file in */usr/lib/help/auths/locale/C*.
- auths: Comma-separated list of authnames from auth_attr. Wildcarding permitted with an *.

user_attr

The user_attr database supplements the information in the passwd and shadow databases. The format for user_attr entries is:

user:qualifier:res1:res2:attr

The meanings of each of these fields is:

- user: Name of the user or role; matches passwd database entries.
- qualifier:res1:res2: These fields are not currently in use.
- attr: Semicolon-separated *key=value* pairs for the following key types:
- type=[normal|role] (Normal means regular user; role means role.)
- auths=comma-separated linst of authorizations from auth_attr.
- profiles=comma-separated, ordered list of assigned profiles from prof_attr (Profiles are matched in the order listed; the first match is the one used.
- roles=comma-separated list of roles assigned to a user. (Roles cannot be assigned to other roles. Roles are as listed in user_attr.)

policy.conf

This configuration file allows us to grant rights profiles, authorizations, and privileges to all users. These are assigned with the following key words in the `policy.conf`:

- `AUTHS_GRANTED`: Authorizations granted.
- `PROFS_GRANTED`: Rights profiles granted.
- `PRIV_DEFAULT`: Inheritable set of privileges for the system.
- `PRIV_LIMIT`: Limit set of privileges for the system.

RBAC Management

While the GUI can be useful, the full power of RBAC cannot be exploited without digging into the command line commands, databases, and configuration files that define RBAC. In this book, we will continue to focus on terminal-based commands wherever possible.

> The role permission infrastructure can be managed by the GUI, the command line interface, or by directly interacting with the RBAC configuration files. These mechanisms should not be used at the same time; the resulting behavior would be unpredictable. Only use one control mechanism at a time.

Table 15-2 lists the key commands used to manage RBAC. The table distinguishes between commands that are used to manage local RBAC databases, those that manage distributed RBAC databases (on NIS, NIS+, or LDAP), and those that are used in all RBAC environments.

Table 15-2. RBAC Management Commands

Command	Description
`auths`	Displays authorizations for a user.
`pam_roles`	Role account management for PAM.
`pfexec`	Used by profile shells to execute commands associated with security attributes.
`ppriv`	Privileges for a process. (`$$` is the current shell.)
`profiles`	Lists rights profiles for a user.
`roles`	Displays the roles a user can assume.
`roleadd`	Adds a role (local database only).
`roledel`	Deletes a role (local database only).
`rolemod`	Modifies a role (local database only).
`smattrpop`	Populate security attributes on a distributed database from a local database.
`smexec`	Manages entries in a distributed `exec_attr` database.
`smmultiuser`	Bulk operations on multiple users' accounts in a distributed environment.

Command	Description
smprofile	Manages rights profiles in prof_attr and exec_attr in a distributed environment.
smrole	Manages roles in a distributed environment.
smuser	Manages users in a distributed environment.
useradd	Adds a user account to the local system. -P assigns a role to the new user account.
userdel	Deletes a user account from the local system.
usermod	Modifies a user account on the local system.
usermod -K type=role \ username	Convert a username (such as root) to a role. This role would then be granted to other userids.
usermod -u *UID* -R *role*	Add a role to a particular userid.

After each RBAC configuration modification, name service caching should be restarted with **svcadm restart system/name-service-cache.**

In Example 15-1, we create a role to which we assign the Operator rights profile. The role is then assigned to the user "testuser." To help make it clear what the user context is, the prompts for root are "#," the prompts for testuser are "testuser$," and the prompts for the nightop role are "$." (This particular scenario was also examined in Figure 15-1 above.)

Example 15-1. Creating a Local Role

```
# roleadd -c "Night Operator" -g 14 -d /export/home/nightop -u 104 \
-s /usr/bin/pfksh -P "Operator" nightop
# grep nightop /etc/user_attr
nightop::::type=role;profiles=Operator
# grep nightop /etc/shadow
nightop:*LK*:::::::
# passwd nightop
New Password:
Re-enter new Password:
passwd: password successfully changed for nightop
# svcadm restart system/name-service-cache
# su nightop
$ whoami
nightop
$ ppriv $$
3995:   pfksh
flags = <none>
        E: basic
        I: basic
        P: basic
        L: all
$ exit
# usermod -R nightop testuser
# su - testuser
testuser$ roles
```

```
nightop
testuser$ su - nightop
Password:
$ whoami
nightop
$ ppriv $$
4063:    -pfksh
flags = <none>
        E: basic
        I: basic
        P: basic
        L: all
$ exit
testuser$ exit
# grep Operator /etc/security/prof_attr
Operator:::Can perform simple administrative tasks:profiles=Printer Management,Media
Backup,All;help=RtOperator.html
# grep nightop /etc/user_attr
nightop::::type=role;profiles=Operator
testuser::::type=normal;roles=nightop
```

Privilege Descriptions

System privileges are classified based on the types of objects affected by the privilege:

- FILE: Operate on file system objects. For example, `file_dac_write` suspends discretionary access control when performing file writes.

- IPC: Override object access permissions for IPC objects. For example, `ipc_dac_read` allows a process to read shared memory protected by discretionary access control.

- NET: Allow access to network functionality. `Net_rawaccess`, for example, allows a device to connect to the network.

- PROC: Allow modifications of restricted characteristics of the process itself. `proc_clock_highres` allows the process to use a high resolution timer.

- SYS: Allow access to system properties. `Sys_linkdir`, for example, allows a process to make and break hard links to directories.

The privilege limits reported by **ppriv** are:

- E (Effective privilege set): Privileges currently in effect. Privileges may be added or removed as needed during the life of the process.

- P (Permitted privilege set): Privileges available for use. These may have been inherited or assigned. (For example, an SUID root program assigns all privileges that root would have to the permitted privilege set.) Privileges may be removed from, but not added to this set. All privileges removed from the P set are also removed from the E set.

- I (Inheritable privilege set): Privileges that a process can inherit across an exec() system call.

- L (Limit privilege set): The maximum privilege set that would be available to the process and its children. The default is ALL. L can shrink, but can never grow.

The **ppriv -v** *PID* command prints out a specific list of privileges in each set. If needed, a privilege can be removed from a user or role's default privilege set:

usermod -K defaultpriv=basic,!*privname* *username*

Similarly, a privilege can be added:

```
usermod -K defaultpriv=basic,privname username
```

Adding or removing a privilege from the limit set would be similar; it would just use the `limitpriv` key word.

Programs that are capable of respecting privileges are called **privilege aware**. Such programs only turn on required permissions for each step and turn off unnecessary permissions when they are no longer needed..

Troubleshooting Privileges and Authorizations in RBAC

Permissions problems are notoriously difficult to troubleshoot. With these, the devil is in the details. Permissions problems have a habit of hiding in plain sight. Double-check all of your assumptions. Make sure all of the details are right. If all else fails, ask a colleague for a second set of eyeballs to see something that you may have missed.

A few comments may be helpful in troubleshooting these problems:

- The database that is used in a particular case will be the first match specified in */etc/nsswitch.conf*. If there are multiple matches, make sure you are going after the database scope that you are looking for.

- Make sure that the following is specified in the proper */etc/nsswitch.conf* lines if you have distributed databases in the search path:

  ```
  [TRYAGAIN=0 UNAVAIL=return NOTFOUND=return]
  ```

  This entry allows the name service search to return in the event of a failure.

- The first occurrence of a command in a rights profile is the one that will be used. In the `prof_attr` database, the rights profile with the most capabilities should be listed first in the collection of supplementary rights profiles. (The `exec_attr` lists the rights profiles and their associated privileged commands.)

- `ppriv` and `truss` provide information about which privileges are missing when a process fails. In particular, `ppriv -eD failed-command` will list the missing privilege. If we want to find out how the privilege is problematic, we can find the name of the failing system call in */etc/name_to_sysnum* (`ppriv -eD` reports a system call number). We can examine how the failure occurs with `truss -t syscall failed-command`. We would then add the missing privileges to a rights profile, assign the profile to a role, and have the user assume the role.

Risk Analysis

About the only way to totally secure the information on a computer is to destroy it. This would obviously have an adverse effect on data integrity, let alone service availability.

Seriously, we will always have some level of risk associated with any usable information system. We need to reduce this risk to a level that is acceptable to the organization.

A security **vulnerability** is something that could potentially reduce the confidentiality, integrity, or availability of an asset in our information system. A **threat** is a mechanism by which a vulnerability may actually result in a reduction of an aspect of the CIA Triad. The **risk** of a threat is determined by the likelihood of the threat occurring and the cost per incidence.

The likelihood of the threat's occurrence is measured as an **annualized rate of occurrence** (ARO) which represents the number of occurrences we would expect in a given year. The expected cost per incident is known as the **single loss expectancy** (SLE). Risk is usually measured in terms of the **annualized loss expectancy** (ALE), which is the product of the ARO and the SLE. In other words:

```
Risk = (Expected Number of Occurrences) x (Expected Cost per Occurrence)
```

This definition of risk can be used to decide how best to protect our information assets. In particular, the ALE provides a good way to prioritize which risks to attack first. The ALE also gives us a good way to gauge how much to spend. It would not make sense to spend more money avoiding a risk than we would expect to lose if the risk came to fruition.

Three ways to deal with a risk are:

- **mitigation**: Implement changes to reduce the likelihood or impact of a risk. A firewall is an example of a mitigation measure, since it reduces the likelihood of a network-based attack. Partitioning the network would be another example of mitigation, since this would reduce the impact of a successful network penetration. Insurance policies and service contracts are also mitigation measures, since they reduce the financial impact of an event.

- **avoidance**: Sometimes we can avoid a risk by doing things differently. If we are concerned about a developer typing commands as root on a production server, for example, we can provide a mechanism (like `sudo`) to limit root access to a few acceptable commands.

- **acceptance**: Some risks are deemed so unlikely that the business is willing to gamble on them never happening. Other risks may carry a low enough cost that they can be ignored.

Types of Attacks

Attacks may be classified into a few basic types. Different types of attack profiles should be protected against in different ways. The most important attack profiles include:

- **Access Control Circumvention**: This type of attack may involve bypassing logon restrictions, or it may involve masquerading as another user who has different access privileges.

- **Eavesdropping**: Typically this sort of attack involves intercepting or otherwise viewing communications that the person is not authorized to participate in.

- **Denial of Service**: This sort of attack is aimed at disrupting services. This may come as a result of swamping available resources of some sort, or it may come as a result of triggering a technical problem in a network or computer resource.

- **Network Intrusion**: If someone succeeds in gaining access to a secured network, it may become possible to leverage the access to steal, modify, or corrupt our information. Some approaches for performing a network intrusion attack include spoofing (providing false information to gain access), piggy-backing (using a legitimate user's access), or back-door (using undocumented and/or unauthorized connections to the network).

Network Security

Network access can be controlled through firewall and router port limitations. These prevent systems on the external network from directly contacting systems on the internal network. They are not the be-all and end-all of security engineering, but they are an important first step.

There are five distinct types of firewalls that we might deploy in our network:

- **Packet Filtering Firewall** (1st Generation): Examines source and destination addresses and ports and allows or disallows connections based on an access control list (ACL).

- **Application Level Firewall** (2nd Generation): Transfers a copy of acceptable data packets from one network to another. This type of firewall is usually configured as a proxy server. It operates at layer 7 of the OSI model.

293

- **Stateful Inspection Firewall** (3rd Generation): Packets are queued and analyzed at all OSI layers. It allows us to examine both the state and context of a communication stream, allowing us to examine connection-oriented protocols.
- **Dynamic Packet Filters** (4th Generation): This type of firewall remembers packets for a brief period of time, allowing us to filter UDP-based connections.
- **Kernel Proxy** (5th Generation): Uses dynamic, custom kernel-level proxies to inspect packets and enforce security policies.

Firewalls and router port settings can also be used to partition the internal network into different zones. Not every system needs to be able to hit every port on every other system. By partitioning the network, we can limit the impact of any security breach on a single system or group of systems.

In particular, most secure network designs use one or more **demilitarized zones** (**DMZ**s) to hold hosts which communicate outside of the secure network. Systems located in the DMZs only have limited connectivity to the internal, secure network. A DMZ serves to limit the impact of a compromise of one of the systems that can talk to the outside world.

Traffic across public networks should never be sent in the clear if it can possibly be avoided. **Virtual Private Network (VPN)** technology allows remote sites to communicate with each other across a public network in a secure way. An encrypted connection, known as a tunnel, is created between the two sites. When combined with secure authentication, VPNs are a much cheaper way to tie together remote secure networks than would be possible with a dedicated connection. VPNs may be implemented in hardware appliances or in software.

Wireless Networking

Wireless networking technologies have the ability to unleash people from working only where network drops have been run. The downside to wireless networks is that physical security is not sufficient to ensure that the network has not been breached.

Wireless LANs are defined by a **Service Set Identifier (SSID)**. Public wireless networks broadcast their SSIDs to allow people to connect easily without any special configuration; this is obviously not desirable for a private network. Some key suggestions for keeping a WiFi network secure are:

- Restrict wireless access points (WAPs) to a DMZ. Access to the internal network should require additional authentication.
- Restrict wireless access to known MAC addresses.
- Disable SSID broadcasts. This means that the SSID will need to be manually entered on each client.
- Use strong encryption, such as AES. Do not rely on WEP encryption, which is extremely weak, even with large key sizes. Set the key be long and not easily guessable.

Host Security

Host security should not be overlooked. A few key security settings are:

- Turn off stack executability: This setting is the default in Solaris 10.
- Set NFS to require a privileged port.
- Set file permissions appropriately.
- Set randomness on sequence number generation.
- Limit SUID permissions.

Stack Execution

A common type of attack in the Unix world is called a "stack overflow." In this sort of attack, an attempt is made to push custom-made information onto the stack, then execute it. If a hacker can do this from an SUID root program, the system can be compromised.

Fortunately, the stack defaults to not being executable in current versions of Solaris. It is also useful to log attempts to execute on the stack, since nobody should be trying. Attempts to execute on the stack indicate either a program bug or an attempt to exploit a security hole. The /etc/system settings to enable stack protection and log stack execution attempts are:

```
* Enabling hardware protection for stack overflow exploits
set noexec_user_stack = 1
set noexec_user_stack_log = 1
    • End of stack overflow protection
```

After a reboot, an attempt to execute code on the stack will generate an error something like:

```
May  8 21:15:16 soltest genunix: [ID 533030 kern.notice] NOTICE: x[11686] attempt to execute
code on stack by uid 666
```

File Permissions

Generally speaking, no program that is run by root should ever be writable by another user or be located in a descendant of a directory where another user has write permissions. If another user has this level of permissions, it is only too easy to drop a trojan horse program into place to gain root permissions over the sytem.

The same is true of other key system accounts or application accounts such as oracle or sybase. Breaking this rule should be considered the same as giving someone control over the administrative account.

The **Automated Security Enhancement Tool (ASET)** is a Solaris-provided mechanism for limiting the file system permissions of key files. It also performs some elementary checking of the contents of these files on a regular, scheduled basis. (In particular, it makes sure that default $PATH settings do not include the current directory.)

Unfortunately, ASET is an extremely blunt instrument. It allows settings of low, medium, or high. Arbitrarily setting the security level to high is guaranteed to make some services break. I have even seen ASET levels of medium result in odd system behavior. Sun recommends a "medium" setting for most servers in a security-conscious setting; "low" is the OS default setting. The program can be run interactively with the `aset -l level` command. `aset -p` adds a line to the root crontab to re-run ASET periodically.

The specific actions associated with ASET are defined in the */usr/aset/asetenv* configuration file and the master files in */usr/aset/masters*. In addition, ASET does report the actions taken to */usr/aset/reports*, so it should be possible to search through the list to find some candidate causes of whatever problems result. If all else fails, the `aset.restore` program will back out the changes.

The Sun-provided `fix-modes` script provides another way to go after file and directory permission problems. (This script is provided in the *Solaris Security Toolkit* from the Sun web site.)

The `fix-modes` script uses the package-specified permissions in */var/sadm/install/contents* as a point of departure and saves the results of its changes in */var/sadm/install/contents.mods*. These changes can be reverted by using the `-u` option.

SUID Permissions

One particular type of file permission merits its own section. SUID and SGID permissions are granted to a number of programs to allow users to access resources that are otherwise controlled by an administrative user. Files with the

SUID or SGID bits allow other users to execute the program with privileges normally reserved for the administrative user or group.

Programs with SUID permissions are frequent hacker targets; it is only too easy to get past the programmed protections through a bug on such a program. The best protection is to reduce the number of SUID programs to a minimum.

It is relatively easy to identify SUID programs on the system. The following find command will do the trick:

```
find / \( \( \( -perm -2000 -o  -perm -4000 \) -type f -print \) \
-o \( -fstype cachefs -prune \) -o \( -fstype nfs -prune \) \
-o \( -name proc -print -prune \) -o \( -name xfn -print -prune \) \
-o \( -name atjobs -print -prune \)
```

> This command actually prints out several directories which are pruned in addition to the names of the programs. This is to get around the potential problem of a hacker naming a SUID file **xfn** and not having it picked up by the command.

If there are any programs in this list which would only be run from the administrative account anyway, remove the SUID permissions. The fewer such programs on the system, the better.

It is relatively straightforward to use the output of the above **find** command to compare the findings to a list of "approved" SUID programs. This may need to be done each time that patches are applied, and it makes sense to run a monitoring command like this on a regular, scheduled basis.

Access Control Lists

Access Control Lists (**ACLs**) are used to provide more granular file permissions than are possible with standard Unix-style permissions. Unix-style permissions really only allow us to apply read, write, and execute/directory search permissions to a file or directory for the owner, a specific Unix group, and everyone else. Sometimes more flexibility is needed.

> ACLs are file system specific. If a file is restored or copied to another type of file system, the ACLs may well disappear. For example, if a file lives on a UFS file system, but is copied to a tmpfs-mounted /tmp directory, the ACL will be lost.

The **setfacl** command is used to create or modify an object's access control list. The types of file and directory access controls that may be specified are listed in Table 15-3.

Table 15-3. Access Controls

File Access Control	Description
u::*perms*	File owner permissions (standard Unix "u" permissions)
g::*perms*	File group permissions (standard Unix "g" permissions)
o:*perms*	File permissions for all others (standard "o" permissions)
m:*perms*	Mask indicating maximum file permissions allowed for users other than the owner.
u:*uid*:*perms*	Permissions for a specific user.
g:*gid*:*perms*	Permissions for a specific group.
d:u::*perms*	Default directory owner permissions (standard Unix)
d:g::*perms*	Default directory group owner permissions (standard Unix)

File Access Control	Description
`d:o:`*`perms`*	Default directory permissions for all others.
`d:m:`*`perms`*	Default directory permissions mask.
`d:u:`*`uid`*`:`*`perms`*	Default directory permissions for specified user.
`d:g:`*`gid`*`:`*`perms`*	Default directory permissions for specified group.

When a file is created in a directory with default access controls set, the ACL will consist of the permissions that exist both in the default ACL and the permissions that are requested when the file is created. In other words, the "default" directory permissions are the maximum discretionary access controls that will be allowed.

The values set in the mask may override explicitly set group permissions. Example 15-3 below includes a demonstration of how masks work in an ACL context. Pay particular attention to the "`effective`" permissions in the `getacl` output:

Example 15-3. ACL Manipulation

```
test# setfacl -s u::rw-,g::r--,o:---,m:rw- create-user.sql
test# ls -l create-user.sql
-rw-rw----   1 scromar  sysadmin    270 May 17 19:29 create-user.sql
test# getfacl create-user.sql

# file: create-user.sql
# owner: scromar
# group: sysadmin
user::rw-
group::rw-            #effective:rw-
mask:rw-
other:---
test# setfacl -m m:r-- create-user.sql
test# getfacl create-user.sql

# file: create-user.sql
# owner: scromar
# group: sysadmin
user::rw-
group::r--            #effective:r--
mask:r--
other:---
test# ls -l
total 2
-rw-r-----   1 scromar  sysadmin    270 May 17 19:29 create-user.sql
test# setfacl -m u:1002:rw- create-user.sql
test# getfacl create-user.sql

# file: create-user.sql
# owner: scromar
# group: sysadmin
user::rw-
user:oracle:rw-       #effective:r--
group::r--            #effective:r--
mask:r--
other:---
```

If `setfacl -s` is used, it is important to set the user, group, other, and mask permissions at that time. The `-s` option specifies that any existing ACL is to be overwritten with the access controls specified in this command.

297

`setfacl -m` may be used to replace any access control or group of access controls. `Setfacl -d` is used to delete a particular control from the list. The `getfacl` command is used to display the current ACL for a file.

Encryption

Encryption is only worth doing when it is done properly. When not done properly, it can give a false sense of security and lead to laziness. We need to use an appropriate algorithm with a long key. (What constitutes a "long" key will vary between algorithms.) Examination of encryption algorithms is a specialized discipline; the best way to evaluate algorithms is to look at reviews in independent trade publications.

Solaris 10 includes an implementation of RSA's PKCS#11 Cryptographic Token Interface. This framework allows easier integration of different encryption algorithms. These algorithms have been well-studied, and are well-understood. Solaris 10's *Security Services* manual includes a discussion of this interface.

AES is widely considered to be a very secure, widely available encryption algorithm. DES, the previous standard, is no longer considered to be state-of-the-art, and is vulnerable to some brute force attacks. (DES3, also known as "triple DES," is still considered to be secure enough for production use.)

Three places that encryption makes sense are on the backup tapes, on the file system, and during network communications.

Every week brings another story of a stolen backup tape with unencrypted data. The potential exposure of the loss of such a tape would be minimized if only the data had been encrypted.

Similarly, if confidential data were properly encrypted on the hard drive, a stolen hard drive or even a compromised server would be less of a problem. This includes data that is left for pickup on an ftp site or a file share.

Network communications on any public network should always be encrypted. This includes high-value communications on a general office network, or even files sent via email.

Auditing

We may believe that we have set up a perfectly secure system, but we need to verify that our protections have not been bypassed. Monitoring need to be done in such a way that a compromise of one component will be noticed by another, separate component.

An easy first step is a separate, limited-access syslog server. The local system logs are valuable, but may be tampered with if the system is compromised. A separate syslog server means that two systems would need to be compromised before the intruder could cover traces of the intrusion.

Authentication events need to be logged on a very fine-grained level. All changes to sensitive data should also be logged. Logging should be done at a number of different levels, including database logging (where appropriate), combined with Solaris audit logging or process accounting.

Audit Logging

Solaris provides a rich, C2-compliant auditing framework via the Basic Security Module (BSM). This module uses the `/etc/security` directory, and is configured in the `/etc/security/audit_control` file. This facility is not enabled by default, and is enabled via the `/etc/security/bsmconv` program.

A full discussion of the Solaris Audit framework is beyond the scope of this book, but is fully documented in the Solaris manuals.

Process Accounting

Process accounting is easier to use, but less explicit than audit logging is. Process accounting was originally designed to see how many computer resources are consumed by a particular process.

Solaris process accounting requires the SUNWaccr and SUNWaccu packages. It is enabled by linking /etc/init.d/acct to /etc/rc2.d/S22acct and /etc/rc0.d/K22acct. The following lines need to be added to the adm crontab:

```
0 * * * * /usr/lib/acct/ckpacct
30 2 * * * /usr/lib/acct/runacct 2> /var/adm/acct/nite/fd2log
30 7 1 * * /usr/lib/acct/monacct
```

The following lines need to be added to the root crontab:

```
30 22 * * 4 /usr/lib/acct/dodisk
```

The resulting logs can be examined directly using acctcom.

Intrusion Detection

Intrusion detection systems are usually based either on the network or host. Network-based intrusion detection systems check for network traffic that either matches attack signatures or looks for anomalous behavior. Similarly, host-based systems may look for activities or files matching known attack signatures, or they may look for activities or file changes that are unexpected.

Either way, a major issue with intrusion detection systems is dealing with false positives. We need to have the threshold sensitive enough to pick up nefarious activity, but also stringent enough that we aren't swamped with messages about regular activity.

File Integrity Checking and BART

One particularly useful type of host-based intrusion detection system is a file integrity checker. When tuned properly, a file integrity checker looks at directories and files of interest to see if any changes are made. Beyond being able to look for unexpected changes made by an intruder, a file integrity checker allows us to look for changes that have not been authorized through the change control system. This can be useful as part of an enforcement mechanism for a change control system.

For files installed as part of a package, the **pkgchk** command provides a way to verify that files are still as expected. Checksums of the current files are compared to what is expected based on the package database. Discrepancies are reported.

Unfortunately, most of the interesting files for our purposes are configuration files that are meant to be changed. We will need to use a more flexible file integrity checker that can check specified files and directories.

Tripwire and AIDE are two popular third-party integrity checkers. In addition, Sun provides the **Basic Audit Reporting Tool (BART)** facility to provide this sort of service. BART creates a manifest containing information and checksums representing the current state of the target. This manifest can be compared to later BART runs against the same configuration file to see what has changed.

Example 15-4 below demonstrates how BART might be used to monitor changes on a particular directory. The bart_rules(4) man page describes how to build a more sophisticated configuration file. Generally speaking, patterns on a particular line are combined with a logical AND. Wildcards allow pattern matching, a ! represents a logical NOT, and a pattern ending with a / is a directory.

Example 15-4. BART File Integrity Checking

```
test# ls -R /export/home/scromar
/export/home/scromar:
afiedt.buf   core          sql          vpd

/export/home/scromar/sql:
create-user.sql

/export/home/scromar/vpd:
vpd.txt   vpd.zip
test# cat bart_rules
/export/home/scromar !core !vpd/*
CHECK all
test# bart create -r bart_rules > control_manifest
test# touch /export/home/scromar/core
test# touch /export/home/scromar/afiedt.buf
test# touch /export/home/scromar/newfile.txt
test# echo "x" >> /export/home/scromar/sql/create-user.sql
test# bart create -r bart_rules > test_manifest
test# bart compare -r bart_rules control_manifest test_manifest
/export/home/scromar/afiedt.buf:
  mtime   control:464da0f5   test:464da5f0
/export/home/scromar/newfile.txt:
  add
/export/home/scromar/sql/create-user.sql:
  size   control:266   test:268
  mtime   control:464da156   test:464da60b
  contents   control:6874d70c539c19a4cf5110c65498bef1   test:4ac05faa5450a49d840b75f9e26737df
```

In the BART example, I used "!vpd/*" to eliminate files from the *vpd* subdirectory. I have previously run into problems with **bart** not being able to parse subdirectory names ending in /, including subdirectory names matching the examples on the bart_rules(4) man page.

Also note that the modification time is reported in hexadecimal seconds from the epoch (January 1, 1970 00:00:00 UTC). I have some difficulty thinking of a more useless way to report creation or modification times. Maybe Sun's next monitoring tool can report dates and times in the ancient Mayan calendar.

Even with these drawbacks, **bart** is a powerful and useful tool to add to your toolbox.

> With any file integrity checker, the baseline data file needs to be protected in order for the comparison to be valid. After all, what's to stop a hacker from editing the baseline data file to match the signatures of the trojaned files? A common recommendation is that the baseline data file should be stored on a read-only NFS mount from a secure server.

Incident Response

We need to establish a procedure for dealing with incidents in a standardized way. We need to know whom to contact, what sort of information to collect, and how to collect it. This procedure needs to be laid down before an incident occurs, while everyone still has a clear head and is able to think through the ramifications of the decisions that are made.

This procedure should be reviewed by the legal or risk management departments to make sure that it complies with any regulatory or corporate requirements. It may even be worth having the procedure reviewed by an outside expert to make sure to cover things that are not immediately obvious.

Resources

- Anderson, Ross. (2001) *Security Engineering*. New York City, NY: John Wiley & Sons.

- Bezroukov, Nikolai. (2007) Solaris 10 Role Based Access Control (RBAC). (http://www.softpanorama.org/Solaris/Security/solaris_rbac.shtml)

- Center for Internet Security. (2005) (http://www.cisecurity.org/bench_solaris.html)

- (ISC)^2. (http://www.isc2.org).

- Krutz, Ronald L. and Vines, Russell Dean. (2001) *The CISSP Prep Guide*. New York City, NY: John Wiley & Sons.

- Miller, Todd and Jepeway, Chris. (2007) *sudo Manual*. (http://www.gratisoft.us/sudo/man/sudo.html)

- Sun Microsystems. (July 2005) *Solaris Security Toolkit*. Santa Clara, CA: Sun Microsystems, Inc. (http://www.sun.com/software/security/jass/)

- Sun Microsystems. (2005) System Administration Guide: Naming and Directory Services (DNS, NIS, and LDAP). Santa Clara, CA: Sun Microsystems, Inc. (http://docs.sun.com/app/docs/doc/816-4556)

- Sun Microsystems. (May 2006) *System Administration Guide: Security Services*. Santa Clara, CA: Sun Microsystems, Inc. (http://docs.sun.com/app/docs/doc/816-4557)

- van der Weerd, Peter. (August 2006) *System Security in Solaris 10: Privileges and Zones in Perspective*. SysAdmin Magazine. (http://www.samag.com/documents/s=9366/sam0608a/0608a.htm)

Appendix A

Common Error Messages

A complete (or even reasonably complete) listing of error messages on Solaris is beyond the scope of this book. For that matter, the nature of an evolving operating system may put it beyond the scope of any printed book. Having said that, this appendix contains a list of several of the most common error messages. Where I have been able to identify a usual cause for an error message, I have included that.

There are several sources that contain listings of error messages that are useful for debugging purposes.

One of the best resources is the *Solaris Common Messages and Troubleshooting Guide* released by Sun with Solaris 8. (See the "Resources" section at the end of this chapter.) It is dated, but there is a lot of good information contained in it.

The SunSolve web site (http://sunsolve.sun.com) is available to anyone with a Sun service contract. Its search feature can be used to look up key words in an error message to look for current bug reports and patches that may resolve them.

The *Intro(2)* man page contains an introduction to system calls and error numbers. The information comes from the *errno.h* include file. Several include files contain at least basic information about different kinds of error messages:

- */usr/include/sys/errno.h* (error messages, including abbreviations and numbers seen in `truss` output.)
- /usr/include/sys/trap.h (software traps)
- /usr/include/v7/sys/machtrap.h (hardware traps, 32 bit)
- /usr/include/v9/sys/machtrap.h (hardware traps, 64 bit)

(Some of these files vary between different server architectures, so it does not make sense to try to define them here, except in the most general terms.)

This appendix contains a bullet list of some of the more common error messages that may appear during Solaris troubleshooting sessions. In order to keep the list a reasonable length, many obscure or software package-specific error messages have been left out. Informational messages that appear during the running of a chatty command like `fsck` or `ufsdump` are also left out, since those messages are detailed on each command's man page.

Alphabetizing error codes is not a trivial exercise, since error codes can be variable. For compatibility's sake, this list is alphabetized similarly to Solaris 8's *Solaris Common Messages and Troubleshooting Guide*. Error messages are listed alphabetically by the first non-variable part of the error message. Since the specific wording of an error message may change over time, it may be necessary to look for the closest match on the list.

Some of these messages may refer to bugs that have been fixed prior to Solaris 10. Where I have been able to confirm that this is the case, I have removed that error message from the list. Where I have not been able to confirm that this is the case, I have left the error message in the list.

I have included troubleshooting tips for many of these error messages. The sources include Sun bug reports, my own troubleshooting notes, online discussion groups, OS documentation, and web resources.

If a particular error message is not in this list, it may be searchable on your favorite web search engine, in the Sun Documentation web site (http://docs.sun.com) or Sunsolve (http://sunsolve.sun.com).

- **Accessing a corrupted shared library** (ELIBBAD): exec(2) was unable to load a required static shared library. The most common cause for this is a corrupted library.
- **Address already in use** (EADDRINUSE): The protocol does not permit using an address that is already in use. This error indicates a software programming bug.
- **Address family not supported by protocol family** (EAFNOSUPPORT): The protocol does not support the requested address. This indicates a software programming bug.
- **Arg list too long** (E2BIG): The argument list includes both the argument list and the environment variable settings. The most common cause for this problem is that so many environment variables are set that it exceeds the size of the argument buffer used by exec(2). The easiest solution may be to unset some environment variables in the calling shell.
- **Argument out of domain** (EDOM): This error appears when an improper argument is submitted to a math package programming function. (For example, an attempt to take a square root of a negative number would probably yield this error.) It may be helpful to use matherr(3M) to diagnose the problem, or the programmer may need to implement argument-checking before the function is called.
- **Arguments too long**: This is a C shell message indicating that more than 1706 arguments follow a command. This may happen if globbing is applied to a large number of objects (eg rm * in a directory of more than 1706 objects). Temporarily switching to Bourne shell may resolve the problem, since Bourne shells dynamically allocate space for arguments.
- **Assertion failed**: This is a result of an assert(3C) debugging command that the programmer inserted into the program. The output will include an expression, a source file number and a code line number. The information may be useful in examining the source code.
- **Attachment point not found**: Use cfgadm to list available attachment points. Check the physical connection to the desired device.
- **Attempting to link in more shared libraries than system limit** (ELIBMAX): The executable requires more static libraries than the current system limit.
- **authentication receive failed**: Initiator unable to receive authentication information. Verify network connectivity to storage device and authentication server.
- **authentication transmit failed**: Initiator unable to transmit authentication information. Verify network connectivity to storage device and authentication server.
- **Bad address** (EFAULT): A function taking pointer argument has been passed an invalid address. This may result from supplying the wrong device or option to a command, or it may be the result of a programming bug.
- **Bad file number** (EBADF): The file descriptor references a file that is either not open or is open for a conflicting purpose. (eg, a read(2) is specified against a file that is open for write(2) or vice-versa.) This is a programming bug.
- **Bad module/chip**: This error message usually indicates a memory module or chip that is associated with parity errors. This is a hardware fault.
- **BAD SUPER BLOCK:** Check the **Trap 3E** entry below to see if there are possible hardware or SCSI configuration causes for this problem.

It may be possible to boot from alternate super blocks. If there is no current backup, boot from a CD and back up the raw partition with `ufsdump` or another similar utility.

Solaris 10's 6/06 release includes enhancements to `fsck` to automatically find and repair bad superblocks. This option should only be used to repair file systems that were created with `mkfs` or `newfs`.

For older systems, an alternate superblock can frequently be found with a
```
newfs -N /dev/rdsk/c#t#d#s#
```
command while booted from a CD. (Note the -N option. Running this command without this option may mess things up beyond repair.) `fsck` can be run against an alternate superblock with
```
fsck -o b=superblock /dev/rdsk/c#t#d#s#
```
If there is a lot of output, it may be necessary to choose the `-y` option to avoid having to answer a ton of prompts. We may need to try several alternate superblocks before finding a working one. Once we are done, we need to re-install the bootblock:
```
cd /usr/platform/`arch -k`/lib/fs/ufs
/usr/sbin/installboot ./bootblk /dev/rdsk/c#t#d#s#
```

- **BAD TRAP**: The causes for bad traps include system text errors, data access faults, data alignment errors or some types of user software traps. These can indicate either a hardware fault or a mismatch between the hardware and its software configuration. They may also indicate a CPU with an obsolete firmware. Bad traps usually result in a panic, sync, dump, reboot cycle. The kernel traceback message on the console will frequently indicate the hardware component that generated the BAD TRAP. If the configuration for this component is correct, it will need to be replaced (or at least reseated).

- **/bin/sh: ... too big**: This Bourne shell message is a variant of "**Not enough space**." Check that message for steps to take.

- **Block device required** (ENOTBLK): A raw device was specified where a block device is required.

- **Broken pipe** (EPIPE): No reading process was available to accept a write on the other end of a pipe. This can happen when the reading process (the process after the pipe) exits suddenly.

- **Bus Error**: I/O was attempted to a device that is unavailable or does not exist. See the "Bus Error" section in Chapter 3.

- **Cannot access a needed shared library** (ELIBACC): Either the library does not exist, the LD_LIBRARY_PATH variable does not include the library, or the user is not permissioned to use it. The library in question can usually be pinned down with `truss`.

- **Cannot assign requested address** (EADDRNOTAVAIL): The requested address is not on the current machine.

- **Cannot exec a shared library directly** (ELIBEXEC): You can't execute shared libraries directly. This error indicates a software bug.

- **Cannot install bootblock**: On an x86 system, this error typically appears when a `newfs` and `restore` operation was carried out without performing a `installboot` before installing the OS. It may be possible to install the bootblock from the CD drive in single-user mode (note that Sun does not guarantee this procedure):
```
cd /usr/platform/` -k`/lib/fs/ufs
installboot ./pboot ./bootblk /dev/rdsk/c#t#d#s#
```

- **Cannot send after transport endpoint shutdown** (ESHUTDOWN): The transport endpoint has been shut down, so data was unable to be sent. The solution is usually to restore the endpoint and re-run the transfer. (We may need to troubleshoot why the remote endpoint became unavailable.)

- **can't accept**: Initiator does not accept the specified data of the given format. Consult storage device documentation to look for compatibility information for the server hardware and OS.

- **can't accept ... in security stage**: Device responded with unsupported login information during login security phase. Verify storage device authentication settings. Consult storage device documentation to look for compatibility information for the server hardware and OS.

- **can't find environment variable**: The specified environment variable has not been set. Check for a typo and/or verify that the variable has been set.

- **Can't invoke /etc/**init: The init binary is missing or corrupted during a reboot. We may be able to complete the boot by copying init from a CDROM during a CDROM reboot.
- **capacity of this LUN is too large**: SCSI partitions must be less than 2TB.
- **Channel number out of range** (ECHRNG): A stream head attempted to open a minor device that is in use or does not exist. We need to make sure that the stream device exists, along with an appropriate number of minor devices, and that it matches the hardware configuration. It may be necessary to schedule jobs differently to allow for limited system resources.
- **check boot archive content**: If **SMF does not start up on its own, this message in response to** svcs -x may indicate a failure of svc:/system/boot-archive:default   To resolve this problem, select the Solaris failsafe archive option in the GRUB boot menu during the next reboot. The failsafe boot option provides instructions for rebuilding the boot archive. Once that is complete, the boot can be continued by clearing the **SMF boot archive with the** svcadm clear boot-archive command.
- **Command not found**: This is a C shell error message that means exactly what it says. It typically means that the command was misspelled or does not live on the PATH.
- **Communication error on send** (ECOMM): The link between machines breaks after data is sent, but before the confirmation is received.
- **Component system is busy, try again: failed to offline**: cfgadm attempted to remove or replace a device with a mounted file system, swap area or configured dump device. Unmount the file system, remove the swap and/or disable the dump device, then retry the cfgadm command. See the cfgadm(1M) man page.
- **Configuration operation invalid: invalid transition**: The incorrect device may have been specified, or there may be a problem with the device or its seating. Use cfgadm to check the receptacle and its state. The card may need to be reseated.
- **Connection refused** (ECONNREFUSED): The target machine actively refused the connection. The service may not be active, or there may be restrictions on connections (such as the hosts.allow and hosts.deny in TCP wrappers).
- **Connection reset** (ECONNRESET): The target system forcibly closed an existing connection. This typically happens as a result of a reboot or a timeout.
- **Connection timed out** (ETIMEOUT): The target host is unreachable due to network problems or the system being down.
- **Core dumped**: A core file (image of software memory at the time of failure) has been taken. See "Core File Management" in Chapter 3.
- **Corrupt label**: This happens if cylinder 0 has been overwritten, usually by a database using a raw partition including cylinder 0. The best solution is to back everything up and repartition the disk with cylinder 0 either not in any partition or at least in a partition with a file system (such as UFS) that respects cylinder 0. This error may also indicate that the disk label is in an unsupported format. If the disk is new, attempt to relabel it with **format**.
- **cpio: Bad magic number/header**: The cpio archive has become corrupted. We can try to recover whatever we can by using the cpio -k command.
- **Cross-device link** (EXDEV): Hard links are not permitted across different file systems. Use a soft link instead.
- **Data access exception**: Mismatch between the operating system and disk storage hardware. This can be due to mis-seated DIMMs or disk problems, so it makes sense to try to identify any hardware problems. Usually, the operating system (and perhaps file system) will need to be upgraded to deal with the newer hardware.
- **DataDigest=... is required, can't accept**: Device returned an improperly processed DataDigest. Verify that storage device digest settings are compatible with the initiator.
- **Data Fault**: This is a particular type of bad trap that indicates a configuration text or data access fault. See **BAD TRAP** above.
- **Deadlock situation detected/avoided** (EDEADLK): A potential deadlock over a system resource (usually a lock) was detected and avoided. The software should be examined to see if it can be made more resilient.

- **Destination address required** (EDESTADDRREQ): An address was omitted from an operation that requires one.
- **/dev/fd/#: cannot open**: Indicates that the file descriptor file system (fdfs) is not mounted correctly. In most cases, the problem is that it is mounted either *no*suid or not at all. The file descriptor file system should have the following options in the vfstab:
  ```
  fd         -        /dev/fd fd         -          no          -
  ```
- **Device busy** (EBUSY): A hard drive or removable media failed to unmount or eject due to an active process using them. The fuser command allows us to see what processes are using the file system or even kill them with a command like **fuser -ck /mountpoint**
  (Make sure that you know what processes are running on a file system before killing them.)
- **DIMMs Manufacturer Mismatch**: DIMMs in the system are not on the hardware compatibility list.
- **Directory not empty**: This is an error from rmdir which means exactly what it says. Non-empty directories cannot be removed. (If a process is holding a file open, it is possible to track down the culprit by looking for the inode of the file in question (ls -i *filename*) in pfiles output.)
- **Disc quota exceeded** (EDQUOT): A user's disk quota has been exceeded. Some of the user's files can be removed or the quotas can be increased with edquota.
- **disk has ... blocks, which is too large**: 32-bit kernels do not support disks of more than 1TB.
- **Disk# not unique**: This error is displayed if there are multiple EEPROM devalias entries for a disk. At the **ok**> prompt, the values of the aliases can be shown with
  ok> **printenv**
  the aliases can be reset with
  ok> **nvunalias disk#**
  ok> **nvalias disk#** *device-path*
- **dquot table full**: The UFS quota table needs to be increased in size. This is done by increasing ndquot in */etc/system* and rebooting. Ndquot defaults to (maxusers x 40)/4 + max_nprocs
- **dr in progress**: This error may occur if a SCSI unconfigure operation fails while only partially completed. The controller may need to be reconfigured with **cfgadm**.
- **driver not attached**: No driver currently attached to the specified device because no device exists at the node or the device is not in use. This may or may not mean that a proper driver is not installed. Make sure that the driver is installed and properly configured.
- **empty RADIUS shared secret**: The RADIUS shared secret needs to be set.
- **Error 88** (EILSEQ): This is an illegal byte sequence error. Multiple characters have been provided where only one is expected.
- **Error code 2: access violation**: This error is due to a permissioning or pathing error on a tftp get.
- **Error: missing file arg (cm3)**: A filename was not included in an sccs command that requires one.
- **error opening dir**: The specified path may not be a directory.
- **error writing name when booting**: */etc/nodename* must contain exactly one line with the name of the system and no blanks or returns.
- **esp0: data transfer overrun:** This error appears when we attempt to mount a CD drive with an 8192 block size as opposed to the Sun-standard 512 block size. Check with the drive manufacturer to see if the block size can be switched.
- **ether_hostton: Bad file number/Resource temporarily unavailable:** These messages may be a result of a mis-matched nodename file. Make sure that the */etc/nodename* entry matches the corresponding */etc/hostname.interface* and /etc/inet/hosts files.
- **Event not found**: The shell reports that a command matching the request cannot be found in the history buffer for the shell session. The history command shows the current contents of the history buffer.

- **Exec format error** (ENOEXEC): This error usually means that the software was compiled for an architecture other than the one on which it finds itself. This may also happen if an expected binary compatibility package is not installed. The *file* command displays the expected architecture for the binary.
- **Failed to initialize adapter**: If the adapter has been correctly identified, this means that the configuration of the adapter is incorrect. In particular, make sure to check the DMA settings.
- **Failed to receive login response**: Initiator failed to receive a login Payload Data Unit (PDU) across the network. Verify that the network connection is working.
- **Failed to transfer login**: Initiator failed to transfer a login Payload Data Unit (PDU) across the network. Verify that the network connection is working.
- **Fast access mmu miss**: This is usually due to a hardware problem. Memory is a possible culprit, as are the system board and CPU. Check the "PROM Monitor Diagnostics" section in Chapter 3
- **File descriptor in bad state** (EBADFD): The requested file descriptor does not refer to an open file or it refers to a file descriptor that is restricted to another purpose. (For example, a read request is made to a file descriptor that is open for writing only.)
- **File exists** (EEXISTS): An existing file was targeted for a command that would have overwritten it improperly. For example, there may have been a request to overwrite a file while the csh noclobber option is set, or there may have been a request to set a link to the name of an existing file.
- **File locking deadlock** (EDEADLOCK): Two processes deadlocked over a resource, such as a lock. This is a software programming bug.
- **File name too long** (ENAMETOOLONG): The referenced file name is longer than the limit specified in /usr/include/limits.h.
- **File system full**: The file system is full. (Error messages sometimes mean what they say.) If the message occurs during a login, the problem is likely the file system that includes the utmpx file (usually /var).
- **File too large** (EFBIG): The file size has grown past what is allowed by the protocol or file system in question, or exceeds the resource limit (rlimit) for file size. The resource limit can be checked by running ulimit -a in Bourne or Korn shells or limit in C shell.
- **Giving up**: In the context of a SCSI command, this means that the timeout has been exceeded. This is usually due to a hardware or connection problem, but it can be caused by contention on the SCSI channel, or even a mis-match in timeout settings between the OS and the device in question.
- **Hardware address trying to be our address**: Either we have two systems on our network with the same IP address, or we have snooping enabled on a device on the network.
- **HeaderDigest=... is required, can't accept**: Device returned an improperly processed HeaderDigest. Verify that storage device digest settings are compatible with the initiator.
- **Host is down** (EHOSTDOWN): A connection attempt failed because the target system was unavailable.
- **Host name local configuration error**: sendmail wants to have a fully qualified domain name for the local host. It is good practice to include a fully qualified domain name in the *hosts* file entry for the local server.
- **Hypertransport Sync Flood occurred on last boot**: Uncorrectable ECC error caused the last reboot. For x64 systems, check the service processor's System Event Log and BIOS log to identify the culprit.
- **Identifier removed** (EIDRM): There is a problem accessing a file associated with messaging, **semaphores or** shared memory. Check the msgctl(2), semctl(2) or shmctl(2) man page for more details.
- **ieN Ethernet jammed**: The number of successive failed transmission attempts has exceeded the threshold. Check whether the network is saturated or check for other network problems.
- **ieN no carrier**: The carrier detect pin died during a packet transmission, resulting in a dropped packet. Check for loose connections and otherwise check the network.
- **If pipe/FIFO, don't sleep in stream head** (ESTRPIPE): There is a problem with the STREAMS connection.
- **ifconfig: bad address:** Check */etc/hostname.interface* to make sure that the entries match the hosts file. When this error occurs early in the boot process, make sure that the file system containing hostname.*interface* and hosts is online at that stage of the boot process. If "files" is not the first entry in

the "hosts" line of */etc/nsswitch.conf*, the hostname lookup will not be possible until the interface comes online.

- **ifconfig: no such interface**: Make sure that the */etc/hostname.interface* file exists.
- **Illegal instruction:** This error message means exactly what it says. This may come about because the binary is not compiled for this architecture (see "Exec format error" above), or it may come as a result of trying to run a data file as a program. If this appears during a boot, it means that the system is trying to boot from a non-boot device, that the boot information has become corrupted, or that the boot information is meant for a different architecture.
- **Illegal seek** (ESPIPE): There is a problem with a pipe in the statement. A workaround suggested by Sun is to redirect the output of the source command to a scratch file, then process the file.
- **Initiator could not be successfully authenticated**: Verify CHAP and/or RADIUS settings, as appropriate.
- **Initiator is not allowed access to the given target**: Verify initiator name, masking and provisioning.
- **initiator name is required**: The initiator name is improperly configured.
- **Interrupted system call** (EINTR): An signal (like an *interrupt* or *quit*) was received before the system call had completed. (If we try to resume, we may error out as a result of this condition.)
- **Invalid argument** (EINVAL): System cannot interpret a supplied parameter. Depending on the context, this may be an indication that the object named by the parameter is not set up properly.
- **Invalid null command**: This may indicate that there were two pipes in a row ("||") in the referenced command.
- **I/O error** (EIO): This references a physical I/O fault. Depending on the context, it makes sense to replace the removable media, check all connections, run diagnostics on the referenced hardware or fsck the file system. If this error occurs during a write, we must assume that the data is corrupt.
- **Is a directory** (EISDIR): We tried to treat a directory like a file.
- **iSCSI service or target is not currently operational**: Run diagnostics on the storage device hardware; check storage device software configuration.
- **Kernel read error**: savecore is unable to read the kernel data structures to produce a crash dump. This may indicate a hardware problem, especially a memory problem. This problem may accompany a **BAD TRAP** error.
- **Killed**: This may happen as a result of a memory allocation attempt where either there is insufficient swap space or the stack and data segment size are in conflict. A "Killed" message may also appear when a program is sent a SIGKILL by other means, such as a kill command.
- **kmem_free block already free**: This is a software programming bug, probably in a device driver.
- **ld.so.1 fatal: can't set protection on segment**: Sun reports a case where this error occurred due to a lack of swap space. Ld.so.1 complained because there was no segment on which to set protections.
- **ld.so.1 fatal: open failed: No such file or directory**: The **linker was unable to find the shared library in question. Make sure that** LD_LIBRARY_PATH is set properly.
- **ld.so.1 fatal: relocation error: referenced symbol not found**: The symbol referenced by the specified application was not found. This error most frequently occurs after installations or upgrades of shared libraries. Ldd -d on the application will show its dependencies. Depending on the nature of the conflict, it may be resolvable by changing the LD_LIBRARY_PATH or installing an appropriate version of the shared library.
- **Link has been severed** (ENOLINK): The connection to a remote machine has been severed, either by the remote process dying or a network problem.
- **login failed to authenticate with target**: Initiator unable to authenticate the storage device. Verify initiator and storage device authentication settings.
- **Login incorrect**: This error means that an appropriate username and password pair was not entered. This may be due to a problem with the passwd and shadow file, the naming service, or the user forgetting login credentials.
- **login redirection failed**: Storage device attempted to redirect initiator to an invalid destination. Verify storage device redirection settings.

- **Memory Configuration Mismatch**: Can be caused by damaged or unsupported DIMMs, or by running non-identical DIMMs within the same bank.
- **Message too long** (EMSGSIZE): A message was sent that was larger than the internal message buffer.
- **Miscellaneous iSCSI initiator errors**: Check the initiator.
- **Missing parameters (e.g, iSCSI initiator and/or target name)**: Verify that the initiator and target name are properly specified.
- **mount: ...already mounted...** (EBUSY): Either the file system is mounted elsewhere, an active process has its working directory inside the mount point or the maximum number of mounts has been exceeded.
- **mount: giving up on...**: The remote mount request was unsuccessful for more than the threshold number of retries. Check the network connection and make sure that the NFS server is sharing the directory to the client as expected.
- **mount: mount-point...does not exist**: The directory specified as the mount point does not exist.
- **mount: the state of /dev/dsk/... is not okay**: The file system should either be mounted read-only or fsck-ed.
- **Network dropped connection because of reset** (ENETRESET): The remote host crashed or rebooted.
- **Network is down** (ENETDOWN): A transport connection failed due to a dead network.
- **Network is unreachable** (ENETUNREACH): Either there is no route to the network, or negative status information was received from intermediate network devices.
- **NFS getattr failed for server...RPC: Timed out**: The NFS server has failing hardware. (For a server that is slow to respond, the **NFS server not responding** message would appear instead.)
- **nfs mount: Couldn't bind to reserved port**: The NFS server has multiple network cards bound to the same subnet.
- **nfs mount: mount:...Device busy**: An active process has a working directory inside the mount point.
- **NFS mount:...mounted OK**: A backgrounded mount completed successfully. This may be an indication that the server response is poor, since otherwise the mount would have completed immediately and not required backgrounding.
- **NFS read failed for server**: This is a permissions problem error message. In addition to checking the permissions on the NFS server, make sure that the permissions underneath the mount are acceptable. (Mount points should have 755 permissions to avoid odd permissioning behavior on mounted file systems.)
- **nfs_server: bad getargs**: The arguments are unrecognized or incorrect. This may be an indication of a network problem, or it may indicate a software configuration problem on the client.
- **NFS server ... not responding**: The network connection to the NFS server is either slow or broken.
- **NFS server ... ok:** The network connection to the NFS server has been restored. This is a followup to "**NFS server ... not responding.**"
- **nfs umount: ... is busy**: An active process has a working directory inside the specified NFS mount. See the "**Device busy**" error message.
- **NFS write error on host ... No space left on device:** If an NFS mount runs out of space, attempts to write to files on the share may corrupt or zero out those files.
- **NFS write failed for server ... RPC: Timed out**: The file system is soft mounted, and response time is inadequate. Sun recommends that writable file systems not be soft-mounted, as it can lead to data corruption.
- **No carrier-cable disconnected or hub disabled?**: This error may manifest due to a physical networking problem or a configuration issue.
- **No child processes** (ECHILD): An application attempted to communicate with a cooperating process that does not exist. Either the child exited improperly or failed to start.
- **No default media available**: Drives contain no floppy or CD media to eject.
- **No directory! Logging in with home=/:** The home directory either does not exist or is not permissioned such that the user can use it. If home directories are automounted, it may be necessary to troubleshoot the automounter.

- **no driver found for device**: A driver has been disabled while the device is still attached. Depending on the type of device, **cfgadm**, **drvconfig**, **devfsadm** or a reconfiguration reboot (**boot -r**) may be required. Check the System Administration Guide: Devices and File Systems document (see the "References" section below).
- **No message of desired type** (ENOMSG): Something attempted to receive a message of a type that does not exist on the message queue. See the msgsnd(2) and msgrcv(2) man pages.
- **No more connections can be accepted on this Session ID**: The storage device is unable to accept more connections for this initiator on the iSCSI target device.
- **No record locks available** (ENOLCK): Any of several different locking subsystems, including fcntl(2), NFS lockd and mail, may yield this message when no more locks are available.
- **No route to host** (EHOSTUNREACH): In practice, this message is not distinguishable from "**Network is unreachable**."
- **No shell Connection closed**: The shell specified for the user is either unavailable or illegal. Make sure it is listed in /etc/shells and that it exists. It may be necessary to change the passwd entry for this user to assign a valid shell.
- **No space left on device** (ENOSPC): The disk, tape or diskette is full.
- **No such device** (ENODEV): An operation was attempted on an inappropriate or nonexistent device. Make sure that it exists in /devices and /dev. The drvconfig or boot -r commands can be used to regenerate many /devices entries.
- **No such device or address** (ENXIO): I/O has been attempted to a device that does not exist or that exists beyond the limits of the device. Make sure that the device in question is powered up and connected properly, including the correct SCSI ID.
- **No such file or directory** (ENOENT): The file or path name does not exist on the system. Make sure that the relevant file systems are mounted and that the expected files and/or directories exist.
- **No such process** (ESRCH): The process does not exist on the system. It may have finished prior to the attempt to reference it.
- **No such user ... cron entries not created**: Even though a file exists in /var/spool/*cron/crontabs* for this username, the username is not present in the passwd database.
- **No utmpx entry**: The file system containing the utmpx file is full. This may need to be resolved in single-user mode, since logins will not be permitted.
- **Not a data message** (EBADMSG): Data has come to the head of a STEAMS queue that cannot be processed. See the man pages for read(2), getmsg(2) and *ioctl*(2).
- **Not a directory** (ENOTDIR): A non-directory was specified as an argument where a directory is required.
- **Not a stream device** (ENOTSTR): The file descriptor used as a target for the putmsg(2) or getmsg(2) is not a STREAMS device.
- **Not a UFS filesystem**: The boot device is improperly defined. For x86, boot the system with the Configuration Assistant/boot CD and identify the disk from which to boot. For PROM-based systems, set the boot-device properly in the PROM environment variables.
- **Not enough space** (ENOMEM): Insufficient swap space available.
- **Not found**: The specified command could not be found. Check the spelling and the PATH.
- **Not login shell**: Use exit to get out of non-login shells. (The logout command can only be used from login shells.)
- **Not on system console**: Direct root logins are only permitted on the system console unless otherwise specified in /etc/default/login.
- **Not owner** (EPERM): Action attempted that can only be performed by object owner or the superuser.
- **Not supported** (ENOTSUP): A requested application feature is not available in the current version, though it may be expected in a future release.
- **Object is remote** (EREMOTE): We tried to share a resource not on the local machine.

- **Operation already in progress** (EALREADY): An operation was already in progress on a non-blocking object.
- **Operation canceled** (ECANCELED): The asynchronous operation was canceled before completion.
- **Operation not applicable** (ENOSYS): No system support exists for this operation.
- **Operation not supported on transport endpoint** (EOPNOTSUPP): Tried to accept a connection on a datagram transport endpoint.
- **Operation now in progress** (EINPROGRESS): Operation in progress on a non-blocking object.
- **Option not supported by protocol** (ENOPROTOOPT): A bad option or level was specified.
- **Out of memory**: System is running out of virtual memory (including swap space). See "**Not enough space**" as well.
- **Out of stream resources** (ENOSR): No STEAMS queues or no STREAMS head data structures available during a STREAMS open.
- **Overlapping swap volume:** Make sure that the additional swap volumes have unique names.
- **Package not installed** (ENOPKG): The attempted system call belongs to a package that is not installed on this system.
- **Paired DIMMs Mismatch**: Checksum mismatch between two DIMMs in a pair. Can be caused by damaged or non-identical DIMMs.
- **Panic – boot: Could not mount file system**: The Jumpstart boot process is unable to get to the install image. Make sure that the Jumpstart configurations and file shares are correct.
- **Panic ... valloc'd past tmpptes**: May occur if maxusers is set to an absurdly high number. It should not be set past the number of MB of RAM or 4096, whichever is smaller.
- **Permission denied** (EACCES): The attempted file access is forbidden due to file system permissions.
- **Protocol family not supported** (EPFNOSUPPORT): The protocol has not been implemented on this system.
- **Protocol not supported** (EPROTONOSUPPORT): The protocol has not been configured for this system. Check the protocols database (/etc/inet/protocols by default).
- **Protocol wrong type for socket** (EPROTOTYPE): Application programming error or misconfigured protocols. The requested protocol does not support the requested socket type. Make sure that the protocols database matches with the corresponding entries in /usr/include/sys/socket.h.
- **quotactl: open Is a directory**: A directory named "quota" can cause edquota to fail. Such directories should be renamed.
- **RADIUS packet authentication failed**: Re-set the RADIUS shared secret.
- **Read error from network: Connection reset by peer**: The remote system crashed or rebooted during an rsh or rlogin session.
- **Read-only file system** (EROFS): We can't change stuff on file systems that are mounted read-only.
- **received invalid login response**: Storage device response was unexpected. Verify initiator authentication settings.
- **Requested iSCSI version range is not supported by the target**: The initiator's iSCSI version is not supported by the target storage device. See if firmware or driver upgrades would be sufficient.
- **Requested ITN does not exist at this address**: The iSCSI target name (ITN) is not accessible. Verify the initiator discovery information and storage device configuration.
- **Requested ITN has been removed and no forwarding address is provided**: The requested iSCSI target name is no longer accessible. Verify the initiator discovery information and storage device configuration.
- **Resource temporarily unavailable** (EAGAIN): fork(2) cannot create a new process due to a lack of resources. These resources may include limits on active processes (see the "Resource Management" section) or a lack of swap space.
- **Restartable system call** (ESTART): The system call has been interrupted in a restartable state.

- **Result too large** (ERANGE): This is a programming or data input error. The result of a calculation is not representable in the defined data type. The matherr(3M) facility may be helpful in debugging the problem.
- **ROOT LOGIN ...**: Someone has just logged in as root or su-ed to root.
- **RPC: Program not registered**: Make sure that the requested service is available.
- **rx framing error**: This error usually indicates a problem with the network hardware. Framing errors are types of CRC errors, which are usually caused by physical media problems.
- **SCSI bus DATA IN phase parity error**: This is a problem related to SCSI hardware or connections. It may have to do with hardware that is not qualified for attachment to Sun servers, connections with cables that are flaky or too long (total length more than 6 meters), bad terminators or flaky power supplies. See the "**SCSI transport failed: reason 'reset'**" message as well.
- **SCSI transport failed: reason 'reset'**: The system sent data that was never received due to a SCSI reset. This may occur due to conflicting SCSI IDs, hardware that is not qualified for attachment to Sun servers, connections with cables that are flaky or too long (total length more than 6 meters), bad terminators or flaky power supplies. These issues have also been observed on systems where the highest capacity DIMMs are not in the lowest numbered slots. Disk arrays wth read-ahead caches can sometimes also cause this problem; turn off the caching to see if the problem goes away. Non-obvious SCSI ID conflicts may be diagnosed using the PROM monitor probe-scsi-all command. (See "**OBP Command Line Diagnostics" in Chapter 3 for more details.)** These errors may also happen when the SCSI device and the server are set to different SCSI timeout thresholds.
- **Segmentation Fault**: These can be produced as a result of programming errors or improperly set rlimit resource settings. (See "Resource Management" in Chapter 9 for how to check and adjust resource settings.) Segmentation faults are an indication that the program has attempted to access an area of memory that is protected or does not exist. Programming causes for segmentation faults include dereferencing a null pointer and indexing past the bounds of an array.
- **setmnt: Cannot open /etc/mnttab for writing**: The system is unable to write to /etc/mnttab. This may be caused by the /etc directory being mounted read-only (which can happen during certain types of boot problems).
- **share_nfs: /home: Operation not applicable**: A local file system is mounted on /home, which is usually reserved for use by the automounter.
- **skipping LIST command – no active base**: A LIST command is present without an associated BASE command. (cachefspack)
- **Socket type not supported** (ESOCKTNOSUPPORT): The socket type's support has not been configured for this system.
- **Soft error rate ... during writing was too high**: The number of soft errors on a tape device have exceeded the threshold. It may be due to a dirty head, bad media or a faulty tape drive.
- **Software caused connection abort** (ECONNABORTED): The connection was aborted within the local host machine.
- **Stale NFS file handle** (ESTALE): The file or directory on the NFS server is no longer available. It may have been removed or replaced. A remount may be needed to force a renegotiation of file handles.
- **statd: cannot talk to statd**: statd has left remnants in the /var/statmon/sm and /var/statmon/sm.bak directories. Files named after inactive hosts should be removed, and statd and lockd should be restarted.
- **su: No shell**: The default shell for root is improper. It may have been set to a nonexistent program or an illegal shell. This problem has been known to occur when an extra space is appended to the "root" line of the passwd file. The passwd file will need to be repaired while booted from CDROM or network.
- **syncing file system**: The kernel is updating the superblocks before taking the system down or in the wake of a panic.
- **System booting after fatal error FATAL**: This can be caused by UPA address parity errors, Master queue overflows or DTAG parity errors. This is going to be due to a bad CPU or possibly a bad system board.

- **tar: ...: No such file or directory:** The specified target (which defaults to TAPE) is not available. This may be due to a hardware problem with the tape drive or connections, or to a misspecified target.
- **tar: directory checksum error**: The checksum of the files read from tape do not match the checksum in the header block. This may be due to an incorrectly specified block size or a bad piece of tape media.
- **tar: tape write error**: A physical write error has occurred on the `tar` target.
- **Target hardware or software error**: Run diagnostics on the storage device hardware; check storage device software configuration.
- **Target has insufficient session, connection or other resources**: Check storage device settings. Check with storage device vendor to see if resource settings can be increased or capacity can be otherwise increased.
- **target protocol group tag mismatch**: Initiator and target had a Target Portal Group Tag (TPGT) mismatch. Verify TPGT discovery settings on initiator and storage device.
- **Text file busy** (ETXTBSY): An attempt was made to execute a file that was open for writing.
- **The SCSI bus is hung**: The likely cause is a conflict in SCSI target numbers. See the "**SCSI transport failed: reason 'reset'**" message as well.
- **Timeout waiting for** ARP/RARP packet: Indicates a network connection problem while booting from the network. This problem can sometimes be observed on subnets containing multiple servers willing to answer a RARP request, which can result in a server without a *bootparams* file receiving a request. (We have had good luck moving Jumpstart targets to an isolated subnet for initial installations.)
- **Timer expired**: The timer for a STREAMS `ioctl` has expired. The cause is device specific, and may be related to a flaky hardware, driver failure or an inappropriately short timeout threshold.
- **Too many links** (EMLINK): A file has too many hard links associated with it. Use soft links instead.
- **Too many open files** (EMFILE): A process has exceeded the limit on the number of open files per process. (See the "**Resource Management**" section of Chapter 9 for methods to monitor and manage these limits.)
- **Transport endpoint is already connected** (EISCONN): Connection request made on an already connected transport endpoint.
- **Transport endpoint is not connected** (ENOTCONN): The endpoint is not connected and/or an address was not specified.
- **Trap 3E**: These are caused by a bad boot disk superblock. This may have been caused by a failing disk, faulty disk connections, software misconfiguration or duplicate SCSI addresses. Check the possible hardware and SCSI configuration issues before attempting to recover the superblock using the methods listed under "**BAD SUPER BLOCK**" above.
- **Too Many Arguments**: This is a variant of the C shell's **Arguments too long** message.
- **unable to connect to target**: Initiator unable to establish a network connection. This message typically accompanied by an error number from /usr/include/sys/*errno.h*.
- **unable to get shared objects**: The executable may be corrupt or in an unrecognized format.
- **unable to initialize authentication**: Verify that initiator authentication settings are properly configured.
- **unable to make login pdu**: Initiator could not make a login Payload Data Unit (PDU) based on the initiator and storage device settings. Reset target login parameters and other settings as required.
- **unable to schedule enumeration**: Initiator unable to enumerate the LUNs on the target. LUN enumeration can be forced via the `devfsadm -i iscsi` command.
- **unable to set [authentication|ipsec|password|remote authentication|username]**: Verify that initiator authentication settings are properly configured.
- **uname: error writing name when booting**: */etc/nodename* must contain exactly one line with the name of the system and no blanks or returns.
- **Unknown service**: Either the service is not listed in the services database (/etc/services by default), or the permissions for the services database are set so that the user cannot read it.
- **Value too large for defined data type** (EOVERFLOW): Argument improperly formatted for the structure allocated to it.

- **WARNING: /tmp: File system full, swap space limit exceeded**: Virtual memory has filled up. A reboot is recommended after we have figured out which process is hogging all the memory and/or swap, since the system may be in an unstable state.
- **WARNING: TOD clock not initialized**: It is likely that the system clock's battery is dead.
- **Watchdog Reset**: This usually indicates a hardware problem. (See the "Watchdog Resets" section in Chapter 3 for a complete discussion.)
- **Window Underflow**: These errors sometimes accompany a trap, especially at boot time. Some program attempted access of a register window that was not accessible from that processor. These errors may occur when differently sized DIMMs are improperly used together, or when cache memory has gone bad. If mismatched memory is not the problem, the CPU or system board will need to be replaced.
- **wrong magic number**: See "**Corrupt label**" above.
- **you are not authorized to use**: A configuration file (eg `at.deny` or `cron.deny`) forbids access to this service.

Resources

- Sun Microsystems. (June 2006) *man pages section 2: System Calls*. Palo Alto, CA: Sun Microsystems, Inc. (http://docs.sun.com/app/docs/doc/816-5167)
- Sun Microsystems. (June 2006) *man pages section 3: Extended Library Functions*. Palo Alto, CA: Sun Microsystems, Inc. (http://docs.sun.com/app/docs/doc/816-5172)
- Sun Microsystems. (February 2000) *Solaris Common Messages and Troubleshooting Guide*. Palo Alto, CA: Sun Microsystems, Inc. (http://docs.sun.com/app/docs/doc/806-1075)
- Sun Microsystems. (November 2006) *System Administration Guide: Devices and File Systems*. Palo Alto, CA: Sun Microsystems, Inc. (http://docs.sun.com/app/docs/doc/817-5093)

Appendix B

Commands and Configurations

Solaris comes with a broad variety of utilities that are extremely useful for troubleshooting. This appendix contains a listing and brief description of the most important utilities and configuration files.

General Commands

The following table contains general OS commands that are useful for system management, configuring, monitoring and troubleshooting.

Table B-1: General Troubleshooting Commands

Command	Description
awk	Useful in filtering log files and other information.
catman -w	Create the *windex* database for man pages.
cpustat	Monitor system behavior using CPU counters.
cputrack	Monitor process and lwp performance using CPU counters.
dtrace	Monitor and trace the kernel and its interactions with processes.
file	Identifies file type.
find	Finds objects of a certain description and performs operations on them.
grep/egrep	Finds a string in a file or data stream.
grpck	Checks the format of an */etc/group* file.
kmdb	Examine running kernel or kernel core dump.
last	List logins to this system.

Command	Description
ls	Display file information.
mdb	Modular debugger. View process and kernel internals.
modinfo	List current kernel modules.
modload/modunload	Load and unload kernel modules.
pargs	Identify process arguments.
pcred	Display process credentials.
perl	Sort and collate text, automate administrative tasks.
pfiles	List the inode and device information for files associated with a process.
pflags	Display tracing flags, signals and status information.
pgrep	Looks for matching processes.
pkgchk	Check package integrity.
pkill	Kill matching processes.
pldd	List dynamic libraries linked into a process.
pmap	Process memory address space information.
preap	Reap a zombie process.
prun/pstop	Restart or stop a process.
ps	Process information.
psig	List signal actions and handlers for a process.
ptime	Time a process.
ptree	Displays process genealogy.
pwait	Display process status after termination.
pwck	Check *passwd* file format.
pwdx	Display process working directory.
sed	Reorganize text data stream.
strings	Identify strings in binary and object files.
tail -f	Display the end of a file while it is being written.
truss	Monitor system calls and durations of a process.

316

Command	Description
uname	Display system identification information.

Device Management Commands

The following commands are useful for controlling, monitoring and troubleshooting devices:

Table B-2: Device Management Commands

Command	Description
arch	Displays architecture and kernel information.
busstat	Interconnect bus hardware information.
devlinks	Creates links from the */dev* tree to the */devices* tree.
drvconfig	Configure the */devices* tree to reflect detected hardware.
eeprom	Modify or view settings on the EEPROM.
intrstat	Shows interrupt-to-CPU bindings and statistics.
isainfo -v	Describes currently supported architectures (32 vs 64 bit) and types of device drivers.
ndd	Modify and view device driver settings.
prtconf -v	Display system configuration information.
prtdiag -v	Display system configuration and diagnostic information.
psradm	Administer CPUs.
psrinfo	Display CPU information.
psrset	Binds process groups to a processor set. (Not usable with pools.)

Storage Management Commands

The following commands are used for monitoring, troubleshooting and managing disk, filesystem and tape storage.

Table B-3: Storage Management Commands

Command	Description
df -k or *df -h*	Displays filesystem disk space usage in KB.
dfmounts	Information on remote mounts.

Command	Description
dfshares	Information on shares.
disks	Creates links in */dev/dsk* and */dev/rdsk* for any detected disk devices.
du -dsk	Reports on disk space usage of a directory, without crossing mount points.
format	Display or manage partitioning information.
fsck	Filesystem checker. (Not required for ZFS.)
fsdb	Filesystem debugger. (Allows manual repair of a filesystem after a crash.)
fstyp	Displays filesystem information.
metastat	Solaris Volume Manager/DiskSuite monitoring.
mkfs	Create a new filesystem.
newfs	Create a new UFS filesystem.
share	Enable or disable remote shares.
showmount -e	Display share information.
swap	Manage and view swap space allotments.
tapes	Create */dev* links for tape devices.
tunefs	Modify and view file system parameters.
vxassist	Veritas Volume Manager (VxVM) volume management utility.
vxdctl	VxVM device management.
vxdg	VxVM disk group management utility.
vxdiskadm	VxVM menu-driven device management utility.
vxprint	Display VxVM configuration.
zfs	Manage and view ZFS filesystem information.
zpool	Manage and view ZFS pool information.

Networking Commands

The following commands are useful for managing, monitoring and troubleshooting network problems.

Table B-4: Networking Commands

Command	Description
arp	For Address Resolution Protocol tables.
ifconfig	Manage and view network interface settings.
inetadm	Administer and observe *inetd*-managed services.
netstat	Check network tuning and routing information.
ping	Check connectivity.
route	Manage and view routing information.
rcpinfo	View information about RPC services.
snoop	View all network traffic on an interface.
svcadm	Administer SMF services.
svccfg	Configure SMF services.
svcs	View and manage SMF services.
tcpdump	Another tool for viewing network traffic.
traceroute	Display information for route to an object.

- The **ifconfig** command is important for verifying the network settings and checking the status of each interface. In particular, we check the output for the *UP* and *RUNNING* flags, as well as looking at the IP address and netmask settings.

- The **netstat -i** command allows us to check the collision, error and packet throughput rates for each interface.

- The **netstat -r** command displays the routing settings for the system.

Performance Monitoring Commands

The following commands are useful for monitoring several aspects of system performance.

Table B-5: Performance Monitoring Commands

Command	Description
iostat	Disk I/O-related statistics.
lockstat	Lock usage and contention statistics.
mpstat	Multiple processor utilization statistics.
netstat	Network-related performance statistics.

Command	Description
nfsstat	NFS-related statistics.
prstat	Resource utilization by process.
sar	Collects and collates a range of performance data.
top	Process resource utilization.
uptime	Reports on load average and length of time since reboot.
vmstat	Virtual memory-related statistics.
vxstat	Veritas Volume Manager-related statistics.

Fundamental Configuration Files

This is a listing of several of the most important configuration files, along with a brief description of what they manage.

Table B-6: Fundamental Configuration Files

Configuration File	Description
/etc/bootparams	Information for network boot clients.
/etc/cron.d/cron.allow, /etc/init.d/cron.deny	Allow access to crontab for users listed in *cron.allow*. If *cron.allow* does not exist, access is permitted for users not in the */etc/cron.d/cron.deny* file.
/etc/defaultdomain	NIS domain.
/etc/default/cron	Sets *cron* logging with the CRONLOG variable.
/etc/default/ftpd	Allows *ftpd* variables, including a login BANNER, to be set.
/etc/default/login	Controls root logins via specification of the CONSOLE variable, as well as variables for login logging thresholds and password requirements.
/etc/default/passwd	Set password length and quality requirements.
/etc/default/su	Determines logging activity for su attempts via the SULOG and SYSLOG variables, sets some initial environment variables for su sessions.
/etc/default/telnet	Allows telnetd variables, including a login BANNER, to be set.
/etc/dfs/dfstab	Determines which directories will be NFS-shared at boot time. Each line is a share command.
/etc/dfs/sharetab	Contains a table of resources that have been shared via *share*.
/etc/group	Provides groupname translation information.
`/etc/hostname.`**interface**	Assigns a hostname to **interface**; assigns an IP address by cross-referencing */etc/inet/hosts*.
/etc/hosts.allow,	Determine which hosts will be allowed access to TCP wrapper mediated services.

320

Configuration File	Description
/etc/hosts.deny	
/etc/hosts.equiv	Determines which set of hosts will not need to provide passwords when using the "r" remote access commands (eg *rlogin*, *rsh*, *rexec*)
/etc/inet/hosts	Associates hostnames and IP addresses.
/etc/inet/inetd.conf	Before Solaris 10, this was the file for configuring `inetd` services. Now this is run out of the Service Management Facility via inetadm.
/etc/inet/ntp.conf	Time service control file.
/etc/inittab	Controls process dispatching by `init`. As of Solaris 10, it is no longer edited directly. It should be edited via the Service Management Facility (SMF).
/etc/logindevperm	Contains information to change permissions for devices upon console logins.
/etc/magic	Database of magic numbers that identify file types for file.
/etc/mail/aliases	Contains mail aliases recognized by *sendmail*.
/etc/mail/sendmail.cf	Mail configuration file for *sendmail*. This is no longer edited directly. It is managed via the */etc/mail/cf/cf/sendmail.mc* file and */usr/ccs/make*.
/etc/minor_perm	Specifies permissions for device files; used by drvconfig
/etc/mnttab	Contains information about currently mounted resources.
/etc/name_to_major	List of currently configured major device numbers; used by *drvconfig*.
/etc/netconfig	Network configuration database read during network initialization.
/etc/netgroup	Defines groups of hosts and/or users.
/etc/netmasks	Determines default netmask settings.
/etc/nsswitch.conf	Determines order in which different information sources are accessed when performing lookups.
/etc/passwd	Local user information file.
/etc/path_to_inst	Contents of physical device tree using physical device names and instance numbers.
/etc/project	As of Solaris 10, used to assign resource management parameters to users, groups and collections of tasks.
/etc/protocols	Known protocols.
/etc/remote	Attributes for `tip` sessions.
/etc/rmtab	Currently mounted filesystems.
/etc/rpc	Available RPC programs.
/etc/services	Well-known networking services and associated port numbers.
/etc/shadow	Hashed passwords for local user accounts.
/etc/syslog.conf	Configures *syslogd* logging.
/etc/system	Customizes kernel operation. As of Solaris 10, many of the resource management parameters are now handled in `/etc/project`.
/etc/vfstab	Default filesystem information. Note that ZFS filesystems are not

Configuration File	Description
	mounted from the *vfstab*.
/var/adm/messages	Default system logging file.
/var/adm/sulog	Default log file for the *su* command.
/var/adm/utmpx	User and accounting information.
/var/adm/wtmpx	User login and accounting information.
/var/cron/log	Default *cron* log file.
/var/lp/log	Default printer log file.
/var/sadm/install/contents	Database of installed software packages.
/var/saf/_log	Logs activity of SAF (Service Access Facility), which manages the serial ports.

Resources

- Sun Microsystems. (June 2006) *man pages section 1: User Commands*. Palo Alto, CA: Sun Microsystems, Inc. (http://docs.sun.com/app/docs/doc/816-5165)

- Sun Microsystems. (June 2006) man pages section 1M: System Administration Commands. Palo Alto, CA: Sun Microsystems, Inc. (http://docs.sun.com/app/docs/doc/816-5166)

- Sun Microsystems. (June 2006) *man pages section 2: System Calls*. Palo Alto, CA: Sun Microsystems, Inc. (http://docs.sun.com/app/docs/doc/816-5167)

- Sun Microsystems. (May 2006) *System Administration Guide: Advanced Administration*. Palo Alto, CA: Sun Microsystems, Inc. (http://docs.sun.com/app/docs/doc/817-0403)

Alphabetical Index

Made in the USA
Charleston, SC
19 December 2013